UNFINISHED BUSINESS

Ayukawa Yoshisuke and U.S.-Japan
Relations, 1937–1953

Harvard East Asian Monographs, 199

UNFINISHED BUSINESS

Ayukawa Yoshisuke and U.S.-Japan
Relations, 1937–1953

Haruo Iguchi

Published by the Harvard University Asia Center
and distributed by Harvard University Press
Cambridge (Massachusetts) and London   2003

Printed in the United States of America

The Harvard University Asia Center publishes a monograph series and, in coordination with the Fairbank Center for East Asian Research, the Korea Institute, the Reischauer Institute of Japanese Studies, and other faculties and institutes, administers research projects designed to further scholarly understanding of China, Japan, Vietnam, Korea, and other Asian countries. The Center also sponsors projects addressing multidisciplinary and regional issues in Asia.

Library of Congress Cataloging-in-Publication Data

Iguchi, Haruo, 1964-

Unfinished business : Ayukawa Yoshisuke and U.S.-Japan relations, 1937-1953/ Haruo Iguchi.

p. cm. -- (Harvard East Asian monographs ; 199)

Includes bibliographical references and index.

ISBN 0-674-00374-8 (cl. : alk. paper)

I. Aikawa, Yoshisuke, 1880-1967. 2. Japan--Foreign economic relations--United States. 3. United States--Foreign economic relations--Japan. 4. International cooperation. 5. Japan--Foreign relations--United States. 6. United States--Foreign relations--Japan. I. Title. II. Series.

HF1602.15.U6 I335 2002

337.52073'09'041--dc21   2002032850

Index by the author

☠   Printed on acid-free paper

Last figure below indicates year of this printing

12 11 10 09 08 07 06 05 04 03

Acknowledgments

During my second or third year in graduate school, Bruce Cumings, my main advisor at the University of Chicago, told us graduate students that in choosing a dissertation topic students should assume that it usually takes a longer time to complete the project than initially anticipated, particularly if that project ultimately ends with a publication of a book. After completing my dissertation in less than six years at the University of Chicago's History Department in the summer of 1995, I now fully understand.

I express my great appreciation to my mentors, Akira Iriye and Bruce Cumings, for their support and encouragement during the past decade or so. I also thank the faculty and staff at Harvard University's Edwin O. Reischauer Institute, who gave me the opportunity to spend one year with financial support as a postdoctoral fellow there, and *The Journal of American–East Asian Relations* (particularly Anthony Cheung) and *The Journal of American and Canadian Studies* for granting me the permission to incorporate my articles published by them into this book. Furthermore, I thank the University of Chicago for providing me financial support, including a Mellon Dissertation Write-Up Grant, during one or more stages in my dissertation project. In addition, I thank the archivists and staff at the various archives I had visited for research for rendering me their kind assistance. Finally, I am very grateful for the fact that John Ziemer, the editor of this book, has been so professional and patient in dealing with my manuscript and slowness.

Last but not least, I express my deepest gratitude to my parents, Iguchi Takeo and Katsuko, for their loving support throughout the years, and to Iguchi Yoko, my wife, who gave me lots of psychological support during the final and crucial phase of this project.

Contents

UNFINISHED BUSINESS

*Ayukawa Yoshisuke and U.S.-Japan
Relations, 1937–1953*

Introduction

This book examines the efforts of Ayukawa Yoshisuke (1880–1967), the founder of the Nihon sangyō (Nissan) conglomerate and of the quasi-governmental Manchuria Industrial Development Corporation (MIDC, Manshū jūkōgyō kabushiki kaisha or Mangyō), to introduce massive amounts of foreign—primarily American—direct and indirect investment into Japan and Manchukuo from 1937 to 1941 and into Japan from 1947 to 1951 and assesses the reasons for the failure of these efforts. Ayukawa's objectives were (1) to reduce state control of industrial development and international trade and commerce in Japan and Manchukuo; (2) to further the economic development of Japan and Manchukuo; and (3) to stabilize relations between Japan and the United States by promoting strong economic ties between the two countries. Ayukawa's activities are highly relevant to Japan's current economic situation. As Nakamura Takafusa and Noguchi Yukio argue, the origin of Japan's current economic system can be traced to the state's regulations for war mobilization. According to Noguchi, the largest obstacle to reforming the present Japanese economy is this system, which he dubs "the 1940-era system." Among its characteristics, he lists corporations' greater dependence on indirect financing through bank loans rather than on direct financing through the issuance of stocks and bonds, strong and broad state intervention in the private sector for economic regulation, the subordination of small- and medium-sized firms to large corporations in a pyramidal subcontracting hierarchy, low dividends, weak stockholder's rights, lifetime employment, seniority-based wages, and company unions.

The historical origins of these characteristics have been debated in Japan by scholars such as Nakamura, Noguchi, Hashimoto Jurō, Okazaki Tetsuji, and Okuno Masahiro and in the United States by researchers such as Chalmers Johnson and John Dower. Both Hashimoto and Dower emphasize that the postwar Japanese economic system is a hybrid of American and Japanese economic models because of American influence during the postwar occupation. Hashimoto argues that the 1950s were the critical period in Japan's transition from a wartime command economy to the postwar market economy. By then the main subsystems of the postwar Japanese economic system were in place. Some of these subsystems were formed during the interwar period and during the war; others were temporarily dismantled during the Occupation and later reactivated; the most important, however, were created through interactions between the American economic reforms during the Occupation and the Japanese absorption of the American economic system during the 1950s.[1]

Ayukawa attempted to modify the Japanese economic system in the prewar years and the postwar years by attracting American capital and technology through direct and indirect foreign investment in Japan and Manchukuo. In addition during the postwar years, he sought to rejuvenate direct financing, which had become far less common than indirect financing during the war mobilization years. Ayukawa's other postwar project was his effort to stimulate the growth of independent small- and medium-sized firms.

Even before the war, Ayukawa was an economic internationalist, a believer in global prosperity and peace through free trade and economic interdependence. This outlook is well reflected in his December 1936 essay "Tsugi no sekai o kataru," which was included in his widely read *Mono no mikata kangaekata*, published in May 1937. This book was translated into English and published as *Searching for Truth* in 1938; the essay was entitled "About the New Era." In this essay, Ayukawa argued that drastic measures were needed to solve the worldwide political and economic crises and that the only way to achieve world progress was to restore the Wilsonian principle of international trade. Specifically, he advocated the elimination of bloc economies and the immediate abolition of tariffs worldwide. His argument was grounded on a Social Darwinian and Fordist (mass-productionist) perspective of world economic competition and based on what he saw as the shrinking size of the world because of advancements in communications through radio and, as he predicted correctly, television.

Although he had been receiving government assistance in nurturing Nissan Motors, Ayukawa in this essay discouraged government aid in exploiting natural resources. "The old economic ideas will have to be radically altered," he wrote, by "discarding all artificial measures of help." With this view of world trade, Ayukawa foresaw a day "when a country with more petroleum than it needs will allow it to flow freely to supply the needs of the world; a country that grows tobacco will produce it abundantly and cheaply for the sake of tobacco lovers; in the same way, the shoes of Czechoslovakia will cover the feet of savages."

This "New Era," a Ricardian world of free trade, was also a world with a Social Darwinian orientation because "important industries will spring up only in those regions most suited to their development." "People who are not favored either with natural resources or with fine brains . . . will adopt the policy of raising their standard of living by utilizing their labor forces more fully." In the New Era, "the exchange of necessary commodities will be perfectly free, and a country poor in certain goods need not despair" because if it has "capable leaders, industries will naturally rise up, and the standard of living will be raised as it has been in the United States." In the end, "Materials, brains, and labor will work to their greatest effect, industries will develop one after the other, and economic expansion will be phenomenal."

On the other hand, in a completely open global trading system, nations faced the danger of trade wars. Although nations would try to avoid this situation by maintaining an open trade system, such an effort would have to overcome tensions that arose from strong international economic competition, a competition so intense that it would result in "suicide" among the losers. Given this situation, in economic matters, he expected the Japanese prime minister in the "New Era" to act like the CEO of a large corporation.[2]

In spite of Ayukawa's Wilsonian orientation, he strongly criticized Woodrow Wilson (1856–1924) for his failure to learn "by experience [that] the economy rules society." To his regret, Ayukawa found that Wilson, "the alleged 'Saviour of the world,' was not a man of great insight, thoroughly versed in the actual workings of finance and economy." Unfortunately, "The chance he had was lost once and for ever!" Ayukawa was also critical of the next three presidents, Warren G. Harding (1865–1923), Calvin Coolidge (1872–1933), and Herbert Hoover (1874–1964), for failing to resolve the issues of European war debts and reparations. Adolf Hitler's (1889–1945) rise to power and the spread of fascism and communism, he argued, were caused by the failure among nations to solve the problems of war debts, reparations, and worldwide protectionism. To remedy the situation, he not only called for the cancellation of war debts and reparations but, as mentioned earlier, also advocated the removal of tariff barriers and the end to bloc economies.[3]

From the Manchuria Incident of 1931 to Pearl Harbor in 1941, Japanese militarism and economic nationalism encouraged greater state control over the economy and discouraged Western direct and indirect investment in Japan's formal and informal empires. Business leaders such as Ayukawa, however, opted for closer economic cooperation with the United States through foreign direct investments, such as joint ventures, and foreign indirect investments. Such cooperation had been the cornerstone of U.S.-Japan relations in the 1920s, a decade when American direct and indirect investments in Japan increased and the Japanese economy enjoyed less state regulation than during the succeeding decades. In the immediate postwar years, Japanese business leaders like Ayukawa, facing a war-devastated economy, renewed their prewar efforts to attract Western, mainly American, investments. By this time, however, the Japanese political economy had experienced a great transformation because of state regulation of its economy for war mobilization.

Despite Ayukawa's preference for free trade, he did not practice it completely in the prewar years, because of both domestic and international changes, opposition from his top executives to his approach, and his ties to the military. As he wooed the American business community to invest in Japan and Manchukuo, his economic views represented a regulated version of free trade, rather like Herbert Hoover's (see Chapter 7). As the Japanese government implemented increasing numbers of regulations for Japan's war effort, Ayukawa admitted that politics was driving economics (see Chapter 8) rather than the other way around; this view was also articulated by his colleagues in the civilian and military bureaucracies (see Chapters 1 through 3 and 8) and by Adolf Hitler, who lectured Ayukawa on this point (see Chapter 6).

Based on this worldwide trend toward state regulation of the economy and on the interaction between the forces pushing for greater state control and Ayukawa's ideas, Manchukuo, from the late 1930s to 1941, pursued a modified Open Door strategy by inviting American business participation in the activities of MIDC and its subsidiaries and by welcoming greater American exports to Manchukuo. Not only Manchukuo but also Japan wanted a modified Open Door whereby America would benefit economically by supporting a Japanese-dominated and state-regulated economic sphere in the Far East and, later, Southeast Asia.

The concept of the Open Door had changed since Secretary of State John Hay's (1838–1905) first announcement in 1899. Initially, it simply was an American call to the other Great Powers for equal commercial opportunities in China, "a negative response to the public demand for positive and vigorous assertion of American rights and interests in China."[4] By the time of the Taft administration in 1909–13, "the Open Door . . . had become synonymous with the principles of equal commercial opportunity and China's territorial and administrative integrity."[5] At the Versailles Conference in 1919, American leaders failed to achieve universal agreement on equal economic opportunity, the third of Woodrow Wilson's Fourteen Points. But during the Washington Conference in 1922, the Open Door policy was codified in the Nine Powers Treaty and its call to respect China's territorial integrity and to uphold equal commercial opportunity there. As Joan Wilson remarks, however, "The doctrine was violated more often than honored by most of the Nine Power signatories, including the United States."[6]

But this comment overlooks the fact that the meaning of the Open Door principle had changed in the 1920s. Wilson is right in arguing that the United States was selective about applying the idea of equal economic opportunity. It favored it in those areas it wanted to penetrate economically, such as China and Manchuria, and tended to apply the Closed Door policy in areas where it enjoyed economic dominance, such as Latin America. This view, however, should be combined with Michael Hogan's argument that "just as combination, cooperation, and bureaucratic administration were displacing individual enterprise and natural market forces as the dynamic and integrative factors in the domestic sphere, so also multinational collaboration and managerial regulation were replacing nationalism and competition in the world economy." Hogan acknowledged the existence of "a tension . . . in American policy between contemporary processes and the older conception of the Open Door," but "more often than not public officials found it necessary to redefine traditional principles because of business insistence upon order, stability, and progress through cooperation."[7] Although Japan's economic and military strategies in the Far East were based on a rejection of the Open Door in the traditional sense, Ayukawa thought he could win American acquiescence to a modified conception of the Open Door and American direct and indirect investment in Manchukuo through joint ventures.

Was it wishful thinking for Japan to try attracting American investments to Manchukuo, a country not recognized by the United States? During the 1920s, when the United States did not recognize the Soviet Union, American businesses such as Ford Motors had built factories there, and hence it was not necessarily unrealistic for Japanese to think Americans might invest in Manchukuo. Nor was it necessarily far-fetched for Japan to believe that opening Manchukuo to American interests might lead to American recognition of that state. American recognition of the Soviet Union in 1934, although motivated in part by the American wish to counter Japanese expansionism in mainland Asia, was also motivated by pressures from business interests hit hard by the Great Depression such as Ford and General Electric to open trade with the Soviets.[8]

Ayukawa thought that American companies would jump at the sudden opening of tremendous business opportunities in Manchukuo because, at the time he embarked on his mission to attract American capital for Manchukuo, the United States was in the midst of the so-called Roosevelt Depression, a recession viewed by Franklin D. Roosevelt (1882–1945) and many other observers at the time as the direct result of a cut in government spending in the middle of an economic recovery. Although by 1937 the national economy had recovered to close to the level it had reached shortly before the 1929 crash, the industrial production index fell from 117 in August 1937 to 76 in May 1938. According to William E. Leuchtenburg, "Industrial activity fell off with the most brutal drop in the country's history. By December 1937, The *New York Times* Business Index had plunged from 110 to 85, wiping out all the gains made since 1935. In the three months, steel fell from 80 per cent of capacity to 19 per cent."[9] By March 1938, unemployment from the recession reached four million and the Federal Board index, at 79, was only 10 points higher than it had been in 1932.

Because the American economy had been sluggish for almost a decade, one mainstream line of thought, a pessimistic one, revived the "frontier thesis" of Frederick Jackson Turner: without an underdeveloped West, there was no longer an opportunity for limitless economic expansion. There was some validity to this notion. On the one hand, the 1930s witnessed the rapid industrial transformation of America's hitherto underdeveloped regions, including the western states, particularly California, and the southern states, especially Texas, as they became primary beneficiaries and targets of the New Deal's massive public investment in roads, irrigation systems, and dams. On the other hand, these regional developments did not stop the Roosevelt Depression. Faced with this downturn, the New Dealers of the late 1930s decided not only to increase government spending but also to implement anti-monopoly measures to realize "efficiency in production and distribution" so that mass consumption, and hence demand, could be stimulated by keeping consumer prices from inflating.

What ultimately saved the New Dealers' political lives was not their economic programs but the World War II economic boom that began in 1940. Although government spending had initiated a slow and painful recovery after the summer of 1938, the war boom pulled America out of the Great Depression by the middle of 1941.[10] Given this slow economic recovery, Ayukawa's idea of economic cooperation with the United States was not without foundation between 1937 and 1940 because the United States might perceive Manchuria as a major outlet for its exports.

Chapters 1 through 8 examine Ayukawa's thought and activities before the Japanese surrender in 1945. Chapter 1 deals with Ayukawa's pre-1937 attempts to engage in joint ventures with American automobile companies. His negotiations with American companies are important background information for understanding Chapter 2, which discusses how and why Ayukawa became involved in Manchukuo's industrialization projects. Chapter 2 emphasizes the continuity in Ayukawa's perceptions regarding the importance of utilizing American capital and technology for the advancement of his and Japan's industries.

Chapters 3 through 5 introduce Ayukawa's efforts to attract foreign investment to Japan and Manchukuo from 1937 to 1940. Chapter 3 demonstrates that both Japan and Manchukuo, particularly the latter, depended on foreign capital and technology to industrialize and that America's export boom to Manchukuo in the late 1930s was the context in which Ayukawa considered his schemes for joint ventures with American firms feasible. But from the outset, Ayukawa's idea encountered many obstacles, such as (1) policy changes in Japan and Manchukuo ensuing from the Sino-Japanese War, changes that conflicted with his ideas; (2) disappointments over the mineral resources of Manchukuo; and (3) the deterioration in U.S.-Japan relations. In addition to discussing Manchukuo's trade relations with the

West, Chapter 3 treats Ayukawa's initial efforts to attract American capital
and technology amid mounting domestic and international difficulties, difficulties that led him to consider attracting Japanese-Americans and American farming equipment to undertake large-scale farming along American
lines, an idea vetoed by the military. Ayukawa's pessimism regarding Manchukuo's potential for industrialization may have been prompted by the re-
nowned American geologist H. Foster Bain (1871–1948), who visited Manchukuo at Ayukawa's request. Bain told Ayukawa that even though he was
optimistic about Manchuria's potential for heavy industrialization in the
long run, he was, at the moment, pessimistic about Ayukawa's chances of attracting American investments to Manchuria.

Chapters 4 and 5 show that Ayukawa, in spite of these negative factors,
did have several good opportunities to secure American capital and technology between 1937 and 1940. Chapter 4 discusses Ayukawa's negotiations
with Ford Motors from 1937 to 1940, a joint venture scheme that was an integral part of Ayukawa's plan for industrialization in Manchukuo. Chapter 5
deals with Ayukawa's other attempts to attract American capital and technology for Manchukuo in the late 1930s.

Although Chapters 4 and 5 also assess why Ayukawa's efforts failed, the
prewar story does not end here because, as Chapter 6 shows, Ayukawa's
search for American capital and technology motivated him to engage in private diplomacy between 1939 and 1940, activities that sought America's tacit
recognition of Manchukuo and U.S. economic cooperation in Japan and
Manchukuo. Despite Ayukawa's occasional flirtation with closer cooperation with Germany, he was much more interested in the possibility of
American economic cooperation with Japan and Manchukuo. Between May
and June 1940, Ayukawa's private diplomacy had a limited but surprising
opportunity for success.

Although Ayukawa's prewar private diplomacy more or less ended with
the downfall of the Yonai cabinet on July 16, 1940, he continued to strive for
U.S.-Japan rapprochement in 1941. Chapter 7 analyzes Ayukawa's view of
U.S.-Japan relations as well as those of Kurusu Saburō (1886–1954), whose
relationship with Ayukawa is discussed in Chapter 6, and Herbert Hoover,
whom Ayukawa had been prodding for assistance since 1938. Although
Hoover and Ayukawa never made direct contact, both men acted behind
the scenes to prevent a war between the United States and Japan. Chapter 7
treats Ayukawa's relations with Hoover and sketches the parallel develop-

ments between Hoover's group and Ayukawa's group in trying to avert a U.S.-Japan war. Although Hoover's and Ayukawa's activities had little impact on U.S.-Japan relations, they are important in thinking about the continuities between prewar and postwar relations between the two countries. From this standpoint, Chapter 6 and 7 are important for understanding the three major themes of Chapter 9 (see below).

In spite of Ayukawa's endeavors, Manchukuo's industrialization did not happen in the way that he foresaw. Chapter 8 examines and analyzes the reasons behind Manchukuo's failure to achieve its objectives in industrialization. Part of this analysis focuses on Ayukawa's efforts to maintain MIDC's central position in Manchukuo's industrialization projects, such as his attempts to gain more control over the automobile industry in Japan and Manchukuo. This chapter also discusses Ayukawa's activities after he left MIDC and his continuing efforts to modify state controls over the economy during the Pacific War.

Chapters 9 and 10 deal with the postwar period when the United States, then the sole economic superpower, for a while pursued American-style economic reforms in Japan, reforms that changed from a liberal to a conservative direction. These changes in U.S. policy were advantageous for Japan's economic recovery, but Japanese business and political leaders still faced the question of how best to achieve this. Given this interest and America's appetite for seeking business opportunities, Ayukawa's idea of attracting American direct and indirect investments gained significant attention in both Japan and the United States. Chapter 9, the continuation of Chapter 7, addresses three themes: (1) the importance of the thought and activities of Hoover and of two men whose prewar encounters with Ayukawa's private diplomacy are discussed in Chapter 6, diplomat Joseph C. Grew (1880–1965) and a former president of the investment banking firm of Dillon, Read and Company, James V. Forrestal (1892–1949), in the debates within the U.S. government over modifying the policy of demanding Japan's unconditional surrender; (2) the roles of Hoover and former executives of Dillon, Read (Forrestal and William H. Draper, Jr. [1894–1974]) in the debates over the reversal of economic reforms in Japan; and (3) the relations between Ayukawa's postwar efforts to attract foreign investments and those of his colleagues within the Japanese business leadership.

Chapter 10 discusses how Ayukawa renewed his efforts to modify state control over the economy by attracting American direct and indirect investments, by nurturing independent small- and medium-sized firms, and by revitalizing direct finance as the primary means of corporate financing. Ayukawa perceived an influx of American capital and technology as an absolute necessity for Japan's postwar economic recovery. As a means of attracting American investments and promoting the growth of Japanese firms through direct financing, he and his colleagues negotiated with Dillon, Read to form an investment bank jointly managed and financed by Japanese and American interests. Ayukawa and his colleagues also strove to create hydroelectric power plants financed by American investments, an effort based on Ayukawa's concept of introducing projects modeled on the Tennessee Valley Authority program of the New Deal era. Both the last section of Chapter 9 and Chapter 10 use Hashimoto's framework (see above). Ayukawa's efforts during the immediate postwar years, when the Japanese economic system was still in flux, are highly relevant to Japan's contemporary efforts, in the midst of a depression that has lasted more than a decade, to restructure its economy by deregulation, attract foreign investment, nurture new businesses through venture capital, and rely more on direct financing.

Much has been written about the collision between Japan's drive for autarky and America's search for a multilateral free trade system in the years leading to the Pacific War;[11] Japan's overtures to foreign capital to aid in the industrialization of Manchuria after the summer of 1937 have received less attention. Previous researchers, such as Hara Akira and Suzuki Takashi, who have written on Ayukawa's activities in Manchukuo in the late 1930s, and Udagawa Masaru, who has written works on Nissan's negotiations for a merger with General Motors during the first half of the 1930s, had limited access to Japanese and English documents in the Ayukawa Yoshisuke papers, which are now available to the general public at the National Diet Library in Tokyo. These resources can augment other primary and secondary materials in Japanese and English and lead to a fuller appreciation of the events in the Japanese political economy not only of the 1930s but also of the 1940s and early 1950s. The outcome of this research will, I hope, lead to a better understanding of Ayukawa's role in U.S.-Japan relations from 1937 to 1941 and from 1945 to 1953 and his attempt to avoid the tragic war that occurred between the United States and Japan.[12]

ONE

Economic Internationalism: Ayukawa and American Business Before 1937

Ayukawa's idea of collaborating with American business in MIDC originated from his experiences with international business before 1937. Although the most immediate factor behind his emphasis on joint ventures was his negotiations with the Ford Motor Company in 1937, which are extensively discussed in Chapter 4, he had a strong record of supporting economic internationalism through international joint ventures. Indeed he started MIDC not only because of business imperatives but also because of his belief in economic internationalism, an idea that often conflicted with the economic policies supported by civilian and military bureaucrats.

Formation of the Nissan Conglomerate

The idea of joint ventures in Manchuria between Japanese and American business interests had a long history. Shortly after the Russo-Japanese War of 1904–5, Count Inoue Kaoru (1835–1915), a relative of Ayukawa's and one of the Meiji oligarchs, supported a tentative agreement between Prime Minister Katsura Tarō (1847–1913) and E. H. Harriman (1848–1909) for joint American-Japanese railway operations in southern Manchuria, an agreement never realized because of opposition from Foreign Minister Komura Jutarō (1855–1911). Instead of welcoming foreign capital for the economic development of southern Manchuria, an area in which Japan acquired the rights to control and develop the railroads and their environs as the result of its war with Russia, this task was concentrated in the South Manchuria Railway Company (SMR), a company established in 1906 and half-owned by the Japanese government and half by private investors, who were guaranteed an annual return of 6 percent on their SMR stock dividends.

Shortly after the Lansing-Ishii agreement in November 1917, an agreement in which the United States recognized Japan's "special interests" in China, especially Manchuria, in exchange for Japan's agreeing to the principle of equal commercial opportunities in, and the territorial integrity of, China as well as non-encroachment upon American and Allied interests in China during World War I, Ayukawa assisted his brother-in-law Kuhara Fusanosuke (1869–1965) in realizing a joint venture for steel production in China with Judge Elbert Gary's U.S. Steel Corporation during their visit to Gary and his company in the summer and fall of 1918. Kuhara's discussions with Gary centered around the participation of Japanese steel companies in the venture. Kuhara was also interested in having the Chinese participate in this operation, and he had asked Ayukawa to be prepared to go to China to discuss this proposal with the head of the Chinese government. This joint venture never materialized, and Ayukawa did not go to China.

During the 1920s several attempts were made by Japan and SMR to attract American capital to Manchuria. After seeing Kuhara, Gary and other American businessmen remained interested in pursuing a joint business operation with the Japanese in China. In 1921 Gary and the president of Japan's Anshan Steel Works in Manchuria, Inoue Tadashirō (1876–1959), negotiated a joint venture, which had the approval of the Japanese cabinet led by Prime Minister Hara Takashi (1856–1921) and the support of Bank of Japan Governor Inoue Junnosuke (1869–1932) and a top American executive at the investment banking firm of J. P. Morgan and Company, Thomas W. Lamont (1870–1948), who was a good friend of Inoue Junnosuke. Gary told Inoue Tadashirō to obtain the consent of Kuhara. This negotiation failed because the project lost its primary Japanese supporters: SMR President Nomura Ryūtarō (1859–1943), who left his post in May 1921 as the result of a major scandal in SMR, the owner of Anshan; Minister of War Tanaka Giichi (1864–1929), who was instrumental in galvanizing enough support within the Army for a joint venture that permitted 51 percent control by Japanese interests and 49 percent by American interests, but resigned in

June 1921 for health reasons; and Prime Minister Hara, who was assassinated in November 1921. Despite these setbacks, in January 1922 SMR
nearly succeeded in obtaining a $50 million loan from two leading American
investment-banking firms, J. P. Morgan and Company and Dillon, Read
and Company. Opposition from the Japanese Ministry of Finance (MOF)
torpedoed this deal. In July 1922 Inoue Tadashirō was forced to resign from
SMR. The U.S. State Department and Herbert Hoover, secretary of commerce during the Harding and Coolidge administrations, opposed American financing of industrial developments in Manchuria in the early 1920s,
but because of military tensions between the Chinese Nationalists led by
Chiang Kaishek (1887–1975) and the United States and Great Britain in
Nanking in March 1927, the State Department began to tacitly approve
Japanese economic control over Manchuria. Hoover, who had since the
mid-1920s ceased to oppose the influx of American capital into Manchuria,
further reinforced this outlook. Despite setbacks, Japan still had hopes of
foreign capital. The State Department advised J. P. Morgan and Company
in summer 1927 to postpone a $30 million loan to SMR because of Chinese
protests and criticisms in American newspapers, and the British Foreign
Office halted a £6 million loan to SMR in August 1928 because of Chinese
protests in the wake of military tensions between China and Japan in mid-
1928 and because of Chinese demands in July 1928 for terminating the un-
equal trade treaties imposed on China by the West and Japan. Even so, the
National City Bank lent $20 million to Oriental Development Corporation
for its business projects, many of them in Manchuria. This probably encouraged Japanese hope of increased American capital inflows in Manchuria. After being appointed SMR president by the Tanaka Giichi cabinet
(April 1927–July 1929), Yamamoto Jōtarō (1867–1936) tried to attract Western, particularly American, capital and Chinese investments for SMR.
Yamamoto believed that the economic development of Manchuria should
be accomplished by privatizing SMR and by alleviating tensions with the
West, particularly America and Britain, and with China. Yamamoto's idea
of economic cooperation with foreign countries, particularly the United
States and China, was further embraced by those who replaced the Tanaka
cabinet in the aftermath of the assassination of Manchurian warlord Chang
Tso-lin (1875–1928): Prime Minister Hamaguchi Osachi (1870–1931), his Finance Minister Inoue Junnosuke, and his choice as SMR president, Sen-
goku Mitsugu (1857–1931). Although a similar effort by the Hamaguchi

cabinet (July 1929–April 1931) also failed, the decade preceding the Manchuria Incident in September 1931, when the Japanese Kwantung Army launched a takeover of Manchuria, was characterized by Japanese attempts to develop southern Manchuria jointly with the West, especially the United States, and China so as to alleviate tensions and restructure SMR into a more efficient and internationally competitive firm.[1]

In March 1928, Ayukawa formed Nissan (Nihon sangyō), a holding company, by merging his business interests, including Tobata Casting Company (Tobata imono kabushikigaisha, initially financed, through the mediation of Count Inoue, Ayukawa's great-uncle, by Ayukawa's relatives [Kuhara and the Kaijima and Fujita clans] and the Mitsui Trading Company, a firm in which Inoue was a major advisor), and Kuhara's conglomerate, which had grown during the economic boom caused by World War I. Ayukawa had founded Tobata in 1910 near the state-owned Yawata steelmill in northern Kyūshū, the largest mill in Japan, after a stay in the United States as a laborer to learn the most advanced iron-casting techniques at the Gould Coupler Company in Depew, New York, and the Erie Iron Foundry in Pennsylvania during 1905–7. He purchased machinery and equipment during a trip to the United States in 1908–9. (In 1988, Japan Energy, a company founded by Ayukawa and Kuhara, purchased Gould Inc., a descendant of Gould Coupler; in the 1990s, Japan Energy, as part of a corporate restructuring, sold many of Gould's assets. Hitachi Metals, another ex-Nissan company, became a major shareholder of Erie Malleable Iron, formerly Erie Iron Foundry, in 1988, owned it outright from 1997 to 1999, and then sold it because of change in corporate strategy.)

Until he decided to succeed Kuhara as president of the Kuhara conglomerate, Ayukawa had sundered his business ties with his brother-in-law after resigning as a director of the Kuhara Mining Company in January 1918. Suspicion had developed between the two over starting Tobata Steelworks under Ayukawa in 1916 because Kuhara, who unbeknownst to Ayukawa was starting a new steel mill elsewhere, was unwilling to finance the expansion of the fledgling company. The final break came after Gō Seinosuke's (1865–1942) Oriental Steel Company took over their failed steel operation in April 1918, although the two men did travel to the United States together later that year. At the time of the merger, Ayukawa became a director of Oriental Steel, but his main business efforts in the immediate post–World War I years centered around Tobata Casting, which had a capitalization of $1 million and nearly a thousand employees by 1920. His other main interest was a holding company

he launched in 1922, Kyōritsu Enterprise (Kyōritsu kigyō), with a capital of
$2.5 million; Ayukawa hoped by this means to diversify his business activities
by acquiring other companies during the postwar recession.

Although relations between the two were awkward, in 1927 Ayukawa
agreed to take over Kuhara's near-bankrupt firm. On December 25, 1926, the
president of the Seiyūkai Party, General Tanaka Giichi, visited Ayukawa to
plead for his assistance in securing enough money to pay the upcoming dividends for the Kuhara Mining Company. Tanaka had been a major recipient
of political donations from Kuhara over the years and had tried to help Kuhara by asking Dan Takuma (1858–1932) of the Mitsui Holding Company,
Ikeda Seihin (Shigeaki; 1867–1950) of the Mitsui Bank, and a top executive
at the Daiichi Bank for a bailout, a request that all three rejected. Ayukawa's
immediate response to Tanaka was the same as that of the other three businessmen. Tanaka argued that Kuhara's failure would jeopardize not only his
political life and ambition to be prime minister but also the future of the
Seiyūkai Party, toward whose growth Ayukawa's relative and benefactor
Inoue Kaoru had contributed so much. After Ayukawa told Tanaka he
wanted to think about the matter overnight, Tanaka left and Ayukawa went
to see another brother-in-law, Kimura Kusuyata (1865–1935), the top executive in the Mitsubishi Holding Company. Since Kimura and Kuhara did
not enjoy amicable relations, Ayukawa thought his brother-in-law's answer
would be the same as his initial response to Tanaka's desperate plea. But
Kimura felt that Kuhara's bankruptcy would worsen the already depressed
economy and this might have repercussions for Mitsubishi. With Kimura's
encouragement, Ayukawa changed his mind.

With the generous financial assistance of the Fujita family, which was
headed by Ayukawa's younger brother, Fujita Masasuke (1889–1983), Ayukawa managed to obtain the necessary funds on the day before the Kuhara
Mining Company's stockholder meeting in late December. After the new
year began, Ayukawa, in addition to his contribution, managed to collect
more money from Kuhara executives, the Hitachi Manufacturing Company, and the Fujita Company; an additional source of generous financial
assistance was another of Ayukawa's relatives, and Kuhara Mining Company's auditor, Kaijima Taiichi (1881–1966), and his family. To secure more
capital, Ayukawa raised money by selling stock in the company publicly.

After Ayukawa took over Kuhara's business interests in March 1928,
Kuhara completely disengaged himself from the companies he had built,

and the business relations between the two again ended. In politics, how-ever, Ayukawa supported Kuhara's failed attempt to become foreign minis-ter in Tanaka Giichi's cabinet in the late 1920s. Ayukawa supported Ku-hara's call in early 1928 for creation of a demilitarized and tariff-free buffer state consisting of Siberia, Manchuria, and Korea. In February 1928 Kubara was elected a Lower House member, and Tanaka appointed him minister of communications in May. After the 1930s, Ayukawa seemed to have avoided further involvement in Kuhara's political activities, although he and his rela-tives did bail Kuhara out from a massive financial bankruptcy in 1938. Ku-hara had become president of the Seiyūkai in 1937, and in the summer of 1940 he succeeded in his political dream of dissolving all the political parties and forming a single political organization under the Imperial Rule Assis-tance Association (Taiseiyokusankai), an authoritarian-style organization to rally and stir Japanese nationalism.[2]

In the early 1930s, Ayukawa's Nissan Holding Company made a spec-tacular entrance into big business. It began with a decision of the cabinet of Inukai Tsuyoshi (1855–1932) to take Japan off the gold standard in Decem-ber 1931. A day before this change, Ayukawa had visited Finance Minister Takahashi Korekiyo (1854–1936) and given him a copy of his essay arguing that the output of gold was directly related to the price of gold. After Ayu-kawa had finished explaining his views, Takahashi, to Ayukawa's delight, ordered his aide to implement the policy to increase the price of gold. As the price of gold went up, Ayukawa's Nissan reaped a tremendous profit by sell-ing half of its stock in the Japan Mining Company, the largest producer of gold in the Japanese empire at the time. The popularity of Japan Mining stock in the market also helped increase the price of Nissan's stock, an in-crease that was also part of the overall stock market boom in Japan follow-ing the Manchuria Incident of September 8, 1931. Ayukawa aggressively pur-chased other companies and sold stock in Nissan and its subsidiaries at a premium, not only to institutional investors and corporations but also to individuals. By 1937, 50,783 small shareholders (less than 500 shares a per-son) owned 51.8 percent of Nissan stock, and large investors (over 10,000 shares), most of them institutional investors, held 18.4 percent. Ayukawa's interests controlled a mere 5.2 percent. By using the funds gained in this boom to acquire other companies, by 1937 Nissan not only became Japan's third largest conglomerate after Mitsui and Mitsubishi in size, but also had a stronger base in the heavy and chemical industries, in comparison to the other conglomerates, when the army became serious about forming partnerships with big business to industrialize Manchukuo. Nissan owned such companies as Nissan Motors, Nissan Chemicals, and Hitachi (which merged with Tobata Casting in 1937). The stock market boom also alleviated the financial situation of Nissan's subsidiary in the automobile industry (renamed Nissan Motors in spring 1934) and put it into the black within three years of the company's establishment.[3]

Ayukawa's Business Negotiations with GM and Ford

Ayukawa's primary interest was establishing a competitive Japanese automobile industry that produced affordable passenger cars. The automobile industry, of course, was one of the most technologically complex of the heavy industries and required the growth and maturation of other heavy and chemical industries. In other words, to manufacture cars successfully, Japan had to develop many other heavy and chemical industries.

Ayukawa was well aware that the United States led in most of the advanced heavy and chemical industries and was pre-eminent in the automobile industry. Ayukawa had been working with American automobile manufacturers even before starting Nissan Motors. After Ayukawa's Tobata Casting began supplying parts to three Japanese companies, subsidized by the military, that manufactured trucks (Tokyo Gas and Electric Company, Ishikawajima Automobile Manufacturing Company, and Dat Automobile Manufacturing Company), he also began selling them to Ford Motors and to General Motors (GM), both of which came to Japan in 1925 and saw Japan as the greatest potential market in the Far East.

Ayukawa had four things in mind in establishing a Japanese automobile-manufacturing company. First, as already mentioned, the company was to manufacture car parts. Second, Ayukawa wanted to foster companies under Nissan that provided special alloys and paints so that Nissan would be vertically integrated in producing cars. Third, Ayukawa hoped to create a single Japanese car company through mergers, a point that is discussed further in Chapter 8. Fourth, before engaging in the manufacture of various types of cars and trucks (taishūsha), as Ford and GM were doing in Japan, Nissan would manufacture small passenger vehicles. In thinking about the fourth point, Ayukawa had to face the hard fact that Ford and GM, along with Chrysler, which came to Japan in 1930, almost completely dominated

Japan's automobile market. Ford consistently ranked first in sales, and GM finished second, except for one year when the ranking was reversed. This American dominance continued until May 1936, when the Ministry of Commerce and Industry (MCI) promulgated the Automobile Manufacturing Industry Law.

From the beginning, Ayukawa depended heavily on American technology, equipment, and personnel. Ayukawa was assisted by the American engineer William R. Gorham (1888–1949). Gorham was an inventor, who, among other things, had created an engine for airplanes. He settled in Japan after World War I, and Ayukawa hired him in 1921 as a consultant, around the time Gorham invented a mechanized rickshaw, which became famous in Japan. For Ayukawa, Gorham designed gas engines for ships and farm equipment.

In the late 1920s, the two began manufacturing small and affordable vehicles. In the winter of 1933, Ayukawa sent Gorham to the United States on a purchasing and recruitment trip. Because of the depression, Gorham found good bargains. About 80 percent of the machinery Gorham purchased was second-hand American equipment. He also hired several engineers, including Harry Marshall, a Ford employee, and George Motherwell, a specialist in forging (on a tour of an Opel factory in Germany in 1940, Ayukawa would discover that Motherwell had introduced casting techniques there after leaving Nissan). Over ten American engineers worked for Ayukawa's automobile projects until the late 1930s. In addition to making purchases, for about a month Gorham visited Ford's factory in Dearborn and General Motors' factory near Detroit, where he observed state-of-the-art production methods in detail.

Although Ayukawa had no specific plans for manufacturing cars and trucks as it was building its Yokohama plant adjacent to Ford's factory, Gorham and Japanese engineers produced the Datsun, the first small passenger vehicle made by a Japanese company, at a factory formerly owned by the Dat Automobile Manufacturing Company. Ayukawa had purchased the factory and the right to manufacture cars in March 1933 through Tobata Casting, which had been managerially and financially involved in Dat since August 1931 as its majority shareholder. In 1933 Ayukawa sold its Dat shares to Ishikawajima because he was not interested in making trucks; this decision was a byproduct of merger talks between September 1932 and March

1933 among the three Japanese truck-manufacturing companies, talks that had led to the merger between Dat and Ishikawajima.

In April 1935, Nissan Motors' Yokohama factory produced its first Datsun. The Datsun sold very well in the Japanese market because it was not in competition with the American cars, which were larger. Datsun's sales growth was aided by the lobbying of three business executives, including President Shibusawa Masao (1888–1942) of Ishikawajima Automobile Manufacturing Company, the third son of the prominent industrialist and statesman Shibusawa Eiichi (1840–1931). They urged MCI not to implement a new definition for a small passenger vehicle in the regulations governing motor vehicles. Had the proposed change taken place, the new definition proposed by MCI and the army would have meant doubling the engine size from 500 cc to 1,000 cc and increasing the car's length and width. One of Ayukawa's men, Yoshizaki Ryōzō, persuaded him that this proposal would permit Austin cars from England to slaughter the fledgling Datsun, a small passenger car with a 500 cc engine. Austin protested to Datsun, but it was too late. Sales of Datsun probably would have continued to increase had the government not decided to allocate more resources to manufacturing trucks after 1938.

Because Ayukawa wanted to move into a market dominated by American companies, he decided that the quickest way was to start a joint venture with either Ford or GM. In 1932, Ayukawa approached Ford about a merger. Although both Ayukawa and Gorham preferred a merger with Ford-Japan to one with either of the two other American companies, the discussions were unsuccessful. The Nissan group wanted to purchase 50 percent or more of Ford-Japan's shares, whereas Ford was willing to sell only 49 percent.

Ayukawa then turned his attention to GM. Compared to Ford, GM was much more willing to adapt to local market conditions. Since GM was the result of mergers of over twenty companies, it tended to adopt the same strategy overseas and actively sought joint ventures and mergers with local companies. At the time of Ayukawa's approach, GM had already contacted MCI in 1932 about participating in the merger of the three Japanese truck manufacturers financially supported by the Army. Ayukawa told Managing Director R. A. May of GM Japan that a merger with the Nissan group had better prospects since the military would never allow GM to participate in the merger of the truck manufacturers. The talks between Nissan and GM led to an agreement on April 26, 1934, for the eventual majority control of GM-Japan by Nissan Motors. The Nissan group and GM agreed not only to an immediate arrangement for cross-ownership between Nissan Motors and GM-Japan by exchanging 49 percent of Nissan Motors stock for 49 percent of GM-Japan stock but also to a deal that would allow Nissan Motors to control 51 percent of GM-Japan's stock in five years.

Although MCI, particularly its minister, Matsumoto Jōji (1877–1954), who was also a prominent lawyer, Vice Minister Yoshino Shinji (1888–1971), and Director of the Industrial Affairs Bureau Takeuchi Kakichi (1899–1953), as well as MOF Foreign Exchange Director Aoki Kazuo (1889–1977), apparently supported this development, the Army did not. During a major Manchuria military operation in February 1933, the Imperial Japanese Army had experienced for the first time a situation in which trucks rather than trains served as the crucial means of land transportation. Because the Army could not procure enough Japanese vehicles, which were not mass-produced, it used Ford trucks, which it found to be lighter, faster, and much more reliable than Japanese trucks. Based on this experience, the military came to see the importance of mass-producing similar vehicles, and it began to research building Japanese-made vehicles comparable to Ford and GM trucks and approached MCI in January 1934.

Although some within the Army believed that the quickest way to procure the necessary vehicles was by purchasing Ford and GM vehicles, this view lost out to the opinion represented by Major Itō Hisao of the Army's Mobilization Section; in a September 1935 report, which he had been working on since the previous year, Ito argued that since Ford and GM dominated over 90 percent of the market for standard-type vehicles in Japan, a government licensing system should be implemented to protect and nurture Japanese car companies. Despite the fact that Itō was aware that small Japanese-made passenger vehicles were competitive as a result of technological advances and foreign-exchange devaluation, he believed that Japanese automobile makers could also become competitive through protectionism. Not only would this protectionist measure serve national security needs, but it would also stem the outflow of precious foreign exchange at a time when Japan was suffering from chronic trade deficits. In order to nurture mass production and an economically competitive Japanese automobile industry, Itō thought that a new company or group of companies should be created to foster mass production. Since the automobile industry used many products from other heavy industries, fostering this industry would also stimulate the growth of other heavy industries. Furthermore, World War I had demonstrated that car factories could easily be converted into aircraft factories.

As part of this movement within the military to strengthen the Japanese automobile industry, the Dōwa Automobile Company was established in Manchukuo in March 1934; among the seven major Japanese companies that were major shareholders of Dōwa were Ayukawa's Tobata Casting Company and Tokyo Gas and Electric. The government of Manchukuo and the Kwantung Army established this company to forestall a proposal from the SMR to start a GM knock-down assembly line operated by the railroad company. Because the Army felt such an action would threaten Japanese security, it was particularly intent on blocking the penetration of American automobile companies into the Manchuria market. Dōwa was to assemble cars from parts manufactured by the three Japanese truck-manufacturing companies (Tokyo Gas and Electric, Ishikawajima Automobile Manufacturing Company, and Dat Automobile Manufacturing Company) that were planning to merge. Between 1936 and 1940, Dōwa assembled 936 Toyota trucks. In 1942 Dōwa was acquired by MIDC's Manchuria Automobile Manufacturing Company and became a knock-down assembly operation for Nissan trucks.[4]

After June 1934, MCI and the Army began to build a consensus on regulatory measures for the Japanese automobile industry. The Army completed a proposal for establishing a car industry on June 23, 1934, and MCI, after the army discussed this proposal in several meetings, presented a counterproposal on July 18, 1934. Both proposals called for tax breaks, a government licensing system for companies entering the automobile industry, lower tariffs for foreign machinery needed at car factories, and higher tariffs for auto parts. The two proposals also called for the establishment of a new car factory that could mass-produce standard-type vehicles and important parts for them. The existing automobile companies were to invest in or provide parts for this factory. Although the Army thought in terms of establishing a new company for this task, as it had in Manchukuo, MCI did not favor this option. Both groups clearly wanted to prevent an excessive number of companies, because that would induce chaos in that industry. Meetings among officials from the Resource Agency, MCI, and the Army, Navy, Railroad, Finance, Interior, and Foreign Affairs ministries led to a proposal on October 9, 1934, that called for a government licensing system for the manufacturing of automobiles and major car parts, as well as tax breaks, subsidies, and low-interest loans to foster a Japanese car industry.

Major Itō would later recall that during the course of the discussions that resulted in this proposal, "representative" automobile companies were invited to submit opinions, but they apparently showed no interest in the proposals that were being discussed, except for the provision of subsidies. It is unclear (though highly likely) whether Nissan was a participant in these policy deliberations, but it is clear that the government was tilting to the army's viewpoint. In the fall of 1934, MCI, presumably at the behest of the army, pressured Nissan Motors to acquire immediate majority control of GM-Japan. GM conceded to Nissan by selling it 51 percent of GM-Japan's stock and making other modifications in the terms agreed on April 26. It seemed a done deal. But when Nissan asked the government to approve the merger, it discovered that the government would not permit it to pay GM the dollar equivalent of the ¥8 million to purchase a controlling share of GM-Japan (MOF official Aoki had left his post as foreign exchange director in July 1934). The government was concerned about declining foreign exchange reserves as the result of chronic trade deficits. As the result, GM headquarters in New York informed Ayukawa on January 2, 1935, that it was ending the negotiations.

Despite this unhappy ending, Ayukawa was glad to learn of GM's willingness to resume discussions in the future. In a cable to GM in New York on January 9, 1935, he remarked that "the most economical and quicket [sic] way to the establishment of commercial automobile industry" was through a joint venture with GM. Ayukawa was at this point unaware that the army and MCI would soon veto his idea of transferring technology through a merger with a major foreign multinational company.

Ayukawa expressed interest in certain aspects of the automobile industry regulations, but not in the idea of removing American car companies from the Japanese market. According to Major Itō's post–World War II recollections, Ayukawa said he wanted a government licensing system to prevent an excessive number of companies in the industry, but he did not want subsidies. Ayukawa, like MCI and the Army, wanted to avoid chaotic competition, because this discouraged businessmen from taking risks in building large-scale plants for mass production.[5]

The year 1935 turned out to be a tug-of-war between those who favored cooperating with foreign automobile companies to develop the Japanese automobile industry and those who opposed it. The catalyst was a decision by Ford-Japan. In August 1934, the Army had found out that Ford was planning to purchase land in Yokohama from the municipal government to start a local manufacturing plant in a few years. Ford intended to manufacture Japanese-made Fords rather than assemble them from imported parts. Benjamin Kopf (1890–?), president of Ford-Japan, was eager to do this because of the great demand for Ford vehicles in Japan. In February 1935, Vice Minister of War Yanagawa Heisuke (1879–1945) told the mayor of Yokohama to cancel the land deal with Ford, and the mayor complied.

Even though the deal fell through, Kopf was determined to build a new factory; he was aware of the trend toward protectionism in Japan, and he wanted to expand Ford-Japan's production before the government implemented programs to keep foreign automobile manufacturers out. In April, Kopf initiated talks with Asano Ryōzō (1889–1965), the Harvard-educated steel executive of the Asano conglomerate, to purchase land from the latter's Yokohama property.

In promoting a nationalistic approach to the Japanese automobile industry, the army found a person in MCI more sympathetic to their viewpoint after April 1935, when Kishi Nobusuke (1896–1987) became director of the Industrial Affairs Bureau after his predecessor Takeuchi left for Manchukuo as an economic advisor to the Kwantung Army. It was relatively easy for Itō to approach Kishi since a classmate of his in the army academy, Kogane Yoshiteru (1898–1984), was Kishi's new and loyal chief of the Bureau's Industrial Policy Section. Kishi seemed to have mixed feelings about joint ventures between Japanese and foreign companies. On the one hand, Kishi intended to realize laws to regulate the automobile and the chemical fertilizer industries so that they could serve as centers of Japan's advancement in the heavy and chemical industries (at the time, among Japan's heavy industries, only shipbuilding and locomotive manufacturing were internationally competitive). On the other hand, Kishi seemed to share Yoshino's view of the massive technological gap in car manufacturing between Japan and the United States and thought it imperative to incorporate foreign technology to catch up.

Nevertheless, in spite of these mixed feelings, Kishi and Kogane were sympathetic to the Army's demands. In the end, they could not or did not oppose its views in any substantive way. Although MCI was initially indifferent, the Army pressured the ministry to take action. Major Itō met with

MCI's Kishi and Kogane in April, and on May 20 MCI announced its opposition to the signing of an agreement for this land purchase. In spite of these negative pressures, Kopf and Asano continued the talks. On July 24, 1935, the two signed an agreement, and Ford proceeded to start construction after Dearborn gave a green light in October.[6]

Meanwhile, the Army intensified its attempt to torpedo the deal. As Miyata Masayoshi, a MCI official who worked in Kishi's bureau at the time, recalled years later, the movement by Ford to open a local factory intensified the activities of those government officials who wanted a protectionist program to stop further expansion of foreign car companies into the Japanese market. There was, however, a major point of contention between the Army and MCI. The ministry supported equal treatment of Japanese automobile companies and joint ventures between Japanese and foreign manufacturers. The discussions between the two ministries led to an agreement on July 12, and after discussions with other relevant ministries, the cabinet approved the Outline for the Japanese Automobile Industry Law on August 8, 1935, shortly after Kopf and Asano reached their agreement. The outline stated that the existing car companies in Japan were permitted to operate within the limits of current production levels. To be eligible to expand after the law went into effect, a company had to meet one condition: a majority of its stock had to be in Japanese hands. Companies that did not meet this requirement would fall outside the government's licensing system. The companies that came under this system were to abide by new regulations on industry and national defense. The Army and MCI were to discuss ways to favor the growth of Japanese automobile companies, including tax breaks.[7]

This cabinet decision was significant for its intent to implement protectionist measures. The outline's provisions were incorporated into the Automobile Manufacturing Law, which was enacted in May 1936 and put into force two months later. The law was based on the national defense argument, which was used for the second time (the first was the 1934 Petroleum Industry Law). MCI official Kogane had apparently gotten this idea from a friend at the Foreign Ministry, First Section Chief of Commerce and Trade Matsushima Shikao (1888–1968); they had to argue against Matsushima's boss, Director of Commerce and Trade Kurusu Saburō, who argued that the protectionist proposals violated the 1911 commerce and navigation treaty with the United States. Furthermore, they had to overcome the same argument as Kurusu made by the Cabinet Legal Section and also ignore the Navy Ministry's favorable view of Ford-Japan as a semi-Japanese company.

In October, despite the government's announcement of the outline on August 9, Ford went ahead with its plans to build a factory. In the meantime, there was another significant event: GM and Nissan resumed talks during the summer. Ayukawa proposed a merger between Nissan Motors and GM-Japan, in which 51 percent of the newly merged company would be controlled by Nissan and 49 percent by GM; this would avoid the need to send foreign exchange to GM in New York. In September and October, Harry B. Phillips, a top GM executive, Managing Director May of GM-Japan, and two other executives met with MCI officials Kishi, Kogane, and Vice Minister Yoshino regarding the merger. Ayukawa, along with his aide Kishimoto Kantarō, met separately with these MCI officials. On September 21, Kishi conveyed to Ayukawa MCI's four conditions for the merger and asked Ayukawa to show them to May. First, if Nissan Motors merged with GM-Japan, Nissan had to agree to abide by the government's policies on establishing a Japanese automobile industry. Second, the two parties had to agree to restrictions on distribution channels for cars, probably because Kishi and those who were less sympathetic to this merger wanted to limit the competitiveness of the new company. Third, the agreement had to include a clause that stipulated that the assembly of cars be part of a manufacturing department controlled by a Nissan board member and that the distribution of cars be under the authority of a GM board member for some time; Kishi probably intended this arrangement to satisfy both Nissan and GM. Fourth, after the merger, the new company would start mass production of cars and automobile parts as soon as possible under the government's regulations for the automobile industry.

Although Yoshino stated later in an oral history interview that his only contribution to the merger discussions was to make his house available as a place for Ayukawa and Phillips to carry out their negotiations and that he was not present in the meeting room, a memorandum written by Kishimoto reveals that he not only was present but also argued for the merger. In front of Ayukawa, Phillips, and Kishimoto, Yoshino said the military wanted intensely to establish an automobile industry in Japan run only by the Japanese themselves. Although the success of Nissan Motors in producing Datsun confirmed Yoshino's thinking that the Japanese could establish an industry by themselves, he thought a merger between Nissan and GM would be both a better approach and a shorter and quicker way to establish it. Yoshino agreed with Ayukawa that both GM and Ford had contributed enormously to Japan and indicated that he thought it would not be good to kick GM and Ford out as soon as it seemed Japan could go it alone. Yoshino said MCI did not favor an excessively nationalistic line on this issue and saw the importance of retaining international cooperation. In reply, Phillips asked if the merged company would enjoy equal treatment with other Japanese car companies, and the vice minister confirmed this.[8]

On October 20, 1935, both Nissan and GM reached an agreement in principle. The two sides met further to iron out the details, and Ayukawa indicated that he wanted to finalize an agreement by November 20. But problems arose. According to a draft memorandum of January 24, 1936, the two sides disagreed over such issues as corporate organization, manufacturing arrangements, and the importation of auto parts. Underlying this disagreement was the issue of profits; GM thought profits were going to be sacrificed to the Japanese government's priorities. Nissan thought that in peacetime it would be possible both to generate a profit and to establish a Japanese automobile industry. But boosting Japanese production had become such a national imperative that it needed to be done quickly, and therefore the principle of profit maximization had to be sacrificed.

In December, at Ayukawa's order, two directors of Nissan Motors with technical expertise, Asahara Genshichi (1891–1970) and Kubota Tokujirō, traveled to New York City to hear GM's final thoughts on the merger. GM declined to make an agreement. It worried that any joint venture with Nissan would be nationalized, as had been its venture with Opel in Germany, which had been taken over by the government. GM feared the Japanese Army's pursuit of import-substitution measures against foreign cars would lead to the same situation. After the two companies announced that talks were being postponed, Asahara and Kubota were allowed to tour all the GM factories they had hoped to see in the United States and many GM factories in Europe as well.[9]

Nissan now was ready to pursue a contingency plan of relying on the assistance of the Japanese government. Nevertheless, Ayukawa continued efforts to acquire advanced American technology, and this led to Nissan's purchase of equipment and technology from U.S. automaker Graham-Paige through the introduction of an American businessman, President John Biggers of Libbey-Owens-Ford Glass Company. Because of the coup attempt in 1936 known as the February 26 incident, Biggers had to extend his stay in Japan. He had been visiting Japan to find out why Japan Plate Glass Company, which used Libbey's production methods, had achieved higher productivity than Libbey. Because Biggers had time to kill, the Sumitomo family, who owned Japan Plate Glass, introduced Biggers to MOF official Ishiwatari Sōtarō (1891–1950). Ishiwatari asked him if he knew of an American car company that could facilitate the purchase of machinery needed for the production of automobiles. One of the major stockholders in Libbey-Owens was Joseph Graham of Graham-Paige. Biggers was more than glad to introduce Graham to executives from Nissan because Graham-Paige was close to bankruptcy and needed to sell its facilities.

Through Ishiwatari, Ayukawa met Biggers, and after a friendly conversation he ordered Asahara in London and Kubota in the United States to meet with Graham. The two men purchased all the machinery that was needed to modernize Nissan's Yokohama factory, including the manufacture of engines. And from a Graham-Paige subcontractor, they purchased the machinery to build a foundry next to the Nissan Motors plant. Graham remarked that although he had lost out in competition to GM and Ford, he wanted Nissan to do what he had been unable to do and to manufacture cab-over trucks as well. Kubota, Asahara, and Hatakemura Eki brought back what they had purchased from Graham-Paige, as well as an engineer from that company to help set up the new Nissan facility in Yokohama. In May 1937, Nissan began selling the cab-over Nissan Model 80 truck and the Nissan Model 90 bus; Nissan also built a foundry next to its car factory with the assistance of engineers hired from Graham-Paige and the foundry company from which Nissan had purchased the machines for the new facility.[10]

Even as Ayukawa was acquiring materials from Graham-Paige, the Army, which had gained more political power after the February 26 incident, interfered with Ford's plan to build a factory and passed the Automobile Manufacturing Law on May 29, 1936. In Chalmers Johnson's words, the law "required that manufacturers of cars and trucks in Japan be licensed . . . by the government . . . for the first few firms left in this sector." The two recipients of a license, Nissan Motors and Toyota Motors, received such benefits as government provision of half their capital and the elimination of taxes and import duties for five years. "By 1939 the law had put foreign car manufacturers in Japan (Ford and GM) out of business, as it was intended

to do." This law was one of the first two laws "designed to provide special
governmental financing, taxes, and protective measures for individual industries, and the first that were defended in terms of national defense needs."
According to Johnson, "their importance cannot be overstated" because they
were "part of the prewar heritage most directly relevant to postwar industrial policy." Although "these laws did much to promote the particular industries concerned, . . . politically they represented compromises between
the state-control and the self-control persuasions" because "the business sector was still strong enough to withstand state and public pressure and to insist on private ownership and a large measure of private management, which
is closer to the postwar pattern than some of the other measures enacted by
the state-control group during the 1930s."[11]

Just as the military police had watched Ayukawa during his negotiations
with GM, the military police and the secret police interfered with Ford's factory construction plans and even threatened Ford employees. MCI official
Kogane also hindered Ford's program shortly before the Automobile Manufacturing Law was put into force in July 1936.[12]

Meanwhile, faced with government encroachment in the automobile industry, Nissan approached Lower House member Asakura Tsuneto (1882–
1971), formerly a prominent business executive in the textile industry, to
lobby on its behalf. With the promulgation of the Automobile Law on July
11, 1936, automobile companies had to have a government-issued license to
survive in the industry. Asakura was a good friend of Commerce Minister
Ogawa Gōtarō (1876–1945), and Ogawa relied on Asakura for advice on
various policy issues concerning industry. On August 19, 1936, Nissan executive Yamamoto Sōji invited Asakura for a discussion and asked for his assistance in the merger of Nissan Motors, Jidōsha kōgyō (which was based on a
merger between Dat Automobile Manufacturing Company and Ishikawajima Automobile Manufacturing Company), and the Tokyo Gas and Electricity Company. Nissan wanted to enhance its chances to receive a
government license under the new law and wanted to appeal to the government's wish to avoid untrammeled competition in the automobile industry.[13] After Nissan, along with Toyoda Automatic Loom Company, received government licenses on September 19, it continued to prod Asakura
for assistance in the merger of the three companies, and on November 3,
Minister Ogawa expressed his approval on the grounds of national interest.

In the end, however, the other companies rejected Nissan's offer and merged in 1937 to form the Tokyo Automobile Industry Company.[14]

MCI Minister Ogawa, a supporter of international cooperation in building Japan's automobile industry, apparently felt disgusted by the fact that the law retroactively applied the production levels of August 9, 1935, when the cabinet had approved the automobile regulation; under this provision, Ford-Japan could not expand its production because its new factory had not been built at that point.

Ogawa now had a perfect pretext to move against the Yoshino-Kishi group in MCI and to increase his control over the ministry.[15] In a round of personnel changes in October, Kogane was sent to a post in Kyūshū. Yoshino decided to resign; he felt five years of service as vice minister was long enough, and he took a new job as president of the Northeast Development Bureau, a public holding company established in May 1936 for the economic development of the underdeveloped Northeast region, his native area.

As a precursor of the MIDC, the Northeast Development Bureau formulated and implemented policies for creating industry in the Tohoku region. It produced such important materials for the military as magnesium, aluminum, and alcohol. The military supported Yoshino and his longtime colleague and economic guru Matsui Haruo (1891–1966) because they were working to strengthen national defense and to industrialize this overwhelmingly agricultural region. Like Ayukawa, Yoshino looked to the United States as a model of economic development and industrialization and faced difficulties in implementing his ideas. Yoshino envisioned a Japanese version of a TVA, one of the New Deal programs. To his disappointment, the Interior Ministry's programs for the region fell far short of a comprehensive economic development plan. Yoshino went along with these pre-existing plans, although he insisted to MCI Minister Ogawa that a businessman such as Mori Naoteru (1884–1941) of Shōwa Fertilizer Company rather than bureaucrats should manage the project when it was time to decide what to do with the hydroelectricity generated from the new dams in the Tohoku region; in the end, Mori's Shōwa Electric Works created and ran electric-powered factories that produced aluminum in Fukushima prefecture.[16]

Following Ogawa's reorganization of MCI, Kishi went to Manchukuo in October 1936 to oversee industrialization there, and in July 1937 he gained full authority as deputy directory of industry, a vice-ministerial position

overseeing commerce, industry, and agriculture. Because the minister was a
Manchu and had no real authority, Kishi became the most powerful civilian
official in Manchukuo after Hoshino Naoki (1892–1978), secretary of the
General Affairs Agency since December 1936 and secretary general of that
agency from July 1937 to July 1940. Kishi was welcomed in Manchukuo by
both the Kwantung Army and the Japanese Army. When the Japanese government was preparing in 1930 to reinstate the gold standard, Kishi's 1927
report on the German and American rationalization movements drew
attention among civilian and military policymakers. Army officers such as
Akinaga Tsukizō (1893–1949) and Katakura Tadashi (1898–1991), who
played central roles in running Manchukuo, wanted Kishi to work in
Manchukuo, and Katakura had visited Yoshino for about a year to gain his
support.

Interested in the developments in Manchuria after 1931, Kishi wanted to
take over the administration of the industrial affairs of Manchukuo from the
Army; in 1933 he was instrumental in sending MCI officials, including Shiina Etsusaburō (1898–1979), who will reappear in Chapter 8, to undertake
this task. When Kishi arrived in Manchukuo, he told General Itagaki Seishirō (1885–1948) he wanted the Kwantung Army to give him full authority
over industrial affairs for the good of both Manchukuo and Japan. Itagaki
concurred. Soon, however, Kishi realized his limitations and began supporting the idea of letting a businessman manage Manchukuo's industrialization.[17] Both the leading civilian and military bureaucrats, as represented by
Kishi and Ishiwara Kanji (1889–1949), who will appear frequently in the
next chapter, respectively, chose Ayukawa for that task. For Ayukawa, the
problem then became addressing the idea of economic internationalism
within the confines of economic projects in Manchukuo.

TWO

Ayukawa's Involvement in Manchukuo

Shortly after the outbreak of the Sino-Japanese War in July 1937, Japan began a desperate and ambitious attempt to attract direct and indirect American investment in Manchukuo based on Ayukawa Yoshisuke's ideas. Ayukawa probably would not have become deeply involved in Manchukuo, or
perhaps not even involved at all, had not General Ishiwara Kanji, the mas-
termind of Japan's conquest of Manchuria,[1] wooed him into helping the
military with Manchukuo's industrialization programs. Led by Ishiwara, the
Japanese military and civilian bureaucrats who dominated Manchukuo were
in desperate need of talented business managers as well as technology,
equipment, and capital. Many of these bureaucrats were aware that Manchukuo, like Japan, was dependent on Western capital, equipment, and
technology for creating and running its heavy and chemical industries. They
also tended to view the SMR's non-railroad operations as a hindrance to
Manchukuo's industrialization. Ayukawa persuaded them that in order for
Manchukuo to achieve its goals in these industries, it had to rely heavily on
Western, particularly American, inputs. He increasingly took the lead in the
direction of Manchukuo's industrialization, as elite civilian and military bureaucrats called on him for help with their economic programs.

Military Imperatives and Bureaucratic Bungling

In April 1937, under the guidance of the Kwantung Army, Manchukuo
launched an ambitious economic plan for the heavy industrialization of

Manchuria. Although that year marked the beginning of concentrated efforts for that purpose, less ambitious efforts had been under way since 1933. The five-year economic plan for heavy industrialization begun in 1937 was formulated under the leadership of General Ishiwara. Realistic military officers like him had come to realize in the mid-1930s the futility of the anti-*zaibatsu* policy they had imposed in Manchukuo because of their frustrations with the SMR as the central organization in Manchukuo's economic development. Military officers and upper-level civilian bureaucrats began to seek the ideas of businessmen.

Ishiwara was a proponent of the industrialization of Manchukuo because he believed that Japan would have to fight a long and protracted "Final War" with the United States, the war to end all wars and achieve world unity. He formulated and articulated this idea as an instructor at the Army Staff College between 1925 and 1928. Ishiwara believed that the United States and Japan would dominate Western civilization and Asian civilization, respectively, and that the decisive factor in the Final War would be airpower.[2] In order to prepare for this war, Japan had to establish a self-sufficient industrial base in the Asiatic continent for its military buildup by whatever means were necessary—military operations, diplomacy, economic pressures, alliances, political maneuvers.[3]

As for the location for such an industrial base, Ishiwara thought Japan had to conquer not only southern Manchuria, where Japan had a sphere of influence, but also northern Manchuria, the area within the Soviet sphere of influence. He believed that Japan would be pushed out of Manchuria unless it conquered it. Economically, Manchuria would solve Japan's overpopulation problem, and its abundant economic resources could be used for both Japanese and Manchurian industrial development. Militarily, the occupation of all of Manchuria would check the southward expansion of the Soviet Union.[4]

For Ishiwara and the middle echelons in the Kwantung Army, Manchuria also provided a unique opportunity for social and economic experimentation. The new state was to be a "paradise" based on the "righteous way" and "harmony" among the five Asiatic races living there—Japanese, Chinese, Koreans, Manchurians, and Mongolians. The new country would also be free of the corruption and compromises pervasive in the liberal polity of Japan, as well as of the zaibatsu, who pursued profits at the expense of the Japanese masses.

However, these social ideals never materialized. As Yamamuro Shin'ichi has pointed out in detail, Manchukuo was a garrison state. There was no "righteous way" and no "paradise" there.[5] And it is questionable whether Kwantung Army officers in policymaking circles fully espoused racial harmony.

On the economic front, between January 1932 and March 1933, the Kwantung Army formulated the following policies: (1) control business activities and achieve effective allocation of resources for the creation of basic industries important for national defense without taking the market mechanism into account; (2) discourage the profit motive and solve economic inequalities, a situation, if achieved, that would serve as a model for Japan and elsewhere; and (3) maintain the Open Door policy in Manchukuo and welcome foreign capital and investment so long as it contributed to strengthening national defense and Japanese economic interests were protected.[6]

Policymakers within the Japanese Army around the time of the Manchuria Incident wanted to avoid conflict with the United States and were open to the idea of cooperating with American economic interests, which they perceived as increasingly interested in expanding into Asia; they thought that this was the United States' reason for advocating the Open Door policy.[7] Likewise, around April or May 1932, the Kwantung Army Chief of Staff Itagaki Seishirō (1885–1948), Ishiwara's boss and an instigator of the Manchuria Incident, issued a policy analysis that called for economic cooperation with the United States. Itagaki perceived that the Great Depression would propel American business to seek markets not only in its "backyard" in Latin America but also in China, where the levels of U.S. trade and investment were only 40 percent and 20 percent, respectively, of U.S. activities in Japan. For Itagaki, the United States was using the Open Door as a cloak to promote its own economic interests, and Japan should accept that principle as long as it did not create American economic dominance in Asia. He recommended cooperation with the United States as long as it did not threaten Japanese economic interests and as long as it prevented the United States from cooperating with Great Britain and France and against Japan on the Manchukuo question.[8]

In March 1933, the Kwantung Army announced the "Basic Outline for the Economic Construction of Manchukuo" ("Manshūkoku keizai kensetsu kōyō") through the Manchukuo government and made public for the first time its fundamental principles for economic development and its goal of doubling production in each industrial sector in ten years without guaranteeing profits or the free flow of capital within the country.[9] The outline justified the imposition of state control over the market economy as needed to achieve "healthy" domestic economic development and create a model state for other countries. It proposed four actions: (1) the elimination of concerns in which the few profited at the expense of the many; (2) the effective development of resources and the comprehensive development of each economic sector through government control of "important economic sectors" and rationalization; (3) the use of foreign capital and foreign technology based on the Open Door principle; and (4) the strengthening of economic cooperation with Japan as one means to integrate and rationalize the East Asian economy. On the second point, industries considered nationally or publicly important were in principle to be managed by public or special companies based on the principle of one company per industry, which meant control by one firm over an industry. Companies in other sectors were allowed to operate freely.[10] In spite of the anti-zaibatsu stance underlying the outline, the military understood the need to attract capital from outside Manchukuo, both Japanese and foreign.

Contrary to the military's hopes, capital, particularly direct investments, was not forthcoming from Japan to the extent they wanted. Japanese businesses were reluctant to invest in Manchukuo because of their uncertainty over which industries were to come under strict government regulation based on the vague criterion "important for national defense or as a public good," the rampant social disorder due to bandit and guerrilla activities in Manchukuo during the early 1930s, and the unstable exchange rate between the Japanese yen and the Manchukuo yuan until the two were fixed in 1935.[11] Furthermore, Japanese companies were reluctant to invest in companies that fell into the category of special or semi-special companies in Manchuria. Although they were not nationalized companies, they were heavily regulated, quasi-governmental companies in a state that discouraged companies from making profits.[12]

Although the SMR played a central role until 1936 in channeling capital from Japan and managing and directly investing in all industries the Kwantung Army considered important for building a national defense state against the Soviet Union, it suffered from capital deficiency. The Kwantung Army knew that the SMR could not simultaneously pursue industrialization and aggressively expand the railroad system under its control.[13] In order to obtain an adequate amount of capital, the military, through the Manchukuo government, announced in April and June 1934 that it would welcome private investment from Japan. This, however, did not solve the capital-shortage problem because the announcement remained ambiguous on the issue of profits, which were permitted only to the SMR. The SMR was also not helped by the fact that Japanese economic recovery, which happened earlier than in most Western nations, caused a decrease in exports of surplus capital and products to Manchuria.[14] Both new and old Japanese conglomerates, as well as smaller firms, began making significant investments in Manchukuo after 1934,[15] but they were not enough to satisfy the demand for direct investments. Japanese companies tended to focus on indirect investments such as financing SMR, while SMR made the bulk of direct investments.[16]

Since the Army faced mounting difficulties in steering the Manchukuo economy to its satisfaction, policymakers in the Army realized that as long as the SMR functioned as the central organization for Manchukuo's industrialization, the Army could not exercise firm control over the economy. The Army had begun moving to weaken the SMR as early as 1933 when it secretly formulated a plan to reorganize the SMR into a company involved solely in railroad and harbor businesses and convert SMR subsidiaries engaged in other industries into special companies. Furthermore, the Army proposed to strip the SMR of autonomy in the railroad zone by abolishing extraterritoriality in the zone as well as SMR administrative authority over it. Manchukuo was going to gain that authority, and this meant the Army would gain command over the economic and administrative affairs of Manchukuo.

Although the Army failed to carry out the reorganization of the SMR until Ayukawa's Nissan moved to Manchukuo in 1937, it had succeeded by December 1934 in dominating military, diplomatic, and administrative matters in Manchukuo as well as Japan-Manchukuo relations. The Army achieved this through an expansion in the authority of the commander of the Kwantung Army, who now was simultaneously the ambassador to Manchukuo, and through the creation in Japan of the Steering Committee on Manchurian Affairs (Tai-Man jimukyoku), which consisted of ministries having jurisdictions in Manchukuo and in which the Army was the dominant voice.[17]

The Origins of MIDC

Although not necessarily formulated as an alternative to the SMR in carrying out investment projects for Manchukuo's industrialization, the idea of the Manchuria Industrial Development Corporation (MIDC) probably originated in 1934 when Asakura Tsuneto, a prominent businessman in the textile and electric power industries, proposed to the Army that a large, joint Japan-Manchukuo investment company be formed. Asakura started thinking about this on November 29 and submitted his proposal to his longtime friend General Minami Jirō (1874–1955) on December 10, the day Minami was appointed commander of the Kwantung Army.[18] Asakura envisioned a quasi-governmental company responsible for carrying out research on and investments in forestry, mining, commerce, and industry. He favored government subsidies for a certain period to guarantee a return on investments.

Asakura, however, differed from Ayukawa in that he wanted Manchukuo to become less dependent on foreign imports and wanted it to continue importing Japanese goods. As we shall see below, Ayukawa advocated the active participation of Western countries, although he supported the goal of a self-sufficient Manchukuo economy. In addition, he, unlike Ayukawa, preferred regulating the economy. But he did not want government dominance of the economy and argued, in December 1935, that this company should advise the government on whether a particular industry should be regulated or not.[19]

This view must have been heard by other influential figures aside from Minami. Asakura was well connected with prominent businessmen, high-ranking Army officers, and government officials in Japan and Manchukuo. For example, in Manchukuo he knew Matsuoka Yōsuke (1880–1946), whose appointment as SMR president on August 1, 1935, Minami had backed.[20] On May 10, 1935, Minami wrote Asakura that his views were being given careful consideration as Manchukuo organized the Japan-Manchukuo Economic Committee (Nichi-Man keizai kyōdō iinkai).[21]

As he witnessed these, Asakura found himself increasingly interested in finding an influential business position in Manchukuo.[22] In the spring of 1936, his and Ayukawa's paths crossed through Minister of Commerce and Industry Ogawa Gōtarō. Asakura by then had won a seat in the Lower House as a representative from Ōita prefecture in February 1936. During his thirteen-month career as a politician, he used his experience as a businessman in formulating economic policy. In early 1936 Asakura was arguing for the establishment of an investment company that would take over the stock of SMR's subsidiaries as a way to industrialize Manchukuo, Mongolia, and northern China. Although Matsuoka rejected this new proposal, Ayukawa indicated that he agreed with it shortly before he visited Manchuria on the invitation of the Kwantung Army.[23] Ayukawa went to Manchukuo because of Ishiwara's scheme to accelerate Manchuria's industrialization.

As the first phase of Manchukuo's industrialization came to an end, Ishiwara reappeared at the center of policy formulation. He became chief of the Operations Section in the General Staff on August 1, 1935. Following the assassination of Nagata Tetsuzan (1884–1935), director of military affairs, on August 12, an incident that resulted from infighting between the State Control and the Imperial Way factions in the Army, Ishiwara succeeded Nagata in articulating the integration of the long-term military and industrial planning for the creation of the national defense state to prepare for the total mobilization of the country for war.[24] Ishiwara's ideas were close to those of Nagata's State Control faction. He and the middle echelon in the Army in this faction supported state socialism and opposed immediate war with the Soviet Union, which was supported by the Imperial Way faction.[25]

In the fall of 1935, Ishiwara was shocked to find out that Japanese troop strength in Manchukuo was 36 percent of the Soviet Union's in the Far East and Japanese airpower was 23 percent of the Soviet Union's. Realizing that neither the government nor the private sector had comprehensively surveyed Japan's economic capabilities, he asked Miyazaki Masayoshi (1893–1954), a researcher in the Tokyo office of the SMR, to head his private research organization, the Japan-Manchuria Finance and Economic Research Association (Nichi-Man zaisei kenkyūkai; the "Miyazaki group"), to investigate secretly, among other things, both this issue and economic planning;[26] Ishiwara approached Matsuoka Yōsuke and started this group with annual subscriptions of ¥50,000 and ¥10,000 by SMR and by the General Staff, respectively. Ishiwara wanted the military capability of Japan in the Asian continent to increase to at least 80 percent of the Soviet forces in the Far East, a financially overambitious goal.[27] By June and July 1936, Ishiwara was arguing for completing preparations for the war with the Soviet Union by 1941. Until then he prescribed continued diplomatic isolation of the Soviet Union, economic cooperation with Manchuria and North China, and the maintenance of friendly neutrality with the United States and Great Britain.

Following the suppression of the February 26 rebellion in 1936, Ishiwara was one of the most powerful military figures until the outbreak of the Sino-Japanese war in July 1937. Because of his opposition to that war, he became completely isolated within the policymaking group in the Army.[28] Although Ishiwara flirted with the idea of carrying out the Shōwa Restoration during the February 26 rebellion, because he saw the restoration as important for the establishment of the national defense state, he nevertheless perceived the rebellion as undermining that effort and sided with those who suppressed the uprising.[29] His political influence was at its apex after he became chief of the War Leadership Section in the General Staff, which was responsible for economic planning for military buildup. Mutō Akira (1892–1948), a Military Affairs Bureau officer and one of his two chief opponents, was transferred to the Intelligence Section of the Kwantung Army. The other, Umezu Yoshijirō (1882–1949), vice minister of war, lost his influence over the Military Affairs Section, whose functions overlapped those of the War Leadership Section, as Ishiwara won the support of the new chief of the Military Affairs Section, Isogai Rensuke (1886–1967). The Army as a whole had emerged as the most powerful group in the country after the failed rebellion, and with the decline of the Imperial Way group, Ishiwara was well placed to create the national defense state.[30]

In August 1936, the Miyazaki group completed the "Plans for Revenues and Expenditures and the General Outlines Regarding Emergency Measures for the Empire for 1937–41" ("Shōwa jūninendo ikō gonenkan sainyū oyobi saishutsu keikaku jisshi kokusaku taikō"), which became the basis for the Five-Year Plan for Manchuria in 1937 and the Four-Year Plan for Japan in 1939.[31] The document discussed financial plans, emergency measures for administrative reform and economic control, and the expansion of defense industries. The document focused on the last two, and it formulated a comprehensive plan for building military industries in Japan and Manchuria. The outline aimed to strengthen both the Japanese and the Manchurian economies through the development of natural resources such as steel and oil vital to military industries.[32]

April 1937 marked the beginning of the Five-Year (Original) Plan. Under this plan, from 1936 to 1941 the production of pig iron was to expand 200 percent, of steel products 270 percent, of coal 100 percent, and of weapons 400 percent. By 1941 Manchukuo was supposed to produce 0.8 million tons of liquefied coal and oil shale, 4,000 automobiles, and 340 aircraft annually. Including expenditures on agriculture, communications, transportation, and immigration, the total cost of the operation was estimated at ¥2.5 billion.[33]

Ayukawa's Involvement

By the time Manchukuo began to implement the Five-Year Plan, Ishiwara and other civilian and military bureaucrats wanted Ayukawa to participate in Manchukuo's industrialization. The old bureaucrats and military men who ran the special companies and semi-special companies were simply incompetent, and Ishiwara Kanji's men began to solicit opinions confidentially from leading figures in business and politics regarding the Miyazaki Plan drafted in August 1936. Among those who saw this document were Prince Konoe Fumimaro (1891–1945), chairman of the House of Peers; Ikeda Seihin (Shigeaki), the top executive of the Mitsui conglomerate; Yūki Toyotarō (1877–1951), president of the Industrial Bank of Japan; Tsuda Shingo (1881–1948), president of the Kanegafuchi (Kanebō) Textile Company; Noguchi Jun (Shitagau) (1873–1944), president of a major conglomerate; Kido Kōichi (1889–1977), head secretary to the Lord Keeper of the Privy Seal; Ogura Masatsune (1875–1961), the top executive of the Sumitomo conglomerate; and Ayukawa.[34]

But even before this, among the businessmen Ishiwara had contacted,[35] he had his eyes on three businessmen: Ikeda Seihin, one of the most powerful figures in the Japanese business world at the time, Tsuda, and Ayukawa. These men had representatives working in the Miyazaki group. In dealing with these men, Ishiwara from the beginning focused his attention on Ayukawa.

Although the Army asked for the opinions of zaibatsu leaders, Mitsui and other zaibatsu were not suited for the task because of the strong anti-zaibatsu sentiment among the middle echelons and below of the Kwantung Army. For those in the Army who sought cooperation from big business, it was easier to argue that the new conglomerates such as Nissan did not contradict this anti-zaibatsu ideology since they had to rely heavily on financing from government banks such as the Industrial Bank of Japan and publicly issued stocks and bonds. In other words, they did not possess their own private banks and hence could not be privately managed as much as zaibatsu companies. Because Nissan was owned by over 50,000 stockholders, its supporters in the Army argued that this was an indication that it benefited many, not few.

Another important factor was that these new conglomerates had become corporate giants in the 1930s by concentrating primarily in the heavy and chemical industries, the centers of Japan's economic growth.[36] By 1937, 54.9 percent of Japan's production was in the heavy and chemical industries, and this jumped to 65.6 percent by 1941.[37] Although the zaibatsu had monopolies in some heavy industries such as shipbuilding, electric wire, steel, and electric machinery, it was the new conglomerates such as Nissan, Japan Nitrogen, Nissō, and Riken that invested and took risks in the 1920s in the technologically sophisticated heavy and chemical industries; they survived the competition with the zaibatsu by establishing niches in areas using sophisticated technology. Between 1930 and 1937, although the share of heavy and chemical industries as a percentage of total industrial operations for Mitsui, Mitsubishi, and Sumitomo increased from 14.2 to 21.4 percent, the percentages for the four new conglomerates stayed at a much higher level: 50.3 percent in 1930 and 50 percent in 1937.[38]

Around January or February 1936, Ishiwara sent Asahara Kenzō (1897–1967) to ask Ayukawa's opinions on starting an automobile industry in Manchukuo. Asahara, at age 23, had led the strike in 1920 that stopped the furnace at the Yawata Steelmill. In the 1920s he was active in the labor movement, and from 1928 to 1932 he served in the Lower House as a socialist politician; in January 1936 Asahara broke his ties to the Social Mass Party (Shakai taishūtō), a socialist party, and henceforth devoted his efforts to furthering Ishiwara's cause. Ayukawa had known Asahara since 1927, when the latter, at Ayukawa's request, had helped prevent a strike at Hitachi's Kudamatsu factory in Yamaguchi prefecture. Asahara conveyed Ayukawa's opinions to Ishiwara, and in May or June 1936 Ishiwara again asked Ayukawa about setting up an automobile industry in Manchuria. Ayukawa told him a comprehensive economic development plan centering around the heavy industries was needed because Manchuria did not possess an adequate infrastructure and basic industries to start an automobile industry. Unless the infrastructure was created, the automobile industry should stay in Japan.

From reading secret reports that the SMR Research Committee had compiled for Ishiwara and the Miyazaki group, Ayukawa was aware of the abundant natural resources in Manchuria. Yet, like Ikeda, Yūki, and Konoe, Ayukawa was skeptical about achieving the goals under the Five-Year Plan. After Asahara gave him a copy of the economic plans drafted by the Miyazaki group, Ayukawa had his aide Yano Yoshiaki examine them. Yano reported that they failed to consider the issues of timing and the coordination of the allocation of resources and goods.

In spite of this negative finding, Ayukawa was pleased to become acquainted with Ishiwara and to have a chance to confirm at first hand what he had indirectly heard about Ishiwara's opinions regarding the economic management of Manchuria. Ishiwara told him the Japanese bureaucrats in Manchuria should be replaced by Chinese and Manchurian bureaucrats as soon as possible and that the bureaucracy and the military should stop intervening in the Manchurian economy and let Japanese businessmen take it over.[39]

Ishiwara and Katakura Tadashi, a member of the Steering Committee on Manchuria and the husband of General Minami's niece, discussed Ayukawa's opinions and then told Asahara to request Chief of Staff of the Kwantung Army Itagaki to invite Ayukawa to Manchukuo. After receiving Itagaki's telegram in September, Ayukawa flew to Manchukuo in November,[40] without being aware that the Kwantung Army was approaching other industrialists for their opinions and that by September the Army had already reached a consensus on Manchukuo's industrialization plans.

During his month-long stay in Manchukuo, Ayukawa talked with Matsuoka Yōsuke and executives from 77 SMR subsidiaries and inspected SMR's industrial development projects. Although Matsuoka had approached Ayukawa around the same time as the Army and had advised Itagaki to invite Ayukawa, the Army and the SMR later came into conflict when the Army wrestled economic power away from SMR. Matsuoka wanted Ayukawa's advice, whereas the top military officials in the Kwantung Army such as Itagaki and Commander Ueda Kenkichi (1875–1962), who were influenced by Ishiwara, Katakura, and Asahara, supported the idea of having a businessman take over the management of Manchukuo's industrialization. Ayukawa distrusted Matsuoka and believed that his invitation to Manchukuo had originated with the Kwantung Army and Ishiwara.[41]

In November Ayukawa talked with Manchukuo's top policymakers, including Itagaki Seishirō and Akinaga Tsukizō from the Kwantung Army and Hoshino Naoki, secretary general of Manchukuo's most powerful civilian agency, the General Affairs Agency.[42] During his meetings with these men, Ayukawa advocated, among other things, an increase in gold mining, most likely because Japan needed to increase its foreign reserves given its worsening balance-of-payments position and because his Japan Mining Company reaped enormous profits from Japan's urgent need for gold. Ayukawa also confirmed with Itagaki that Manchukuo would uphold the Open Door principle.

Ayukawa advocated close economic cooperation with the United States in Manchukuo's industrialization. During his discussions with Itagaki, he estimated that this project required $3 billion, out of which at least one-third, and if possible half, had to be Western, namely American, capital. He thought that Japan and Manchukuo could not supply adequate funds for this ambitious economic plan and that Japan lagged in technology in the heavy industries compared with the West. To obtain foreign capital, he preferred selling stocks over bonds since he believed that stocks would make foreign countries more interested parties in Manchukuo, a situation that would deter war. Ayukawa told Akinaga that all industrial sectors in Manchukuo should welcome foreign investments; Manchukuo should be less dependent on Japanese investment and welcome first-class foreign goods, personnel, and capital based on the principle of Open Door and joint ventures through stock ownership. From this industrialist's viewpoint, Manchukuo's ideal of the righteous way (*ōdōrakudo*) could not be achieved without his economic approach.[43]

Shortly after returning from Manchukuo, Ayukawa was invited by Minister of War Sugiyama Hajime (1890–1945) to give his opinions about the industrialization of Manchukuo. In front of the minister and generals, Ayukawa talked frankly and reiterated what he had said to Ishiwara prior to the trip. In his view, the Five-Year Plan lacked horizontal coordination among the various sectors; the plan ignored timing issues and the linking of industries for producing goods. For example, producing a given amount of steel required fixed inputs of coal and iron ore. And for the efficient production of steel, the production of iron ore and coal had to be coordinated. To solve this problem, Ayukawa suggested coordinated production of different goods in different industries. Through this measure, he believed that higher value-added products such as cars could be manufactured.[44]

Ayukawa's opinion gained support in the military, and he became an advisor to the Military Affairs Section of the Kwantung Army Command Bureau in January 1937. In asking Ayukawa to assume this responsibility, General Itagaki seemed to have had in mind a more formal arrangement, whereas Ayukawa, although willing to cooperate, managed to keep some distance from the military. At the time, Ayukawa was not thrilled that the military had asked Nissan Motors to help Dōwa Automobile, the quasi-government entity in Mukden in which Ayukawa's Tobata Casting Company was a major shareholder, although he and other Japanese automobile manufacturers allowed military and civilian officials from Manchukuo to visit their factories to get ideas on solving Dōwa's managerial problems.[45]

The Army narrowed its list of candidates for director of the heavy industrialization program to Yasukawa Yūnosuke (1870–1944) of the Mitsui Trading Company and head of the Oriental Development Company, a major institutional investor in China, Korea, and Manchuria; Noguchi Jun (Shitagau), of the Japan Nitrogen Company; Mori Naoteru of the Shōwa Fertilizer Company; Tsuda Shingo of the Kanebō Textile Company; Ikeda Seihin of the Mitsui conglomerate; and Ayukawa. Although Ayukawa initially proposed a joint project in Manchukuo with Mitsui in order to avoid possible feuds between the two business rivals, Mitsui representative Izumiyama Sanroku (1896–1981) failed to respond because Ikeda never gave him any suggestions. (Mitsui eventually lost interest in the project.) Tsuda was unqualified to give opinions on heavy industries since Kanebō specialized in textiles. The policymakers in the Army felt Mori and Yasukawa were too specialized. From the Army's standpoint, Ayukawa was an experienced manager with vision and a leader of a rapidly rising new conglomerate that not only manufactured automobiles but also engaged in a whole range of operations centered around the heavy industries and chemicals.

Ayukawa initially was reluctant to cooperate with the Army beyond being an advisor, but he indicated that he would be willing to undertake a greater role if the Army supported his idea of attracting foreign capital to Manchukuo. Through Ishiwara Kanji's persuasion and influence, Ayukawa's opinion won enough support from the military in spite of some antagonism from those in the military and in the right wing.[46]

Although Ayukawa did not decide to move Nissan to Manchuria until June 1937, his holding company had been encountering increasing financial difficulties. Even as Nissan invested aggressively in new businesses, acquired companies, and reorganized its subsidiary companies, the slump in the stock market between April 1934 and July 1935 had decreased its capital gains earnings from ¥17.4 million in 1934 to ¥1.2 million in 1935. Nissan began borrowing money from banks, and its indebtedness increased from ¥15 million in 1932 to ¥72 million in 1937; interests payments grew from 30 percent of overall payments to 63 percent during the same period. Nissan's profit rate decreased between the second half of 1934 and the first half of 1937, as did the value of its stock between 1934 and September 1937.

Nissan also faced an increased tax burden under the new tax policy implemented shortly after the Army's murder of Finance Minister Takahashi Korekiyo during the attempted coup in February 1936.[47] Japan lost the one person who could check the military's demands for increases in the military budget; during Takahashi's tenure as finance minister from December 1931 to February 1936, he contained budgetary increases and moderated the rapid increase in the military budget by refusing to countenance increased taxation as a means of preventing a runaway budget deficit. After Takahashi, his successors, Baba Eiichi (1879–1937) in the Hirota cabinet and Yūki Toyotarō in the Hayashi cabinet (February–May 1937), proposed increased taxation, which was implemented under the Hayashi cabinet. Of the 1937 budget of about ¥2.8 billion, the military took about ¥1.2 billion. Under the new tax policy, Nissan faced both taxes on its corporate income and taxes on the dividends paid by its subsidiaries to the holding company. Nissan had to respond drastically to this crisis.[48]

Although it is unclear when the Army first asked Nissan for help in producing automobiles in Manchukuo, by April 1937 Nissan seemed to have had some interest in cooperating with the Army under certain conditions. On April 22, Asakura noted that Nissan was "going to skillfully dodge [the Army's] request since it is too early to consider it."[49]

In May 1937, at the order of Shibayama Kaneshirō (1889–1956), chief of the Military Affairs Section at the Ministry of War and an ally of Ishiwara, Suzuki Eiji, head of the Military Affairs Bureau's Manchuria group, visited Ayukawa to request his participation in manufacturing automobiles and aircraft in Manchukuo. The two special companies in these industries had failed to progress beyond repair and parts factories. Suzuki told Ayukawa that the Manchukuo government was willing to allow him to make "necessary changes" in the industries.

At this point Ayukawa did not seem particularly interested in this project. Instead, he was involved in a project with the Navy to produce airplanes in Japan. In the same month the Army approached Ayukawa, he asked

Minister of Commerce and Industry Yoshino Shinji to persuade President Odaira Namihei (1874–1951) of the Hitachi Manufacturing Company to agree to the Navy's request to start manufacturing aircraft; although Hitachi was a Nissan subsidiary, it, like many other Nissan subsidiaries, enjoyed considerable autonomy from the parent company. Vice Minister of the Navy Yamamoto Isoroku (1884–1943) had made the same request of Yoshino in May.[50]

After the Ministry of War approached Ayukawa, Hoshino Naoki, of Manchukuo's General Affairs Agency and the most powerful civilian official in Manchukuo, visited Ayukawa; Hoshino, who had been in touch with Suzuki and Ishihara's confidant Asahara Kenzō, had the full support of the Ministry of War and the General Staff to persuade Ayukawa to plan and manage Manchukuo's automobile industry. Aware that the lack of technology, capital, and industrial facilities were the major causes slowing Manchukuo's industrialization, Hoshino was attracted to Ayukawa's idea of importing foreign, especially American, capital, technology, facilities, and personnel in addition to Japanese capital and technology; Hoshino, however, was interested in attracting foreign credits rather than other foreign economic resources.

Initially, Ayukawa responded negatively to Hoshino's plea to help establish an automobile industry in Manchuria. Ayukawa gave three reasons for his answer. First, the Japanese automobile industry had not achieved mass production, and it would be far more difficult to reach that goal in Manchuria, where the market was smaller than in Japan. Second, an automobile industry needed many subcontracting firms, and Manchuria did not have them. Third, an automobile industry had to be established through an industrial organization not by a single person. In spite of this response, Hoshino explained road conditions in Manchuria and pleaded repeatedly for Ayukawa's assistance.[51]

In June, Ayukawa started to change his mind. On June 23, Ayukawa and Nissan Motors' board members officially decided to cooperate with the Army. As part of this cooperation, Ayukawa decided that the Nissan Group should eventually take over the non-transportation subsidiaries of the SMR, including its light and heavy industries and its mining operations. In pursuing this objective, Ayukawa agreed to produce trucks for the Army and start supplying them to Manchuria in two or three years. Given this cooperation, after the approval of the MCI, Ayukawa planned to curtail the production of all passenger cars except Datsun, which was enjoying increased popularity in Japan.[52]

Around this time, Ayukawa indicated he would be willing to participate in Manchukuo's industrialization program if he could be in charge of a comprehensive industrialization of the country rather than solely automobile or aircraft manufacturing. Specifically, he wanted to move Nissan's head office to Manchuria and establish a holding company that controlled all natural resources and manufacturing in order to pursue the most efficient means of extracting raw materials and producing semi-finished and finished manufactures. The holding company would coordinate resource allocation and production.

Ayukawa thought it would be impossible to introduce large-scale American production methods in Japan's heavy industries because of the limited availability of land and the scarcity of natural resources. Japanese technology and equipment could not accommodate the American style of industrial production. In contrast, Manchuria's abundant land and natural resources made it possible to establish American-style factories in heavy industries there. Moreover, Manchuria's rich natural resources could serve as collateral for loans and bond issues in American, Japanese, and European financial markets. Both the holding company and its subsidiaries could attract foreign capital, technology, and equipment, and foreigners could hold up to 49 percent of the stock. As long as final decisions on managerial issues were left to the holding company, he believed foreign companies could do business as they desired. And they should be allowed to make an adequate return on their investment. Through these measures, he hoped not only to industrialize Manchukuo but also to re-establish amicable relations with the United States and, through its good offices, the United Kingdom. In spite of his misgivings about the Five-Year Plan, he thought it had potential. He was willing to move Nissan to Manchukuo to pursue industrialization programs there.[53]

The Army agreed to Ayukawa's demands. On June 17, 1937, Suzuki informed Commander of the Kwantung Army Ueda Kenkichi and Chief of Staff Tōjō Hideki (1884–1948) of the decisions of the central Army authorities in Tokyo. Both men initially protested this shift in policies. First, they did not believe it necessary to change existing control measures over industries based on the principle of one company per industry.[54] Second, they feared younger officers and those in the middle echelons who opposed zaibatsu would object. Third, they knew this would fuel the protests among SMR employees over the issue of reorganizing the SMR; since 1933 the Kwantung Army had gradually overcome their resistance, particularly after Matsuoka Yōsuke became SMR president in August 1935, and he agreed to concentrate its operations in railway construction and management after an informal agreement was reached to permit the SMR to operate industries other than railroads in North China. After its reorganization in September 1936, the SMR ceded its administrative authority over the SMR zone to the Manchukuo government.[55]

In July, the key civilian and military bureaucrats moved quickly to cement Ayukawa's cooperation in Manchukuo's industrialization. At Hoshino's request, Kishi Nobusuke, at this point the deputy director of the Industry Department of Manchukuo, talked with Ayukawa and drafted a proposal for Nissan's move to Manchukuo. Ayukawa's response to the draft was to suggest to Kishi and Itagaki that Manchukuo must take over all the non-transportation subsidiaries of the SMR. Kishi listened to Ayukawa and drew up a basic proposal for the creation of the Manchuria Development Corporation (MIDC) in Ayukawa's office. This proposal received the support of both Chief of the Military Affairs Section Shibayama and head of the Military Affairs Bureau's Manchuria group Suzuki Eiji; Shibayama's backing was important because the director of that department was busy handling the outbreak of the Sino-Japanese War, and Ayukawa managed to get the approval of that director through Shibayama. Ishiwara, of course, did his best to woo Ayukawa; at one point, this proud military man served Ayukawa beer during one of the last-minute meetings in Tokyo. In the meantime, Shibayama obtained the approval of Minister of War Sugiyama Hajime for Kishi's proposal.[56]

In mid-July, the Konoe cabinet enthusiastically approved the "Proposal for the Establishment of MIDC and Comprehensive Economic Development," which called for the transfer of all industries, aside from railroads, to the new holding company. Minister of the Interior Baba Eiichi stated during the meeting that this should be pushed through even if SMR employees protested, and he demanded the resignation of Matsuoka. Finance Minister Kaya Okinori (1889–1977) emphasized the need to introduce foreign capital. Around the time of this cabinet meeting, Hoshino and Suzuki lobbied for support from the SMR as well as the civilian and military bureaucrats.

Matsuoka apparently gladly consented and stated that the SMR would concentrate its industrial operations in North China.[57]

Given the consensus among the Japanese government, the Manchukuo
government, and the SMR, as well as the greater priority placed on using
Japanese resources for the war effort in North China rather than for Manchukuo's industrialization, Commander Ueda relented. On October 22, the
Konoe cabinet approved the "Outline for the Establishment of Heavy Industries in Manchuria" ("Manshū jūkōgyō kakuritsu yōkō"), and the Manchukuo
government approved a document with similar content on October 26. On
the evening of October 29, SMR President Matsuoka made the first public
announcement of the outline, causing a huge media sensation. Matsuoka
agreed to transfer all of the SMR's non-railway subsidiaries to MIDC.

The outline stated that under present internal and external circumstances, Manchukuo urgently needed to expand its productive capacity, particularly in the heavy industries. In order to do this, Manchukuo had organized a new and powerful holding company under Ayukawa. Manchukuo
allowed this company, half capitalized by the Manchukuo government and
half by Nissan, to dominate the investment and management of the following industries: iron and steel; light metals; heavy manufacturing, primarily
automobiles and airplanes (Nissan had suspended its talks with the Navy
by this point); and coal mining. The holding company could also invest in
and manage other mining industries, such as gold, zinc, lead, and copper.
Although the SMR managed to retain its rights over the Fushun coal mine,
it planned to transfer its other non-railway subsidiary companies to the new
holding company through the Manchukuo government.

On the issue of financing, the Manchukuo government planned to
provide preferential treatment to the holding company and its subsidiaries
by using private Japanese capital, government funds, and foreign capital.
The Japanese government planned to assist the flow of capital into Manchukuo by such measures as facilitating the liquidity of financial instru-
ments, including stocks, in the international market. The outline emphasized the importance of participation by foreign capital and the introduction
of foreign capital, equipment, and technology. It recommended that foreign
investors could acquire stock with voting rights in the subsidiary companies
as long as their holdings did not reach 50 percent. This limitation did not
apply to foreign acquisition of non-voting stock issued by the holding

company. No limits were to be placed on the foreign purchase of corporate bonds and other forms of borrowing.

Although the outline represented a major break from the previous principles underlying Manchukuo's economic development, the Manchukuo government reserved the right to implement "appropriate" supervisory measures over the holding company and its subsidiaries; on this issue, the Manchukuo government decided to maintain close relations with the Japanese government.[58]

After Ayukawa returned to Tokyo on November 14, 1937,[59] he proposed the following in an interview with *Nichi Nichi*, which in turn appeared in a front-page article in the *New York Times* on the same day: (1) purchase of American materials, machinery, and patents; (2) purchase by foreign interests of shares in the new holding company in Manchukuo; (3) the admission of American directors to the new holding company's board; (4) the formation of an American syndicate consisting of finance companies, Ford, and General Motors; and (5) American provision of capital worth ¥1 billion or about $300 million.[60]

The *New York Times* in a front-page article correctly reported on January 16, 1938, that policymakers who had participated in establishing this outline had tacitly admitted on October 22 the failure of "state socialism" in Manchukuo. Led by Ayukawa and his men from Nissan, MIDC was a special company to lead the heavy industrialization programs there. The *Times* article pointed to the views among "political" leaders in Japan that "this return of a large portion of Manchurian industry to the care of private initiative is tantamount to restoration of open door in the new State."[61]

December 1937 marked a new beginning for Ayukawa and Nissan. With the approval of the Nissan stockholders meeting in November, Nissan became a company incorporated in Manchukuo[62] following the abolition of extraterritoriality in Manchuria on December 1.[63] On December 20, 1937, the Manchukuo government promulgated the Manchuria Industrial Development Corporation Administration Act, whose content for the most part mirrored that of the October outline. It went into effect on December 27. Nissan changed its name to Manchuria Industrial Development Corporation (Manshū jūkōgyō kaihatsu kabushiki kaisha [Mangyō], or MIDC); the holding company and its subsidiaries came under government regulations since they were registered as special companies.

Unlike the outline, the act did not directly discuss the introduction of foreign capital. It neither discouraged nor encouraged the participation of foreign capital in MIDC; Article VI stated that "shares with voting power in the Manchuria Industrial Development Corporation may be transferred to persons of Manchoukuo and Japanese nationality only, or to juridical persons organized under the laws of either of these countries, the majority of voting power of which juridical persons belong to a person or persons or a juridical person or persons of Manchoukuo or Japanese nationality." Ayukawa became the chairman of this holding company, which was capitalized at ¥450 million, half of which came from Nissan; Manchukuo completed its payment of the other half around March 1938.[64] Ayukawa commented in an interview with the *Oriental Economist* that in order to coordinate the production of higher value-added items such as cars, he wanted to introduce "the Ford system of supplying materials and parts . . . since obviously this manufacturing industry cannot be carried on successfully if the essential materials are beyond the manufacturers' control." He wanted "an accurate program for the supply of necessary materials," and "capital requirements" had to "be measured accordingly." He argued that "all activities must be interrelated and coordinated, and therefore we must have a central organization whose guiding principle will underlie all these activities that are to be brought under a single control and which will emphasize the unity of the whole mechanism."[65]

Reacting to this new development, SMR employees expressed their opposition as they saw their economic empire narrowed to the operation of railroads. President Matsuoka also reversed his earlier position regarding MIDC after he realized that there were far fewer business opportunities in North China than he had thought because other special companies formed by the Japanese government were shutting the SMR out.[66]

In addition to this negative pressure, Ayukawa lost a leading supporter of MIDC; although Ishiwara had been vice chief of staff of the Kwantung Army since September, he had lost much of his influence in economic planning and politics. Nevertheless, leading civilian bureaucrats, such as Kishi and Hoshino, backed Ayukawa, and so did Ishiwara's former allies in the Army in Japan and Manchukuo such as Major Katakura of the Kwantung Army staff and other officers, including Commander Ueda and Chief of Staff Tōjō, who was a foe of Ishiwara. Shortly after the founding of MIDC, Ueda released an official statement that seemed to share Ishiwara's thinking and supported Ayukawa's scheme. It recognized Manchukuo's need for Ayukawa and Nissan and called for the reorganization of SMR and the introduction of foreign capital, technology, and equipment for the rapid, comprehensive, and efficient development of heavy industries for strengthening the national defense state. Ueda claimed that Ayukawa and his company were best qualified for this task partly because over 50,000 stockholders owned Nissan, which meant a broad participation of Japanese in the building of Manchukuo.[67]

For Ayukawa, MIDC's start meant not only a new challenge but also relief from Nissan's financial troubles. First, Manchukuo had guaranteed the principal invested in industries in Manchuria and an annual return of 6 percent from operations in Manchuria for investments in Manchukuo for the first ten years. Second, MIDC paid substantially lower taxes in Manchukuo than Nissan had in Japan. Third, the Bank of Japan and the Industrial Bank of Japan backed financing of MIDC. Fourth, both the Manchukuo and the Japanese governments helped MIDC secure the liquidity of its stock. Fifth, profits were divided between MIDC and Manchukuo in a two-to-one ratio if dividend payments were below 7.5 percent, and equally if over 7.5 percent. Sixth, whereas Manchukuo had previously capped dividend payments by special companies at 6 percent, MIDC could pay more than that if it wanted to. Finally, when MIDC was dissolved, the assets were to be divided between Nissan and Manchukuo in a two-to-one ratio. These benefits far exceeded those provided by a 1906 law to SMR, which received a guaranteed 6 percent annual dividend payment, as well as a guarantee by the Japanese government to make payments on the interest and, if necessary, on the principal, of bonds issued up to twice the amount of the company's paid-in capital.[68]

The state offered such generous conditions because it desperately needed Ayukawa, and such benefits were necessary to carry out the rapid and comprehensive industrialization of Manchukuo. Ayukawa had to have state backing to take the risk and to attract investors. He believed that by gaining control over mineral resources in Manchukuo and the SMR's heavy industries, he had enough resources under his company to launch a full-fledged automobile industry. In Japan, many mineral resources were already controlled by the older zaibatsu. In Manchukuo, the discovery of potential mineral deposits in Tungpientao seemed promising, and this could serve to attract foreign capital and technology, including Ford. On top of these possibilities, the company was saving a lot in taxes.[69]

Observing these changes, American Consul General Richard F. Boyce in Yokohama sent a report in early 1938 on Ayukawa and MIDC. Although Boyce thought Ayukawa might succeed in attracting more private capital than SMR because "the Nippon Sangyō [Nissan] and its subsidiaries in Japan probably possess reserves and borrowing power which may be milked for the benefit of the Manchurian enterprises," Boyce's report undoubtedly contributed to the State Department's policy of continuing not to recognize Manchukuo and discouraging the strengthening of economic ties between the United States and Manchukuo through direct and indirect investments, although the trade between the two nations was booming (see Chapter 3). His pessimistic outlook on the Manchukuo economy was in contrast to Ayukawa's initial optimism.

Boyce cautioned "that Americans who may be approached by Mr. Aikawa [Ayukawa] should keep in mind the uneconomic nature of many of the enterprises controlled by the Company, the Army control, the almost inevitable financial difficulties of Japan in the next few years, the possibility of war with Russia, and other considerations," which he listed. First, MIDC did not mark a "material change in the opportunities for private capital in Manchuria" because Japanese companies had always participated as minority shareholders in most SMR subsidiaries. Second, just as it had with the SMR, the Kwantung Army, through its control of the Manchukuo government, would exercise control over MIDC's operations. The real winner in the establishment of MIDC was the military because "in view of the world-wide trend toward increased military influence in industry," the Japanese Army had acquired control not only of Manchukuo but also of Nissan's subsidiaries in Japan. Because of "military domination of the business management of the South Manchuria Railway Company and the vast expansion of enterprise since 1931 along strategic and military rather than economic lines," Boyce doubted "that the transfer to new management (control remaining the same) of the heavy industries requiring extension in Manchuria will attract private capital, either Japanese or foreign, in substantial quantities." Boyce doubted "the soundness of extensive heavy industries in Manchuria upon economic grounds."

In addition, Boyce portrayed Ayukawa as rather a dubious figure because he was a relative of Kuhara and because he had established close economic affiliation with the military. "Messrs. Aikawa [Ayukawa] and Kuhara have been favored by substantial Army support for the last few years and several of the more important industries controlled by Nippon Sangyō depend largely upon military orders." Kuhara was not only "associated with Mr. Aikawa [Ayukawa] in many of his more important enterprises" and "the more reactionary elements in the Japanese Army, but also recently sentenced to prison for his connection with the attempted army coup of February 26, 1936." But, as noted in the previous chapter, Ayukawa, contrary to Boyce's assertion, was not a "son-in-law" of Kuhara and Kuhara did not supply "much of [Ayukawa's] capital." Although Ayukawa's business interests had become intertwined with the military, Boyce acknowledged that such an interdependence was a worldwide trend. Finally, although Boyce was correct in saying that foreigners would not obtain a majority interest in MIDC's subsidiaries, he was wrong in saying they would not have any say in management.[70]

In an interview with the *New York Times* in March 1938, Ayukawa launched a proposal that would enable U.S. and foreign interests to offer machinery, patent rights, and technical services worth up to $300 million (about ¥10 billion) in a ¥30 billion project for Manchukuo's heavy and chemical industries. Ayukawa told news reporter Hugh Byas in Manchukuo that "he intended to follow Japan's example in the early days and employ an unlimited number of foreign experts." He also stated that although "details would have to be negotiated with American leaders according to market conditions," he was going to attract American capital by issuing stocks "of no par value or without voting power" as well as bonds.

Skeptical about Ayukawa's scheme, Byas asked why he expected Americans to respond positively to his proposal given that Americans thought Manchukuo practiced a closed door policy as evidenced by the 1935 decision to limit American oil firms, firms that until then had dominated Manchukuo's petroleum business, to supplying only crude oil. Although Ayukawa defended this decision, he pointed out that negotiations were under way to compensate the American firms for their losses. Indicating his confidence in the improvement in U.S.-Manchukuo business relations, Ayukawa stated: "I am going to open the closed door." Ayukawa wanted "to construct a model, modern industrial State under conditions he considers ideal from the producer's viewpoint."

When Byas asked Ayukawa about the issue of providing higher returns on MIDC-related bonds than on Japanese government bonds issued in the United States, Ayukawa stated that whereas the latter entailed investing

only money, the former also meant opportunities to sell Manchukuo technology and equipment. Ayukawa argued the two bond issues could not be
compared because Americans could look forward both to selling their surplus commodities and to gaining higher returns on their investments in the
future. Ayukawa painted a rosy picture: "Manchukuo is the world's industrial frontier today, and it is a safe frontier where law, order, and security are
guaranteed by Japan." If Manchukuo's industrialization took off, the economic boom would "raise the living standards of 70,000,000 Japanese,
thereby indirectly increasing their demands for American luxuries." "I am
not transferring my interest because Manchukuo is a risk but because it is
safe—not only my own interests but those of my 50,000 shareholders. If I
let them down, I could never show my face in the streets of Tokyo again."[71]

As this chapter demonstrates, Ayukawa was taking the lead in the direction
of Manchukuo's industrialization as elite civilian and military bureaucrats
desperately sought his assistance in the face of growing economic troubles in
Manchuria and the escalating war with China. Asakura viewed the establishment of MIDC with satisfaction; he wrote in his diary that he had made
a similar proposal to General Minami and Matsuoka between 1934 and 1936.
On the other hand, Asakura, unlike Ayukawa, was suspicious of the West
and was wary of cooperating economically with the United States, such as
proposed in Ayukawa's scheme to introduce American capital to Manchukuo by talking Ford Motors into a joint venture, a proposal that will be discussed extensively in Chapter 4. He was also worried about Anglo-
American intervention in the Japanese sphere of influence in China and
about the reaction of the SMR and its employees to the coming reorganization. By the end of the year, in addition he became concerned about negative
rumors regarding MIDC based on what he viewed as jealousy over its promised economic pre-eminence in Manchukuo as well as blind xenophobia to
the idea of bringing in Western capital to Manchukuo.[72] As Ayukawa embarked on his grand task, he had to fight these negative attitudes.

But policymakers maintained high hopes for foreign capital, an attitude
reflected in one of the Japanese government proposals made in August
1937.[73] Although the version approved by the cabinet on October 22 did not
include estimated figures, the August proposal projected that out of the
planned ¥641 million increase in the capitalization of the special and semi-
special companies that engaged in coal mining and iron ore extraction that

MIDC would acquired from SMR, Nissan was to provide ¥200 million and foreign capital the remaining ¥441 million. In the automobile, mining, and airplane industries, out of the planned capitalization of ¥1.25 billion, Nissan planned to provide ¥378.5 million and foreign capital ¥612.5 million. Furthermore, out of the planned ¥750 million increase in capital for the second year of the Five-Year Plan, Nissan was to provide ¥382.5 million and foreign capital ¥367.5 million. In total, Nissan was to provide ¥961 million (40 percent) and foreign capital, ¥1421 million (60 percent).[74]

THREE

Ayukawa's Initial Overtures to American Business

After 1937, as I hope to show, Manchukuo's industrialization depended on securing Western, especially American, capital and technology. Ayukawa thought this was possible because the severe economic depression in America meant that many American firms would be eager to export their goods to foreign areas that were enjoying an economic boom. His early efforts, discussed in this chapter, included a proposal to invite Japanese Americans to Manchukuo to start American-style, large-scale, mechanized farms, and his hiring of a famous American geologist, H. Foster Bain (1871–1948), to survey Manchukuo's mineral resources and evaluate Manchukuo's potential for industrialization.

American trade with Manchuria and investments in it were only a small part of the United States' overall international trade and investment portfolio in Asia. The U.S. trade with Manchuria was no more than 7 percent of its total trade with all of China in 1929, and its investment in Manchuria was 8 percent of all investment in China by 1931 (Shanghai, in comparison, absorbed 65 percent).[1] After 1931, Japanese investment in Manchukuo and trade with it increased, and non-Japanese investment in Manchukuo decreased and non-Japanese trade with Manchukuo fluctuated.[2] Yet, on the basis of these figures and the share of American imports in Manchukuo's total imports, one should not judge as unimportant trade relations between Manchukuo and the United States from the 1930s to the outbreak of the Pacific War in 1941.

Manchukuo's Trade with the United States

After 1937, Manchukuo exported primarily soybeans and imported mainly capital and consumer goods. The share of agricultural products in total exports declined between 1931 and 1940; whereas the average share for 1931–36 was 74.2 percent, it was 65.6 percent between 1937 and 1940. Over the same period, the average share of minerals and industrial goods in total exports increased from 15 percent in 1931–36 to 18.6 percent in 1937–40. Because of the increased effort to industrialize, the average share of capital goods in all imports rose from 29.7 percent in 1931–36 to 40.1 percent in 1937–40, while the share of consumer goods dropped during the same period from 54.7 percent to 45.6 percent. In 1940, the share of consumer goods stood at 43.8 percent, and that of capital goods at 41.7 percent. In other words, by 1940 the two most important categories of imports held an almost equal share. Japanese investment in Manchukuo jumped from ¥348 million in 1937 to ¥1.3 billion in 1940, and the percentage of investment in capital goods was 42 percent of total Japanese investment in 1939 compared with 25.4 percent in 1930. Since Japanese investment in Manchukuo made up the overwhelming portion, it is safe to assume that after 1937 a significant portion of investment in Manchukuo went toward capital goods.[3]

To achieve the rapid industrialization envisioned in the Five-Year Plan, Manchukuo desperately needed foreign capital, technology, and equipment from the West and Japan. In response, Manchukuo increased its imports of industrial products from Western countries, notably Germany and the United States. Between 1938 and 1940, Manchukuo became dependent on the United States to acquire Western capital and technology, and among the Western nations, America became the second largest customer after Germany for Manchukuo's exports.[4]

Non-Japanese foreign direct and indirect investment in Manchukuo generally declined in the 1930s. Many Western firms and financial houses withdrew from Manchukuo, including the Jardine Engineering Company (Britain), the Skoda Steelworks (Czechoslovakia), the Siemens Schukert Company (Germany), and Anderson, Meyers, and Company (the United States), and the National City Bank (the United States) closed its Mukden office. (In contrast to other American banks, this bank remained active in China and Manchuria until the Pacific War.) Although the Great Depression contributed to the negative business atmosphere, Manchukuo's economic policies were also a factor. For example, the Oil Monopoly Law of 1934 forced the previously dominant firms—Standard-Vacuum Oil Company of New York, Texas Oil Company, and the Anglo-Dutch Asiatic Petroleum Company—out of the oil distribution trade in Manchuria, although they continued to sell naphtha, petroleum, and crude oil and were encouraged by Manchukuo to do so.[5] Other examples are the Law for the Control of Key Industries, the Foreign Exchange Control Law, and the Capital Control Law, which were administered in favor of Japanese and Manchurian companies. Furthermore, foreign exchange regulations made it difficult for companies to repatriate profits, and Manchukuo encouraged them to reinvest their earnings in Manchuria.[6] Yet, despite these hindrances, the trade statistics cited above imply that business opportunities in Manchukuo outweighed the disadvantages. The annual absolute figures in yen for the import and export trade with the United States during 1931–40 were higher after the Manchurian Incident of 1931 than before.[7] Finally, according to an October 1938 survey by the Manchukuo Transportation Department and the SMR Research Department, American cars dominated Manchuria.[8]

Many American policymakers were unhappy about this American trade boom with Manchukuo or puzzled by it. For example, on April 4, 1939, Senator Gerald P. Nye (1892–1971) of North Dakota, a member of the Military Affairs Committee, accused the State Department of exaggerating Japanese violations of American commercial rights in China and Manchukuo. In testimony the following day, Secretary of State Cordell Hull (1871–1955) had difficulty refuting this fact. Although he emphasized that Japan had been violating American trade rights in the Far East, he admitted that American exports since 1937 had been abnormal and wondered whether the isolationist Nye looked with enthusiasm on Japan's use of American goods to wage war against China.

Following the exchange between Nye and Hull over the Manchukuo trade, the *Far Eastern Review* in its July 1939 issue not only supported Nye but also criticized Hull for not admitting that American companies were encountering discrimination in Manchukuo. Because Hull made only a vague statement that Japanese actions in Manchukuo violated American business, the *Review* argued that he had incorrectly claimed that Americans exported war materials to Manchukuo since "American exports to Manchuria of metals and machinery for new factories, steel mills, mines and power plants can no more be considered war materials in the narrow sense than similar American shipments to other parts of the world." Although unsure about the general effect of this trade boom on American business and wondering whether the boom would last, the *Far Eastern Review* questioned the State Department's understanding of the Open Door policy. The *Review* defined this principle as "concerned only with trade" and concluded that the Open Door policy was observed in the Far East because American exports to Manchukuo had increased. If this principle were broadened to include the issue of "who handles the trade," then Japan violated the policy because Japan discriminated against American traders in China and Manchukuo. On the other hand, if the Open Door principle was a matter of "the earnings of workers in American factories producing goods for the Far East, and . . . the sales volumes of the American manufacturers who sell the goods to the Far East," then Japan did not violate it.[9]

The State Department, however, viewed the U.S.-Manchukuo trade statistics with skepticism. It thought they "warrant[ed] no inference that Japan's occupation of Manchuria ha[d] more widely opened the doors of commercial opportunity or benefitted American enterprise in Manchuria." Although the department could not explain the cause of the increase in American exports to Manchukuo, it did point out that the Sino-Japanese War had prompted the Japanese to stockpile American goods.[10]

The U.S.-Manchukuo trade boom did not prompt the State Department to grant Japan's wish that it recognize Manchukuo, although in February 1934, that is, before the U.S.-Manchukuo trade boom, even Stanley K. Hornbeck (1883–1966), chief of the Far Eastern Division of the State Department and a leading critic of Japanese aggression, thought he could not dismiss the possibility that America in "a considerable distance in the future" might recognize Manchukuo.[11] As Errol Clauss points out, "Between 1933 and 1941, Roosevelt's policy toward Manchukuo involved a confused mixture of moralism, legalism, and pragmatism." "Throughout the period, the State Department was willing to go to tortuous lengths in instructing consuls [in Manchukuo in] the art of unofficially acquiescing in Manchukuo's exercise of sovereign powers." The State Department feared that China's "anti-Western feelings that had been relatively dormant since

1931" might be stimulated by "official acquiescence" to the trade with Manchukuo's industrial monopolies and by Japan's abolition of extraterritorial
rights in Manchukuo in December 1937. Americans did not want to stir up
anti-American feelings in China and wanted anti-foreign sentiments there
channeled solely against the Japanese; this was the practical reason behind
the State Department's protests against Japan's violations of American
treaty rights and of international agreements.[12]

In formulating Far Eastern policy, the State Department did tend to
view with sympathy American business in China, which "was well organized
and was able to secure wide expression of its views in the United States," including "the State Department, White House, and Congressional commit-
tees." In spite of their relatively small size, the Shanghai and Tientsin
American Chambers of Commerce as well as the Shanghai American Junior
Chamber of Commerce exerted a considerable influence in the American
press. They conveyed their views and demands for U.S. government action
through the Chamber of Commerce of the United States to government officials and the media.[13]

The majority of American commercial interests, however, were aware
that Japan was the United States' leading trading partner in the Far East.
Although they protested Japanese discrimination against American economic interests in China, they did not believe the Chinese market would be
lucrative for years to come because of China's history of political, economic,
and social instability. The American business community tended to believe
that trade with China would continue no matter who was in power. Many
thought that the Japanese would provide the law and order China needed.[14]
To judge from an opinion poll of nearly 15,000 leading businessmen reported in the September 1940 issue of *Fortune* and John W. Masland's 1942
article in the *Pacific Historical Review*, the majority of American businessmen
were willing to compromise with the Japanese demands for a sphere of influence in the Far East. The American business community tended to oppose economic sanctions and other stiff measures against Japan, although it
did not orchestrate an organized effort to influence U.S. policy toward Japan and tended to accept the dictates of U.S. foreign policy. After President
Roosevelt abrogated the trade treaty with Japan in July 1939, for example,
the American business community did not lobby for its restoration, even
though it would have preferred an expansion of trade. Although the business community showed some concerns about checking Japan's expansion-

ism in the Far East, it was also interested in maintaining good trade relations. It is likely, however, that the American business turned increasingly
against Japan after it signed the Axis Pact with Germany in September
1940.[15]

Ayukawa's Initial Efforts to Contact American Business

Ayukawa knew he was racing against time because American businessmen
would lose interest in exporting to Manchukuo when the U.S. economy began to recover.[16] In October 1937, Ayukawa secretly sent his confidant Miho
Mikitarō (?–1946), a former executive of Mitsui Trading Company, and
James Murray, former financial officer for Columbia Record Company
and Victor Record Company (Nippon Victor), to the United States and
Europe. Their mission was to secure foreign capital for Manchukuo. Later
that year, Ayukawa himself planned to visit the United States and made
reservations on the *Asamamaru*.[17] But he, like many other Japanese over-
estimated the strong American isolationist sentiment. After the *Panay* incident on December 12, when Japanese bombers attacked and sunk several
American ships on the Yangtze River, he perceived the surge of anti-
Japanese sentiment among some groups in the United States as representative of general American sentiment and canceled his trip.

Robert Moss, the Japan representative for Republic Steel and president
of a local American company, Truscon Steel, suggested to Ayukawa that it
would be better for Japan to work on public relations and its image among
the American public and indicated that he thought the Chinese were doing
a better job of this than the Japanese. Furthermore, Moss wondered if Ayukawa could attract American investment, when Japanese government bonds
were trading in London and New York for annual yields of over 10 percent
but the dividends from MIDC were only 6 percent. Ayukawa, however,
stated that he could arrange a better yield for MIDC's subsidiaries and
would minimize the difficulties of repatriating profits under the Japanese
foreign-exchange regulations.

While he was consulting with Moss, Ayukawa was also quite active
in promoting his idea to American contacts. On January 16, 1938, the *New
York Times* reported in a front-page article that MIDC was wooing Thomas
J. Watson (1874–1956), president of the International Business Machine
Corporation and president of the International Chamber of Commerce, to

provide a $50 million credit to purchase "plant equipment." In 1937, Watson's company had established a wholly-owned Japanese subsidiary called Nippon Watson tōkei kaikei kikai. In order to promote dealings between MIDC and American businesses, Ayukawa proposed as a "feeler" that the Japanese government offered to "exempt payments against the credit from the restrictions of Exchange Control Act" and that "American experts would be retained to install the equipment and possibly to operate it during the training of the Japanese and Chinese staffs."[18]

Ayukawa probably contacted Watson through Herbert S. Houston, who was an organizer of the International Chamber of Commerce, a founding member of the Chamber of Commerce of the United States, a member of the Education Committee of the National Foreign Trade Council, and chair of the Institute for the Advancement of Visual Education and Vocational Training in New York City, which made educational motion pictures for mass education. He was friends not only with Watson, who assisted him in the educational films venture, but also with other influential business figures such as Thomas W. Lamont (1870–1948), the head administrator of the J. P. Morgan banking firm; Owen D. Young (1874–1962), former president of General Electric; and Frank A. Vanderlip (1864–1937), former president of the National City Bank. Ayukawa and Houston must have had a meeting of minds because, like Ayukawa in his "New Era" essay, Houston actively supported the idea of achieving peace and open trade based on the spirit of understanding among competitors in international and domestic trade, an idea also shared by the International Chamber of Commerce and the Roosevelt administration. The two men had probably met in August 1937 when Houston visited Tokyo to attend, as commissioner of the New York World's Fair to the Far East, the Education Congress held by the World Education Congress.

Although Lamont wrote to Houston on September 9, 1937, that "Japan is losing all her friends," Houston tended to sympathize with Japan's position in the Far East.[19] On his return to the United States, in a speech delivered at the University of Oregon, Matsuoka Yōsuke's alma mater, Houston proposed the establishment of a Far Eastern Studies Department at Oregon in honor of Matsuoka and at Wellesley in honor of Chiang Kaishek's wife, Mayling Soong Chiang (1898–), in order to promote better understanding of the Far East among the American public. Houston also supported Matsuoka's idea to implement in China, with Chinese cooperation, a modified form of the economic programs found in Korea and Manchuria; Houston told his audience at the University of Oregon that he had been impressed by the economic progress of Korea and Manchukuo.

Although Ayukawa probably would have welcomed Houston as an excellent public relations person for Japan, Houston's speech was not welcome to State Department officials, particularly Hornbeck. In an internal memorandum for the State Department, Hornbeck wrote: "Normally the speech could be dismissed as the mumbling of an old man but because of his position as Commissioner to the Far East for the New York World's Fair some importance may be attached to it by certain uninformed sections of the public." Hornbeck was vexed because Houston's proposal came shortly after the *Panay* incident and the Japanese war atrocities in Nanking. Furthermore, Hornbeck was not fond of Matsuoka, whom he described as a "comparatively rough and 'hard-boiled' type, resembling [in] general attitude and manner certain of our typical political 'bosses.'" He was aware that Matsuoka had "spent his boyhood in straitened circumstances and more or less fighting his way, in Portland, Oregon."[20]

As a result of a *New York Times* report of his failure in wooing Watson, Ayukawa approached with caution an offer by a San Francisco businessman named J. H. Anderton to mediate with the investment banking firm of Kuhn, Loeb and Company. Claiming to have good business relations with Kuhn, Loeb, Anderton proposed to issue bonds in the American market. Anderton apparently had experience in issuing Japanese utility bonds in the United States. Through a Japanese friend, businessman Muraki Kenkichi, Anderton claimed that the issuance of Japanese bonds in the United States was not necessarily impossible. After meeting Muraki in early 1938, Ayukawa in April decided not to pursue this proposition since he doubted its prospect; failure would create the further impression in the United States that Manchukuo was desperate for foreign credits. (As discussed in Chapter 5, in spite of this cautious and rather negative reasoning, by spring he was quietly approaching Kuhn, Loeb through another channel.) After hearing from Muraki that Ayukawa stated that "time was not ripe" for seeking foreign credit, Anderton informed Muraki and Ayukawa that in spite of ample cash reserves at American financial institutions, people were afraid of making investments and the government was encouraging domestic instead of foreign investment to speed up the economic recovery. Anderton expressed pessimism about a public bond issue because of the negative public opinion toward Japan's military actions, Japanese infringement on American rights and investments in China, and the public perception that the Sino-Japanese War was undermining the Japanese economy. Anderton also thought that flotation of Manchurian or Japanese bonds would be impossible until Japan settled its conflict in the Far East, regained fiscal health, achieved better relations with the United States, and arranged satisfactory protections for foreign investments.[21]

American-Style Agriculture and Japanese Americans

From the outset, Ayukawa's MIDC encountered difficulties not only in attracting American capital but also in handling domestic politics. Although Ayukawa thought the Manchukuo government had designated him the sole person responsible for managing MIDC, both the Kwantung Army and the Manchukuo government intervened in the management of the holding company as Ayukawa found it difficult to attract foreign capital. Furthermore, serious threats to MIDC's operations were posed by the Japan-Manchuria Trading Company (Nichi-Man shōji), which increasingly controlled distribution of raw materials, semi-finished products, and finished products, and by the lack of cooperation from MIDC's subsidiary Manchuria Coal Mining Company (Manshū tankō, or Mantan), which was led by Kōmoto Daisaku (1883–1953), who, as a colonel, had assassinated the Chinese warlord Chang Tso-Lin in 1928.[22]

Furthermore, the prolonging of the Sino-Japanese War rapidly undermined Manchukuo's plan to establish an independent national defense state. Instead, its primary role increasingly became the provision of food, raw materials, and semi-finished products to Japan, a trend that continued until the end of the Pacific War. This pattern became very apparent after the Japanese cabinet approved the "Outline for the Cabinet Planning Board Plan to Expand Production Capacity" ("Kikakuin seisanryoku kakujū keikaku yōkō") in January 1939, which was based on the War Ministry's "Guideline for the Five Year Plan for Important Industries" ("Juyō sangyō gonen keikaku yōkō") of May 29, 1937, a document that was influenced by Ishiwara's proposal for a comprehensive economic plan in Japan but was nonetheless formulated apart from the work by Ishiwara and the Army chiefs of staff. The outline was used to plan the expansion of important industries in Japan, Manchuria, and North China, and unlike the Manchukuo Five-Year Plan, it prioritized the needs of Japan over Manchukuo.[23]

Faced with these international and domestic problems, instead of focusing only on industrialization centered around the heavy and chemical industries, in mid-1938 Ayukawa came up with the idea of promoting American-style, large-scale, mechanized agriculture. Ayukawa discussed this idea with Murakami Ryūsuke, an official in the Colonial Ministry and a graduate of an agricultural college in Japan, who had studied at an American agricultural college, and Takasaki Tatsunosuke (1885–1964), managing director of Oriental Can Company (Tōyō seikan kaisha) and a follower of Herbert Hoover and his Standardization and Simplification movement. The three men agreed that since the growing season was short in Manchuria (May through October), a maximum yield could be achieved efficiently only through mechanized farming similar to that practiced in the United States. The three men disagreed with the Japanese government's plan to promote small-scale, non-mechanized family farms in Manchukuo by sending five million Japanese farmers there over the next ten years. When Takasaki and Ayukawa met during the former's visit to Manchukuo in May 1938 to check on the activities of MIDC, Takasaki suggested promoting mechanized agriculture in Manchuria. (Takasaki was visiting Manchuria in search of steel for his cannery business but could not obtain it because of strong demand for steel there.) Both men agreed to provide ¥500,000 each and purchase land for large-scale farming.[24]

Based on Ayukawa's and Takasaki's scheme, the Manchuria Agricultural Development Corporation (Manshū nōgyō kaihatsu kaisha), starting with paid-in capital of about ¥30 million, was to raise $10 million from Japanese Americans and to recruit about 100 second- and third-generation Japanese Americans who had graduated from agricultural colleges and who would be required to bring $10,000 worth of agricultural machinery. The assumption that each Japanese American could bring that quantity of machinery was dubious, given the fact that most Japanese Americans were poor. The figure of $10 million was based on the supposition that the scheme could tap the deposits of Japanese Americans at the California branches of the Sumitomo and the Yokohama Specie banks, which together totaled $70 million. Both men thought that they could promote the idea of racial harmony, one of the state ideologies of Manchukuo, by encouraging the immigration of Japanese Americans, who were talented but faced discrimination in the United States; in the 1920s, Ayukawa's brother-in-law Kuhara Fusanosuke had run a foundation that provided an annual scholarship for one Japanese American from Hawaii to study at an American university, and Ayukawa knew there were many prospective candidates.

Ayukawa asked Murakami and Takasaki to execute the plan. He asked Murakami to travel to the United States because his knowledge would help in recruiting Japanese American college graduates. While Murakami got ready for the trip, Takasaki, upon his return to Japan, also prepared for a visit to the United States and contacted Japanese Americans living in cities such as Seattle and San Francisco in hopes of recruiting about a hundred of them. Ayukawa and Takasaki came up with such ideas as using water from the Amur River to irrigate a stretch of unfertile land along the South Manchuria Railway track between Harbin and Chihli. They also thought of having the Japanese American immigrants start fruit farms and fruit-related industries in Chin-chou. Takasaki calculated that the American methods would boost Manchurian agricultural production fourfold. This figure was later revised to twenty- to thirtyfold in a report written by Ayukawa.

This idea, however, was rejected by the top officers in the Kwantung Army, including Commander Ueda, Chief of Staff Tōjō (vice minister of war after May 1938), and Vice Chief of Staff Ishiwara (who resigned in August 1938). They believed in addressing Japan's overpopulation and supported the migration of five million Japanese (one million Japanese households) over the next ten years. Under this plan, land had to be divided into small plots. The economic-efficiency argument had again lost out to political and military needs. Ayukawa told Murakami to cancel his trip to the United States. (One final attempt to recruit Japanese Americans occurred when a mission headed by former Navy vice-admiral Maebara Kenji [1882–1963], chairman of Ayukawa's Manchuria Aviation Company, toured the United States, Italy, Germany, France, and Switzerland in 1938 to inspect aircraft factories, such as the ones run by Boeing in Seattle and Beech in Los Angeles; the *Japanese American*, a local Seattle newspaper, reported on October 22 that Manchukuo needed second-generation Japanese Americans with technical and engineering skills in aviation as well as those with an interest in aviation.)[25]

H. Foster Bain

Ayukawa's interest in exploring agro-business arose partly because he had learned that the mineral resources of the Tungpientao region were not as promising as the Kwantung Army had claimed. Shimada Toshikichi, an able mining engineer from MIDC's Japan Mining Company, told him: "Even the red iron ores, though of good quality, are types unsuitable for mining. The area has all types of minerals, but basically it is like a collection of rocks at a museum."[26]

Ayukawa was hesitant in revealing this information since it could hamper his efforts to attract foreign capital, equipment, and technology; he had planned to use these mineral deposits as collateral for securing Western economic assistance. At about the time Shimada made his report, as part of the effort to interest American business in Manchukuo, MIDC invited the vice president and engineers from a Chicago-based engineering consulting firm, the Brassert Company, which had designed the Göring steelmill in Germany. MIDC asked Brassert not only to map out plans for enlarging the Shōwa Steelmill in Anshan, which was one of the largest in Asia, but also to make appeals to American investors.

While Ayukawa contacted Brassert, he wanted a third party to confirm Shimada's finding and conduct another comprehensive geological survey. In the summer of 1937, he had been introduced by Herbert Houston to the famous American geologist H. Foster Bain. On March 1, 1938, Ayukawa sent a telegram to Bain in Manila and asked him to survey the mineral resources of Manchukuo beginning in the middle of March and to submit a report within a month after the end of his survey. Bain arrived in Yokohama on March 16, and he was greeted by Miho. The two then flew to Hsinking to meet Ayukawa. Although Bain also thought the mineral resources of Tungpientao were not promising, he reached more optimistic conclusions about Manchukuo's potential to industrialize.[27]

Ayukawa's faith in Bain's ability was based on solid evidence. Born in Seymour, Indiana, on November 2, 1871, Bain studied at Moore's Hill College and Johns Hopkins University before starting his professional career as a geologist at the Geological Survey in Iowa. It was during his career in Iowa that he received his Ph.D. in geology from the University of Chicago in 1897. In 1903 he joined the U.S. Geological Survey, and two years later, he was appointed director of the Illinois State Geological Survey. From 1909 to 1915 Bain served as editor of the Mining and Scientific Press, and between 1915 and 1916, he worked with T. A. Rickard, a mining engineer of international experience and reputation, in wartime London as editor of *Mining Magazine*. There, Bain established a friendship with Herbert C. Hoover. Bain worked for his Commission for Relief in Belgium "and gave much spare time to that service"; for this work, he received the Medal of King Albert. Between 1916 and 1920, Bain conducted geological explorations in South Africa and the Far East, including remote parts of China. In 1919–20, he was an assistant director of the U.S. Bureau of Mines "and worked on war minerals, helium production, war gases and other subjects pertaining to the war." While serving as director of the bureau between 1921 and 1924 during Herbert Hoover's tenure as head of the Commerce Department, Bain went to Chile "to investigate the cost of producing nitrate." Bain also advised the Argentine government in the winter of 1924 "on the establishment of a steel industry," and in 1929 he was a member of an international commission created in Colombia to advise that nation on petroleum laws. From 1925 to 1931, Bain was secretary of the American Institute of Mining and Metallurgical Engineers. Later, Bain became managing director of the Copper and Brass Research Corporation and "between 1934 and 1936 he was in consulting work chiefly if not entirely on Far East problems, and he became a partner in Wright, Dolbear and Company, New York." At the time Ayukawa first met him in the summer of 1937, Bain had just started working in Manila to set up the "newly authorized Bureau of Mines, including a Geological Survey." President Manuel L. Quezon (1878–1944) of the Philippines would shortly thereafter appoint him as advisor on mines.[28]

Manchukuo and Ayukawa impressed Bain. Bain thought Ayukawa "one of the most interesting men with whom I have ever worked and I think is likely to continue to have a strong influence behind the scenes. We seem to have liked each other from the first."[29] Bain perceived Ayukawa as practical and devoted to peace because of

not only the business man's impatience with the disorder of war, its waste, and its useless sacrifice, but something deeper; a feeling that it is the natural order.... His business experience too has taught him to accept people as they are and to work with the means at hand to accomplish results. He knows intimately the limitations of the Chinese, the Japanese and the "Young Officers" group which is playing such an important role in affairs now. He recognizes equally though the deep idealism which has captured the imagination of these young men; their feeling that industrialization in Japan has not benefitted the common people nearly so much as it might have done, and their determination that Manchuoukuo [sic] shall start with a clean slate and realize just as far as may be possible the ideal that resources should be developed for service rather than primarily for profit. Aikawa [Ayukawa] has been in big business long enough to realize that it has in truth a seamly [i.e., "seamy"] and selfish side but he also realized—which . . . young men do not fully—that selfishness provided only that it be enlightened, is a most powerful motive and is in fact the major actuating force in world affairs. I think he believes—as I do—that we can only gradually approximate to a better order and usually lose when we try short cuts. However here is the actual force and idealism of these officers and he believes that by friendly guidance they can be brought to a much better realization of how to accomplish the ideal we all have, by use rather than abuse of business men and methods. He is a man of vision, energy, and willingness to work. Has a keen sense of humor though dominantly serious. It is a great pleasure indeed to work with him whether much or little be accomplished.[30]

Bain was also impressed by economic developments in Manchukuo. Hsinking, with lots of construction under way, reminded him of "a boom town in Texas, or maybe more of an unfinished exposition." Manchuria "reminded me of America in physical aspects, wide plains and big fields— you could have an Iowa farm here. Then there are mountains and some ores and lots of coal. A lot can be done to develop this country and it is real pioneering so naturally it appeals to me." Bain regretted that his visit had been so short since he wanted to explore this land further. On the other hand, Ayukawa's offer came just before he was leaving for a previously scheduled home leave from Manila to see his family in the United States. In mid-April, Bain boarded the Canadian Pacific's *Empress of Asia* in Tokyo, and he arrived in Vancouver in early May.[31]

Bain's recommendations for Manchukuo were made in an April 9 memorandum to Ayukawa; an April 10 report on the mineral resources of Manchukuo; and two reports in May that consisted of the main text and a precis and recommendations under the common title "Mineral Resources of Manchuria as a Basis for Industry." In his final report, Bain stated that Manchukuo's heavy industry "may, with patience and care, be built up on a solid basis to a position hardly to be equalled in the Far East nearer than Australia or India."[32]

Although Ayukawa had invited Bain as part of his scheme to secure American funds for industrialization projects in Manchukuo, Bain was not hopeful about this and stated in a letter to Ayukawa, "I find no reason to change my belief that any public financing is for the present impossible, and that the only available line of approach now is through cooperative enterprises working with individual companies." Bain did not think "there is any fundamental dislike here of Japan or any considerable lack of appreciation among informed men of the fact that your people are the big constructive force in the Far East." He stated, however, that these Americans, including himself, thought "the military approach to the problem is wrong, will defeat its own purpose, and that anything which strengthens them is a danger to the whole world, including yourselves and ourselves." Bain commented: "The popular sympathy, as you know, is very strongly with the Chinese in this scrap, but I really think a large part of that is because we are not convinced that 'the dog knows he won't bite.'"

The good news was that Bain concurred with Ayukawa's call for joint ventures between the latter's business interests and American companies. Bain's report included comments on business prospects in such areas as railway equipment, oil, magnesite, dredges, coal, iron ores, and mining geology. Bain "[found] it . . . feasible to secure at least some railway equipment on the general terms which [he had] suggested to [Ayukawa] and to . . . Matsuoka [Yōsuke]." Bain "arranged [in New York] for a particular competent associate of [his] to take this up if [SMR] wishes him to do so." As for oil, Bain suggested during two visits to President Philo W. Parker of Standard Oil "an arrangement where [Standard Oil] furnish the technical staff and any equipment which might be needed abroad, and one of [Ayukawa's] companies supply the labor and other things which could be paid for with local currency, and the profits be divided." Although Parker and his director "thought fairly well of the idea," Parker indicated only the matter would be kept open. Bain thought Parker might directly contact Ayukawa, but in the meantime he was going to look for other candidates. As for magnesite deposits, Bain's business associate S. H. Dolbear, a consultant specializing in magnesites, evinced interest in introducing Ayukawa to American firms for which Dolbear had previously done consulting work. As for dredges, which were needed to explore and exploit new gold mines, Bain stated that provided he had time in San Francisco, he would ask companies there in that field if they "would be interested in joining in such an enterprise." Although Bain thought the Japanese companies already undertaking this business in Manchukuo could carry this out by themselves, he suggested time could be saved "by having as an associate an American company with a mass of accumulated data, designs, and which keeps in constant touch with operations all around the world." Finally, as for coal, iron ores, and mining geology, Bain recommended hiring American specialists for further studies. Bain thought "costs should be lower than they seemed to be, . . . [and] it would be well worthwhile for [Ayukawa] to have [the] Fushin [coalmines] visited by a first class American specialist . . . ." With regard to iron ore and mining geology, Bain felt "keenly there is a gap here that should be filled, and that various companies may spend larger sums that [sic] are really necessary for lack of data previously systematically collected and recorded."[33]

When he came to Manchukuo, Bain was convinced of the need to make Manchukuo interdependent on the world economy. This thought linked to his concerns to prepare the Philippines economically for its upcoming independence. In an article "Problems of and Adjustment in the Mining Industry" in the September bulletin of the National Research Council of the Philippines, Bain recommended that the Philippines iron ore industry target Japan as a primary export market in the future. There was a potential demand for these ores from Japan's steelmills, especially given the low level of iron ore consumption in the Philippines. Although these ores were being exported to the east coast of the United States and Europe, "their principal handicap is the ocean freight rate. . . . Growth of this industry will depend more upon steps that may be taken to assure lower, or at least steady freight rates, than on tariff favors." Shipping to Japan was obviously cheaper than shipping to the United States or Europe.[34]

Philippine iron ores could also be exported to Manchukuo. In return, the Philippines would obtain coal from Manchukuo; as Bain wrote in his May report to Ayukawa, although further investigations were needed, he had tentatively concluded that the "total would place Manchuria, from the point of view of coal reserves, above Japan including Korea, and below Belgium." Because Manchuria possessed "many coalfields of commercial importance, that is widely distributed, and lies in generally good situations for mining, and that in certain districts very large quantities are available under such favorable conditions [this] should permit production at as low a price per ton as anywhere in the world." If the price could be lowered through American technical advice, Bain thought not only would Manchuria coal become world competitive, but the competition also would force a decline in the price of Japanese coal exported to the Philippines by Japanese syndicates. Bain suggested in the summary and recommendation section of his May report that if a new steel district could be built around the harbor of Hulutao, which he thought feasible, the furnaces should be fed with "imported iron ore . . . available at Surigao in the Philippines." Bain argued: "The ore can be supplied cheaply, the ocean freight haul is shorter than from competing mines to Japan, and the ore movement can be to some extent offset by coal shipments south." Bain argued that "the Surigao ore differs in character from the ores commonly used in Japan and Manchuria, but the technic [*sic*] of its treatment has been fully worked out and tested in practice through some years of operation in the United States." Bain thought Hulutao would be able to produce marketable pig irons by using Surigao ores, and he argued that Manchuria should conserve some of its own iron ore resources for long-term usage by importing the ore from the Philippines.[35]

On the issue of importing Surigao iron ores, Ayukawa seemed to have had little interest in creating an economic interdependence between Manchukuo and the Philippines. Bain, concerned about utilizing Surigao iron ores for the development of the Philippines, continued his discussions and research on these ores with his business associates in the United States. Then, in April 1940, Bain sent Miho a letter explaining his plan to build an iron-processing plant in Surigao with money from the Philippine government. Bain and the government wanted an advance commitment from Ayukawa to agree on a barter arrangement for these ores, presumably for Manchurian coal. Although Bain indicated that the successful creation of such a processing plant was as yet uncertain, he wanted Ayukawa to commit himself to a barter arrangement if the plant went into operation. Bain hoped that if his plan worked out, it would help revive the project for blast furnaces at Hulutao. Bain pursued his plan to build a pilot processing plant, which had the backing of the National Development Company of the Philippines, and contacted his business connections at the Dorr Company in New York, H. A. Brassert & Company in Chicago, and the Battelle Memorial Institute in Columbus, Ohio. Ayukawa, however, apparently never responded to Bain's proposal, and the project had died by the end of 1940.[36] As we shall see in the succeeding chapters, Ayukawa may have been too busy with his other projects to consider Bain's scheme.

Had politics not intervened to the extent that it did in U.S.-Japan relations, Ayukawa probably could have enticed American investment on a large scale and enhanced trade between the United States and Manchukuo. An early end to the Sino-Japanese War would have facilitated this, since most of the laws to regulate foreign exchange and trade resulted directly from the escalation of that war. As the Sino-Japanese War turned into a quagmire, however, Manchukuo could not import enough of the Japanese goods, capital, technology, and skilled and unskilled manpower that it needed for its industrialization programs, because the Japanese economy had little to spare; this increased Manchukuo's need for Western goods and capital. After the outbreak of World War II in Europe in 1939, the United States was the only industrialized power in the West from which Manchukuo could secure capital and technology.

As Ayukawa undertook to attract American investment to Manchukuo, he realized that securing American capital and technology had become more important than he had initially thought. Policymakers in both Manchukuo and Japan initially had had high hopes for MIDC's role in Manchukuo's industrialization and joint venture schemes with foreign, particularly American, companies. Manchukuo policymakers also wanted the companies in Ayukawa's Nissan group to provide products and skilled manpower for its industrialization programs. But because the war with China increasingly made meeting Japan's own domestic needs a higher priority, such assistance became impossible. Ayukawa and Nissan were instead relying on the resources of the SMR's former subsidiaries that now fell under MIDC's umbrella and from the investments Ayukawa sought from the West.[37]

FOUR

Ayukawa's Negotiations with Ford, 1937–1940

Between 1937 and 1939, some major American corporations factored into their business risk calculations for the Far East the possibility that Japan might succeed in subjugating the Nationalist regime in China. This chapter and the following one discuss Ayukawa's negotiations with these American business companies that were reconsidering the environment in which they might have to operate in the Far East. If Japan gained full control over China, should not American business be "realistic" and pursue greater economic cooperation with Japan? Only the outbreak of World War II in Europe, which stimulated a gradual economic recovery in the United States, drew the attention of American business away from U.S.-Japan and U.S.-Manchukuo economic cooperation. This trend accelerated after Japan signed the Axis Pact in September 1940.

Among the schemes MIDC considered in 1938–39, it vigorously pursued a joint venture with Ford, a project that was an integral part of Ayukawa's plans to industrialize Manchukuo and to dominate the Japanese automobile market. Because Ayukawa had previously succeeded in obtaining machinery and technology for Nissan Motors from an economically depressed America, he thought he could take similar advantage of this situation to further Manchukuo's industrialization program. Ayukawa's idea of joint ventures originated from his experiences in dealing with American companies, particularly his attempts to form a joint venture with GM, and from the fact that Ford proposed a joint venture with Nissan in May 1937, partly because the Japanese government had in effect frozen all assets of Ford-Japan by mid-1937.

Ford, which had previously ignored merger proposals from Japanese companies, proposed that it sell 50 percent of Ford-Japan's stock to Nissan Motors; this would enable Ford to meet the requirements for receiving a license under the Automobile Manufacturing Law. Despite the restrictions imposed by this law, sales of Ford cars and trucks made at knock-down assembly plants in Japan increased from 6,505 vehicles in 1932 to 18,379 vehicles in 1937. Many of these vehicles probably ended up on battlefields in China. As part of the agreement, Ford wanted Nissan to remit the payment for the stock in dollars to the United States. It also wanted to renew the aborted factory plan (see Chapter 1) and demanded that Nissan provide capital for its construction. Nissan Motors informed Ford-Japan that the Japanese government would not approve these conditions. Although Nissan did not elaborate, it undoubtedly based this opinion on its previous experience with the foreign-exchange issue during the first GM negotiations and its awareness of government interference in Ford's factory plans only a year or two earlier. As an alternative, Nissan Motors proposed a merger between Nissan and Ford-Japan like that Nissan had sought during the second Nissan-GM negotiations.[1]

Ayukawa wanted to assemble Ford vehicles from parts at Nissan's automobile factory; the arrangement would meet the strong demand for trucks in Manchukuo and the Chinese war front. Nissan's Model 80 would have served fine during peacetime in places where the roads were paved. But, in the muddy battlefields in China and Manchukuo, Nissan trucks shook excessively because their front axle was wider than their back axle, which made it impossible to follow the ruts made by standard trucks. Many Japanese military drivers preferred Ford trucks because they felt uncomfortable driving Nissan 80 and Toyota trucks. Sharing Ayukawa's thinking, Ogura Masatsune of the Sumitomo Holding Company was realistic about the level of Japanese technology and questioned the wisdom of shutting American companies that possessed advanced technology out of the Japanese market. Both men preferred cooperating with American companies in order to absorb new and advanced technology.[2]

On July 29, Ayukawa and Benjamin Kopf, president of Ford-Japan, held a general discussion. At that time, Kopf had intentionally overstocked 6,000 Ford vehicles, undoubtedly because of the outbreak of the Sino-Japanese

War. Although this action exceeded the production quota imposed by the Automobile Manufacturing Law on Ford, both Ayukawa and Kopf wanted to find a way not only to sell these vehicles but also to use their discussions as a way to gain the Japanese government's support for a joint venture. Both men thought the government would favor a joint venture because of the Sino-Japanese War. Ayukawa believed in the superiority of Ford technology, including Ford's ability to develop and produce quality car parts, and he was dissatisfied with the poor performance of Nissan 80 trucks, which were produced using the technology and equipment purchased from Graham-Paige, which, except for engines, relied on automobile parts from other companies. Finally, although Kopf expressed skepticism about the ability of this joint venture to win distribution rights outside Japan, except possibly North China, Ayukawa wanted the joint venture to enjoy the distribution rights for not only Japan but also China, the Philippines, the Dutch East Indies, Singapore, Malaya, and India, provided that this venture could produce quality cars more cheaply than Ford America, which had the distribution rights for China and the Philippines, and Ford Canada, which covered the rest of the area Ayukawa had in mind.[3]

MCI approved a joint venture between Nissan Motors and Ford-Japan, and both parties agreed in an August 4, 1937, contract that Nissan Motors would lease Ford's assembly plant in Japan from that day until October 10, 1937. Under this agreement and an additional contract signed on September 20, Ford produced 2,800 trucks and buses. Since the 1936 Automobile Manufacturing Law imposed a strict quota on Ford-Japan, Ford utilized its own automobile parts approved for importation by the government for Nissan Motors; because of the automobile regulations, this was the only joint venture that Nissan and Ford could arrange. Cars and trucks assembled under this scheme were sold by Nissan Motors to Ford-Japan, which in turn sold them in the Japanese market.[4]

The dilemma for Ford-Japan was how to stay in the Japanese market. Because the U.S. State Department could not effectively assist Ford's head office in Detroit in its request that the Japanese government issue a foreign-exchange license to Ford-Japan so it could remit dividends and profits back to Detroit, Ford Motors had to protect itself by cooperating with Japanese authorities and interests if it wanted to survive in Japan. In early 1938, when Ford-Japan, after receiving authorization from Detroit, agreed to the MOF's informal request that it purchase "China Incident" bonds, which were used to finance Japanese war efforts in China, the Japanese government allowed Ford-Japan to send $1.5 million to the United States.[5]

Later, in August 1938, Nissan Motors and Ford-Japan began discussing more extensive forms of cooperation in Japan and Manchukuo; the talks were held in Tokyo between Kopf, on the one hand, and Miho Mikitarō and James W. Murray, on the other hand. Although the importation of foreign cars and trucks became increasingly more difficult after February 1938 because of heavier government restrictions, the military needed all the vehicles it could secure for the war effort in China. In late October, Kopf informed Ayukawa that his superiors in Detroit, in Kopf's opinion, had made an unprecedented decision to defer payment in dollars for two years for both Ford cars assembled and shipped to Manchukuo from Japan and Ford cars shipped directly to Manchukuo from the United States. Shortly thereafter, MIDC and Ford-Japan discussed the possibility of Nissan Motors' buying up to 51 percent of Ford-Japan's stock and remitting the dollar equivalent to the United States under a two-year payment plan. The merged company would build a new manufacturing plant in Japan that could manufacture 50,000 Ford cars and trucks a year; the new company would also take over Dōwa Motors in Manchukuo and build a new plant there, possibly in Hulutao, to produce Ford cars from scratch. The plans called for the eventual production of some 20,000 vehicles a year.

Kopf, however, was skeptical. On September 13, he told Ayukawa that he did not anticipate a jump in demand for cars in the Japanese empire and the areas it occupied in China because of restrictions on private ownership, high taxes, low income levels, the difficulty of obtaining a driver's license, and poor road conditions. As for the MIDC's desire to assemble cars in Manchukuo, Ford's preference was to build a knock-down assembly plant first and defer a manufacturing plant until later, provided that the Manchukuo-made vehicles were not subject to Japanese tariffs when exported to Japan. Based on proposals exchanged between Ford-Japan and Nissan on October 22 and October 26, 1938, the two firms began to formulate conditions for a Nissan-Ford merger and think of ways to initiate joint Ford-MIDC automobile operations in Manchukuo.

On November 17, 1938, the two sides came up with a scheme to create a Ford knock-down assembly plant under the Dōwa Motor Company's name at either Dairen or Mukden for the production of 5,000 Ford trucks and buses. Ford-Japan and MIDC devised a payment plan of $5 million with a two-year deferment. As this negotiation continued, in part to augment Ayukawa's efforts to attract direct and indirect American investment in Manchukuo, MIDC, the Japanese Foreign Ministry, and the Manchukuo government managed to have the November 30, 1938, issue of the *Journal of Commerce and Finance*, an American trade magazine, devote an entire section to various issues concerning U.S.-Manchukuo trade relations, including Manchukuo's economic potential and the call for American direct and indirect investment in Manchukuo.[6]

Although Kopf believed he was making decisions that would prevent Ford from being completely excluded from the Japanese market, Ford executives in the United States were apparently dissatisfied with MIDC's proposal for joint ventures in Japan and Manchukuo. Ford demanded a larger payment by MIDC for a joint venture and a more equitable arrangement. Ford also refused Ayukawa's wish to permit the merged company to sell its manufactures outside the Japanese empire and the area it occupied in China. It also expressed its unwillingness to make new investments in Japan; although Ford executives were willing to sell machinery to Japanese companies, they were unwilling to do this by extending credits because as long as the current foreign-exchange control laws were in force, they would not approve new dollar investments and wanted to liquidate existing yen credits. In further negotiations, the two sides discussed the purchase of American machinery for automobile-manufacturing plants operated by a joint venture company and evaluated the possibility of long-term credits jointly provided by the machine manufacturers and financial institutions in America. Nissan Motors thought that this credit arrangement might be facilitated with the assistance of Ford Motors in America. In the end, Nissan convinced Ford to withdraw its demand for the liquidation of existing yen credits.

Ford's unwillingness to extend new credits arose in part from "publicity in the American press." Ayukawa received this information from James W. Murray after the latter had held secret talks with top Ford executives in the United States in February. Ford was nervous that news of this meeting might leak, and "Mr. [Edsel] F[ord] expressed many times that if necessary they would rather discontinue all operations in Japan rather than tie up with somebody who would not be satisfactory to them." As Murray explained to Ayukawa, "They have had many unpleasant experiences with other foreign connections."

As an alternative to the Dōwa-Ford arrangement, on February 23, 1939, after discussions that had lasted since November 1938, Nissan and Ford-Japan agreed on a joint venture to supply 4,500 trucks and buses and 500 cars to Dōwa Motors. The agreement was identical to the arrangement made in August 1937, except that Ford-Japan was to supply the vehicles to Dōwa Motors in Manchukuo. MCI approved this contract on two separate occasions, once on July 21, 1939, and again on October 12, 1939. An additional contract signed on May 22 stipulated the production of 500 Ford cars and 3,500 trucks between May 1 and December 31. As stipulated in the February 23 agreement, during 1939 Ford manufactured 4,500 trucks and buses and 500 cars for Dōwa Motors.

The State Department was displeased about the Dōwa-Ford arrangement because it believed the deal involved the provision of credits to a company registered in Manchukuo, an unrecognized country. It based this allegation on information supplied by an informant who had contacted the American embassy in Tokyo. This person stated that the February 23 contract between Nissan and Ford-Japan involved a substantial credit deal. In May the Department summoned Edsel B. Ford (1893–1943), Kopf, and J. Crawford, a top Ford executive, to discuss the February 23 deal. According to Murray, "I am told [Edsel Ford] had considerable difficulty explaining that it was a yen credit granted by the Ford Company of Japan and not a dollar credit granted by the Ford Company of Detroit." J. C. Ankeny, Ford's number-two man in Tokyo, had to visit the American embassy in Tokyo six times to explain the transaction. He, however, got the impression the embassy was reluctant to pursue the matter too deeply since 1,000 of the 5,000 vehicles had already been delivered to Nissan and it feared it would be blamed for not finding this out earlier.[7]

Although Ford expressed unwillingness to make new dollar investments in Japan, after Kopf formulated and showed Miho the "Proposed Basis of Merger Between Ford-Japan and Nissan" on January 26, 1939, the two sides agreed to discuss a joint venture whereby Nissan Motors would provide 60 percent and Ford-Japan 40 percent of the capital. Because of Japanese foreign-exchange regulations, this merger would not involve the purchase of Ford-Japan stock by Nissan and the remittance of the dollar equivalent to the United States. Ford also revived its wish for a new factory at the same site in Yokohama as in 1936; the joint venture planned to sell manufactured passenger cars and trucks in the Japanese empire and the areas Japan occupied in China. If the American shareholders of the new company wished to sell their shares, Nissan was obliged to purchase them within five years at a greater value than the original amount. In the same letter, Kopf argued that because "the policy followed by the Japanese Government in the last few years, and the China Incident, have caused the level of prices of cars and trucks to rise unduly in [Japan]," "one of the primary objects of our contemplated merger should be improvement of quality, increase in quantity, and reduction of cost and prices."[8]

Shortly thereafter, the top-secret talks between Nissan and Ford executives in the United States took place. During discussions on February 16 and 17, 1939, with Ford Motors executives at their head office in Dearborn, James W. Murray learned from Edsel Ford and others present at the meetings that Ford Motors was willing to negotiate with MIDC for a joint venture. Ford executives expressed concern over rumors of the economic collapse of Japan. Murray assured them that was a remote possibility and explained to them in detail "the set-up in Manchukuo and Japan . . . and . . . pointed out in particular the growth of the Japanese companies formerly controlled by the former Nissan Company and now by Maindec [MIDC], and of recent developments in Manchukuo." As Murray argued that Ayukawa's business group was the right choice as Ford's partner if Ford wanted to continue its Japan operations, Ford executives asked him many questions about Nissan Motors' management. Murray "assured Boyer [the code name used for Ford Motors] that they are capable and progressive and that if a merger was made [with Ford-Japan] Mr. Aikawa [Ayukawa] would take considerable personal interest in seeing to it that the progressive policies of Boyer were continued." Murray told them that Ayukawa wanted to "rely on Boyer engineers to a very considerable extent and that they would have a real voice in the management of the company."[9]

As Ayukawa pursued his negotiations with Ford, he became aware of parallel attempts by GM to form a joint venture with a Japanese company. In October 1938 Baron Itō Bunkichi (1885–1951), a friend and confidant as well as a member of the House of Peers and president of Ayukawa's Japan Mining Company, informed Ayukawa that GM had told a friend of Itō's in New York, Lower House member Tsurumi Yūsuke (1885–1973), that it was looking for a joint venture with a Japanese car company in which GM-Japan would have a minority share of a half-million dollars. In June Tsurumi had received a proposal for a joint venture with Toyota Motors from a Mr.

Riley, GM's general manager in New York. GM-Japan was prepared to be a minority shareholder in the new company because it anticipated lucrative future business opportunities in the Japanese empire. GM-Japan now planned to produce in Japan all the component parts of GM trucks, except for the engine, transmission, and rear axle. Initially it planned to import these from GM's plants in Detroit, but it envisioned producing them in Japan eventually. GM trucks made at this Japanese plant were to be sold within the Japanese empire, including the areas Japan occupied in China. MIDC showed no interest in GM's proposal, although in February 1939 it had considered importing GM's Blitz trucks to sell through Dōwa Motors in Manchukuo. When Nissan's merger talks with Ford entered an important stage on April 19, 1939, Ayukawa requested Lt. Col. Akimaru Jirō (1898–1992) of the Kwantung Army's Fourth Section that Manchukuo stop purchasing GM cars and confine its business with GM to the purchase of parts for existing GM vehicles in Manchukuo.[10]

Ayukawa was unaware, however, that Ford-Japan was pursuing negotiations with companies other than Nissan. In July 1938, Ford-Japan had approached Toyota Motors (one of the two government-licensed companies under the 1936 Automobile Manufacturing Law) for a joint venture and told Toyota it was negotiating with other Japanese companies, including the Furukawa and Asano conglomerates. (It was not until March 1939 that MIDC and Toyota became aware of each other's negotiations with Ford-Japan.)

Before negotiating with Ford-Japan, Toyota consulted with MCI and the Army. The Army supported the project since Toyota vehicles were performing poorly on the war front, and the Army needed more trucks as soon as possible. MCI approved this joint venture because of the possibility of technological borrowing and other merits. On February 28, 1939, Ford-Japan and Toyota tentatively reached an agreement on conditions for a merger. Under the proposal, Toyota would purchase 51 percent of Ford-Japan's stock. Toyota not only agreed to remit the dollar equivalent of the value of this stock to Ford in America but also planned to finance 51 percent of Ford's proposed new manufacturing plant in Tsurumi. The new manufacturing plant, to be completed in two years, was scheduled to produce 30,000 vehicles a year to be sold in the Japanese empire and Japanese-occupied areas in China.

During the course of these negotiations, Toyota Motors learned from a November 25 report in the *Ōsaka Mainichi* that Ford-Japan was negotiating with MIDC. When it asked Kopf for an explanation, he stated that he had rejected the proposal because, in his judgment, an automobile industry in Manchuria had few prospects due to the low demand for vehicles there. Although the two parties reached a tentative agreement in February 1939, on March 29 Toyota learned that Nissan and Ford-Japan were still negotiating for a joint venture when MCI ordered Nissan and Toyota to temporarily cease their respective negotiations with Ford, although the two seemed to have disobeyed MCI's demand.[11]

On March 27, 1939, Kopf, on his way to Detroit to confer with Ford executives, visited Ayukawa's MIDC office in Hsinking to discuss the proposed merger. Although Ayukawa expressed his disappointment that Ford had no plans for new investment in Japan under the proposed joint venture, both Ayukawa and Kopf wanted the project to succeed. Although Ayukawa had the support of the Manchukuo government, he continued to worry that Ford might still insist on the remittance of Ford-Japan's yen assets in dollars, a condition that would destroy the proposed merger because of the Japanese government's foreign-exchange regulation. Kopf emphasized that Nissan was Ford's first choice as a partner for a joint venture, although he also mentioned, upon Ayukawa's and Miho's inquiries, that the director of MCI's Industrial Affairs Bureau, Higashi Eiji (1890–1947), had been pressuring Ford to conclude a joint venture with Toyota, which the MCI bureaucrats thought needed strengthening more than Nissan.[12]

On May 18, Murray sent Ayukawa two cables, informing him that after discussions with Ford executives including Kopf, Ford had agreed to let Nissan pay its portion of capital in yen and planned to provide machinery under an arrangement that would not require payments in dollars. Murray elaborated on these points in a May 16 letter to Miho, which Ayukawa received on June 5. According to Murray, Kopf and the other Ford executives proposed a merger that initially allowed Nissan Motors to control 48.75 percent of the new company. Ford Motors felt that given the unfavorable American public opinion of Japan, it could not allow a Japanese company a majority control of the new company. Ford-Japan would control 48.75 percent, and a Japanese employee of Ford-Japan 2.5 percent.

By allowing a Japanese employee of Ford-Japan to hold this share, Ford could explain in the United States it had a 51 percent majority control. Nissan Motors, on the other hand, could also argue to the Japanese government that this Japanese employee fulfilled the requirement that over 50 percent of the shares had to be in Japanese hands. The new plant was scheduled to produce Ford engines, rear axles, and transmissions; although Ayukawa and Miho had hoped for a new plant that produced all Ford components, Kopf thought, in addition to saving money, the other components could be manufactured by Nissan. In creating a new company, Ford demanded the government issue a new license to Ford-Japan or extend Nissan's license to Ford-Japan. Within two years of the signing of the agreement, Ford promised that Nissan would control up to 60 percent of the new company. If Nissan rejected Ford's offer, Ford stated it would make the same offer to Toyota.

On June 19, Ankeny informed Ayukawa of the conditions for a merger as stated by Ford Motors. Ford was prepared to merge Ford-Japan with Nissan Motors to create a company that would have enough capital to erect a new manufacturing plant at the same site that Ford had wanted in 1936. The new company was to meet the requirements of the 1936 Automobile Manufacturing Law as a licensed company, and its products were to be sold in the Japanese empire and the area Japan occupied in China. Nissan Motors would eventually control 60 percent and Ford 40 percent of the company. Ford was willing to broker for the purchase of all necessary machinery and equipment needed for the new factory in Yokohama. Ford was also willing to mediate a favorable credit arrangement. During July, Ford Motors in Detroit agreed to allow Nissan 51 percent of the company from the start and 60 percent within two years after the agreement was signed.[13]

Nissan kept MCI informed of the progress of the negotiations with Ford, even after the ministry ordered a temporary suspension of the talks. For its part, MCI was formulating a new policy for the merger. On July 15, 1939, MCI's Bureau of Machinery issued a memorandum entitled "The Case for the Local Production of Currently Imported Cars" ("Yunyū jidōsha no kokusanka ni kansuru ken"). MCI proposed the merger of Nissan Motors, Toyota Motors, and Ford-Japan. The planned company, whose establishment was subject to MCI approval, had to conform to the conditions stated in the 1936 Automobile Manufacturing Law to become a licensed company. The new company would construct a factory to manufacture everything from auto parts to cars. Ford would provide machinery, equipment, and engineers.

On August 5, Ayukawa told Asakura he had conceded to MCI's request to let Toyota participate on an equal basis with Nissan; Ayukawa, after all, had long entertained the ambition of merging all Japanese companies (see Chapter 8), and a merger of Nissan and Toyota would be a cornerstone for that project. On August 11, MCI, in "Suggestions for the Major Conditions for the Merger with Ford" ("Ford to no shuyō teikei jōken'an"), indicated its willingness to let Ford control 40 percent of the new company with the remainder to be split equally by Nissan and Toyota. In addition to boosting Japanese production of vehicles by creating a new car-manufacturing plant that produced everything from auto parts to vehicles, MCI wanted the new company to produce standard cars that were as good in quality and performance as the models produced by Ford. Ford was also to continue to provide the necessary technology to the new company, as well as to Nissan and Toyota. The new factory was to be completed within two years of the signing of the contract. Foreign-exchange payments to Ford for its machinery, equipment, and technical assistance were to be made in installment payments every six months for three years after the completion of the factory. Finally, Ford Motors was to give the new company the exclusive right to produce and sell Ford vehicles in the Japanese empire and China.[14]

Confronted by these MCI initiatives, on September 1 Ayukawa visited Toyota Motors president Toyoda Risaburō (whose brother-in-law Toyoda Kiichirō [1894–1952], the founder and vice president of Toyota Motors, was married to a sister of Ayukawa's wife; both women came from the Iida clan, owners of the Takashimaya Department Store Company). Ayukawa and Toyoda exchanged views on the proposed merger with Ford-Japan because MCI was about to make its final decision on the merger. According to a report by Toyoda to MCI on September 6, both men agreed that if the government approved, Nissan and Toyota should cooperate to strengthen the Japanese automobile industry. Some arrangement, however, had to be made to shield their two companies lest the merged company re-create Ford's dominance of the Japanese automobile market. The two men differed on how this was to be achieved.

Ayukawa, who seemed more enthusiastic than Toyoda for a merger with Ford, stated that Ford should provide the new company the major auto parts for manufacturing 30,000 vehicles; this idea reflected the earlier negotiations between Nissan and Ford in which Ford agreed to supply engines, rear axles, and transmissions. Toyoda, on the other hand, believed that his company should focus more on developing products under government protection and did not want to be so dependent on Ford. He therefore disagreed with Ayukawa's division-of-labor approach. Ayukawa thought the benefits of the proposed arrangements would outweigh the cost of discarding the machinery and equipment owned by Nissan and Toyota that could produce the vehicle components Ford was to provide, but Toyoda, partly because his company had built a new factory in November 1938, wanted to preserve those machines and use them to improve the Toyota vehicles. Toyoda proposed that the new company should produce 20,000 vehicles, but he also requested MCI to consider, as an alternative to the merger, the hiring of foreign engineers to improve the Japanese automobile industry. He was concerned about indigenous efforts to improve diesel engines and make vehicles powered by heavy oil. Toyoda thought that Japan did not necessarily need to import Ford vehicles. With government protection, Nissan and Toyota could pursue efforts to improve their existing products and car parts. Toyoda worried about saturation of the automobile market, which he considered a strong possibility because of the increased number of licensed companies. He also thought that some other Japanese car company might merge with GM. Although Toyoda thought improved roads, cheaper gasoline, and other improvements would stimulate demand, he was pessimistic that, if Nissan and Toyota each produced its maximum MCI target of 40,000 vehicles and the new company manufactured 20,000 units, the market could absorb 100,000 vehicles annually.[15]

On September 26, MCI announced its proposal for the Nissan-Toyota-Ford merger. Its plan was the outgrowth of the developments discussed above and a proposal Ford-Japan had submitted to MCI on August 24 for merging Ford-Japan with Japanese interests to create a new company that complied with the Automobile Manufacturing Law. MCI took into consideration Kopf's August 26 cable to MIDC in which Ford demanded 51 percent control of the new company for the time being in order to avoid U.S. government interference and public resentment. Ford argued it would be easier to persuade them if it could argue that it still maintained majority control. In the September 26 MCI proposal, Ford was for the time being to control 51 percent of the new company, with the remainder to be split evenly between Nissan and Toyota; as J. C. Ankeny had proposed to Nissan on May 29, Ford would provide a portion of its 51 percent share to a person or persons of Japanese nationality. Although Ford in its August proposal had demanded a 49 percent share even after it became a minority shareholder, the MCI proposal called for Ford to control only 34 percent with the remainder evenly divided between Nissan and Toyota. Ford had also requested a license to produce 50,000 standard vehicles as good as Ford vehicles in quality and in performance annually, but MCI proposed an annual production of 30,000 standard vehicles. The new company would become the third government-licensed company after Nissan and Toyota. Although Ford-Japan in its August proposal asked that the territory of the new concern be limited to the Japanese empire and Japanese-occupied areas in China, MCI stated "the Japanese empire and China" and did not limit the region in China. Finally, although MCI did not explicitly state that it would grant Ford-Japan permission to erect a factory at the site where Ford had been attempting to build a plant since 1935, MCI indicated that it would approve the importation of about $5 million worth of machinery and equipment for a new manufacturing plant to be constructed in two years.

After follow-up discussions, Nissan, Toyota, and Ford-Japan (represented, respectively, by Ayukawa, Toyoda Risaburō, and Kopf) apparently reached an agreement on December 19, 1939, a few days before Ayukawa's departure for Europe (see Chapter 6). It seems the three companies agreed to form a concern that would become the third company licensed under the 1936 Automobile Manufacturing Law. The site of the new factory, which was to be completed within two years after receipt of government approval, was not specified, although it was scheduled to manufacture on an annual basis 70,000 standard cars and trucks under the Ford name. This agreement was to expire in ten years. Ford-Japan would initially hold a majority share as MCI had stipulated on September 26, but within two years after the signing of the agreement, Ford would hold 40 percent, and the remainder would be evenly divided between Nissan and Toyota. If Ford engineers sent from Detroit approved, Nissan and Toyota could supply a portion of their shares of the company's capital in the form of land, machinery, buildings, and equipment. These inputs could be used to supplement the production of vehicle components at the new manufacturing plant. Ford was also willing to broker for securing American machinery and equipment for the new factory under favorable credit terms. These arrangements were similar to those Nissan and Ford had discussed earlier. The new company received exclusive manufacturing and marketing rights from Ford Motor Company for the Japanese empire and Japanese-occupied areas in China.

One problem facing the Japanese side was to secure enough dollars to pay for the new equipment, machinery, patents, trademarks, technical assistance, and stock held by Americans. Nissan Motors continued to talk with Ford into 1940, but by May Ford executives were losing interest in a merger because of inaction on the Japanese side, inaction exacerbated by opposition to the merger within the Army and the Nissan Motors board of directors. The opposition at Nissan was led by Murakami Masasuke (1878–1949), who became Nissan Motors president when Ayukawa moved up to the chairmanship shortly before his departure for Europe in December 1939. Ford had for some time been concerned about securing payments in dollars from the Japanese side and indicated its unwillingness to provide either longer credit terms or dollar investments. Ford was unwilling to relinquish majority control until the Japanese side had enough foreign exchange to make the necessary payments. Murray was told by Ford executive J. Crawford that Ford Motors wanted an initial 60 percent control of the new company under a program that would eventually lead to majority control by Nissan and Toyota.[16]

As far as the issue of providing dollar credits was concerned, Murray had informed Ayukawa in the fall of 1939: "The [U.S.] Government is watching the situation rather carefully and for that reason bank officials and other responsible business men are very reluctant to do something contrary to the Government's wishes, although they would like very much to put to work some idle money that is here in New York." Because of the outbreak of World War II, Murray claimed that big business feared negative publicity that might trigger a domestic boycott of their products by people who were anti-German. Those who opposed Germany felt anti-Japanese; in spite of Japan's loosening of its ties with Germany after Hitler signed the non-aggression pact with Stalin, Murray argued that big business was wary of Jewish Americans, who were thought to have considerable purchasing power and were viewed as anti-Japanese because of the amicable relations between Germany and Japan. The prospects for obtaining large amounts of dollar credits became dimmer after the Import and Export Bank in Washington declined to approve applications for the purchase of goods needed in Japan that used Yokohama Specie Bank notes.[17] After May 1940, Nissan's negotiations with Ford apparently fizzled out. By January 1941, both Ford and GM had practically ceased all business activities in Japan.

FIVE

An Unfinished Dream: Economic
Diplomacy, 1937–1940

In economic diplomacy, Ayukawa's ultimate aim was to avoid war between
Japan and the United States by fostering greater economic interdependence
between the two countries. His business negotiations with American economic interests show that between 1937 and 1939 success depended on those
interests' perception of the direction of the Sino-Japanese War and the U.S.
government's regulations on trading with Japan and Manchukuo. Furthermore, as discussed in the next section, the Jewish refugee question in the Far
East provided an opportunity for arrangements that might partly meet the
needs of Japan's war economy as well as alleviate the plight of European
Jews, a major concern for many influential Americans, notably Jewish-
Americans. MIDC's dealings with Maxwell Kleiman and Franz Moedlhammer and its negotiations with Mesta Machine had a chance of success,
partly because major American firms and banks seriously entertained closer
economic cooperation with Japan and Manchukuo in 1938 and 1939 and
partly because of the Jewish refugee question in the Far East.

The Jewish Refugee Question in the Far East

In December 1937 or January 1938, Kuhn, Loeb & Company, a major Wall
Street investment bank, was approached by Maxwell Kleiman (1904–57), a
New York businessman whose successful consulting work in 1933 for the

Japanese shipping company Nihon yūsen kaisha (N.Y.K.) had won the trust of its president, Kagami Kenkichi (1868–1939). Through Kagami, Kleiman made many contacts in the Japanese business world and government, and these connections helped him to get in touch with influential businessmen such as Ayukawa.

Kleiman was a self-made man. He was born near Kiev in 1904. In order to escape Russia's anti-Semitic pogroms, his family emigrated to the United States in 1910 and settled in New York's Lower East Side. Kleiman became a naturalized American citizen in 1921. Despite encountering economic hardship in the mid-1920s, Kleiman, who never graduated from high school, succeeded under the tutelage of David Kamerman, at Kamerman & Witkin, a major tax consulting firm in New York. Kleiman knew and was apparently trusted by Chairman Walter P. Chrysler (1875–1940) of Chrysler Motors and executives at Hudson Motors Corporation and International Minerals & Metals Corporation. In 1938, Kleiman arrived in Tokyo and met Finance Ministry officials, who in turn introduced him to Ayukawa. Kleiman told Ayukawa that he could mediate loans to MIDC from Kuhn, Loeb and other Jewish financial institutions if Manchukuo would open its doors to Jewish refugees from Germany. Ayukawa showed much interest in Kleiman's proposal not only because of its economic benefits but also because of the positive influence that might be exerted by Jewish Americans on U.S. foreign policy toward Japan and Manchukuo. Ayukawa believed in Jewish economic power, particularly in America and England, and he wanted to use it to further Manchukuo's industrialization.

Japanese authorities were aware that many Jewish refugees in East Asia had American relatives and were seeking their help in obtaining visas to enter the United States. They were also aware that much of the aid to refugees in Shanghai came from American organizations. The Japanese authorities thought that helping the Jewish refugees might bring financial and material support for Japan's industrialization and war effort against China. Even if the attempt failed, it might alleviate the rising tensions with the United States by gaining the goodwill of American Jews, who represented a very influential voting bloc in U.S. politics. By October 1938 there were moves in Shanghai to coordinate the activities of the Navy, the Army, the SMR, and the consul general and conduct studies of obtaining Jewish capital from, for example, the Sassoons (who were British) in Shanghai and of using Jewish refugees to further Japan's industrialization.

Like many other Japanese, Ayukawa had an image of a Jewish-American investment banker at Kuhn, Loeb like Jacob H. Schiff (1847–1920), who had helped finance a major portion of Japan's war against Russia in 1905. Ayukawa knew that many Jewish refugees possessed knowledge and skills that could benefit Manchukuo's industrialization. He himself had letters and documents from refugees asking relatives and Jewish friends working in Japan to intercede with the Japanese authorities on their behalf. Caution was necessary, however, since Germany had recently recognized Manchukuo, and Germany and Japan enjoyed amicable relations.[1]

Ayukawa's opinion was shared by many Japanese leaders. Since 1933, the Kwantung Army had pursued a policy of treating Jews well for pragmatic reasons. After MIDC was established, the Kwantung Army ordered SMR to research the Jews because it supported using Jewish refugees and Jewish economic power for Manchukuo's industrialization.[2] In Japan, this policy received official recognition on December 6, 1938, at the Five Ministers Conference attended by Prime Minister Konoe Fumimaro, Finance Minister Ikeda Seihin (Shigeaki), Foreign Minister Arita Hachirō, Army Minister Itagaki Seishirō, and Navy Minister Yonai Mitsumasa (1880–1948). The conference concluded that although Japan's "diplomatic ties with Germany and Italy" posed difficulties for "embracing the Jewish people," Japan had a "declared policy of racial equality, and their rejection would therefore be contrary to our spirit." Above all, Japan needed foreign capital and wanted to avoid alienating America. Therefore, Japan would treat "the Jews presently living in Japan, Manchuria and China . . . equally with other foreigners" and the Jews entering the country as any other foreigner visiting Japan. Finally, although Japan "will not extend a special invitation to Jews," it would welcome capitalists and engineers.

According to David Kranzler, this meeting "set the tone for the Japanese relations to the Jews for the next three years, and was to have a great effect on the flow of refugees from Austria and Germany." "The policy owes its creation not to the refugee influx, which by December of 1938 had hardly reached the 1,000 mark, but to the earlier Jewish residents of the Far East . . . because plans for it were developed and formulated when the number of refugees entering was hardly more than a trickle." Consequently, "the beneficiaries of this benign policy" were "the large contingent of refugees streaming into Shanghai during the first half of 1939, and the smaller group that came through Japan in 1941."[3] According to Kranzler, Shanghai eventually had more Jewish refugees during World War II than Australia, New Zealand, Canada, South Africa, and India combined. Although Japan did promote anti-Semitism, it did not persecute the Jews but pursued an amoral, self-interested approach to use the alleged economic power of the Jews to further Japan's industrialization, war efforts, and political advantage in the United States.[4]

In March 1938, Kleiman "received a request from Japanese friends in Tokyo," presumably Ayukawa's group, "to study the possibilities of arranging credits [of $30–40 million] either on a short or long term basis" for Japan's economic programs.[5] Kleiman was aware that the State Department could pose an obstacle, but he was also aware that the Soviet Union had received American credits to purchase U.S. machinery and equipment during the years that the United States had not recognized the Soviet state. And despite the Soviet Union's poor record of repaying foreign debts compared to the prompt Japanese repayment, as well as the general tendency of Americans to dislike communism, the United States had recognized the Soviet Union in 1933. Given this history, Ayukawa and Kleiman believed that they had a chance of securing American capital for Manchukuo.

Kleiman decided to approach Kuhn, Loeb & Company through a friend, a banker by the name of Weiss whose father-in-law worked for Kuhn, Loeb. Weiss, however, told Kleiman that it was impossible to float a Japanese or Manchukuo bond because of the current negative American sentiment toward Japan because of its aggression against China. On the other hand, Kuhn, Loeb was willing to discuss Kleiman's proposal that the investment bank extend credits for the Japanese purchase of machinery and equipment.

Kuhn, Loeb seems to have been interested in indirect dealings with Japan, even though the company's de facto head, Lewis L. Strauss (1896–1974), clearly thought that it was impossible to conduct direct financial business with the Japanese. When Strauss received a letter in September 1938 from Wikawa (Ikawa) Tadao (1893–1947), a Finance Ministry official and a good friend, he was not thrilled to hear that "the fall of Hankow would be the turning point of the present troubles" in the Far East and "a new born China, remodelled after U.S.A., will come into existence before long." Although Wikawa asked Strauss to visit Japan to discuss business, Strauss replied, as he had so often to Japanese envoys and financial commissioners, that "Japanese public relations have not been successfully handled here" compared to those of the Chinese. Unless Japan could secure peace with the Chinese, Strauss stated that his firm was unwilling to discuss business with the Japanese government.[6] Officially, Strauss undoubtedly supported the policy of not providing Jewish support for Japan espoused by Rabbi Stephen S. Wise (1874–1949), the president of the American Jewish Congress, a very influential organization in American politics.[7]

Strauss had not always had such a negative view of Japan. In 1926, during a visit to Japan, Manchuria, and China, Strauss had praised Japan's modernization of its leased area in Manchuria. In an internal report to his Kuhn, Loeb partners in December 1926, Strauss had stated that Japanese firms such as SMR, Mitsubishi, and Ōkura, a conglomerate that had been running a 50-50 joint venture with the Chinese since 1910 in producing coal and steel in Manchuria, had "simply transfigured the country," and he emphasized "the remarkable contrast between living conditions in the Japanese Zone and outside of it in Manchuria proper" as "the most convincing evidence of the desirability of Japanese control in that country." During this trip, Strauss had met Ayukawa's brother-in-law Kuhara Fusanosuke, but the two had apparently not kept in touch subsequently.[8]

Despite his official unwillingness to discuss business with Japanese interests, Strauss was willing to pursue informal talks with Ayukawa's group in 1938 because of his wish to save European Jews from Nazi persecution. In the spring of 1938, meetings at the White House on the Jewish refugee question ended with only expressions of concern; the United States was at that time in a severe economic depression, and policymakers had other political priorities. Jewish business leaders such as Bernard M. Baruch (1870–1965) and Lewis Strauss were part of an active movement to find a homeland for Jewish refugees.[9] China, including Manchuria, was one of areas they considered.

Kleiman returned to Japan in September 1938, after spending many months in New York to work on a credit plan for Japan. Kleiman got back in touch with Ayukawa through Vice Minister of Finance Ishiwatari Sōtarō (1891–1950). Kleiman conveyed the news that Kuhn, Loeb was willing to discuss business with the Japanese, although the company would not make an advance commitment. In a memorandum submitted to Ishiwatari on September 22, Kleiman stated that after numerous discussions with Kuhn, Loeb through Weiss between May and August, the investment bank had agreed to start discussions. Kuhn, Loeb proposed the Japanese side designate or create a clearinghouse, preferably a prominent Japanese bank, to take orders from Japanese companies for machinery and other goods. This clearinghouse would then submit the orders to Kuhn, Loeb. A prominent Japanese bank had to guarantee the ability of this agency to pay for the goods. Kuhn, Loeb would approach the relevant American companies and explain to them that the orders came from Japan and that payment was guaranteed by a Japanese bank. While asking these companies to provide credits for the Japanese orders, Kuhn, Loeb would discount the guaranteed notes offered in payment by Japan.[10]

By the end of 1938, Ayukawa was very interested in pursuing this option.[11] Kleiman continued his discussions with Kuhn, Loeb because the proposal was tied to the issue of the Jewish refugee question. Kleiman reported on a preliminary meeting with Kuhn, Loeb in a letter to Ayukawa on February 7, 1939. He stated that although there was "a keen sympathetic interest on Kuhn, Loeb & Company's part," "the actual arrangement of the credit" had "many barriers to overcome and of course many hurdles to jump."[12] In April, Kleiman wrote to Ayukawa of meetings with Strauss and other Jewish leaders. Kleiman "was quite surprised to have . . . Strauss . . . ask me as to the intention of the Japanese Government with regard to Jews" and "whether or not Japan would follow Germany in her stand towards Jews." In reply, Kleiman referred to a report in the *New York Times* on a February 27 speech by Foreign Minister Arita to the upper house in which he declared Japan's policy of non-discrimination against the Jews and their equal treatment with other foreigners. Kleiman informed Ayukawa that he was still talking with Jewish leaders and therefore had yet to form an opinion on the feasibility of gaining support among American Jews for the economic development of Manchukuo in exchange for support by Japan and Manchukuo for Jewish refugees from Europe.

Unfortunately for MIDC, nothing substantial came of its secret negotiations with Kuhn, Loeb. There are no documents on these talks in the Ayukawa papers after Kleiman's April letter, except for a statement in a July 20, 1939, progress report on foreign capital that MIDC was still pursuing talks with Kuhn, Loeb through Kleiman. MIDC's relations with him seemed to have ended with the outbreak of World War II in September 1939. The fact that Strauss had gradually become suspicious of Kleiman's credibility certainly did not help this situation.[13]

Dealings with Franz Moedlhammer

Ayukawa's dealings with Kleiman were paralleled by those with an Austrian named Franz Moedlhammer (1895–?), a man involved mainly in heavy and munitions industries who claimed to have strong business connections in the United States and Germany. Ayukawa hired the Austrian in May 1938 to carry out secret business negotiations in Mexico, the United States, and Germany. In retrospect, the Moedlhammer mission proved more promising than the Kleiman project. Although Ayukawa's hiring of Moedlhammer may seem to indicate that by the middle of 1938 Ayukawa was so desperate for capital that he was cultivating business deals with German concerns, the Moedlhammer project demonstrated that his priority was negotiating with American interests, including Kuhn, Loeb & Company.

Moedlhammer's life centered on the Far East. Born in 1895, he had fought in the Austrian army during World War I and was a prisoner of war in Russia from 1916 to 1921. After 1922 he went into business. From 1923 to 1931, he represented various German industries in Manchuria and North China, and from 1933 to 1934, he worked for Dutch aviation interests in North China and Manchuria. He was also interested in the foreign relations of the Far East and had written a book called *Moscow's Hands in the Far East* at the request of a German anti-Comintern group. Introductions to the book were written by the Japanese ambassador to Germany, Count Mushanokōji Kintomo (1882–1962), and by German Foreign Minister Joachim von Ribbentrop (1893–1946). This book received some attention from the Japanese military, and a Major Saigō, a General Staff officer, ordered its translation and publication.

Moedlhammer first met Ayukawa in 1936 to discuss the purchase of goods from Henschel, the only company the Austrian represented at the time. Then in 1938, as he was about to leave Germany for Japan, Moedlhammer met an acquaintance of Ayukawa, Prince Urach, in Germany. Moedlhammer informed Ayukawa that he could serve as an intermediary between MIDC and his American and German business connections, which he claimed consisted of powerful financiers and industrialists. In Germany he was using Prince Urach as a contact person and proposed a complicated financial scheme that he argued could succeed in Germany. At the time Moedlhammer contacted Ayukawa, he was conducting business for five German firms and one American concern.

After receiving positive testimonials from Moedlhammer's former employer Oskar Henschel, German ambassador to Japan Eugen Ott (1889–1976), Director of Commercial Affairs Matsushima Shikao of the Japanese Foreign Ministry, Lt. Gen. Higuchi Kiichirō (1888–1970), director of the Second Section in the General Staff office, and others about Moedlhammer's background, Ayukawa in a September 26, 1938, letter authorized Moedlhammer to act as a mediator for six months to organize a credit syndicate in Germany. Ayukawa wrote that Moedlhammer was not a legal representative of MIDC or any of its subsidiaries and that he was to avoid publicity. He also stated that Moedlhammer had to follow the arrangements prescribed by the Japan Mining Company regarding a Mexican oil deal.[14]

UNSAN GOLD MINE

Before his planned visit to Germany, Moedlhammer negotiated with American and Mexican business interests. Although he failed in negotiations to import Chrysler vehicles and Mexican oil, Moedlhammer's work led to the purchase in 1941 of the Unsan gold mine in Korea, the largest such mine in the colony, from the Oriental Consolidated Mining Company. At the time Moedlhammer contacted this American company in 1938, it wanted to sell its 600-square-mile property before the termination of the concession on March 27, 1939, partly because Japan's strong foreign exchange controls made it impossible to repatriate the profits (Oriental Consolidated had the right to extend the concession for an additional fifteen years). The company was owned by prominent individuals and their families affiliated with the Republican party and closely associated with Herbert Hoover: Ogden Mills, Jr. (1884–1937), secretary of the treasury in the Hoover administration, prominent Republican businessman J. Sloat Fassett, and newspaperman William Randolph Hearst (1863–1951).

Gold was an invaluable means of purchasing foreign goods much needed by Ayukawa's business interests and the Japanese empire. Ayukawa's Japan Mining Company produced about 30 percent of the gold in the Japanese empire during 1931–41 and owned the second largest gold mine in Korea. Japan Mining was one of Ayukawa's most profitable firms, and he used it as one of the main financial pillars for establishing and operating MIDC. Ayukawa's desire to make Japan Mining more profitable coincided with the Japanese government's drive to boost gold production because of dwindling foreign reserves. As Japan experienced a worsening trade deficit in 1936 and 1937, it began to ship gold in March 1937 as a means of preventing further depreciation of its currency and deterioration of its trade balance. After the outbreak of a full-fledged war with China in July 1937, it became imperative to increase gold output in the Japanese empire. In 1938 Japan implemented a five-year plan to increase gold output in Japan, Korea, and Taiwan. Undertaken primarily by the Japanese government and the colonial government in Korea, this plan sought to boost gold production from 50 tons in 1937 (26 tons in Japan and 24 tons in Korea) to 131 tons (56 tons in Japan and 75 tons in Korea). Korea was to play the most important role in alleviating Japan's trade account and in paying for desperately needed goods for Japan's heavy industries; Japanese leaders wanted Korea to become the Transvaal of the Far East. The main beneficiaries of government incentives such as loans and subsidies were the six major gold-mining companies in Japan—Nissan (Japan Mining), Mitsubishi, Mitsui, Sumitomo, Furukawa, and Fujita (which was headed by Ayukawa's younger brother, who had been adopted by the Fujita family)—and the five major gold-mining companies in Korea— Nissan (Japan Mining), Mitsui, Mitsubishi, Furukawa, and Noguchi.

The initial talks went well. On October 18, 1938, Moedlhammer cabled to Ayukawa that the president of the Oriental Consolidated Mining Company, Lewis Henry, was willing to negotiate with him in New York City in November. Ayukawa responded positively on October 24 expressing his wish to buy the mines at a "reasonable price" and requesting Moedlhammer to ask his New York business contacts to arrange a credit deal over several years for the purchase. Moedlhammer responded in a cable on the same day that his New York financial contacts might offer finance depending on, most notably, how much Ayukawa was willing to pay for the mines. Ayukawa later offered $6 million for the purchase if a satisfactory credit deal could be arranged. He was thinking of using the Yokohama Specie Bank in New York to conduct research on the American company, and he considered secretly sending a representative from the Japan Mining Company to meet Henry.

On November 12, 1938, Moedlhammer reported that his "finance group" planned to purchase the mines and then transfer all mining rights to MIDC. (Ayukawa later learned that one of Moedlhammer's "finance group" who served as his main contact person was a businessman named H. Otto Schundler, who was acquainted with numerous influential businessmen in

New York, including Lewis Strauss of Kuhn, Loeb.) The group wanted MIDC to make an initial payment of $2.5 million in cash to the finance group. The remainder of the sum was to be paid in three years, with an annual interest rate of 5 percent, and the Yokohama Specie Bank was to guarantee payment.

MIDC responded two days later, saying it was willing to pay $6 million. It would remit $2 million in cash upon registration of the transfer of ownership from the finance group and agreed to the finance group's conditions for the remaining $4 million. MIDC stated that the transaction was subject to government approval, but it was confident in obtaining this upon the conclusion of the contract and expected Moedlhammer to finalize his talks on Unsan by the end of the year. The Oriental Consolidated Mining Company, however, wanted more than $6 million and stated that if the total amount could be agreed on, it would accept MIDC's remaining conditions.[15]

Before MIDC could respond, one of the leading members of the American company fell gravely ill, and the talks were suspended on December 22. On January 23, 1939, MIDC informed Moedlhammer that Ayukawa was sending a representative from the Japan Mining Company to negotiate directly with the Oriental Consolidated Mining Company. As the termination date of the concession approached and no deal with Ayukawa's interest had been finalized, Oriental Consolidated exercised its right to extend the concession.[16]

AMERICAN STEEL COMPANIES AND

FINANCIAL INSTITUTIONS

In addition to pursuing the purchase of gold mines, Ayukawa sought to purchase metals, namely iron and steel products, through Moedlhammer. After consulting with the Manchukuo government and the Japan-Manchuria Trading Company (Nichi-Man shōji), on November 22, 1938, MIDC instructed Moedlhammer to purchase two tons of copper and about twenty tons of iron and steel products under a credit arrangement. Although no progress seems to have been made on the purchase of copper, on November 27 Moedlhammer informed MIDC that with the help of the "finance group" he would organize a group of three steel companies, U.S. Steel, Bethlehem Steel, and Crucible Steel, to supply the desired materials.

Among the three companies, Raoul E. Desvernine, the president of the Crucible Steel Company of America, evinced strong interest in doing business with MIDC. Similar enthusiasm was expressed by U.S. Steel and Charles M. Schwab (1862–1939), president of Bethlehem Steel. The financially troubled Schwab tried without success to help Moedlhammer and his "finance group" organize a financial syndicate that included National City Bank, Chase Manhattan Bank, Bank of Manhattan, and Manufacturers Trust to finance the export of steel for MIDC shortly before his death in 1939. Overall, about $15 million worth of iron and steel products was scheduled to be purchased; payment was to be deferred for three years and then made in installments over the following two years.[17]

While these negotiations were taking place, Moedlhammer and his "finance group" tried to organize a finance company with the help of J. & W. Seligman & Company. Moedlhammer's group initially considered using this firm to finance the purchase of iron and steel products, and then later as a general purchasing agent for MIDC. In spite of this seemingly positive development, Ayukawa increasingly began to doubt Moedlhammer's ability to handle sensitive business negotiations and sent his aide Asahara Genshichi to supervise him in December 1938 or January 1939.

Although the steel executives and bankers were interested in the business opportunity offered by MIDC because of the stagnant American economy, in the end they decided against participation because they could not obtain the approval of the State Department. Seligman informed Moedlhammer on February 8, 1939, that the banks had rejected MIDC's counterproposal; contributing to this decision was the negative response that Seligman executive Henry Breck had received during a January 27 discussion with the State Department's Maxwell M. Hamilton (1896–1957) regarding the possibility of selling goods to MIDC and financing the sale. The steel executives and bankers feared that the government might retaliate by cutting them off from the much more lucrative U.S. government defense contracts promised by the government's May 1938 decision to expand the number of warships significantly and to upgrade the army's equipment. Given this shift in the government's defense spending and the economic rewards that could ensue from it, even American businessmen interested in conducting business with Japan became more sensitive to the rising tensions between the United States and Japan and began to take their cue from the State Department. Ayukawa was well aware of this situation; during a phone conversation in February, Asahara had told him that the Seligman project, like the iron and steel proposal, probably would not receive the necessary tacit approval of the government. Asahara had reached this conclusion after talking with H. Otto Schundler and learning that this German-American and Moedlhammer had visited Washington, D.C., two or three times regarding this matter.

But given America's economic depression, both Ayukawa and Asahara believed that Moedlhammer could have concluded an agreement with Seligman for a $20 million loan financed by the National City Bank, Manufacturer's Trust, Bank of Manhattan, and Kuhn, Loeb based on the counterproposal Ayukawa had sent him. Asahara argued that Moedlhammer had blundered. For their part, both Moedlhammer and Schundler thought that Ayukawa had not moved fast enough. Ayukawa spent a week or so consulting with officials—such as leading members of the Japanese Finance Ministry, the president of the Yokohama Specie Bank, and the vice governor of the Bank of Japan—after hearing from Moedlhammer on January 13 about the proposal from Seligman and before sending a counterproposal to him on January 21. Moedlhammer and Schundler thought that this delay had contributed to the failure.

Although Ayukawa wanted to visit Washington to win America's tacit approval of trade with Japan and Manchukuo, Asahara advised against this because he was told by a man from Kuhn, Loeb that the surfacing of a prominent Japanese in the Seligman deal might cause public protest. Because Ayukawa was dissatisfied with Moedlhammer's performance, he did not renew the contract with the Austrian. MIDC no longer saw a need for Moedlhammer to arrange credit and purchasing arrangements in Germany since Manchukuo and Germany now made intergovernmental credit arrangements based on the treaty recently signed by the two states. Embittered by MIDC's unwillingness to heed and follow his advice during the previous three months, Moedlhammer and Schundler filed a lawsuit in New York in the spring of 1939; in a short time the two sides reached an out-of-court settlement.[18]

The National City Bank, U.S. Steel, and the State Department

In spite of this legal fiasco, Ayukawa's dealings with Moedlhammer and Schundler had several unintended repercussions. During the first half of 1939, despite the State Department's interference and the quagmire in

China, the ongoing depression in America permitted Ayukawa to hope for business deals with American firms. Indeed, during the first three months of 1939, U.S. Steel and the National City Bank, both participants in the group underwriting the Seligman proposal, left that group and seemed to be willing to discuss business with MIDC on their own. Ayukawa first learned about this from Asahara, who cabled him on February 1 that U.S. Steel had ordered its representative in Tokyo to start talks with MIDC and that the National City Bank was sending a vice president, Boies C. Hart, who was in charge of the bank's Far Eastern operation.

Then, Moedlhammer, in a February 10, 1939, letter to Ayukawa, stated he and his "finance group" thought that the National City Bank had left the financial syndicate organized by Seligman because the bank judged that it would profit more by negotiating on its own with business interests in Japan, possibly including MIDC. They also thought that U.S. Steel had decided to negotiate directly with Japanese interests because "the Bethlehem Steel Corp. and Crucible Steel Co. assured" them "that the deal [wa]s of highest interest for any steel industry in this country and that they need[ed] this deal." Moedlhammer and his group also knew that Bethlehem's "President Charles Schwab personally made the strongest effort to induce the bank[s] connected with group [sic] to finance this deal and still continue[d] his efforts."

Furthermore, Schundler in a letter to Moedlhammer on February 11, 1939, indicated his opinion that Seligman had probably rejected MIDC's counterproposal, which he thought was a reasonable formula, because the National City Bank had withdrawn from the group. Ayukawa was puzzled by this rejection and thought perhaps Moedlhammer and Schundler were correct in their reasoning; before the withdrawal of National City Bank, Seligman & Company had remarked that the counterproposal was reasonable and businesslike. Schundler was fairly certain that Hart was on his way to Japan to discuss business with MIDC.[19]

It is highly probable that in February the National City Bank was seriously considering doing business with MIDC. Since 1933 the bank had been supporting the recognition of Manchukuo and Japan as a suitable business partner in the Far East. It regarded China as economically unstable, a point clearly indicated in internal reports by the bank's Shanghai branch regarding Chinese financial markets. In one such report, James A. Mackay, assistant vice president in charge of the bank's Shanghai office, to Vice President Boies

Hart of the Far Eastern Division in New York, discussed the terrible financial positions of Chinese commercial banks, corruption in the Chiang family, the economic mismanagement of their banks, and T. V. Soong's (1891–1971) struggle to take over H. H. Kung's (1881–1967) position as finance minister.

In March 1939, however, the bank ran into trouble with the State Department. As Japan began implementing economic policies to establish a new local currency and new central banks in North China and in Shanghai, the department began pressuring the National City Bank and the Chase Bank. The department suggested that the two banks cooperate with British and French banks in those areas in refusing Japanese demands to support the new economic measures in the occupied areas. Although the two banks seemed to have cooperated in North China, the State Department remained suspicious of National City's activities in Shanghai. During a discussion in March with Hornbeck and other State Department officials, Guy Holman, an assistant vice president of the bank, hinted that the department should suspend its application of the Open Door principle in China and avoid opposing Japan. Given the increased tension between the bank and the State Department, when Hart saw Ayukawa in late April 1939, he could not discuss any substantive offer; the banker indicated only his bank's interest in doing business once the situation in the Far East stabilized.[20]

In June 1939, after his talk with Ayukawa, Hart wrote a letter from Shanghai to Stanley Hornbeck of the State Department. The United States, Hart opined, provided that it was prepared with a proper economic strategy, would enjoy tremendous economic benefits in the Far East even if Japan won. Hart argued that when peace arrives, "the trade possibilities to this area of the world are stupendous—it is entirely too much for Japan to handle by herself if she wins a complete victory." Hart was "confident that potentially China will offer us all and more than it has to date" because "the war has brought commerce and industry to areas of China that were practically untouched territories before." He suggested the government advance "credit facilities to our traders . . . through some form of government insurance rather than government financial help" so that American firms could "meet the low cost advantages of Great Britain, Germany and Japan." Hart thought "government financing would be slow and cumbersome and . . . would not benefit American industry and banking as quickly and as effectively as credit insurance," and he wanted "75 percent of the eventual risk . . . underwritten by the Government, the cost of such insurance being a share of the profits on the sales insured." Although the American government had to "eventually do a lot of loaning for currency stabilization," he wanted to confine "commercial long term credit . . . to projects that are in themselves self liquidating and can be most effectively and properly handled by experienced traders on the ground who can work in cooperation and partnership with Chinese bankers and industrialists to see that credit is given where it will do the most good and be most likely paid back."

Apparently amused by Hart's opinion, Hornbeck sent the letter to Secretary of State Cordell Hull on August 1, 1939, with the note: "I am sure that you will find it interesting." This letter seemed to have irritated these two senior officials and probably prompted Gordon S. Renschler, president of the National City Bank, to send representatives to Washington in mid-September for a discussion of the Far Eastern situation with Hornbeck and Ambassador to Japan Joseph C. Grew. After this meeting the National City Bank was much more in accord with State Department policy; in a letter to Hornbeck on October 20, Hart praised Ambassador Grew's denunciation of Japan's "new order" in the Far East.[21]

Like MIDC's talks with National City Bank, nothing seems to have developed between MIDC and U.S. Steel. However, this episode had another interesting twist. Around the time Moedlhammer and his "finance group" in New York were negotiating with executives from U.S. Steel, Crucible Steel, and Bethlehem Steel and bankers from the National City Bank, Kuhn, Loeb, Manufacturers Trust, Chase Bank, and the Bank of Manhattan, Thomas W. Lamont of J. P. Morgan & Co. was contemplating financing $11 million of purchases by Manchukuo from U.S. Steel through its affiliate, the Guaranty Trust Company. It is possible that Lamont and the Guaranty Trust Bank may have heard about Moedlhammer's and Schundler's activities because Morgan had directors on the boards of U.S. Steel and the National City Bank. Lamont told his plans to Hornbeck, who in turn expressed his opposition. A week later Lamont told him the project had been "sidetracked" but "might come up at a later date."

Was Lamont's and Guaranty Trust's proposal related to National City Bank's withdrawal from the Seligman group and the decision by U.S. Steel to act on its own instead of cooperating with Bethlehem Steel or Crucible Steel? Although Lamont was very critical of Japanese aggression against China, he also believed the United States and Japan should try to live peacefully. He was aware that many of his colleagues thought that the trade embargo against Japan would cause war between the two countries, and he himself did not support the embargo, at least publicly, until the autumn of 1940. Regardless of his personal feelings about the Sino-Japanese War, in early 1939 Lamont probably found it difficult, unless the State Department expressed opposition, to veto business dealings between Morgan and Japanese concerns, because of the continuing depression in the United States.[22]

Dealings with H. Otto Schundler

Another event, which occurred in September 1939, can also be traced back to Ayukawa's dealing with Schundler. Around mid-February Schundler contacted MIDC through Moedlhammer. Through his financial and industrial contacts, he had devised a credit proposal to be realized through DuPont and banks affiliated with it for the purchase of non-military-related goods and materials. Although doubtful of Shundler's proposal, Ayukawa nonetheless was willing to consider it since DuPont and the Bank of Manhattan were reportedly involved. In response, Moedlhammer and Schundler stated in a cable on March 6, 1939, that they were willing to organize and send a three-man group—one banker, one industrialist, and one public agency official—to Tokyo to discuss the proposed credit arrangements. These three men could visit as a group or come individually. Ayukawa discussed these proposals with top officials from the Finance Ministry, the Bank of Japan, and the Yokohama Specie Bank. They argued against Schundler's proposal because it assumed that Japan was on the verge of national bankruptcy and it was premised on a fundamental reorganization of trading arrangements between Manchukuo and Japan.

On March 10, Ayukawa sent a cable rejecting the financial offer but indicating his willingness to discuss the visit of three American delegates to the Japanese empire, including Manchukuo, and to sponsor a meeting, provided that they paid their own travel expenses. On March 11, Moedlhammer cabled that the three-member group consisted of a board member of the Bank of Manhattan who had close relations with the DuPont company, an independent businessman who also had close ties to that company, and a senator. Asahara Genshichi knew these people well. Moedlhammer, whom Asahara thought incompetent and whose German nationality made American businessmen suspicious, strongly encouraged Ayukawa not to reject this proposal. He believed that the talks would produce something positive, because he had verified Schundler's strong banking connections.

Schundler argued that this visit might pave the way for U.S. recognition of Manchukuo. Asahara supported Schundler's view that MIDC's search for American capital was stymied by American companies' reluctance to sign contracts with a company from a non-recognized country. On the other hand, Asahara argued that businessmen preferred to deal directly with MIDC rather than indirectly through Moedlhammer and Schundler. Asahara predicted that if the three influential Americans did visit Manchukuo, they would probably pay their own expenses to avoid giving the impression that they were obligated to Japan; he recommended that they visit Japan, Manchuria, and China.

However, after learning in a March 15 cable that Schundler intended to be part of the three-man delegation, Ayukawa decided to sever relations with him. He thought Schundler was not good enough to be part of the delegation.[23] (This also happened in part because of the lawsuit brought by Moedlhammer and Schundler against the MIDC.)

Ayukawa's dealings with Schundler had an unintended effect several months later. Among the series of efforts initiated by Japanese businessmen to invite prominent American businessmen to tour the Far East, the State Department expressed anxiety about a plan to invite three American businessmen to Japan in September, an idea similar to the one entertained six months earlier by MIDC. Because Ayukawa had conferred on the matter with both top government officials and government financial authorities and because he was a leading, influential business executive, this idea undoubtedly was a successor to Ayukawa's previous attempt.

The Japanese financial commissioner in New York offered the chairman of the Chase National Bank, Winthrop W. Aldrich (1885–1974), prior rights in China if the bank refinanced Japan's transportation systems. He suggested forming a "good will mission" to Japan consisting of "a senior vice-president of a leading bank, an important railroad man and a steel man," but the two top State Department officials on Far Eastern affairs, Maxwell Hamilton and Stanley Hornbeck, recommended to Secretary of State Hull that the Japanese proposals be rejected. On September 25, Secretary of State Hull telephoned Aldrich and discouraged him from accepting the Japanese proposals. The department did not see the usefulness of sending special envoys and "good will" missions either from the United States to Japan or from Japan to the United States, since they would create "misinterpretation and serve to arouse undesirable speculation in many quarters." Because the United States had recently announced the termination of the 1911 bilateral trade treaty, a goodwill business mission would signal to Japan that the United States was now conciliatory toward Japan and that both the Japanese and American business and financial interests would misinterpret the situation as a move toward economic cooperation.[24]

Mesta Machine

In another case, Ayukawa did have some success. MIDC managed to sign a contract in January 1940 with Mesta Machine for a joint venture to manufacture heavy machinery. Among the twelve American and European companies with whom MIDC conducted negotiations to establish a joint venture company—four American (Ford for automobiles, Harbison Walker for magnesite processors, United Engineering for heavy machinery, and Mesta for heavy machinery), six German (Daimler-Benz for automobiles, Buessing for diesel cars, Henschel for diesel cars, Reichmetal for light metal alloys, BMW for aviation engines, and Heinkel for airplanes), one Swedish (SKF for high-grade ball bearings), and one Italian (Fiat for automobiles)—Mesta was the only case in which MIDC managed to sign a contract.[25]

In April 1939, MIDC began negotiating with Mesta, whose head office was located in West Homestead, Pennsylvania. The negotiations began immediately after MIDC's talks with United Engineering came to naught; that firm chose Shibaura seisakusho as a partner for a joint venture in which United Engineering would own 49 percent of the stock and Shibaura 51 percent. Mesta had been doing "considerable business with Japan and 'Manchukuo' in steel works equipment." Mesta's relations with MIDC was so important for that company that one of its executives, a Mr. Powell, visited Joseph W. Ballantine (1888–1970), assistant chief of the Division of Far Eastern Affairs in the State Department, and told him that the U.S. government should assist American companies such as his in competition against German exports to Manchuria. He claimed that Mesta was losing to German companies as a result of the barter agreement between Germany and Manchukuo and argued that the United States should stop antagonizing Japan, recognize Manchukuo, provide it with credits for the purchase of American goods, and facilitate trade with Manchukuo. Ballantine was not convinced.

MIDC negotiated with Mesta to buy rolling mills and other heavy machinery for $1 million, and the negotiations progressed to a point that Mesta sent Powell to Manchukuo in late June 1939 to prepare for the specific conditions of the purchase and a joint venture. On January 18, 1940, Yano Yoshiaki, a director of MIDC, and L. Iverson, president of Mesta Machine, signed a "Fundamental Agreement" in New York. Under this and other legal arrangements, the Heavy Machinery Manufacturing Company was established in June 1940. Mesta was a minority shareholder of this company, possessing 10 percent of the non-assessable stocks. MIDC assured Mesta that at least two of Mesta's men would sit on the board and that the 6 percent dividend would be paid in New York in U.S. dollars each year. MIDC also looked forward to obtaining from Mesta blueprints for producing machines. In the end, although the negotiations with Mesta proceeded much better than MIDC's other talks, MIDC succeeded neither in moving the joint venture out of the planning stage nor in obtaining the designs for machinery because of worsening bilateral relations after the summer of 1940.[26]

As demonstrated by the efforts of Kleiman, Moedlhammer, and Schundler and by negotiations between MIDC and Mesta, American interest in economic cooperation with Japan and Manchukuo diminished in 1939 not only because of domestic economic recovery through exports to Europe after the outbreak of World War II and through increased government spending but also because of the interferences in, and objections to, U.S.-Japan trade by the State Department as well as the decision by Congress in July to terminate the bilateral trade treaty with Japan. The only exception was the purchase of the Unsan gold mines in 1941, but this did not involve the American extension of credits or the provision of technology to Japan.

Although the United States remained optimistic that Japan would return to Wilsonian internationalism,[27] after its decision to terminate the bilateral trade treaty, Washington discouraged the extension of credit to Japan; continued and expanded the moral embargo on exports, including airplanes, aviation equipment, material for the manufacturing of airplanes, and technical processes for the manufacturing of aviation gasoline; denied trade agreement rates under the Trade Agreement Act of 1934, which empowered the president to deny the benefits of trade agreement rates to countries whose acts or policies obstructed the expansion of American commerce; and imposed additional duties on imports.[28] Ayukawa's scheme was undermined by Japan's involvement in China as the U.S. State Department became more vocal in condemning Japanese aggression in China and violations of American rights there. For example, on October 6, 1938, Ambassador Grew protested to Prime Minister Konoe that "Japanese authorities in China and . . . Japanese actions and policies . . . deprive American trade and enterprise of equality of opportunity in China [through such measures as exchange controls, tariff revisions, monopolistic practices, preferential treatment of Japanese commercial interests, restrictions on American shipping and on travel, and censorship of mail and telegrams],"[29] and on December 30, 1938, the American government rejected the idea of a "new order" in China, arguing no country had the right to dictate terms and conditions for regions not under its sovereign jurisdiction.[30] Economic relations between the two countries continued to deteriorate.

SIX

Ayukawa's Search for De Facto U.S. Recognition of Manchukuo

In seeking private American investment in Manchukuo, Ayukawa was not at first explicit about his wish for U.S. recognition of Manchukuo. Initially, Ayukawa thought he need not push this issue because the ongoing American export boom to Manchukuo and the economic depression in the United States would induce American investment. Ayukawa did, however, believe that recognition was necessary for the settlement of the Sino-Japanese War, U.S.-Japan rapprochement, and American capital inflows into Manchukuo. Ayukawa hoped for a decision as dramatic as the U.S. recognition of the Soviet Union in 1933. This chapter discusses and analyzes Ayukawa's thinking about the recognition issues and his activities in this area in 1939 and 1940 by examining his meeting with journalist William O. Inglis, his talks with American diplomats Eugene H. Dooman (1890–1969) and Joseph C. Grew, his visit to Germany, his negotiations with Dillon, Read and Company, and his relations with the John O'Ryan mission. The only time in this period when there was a limited possibility for success was during the spring and summer of 1940 as Ayukawa engaged in talks with Dillon, Read and Company and O'Ryan.

William O. Inglis

Ayukawa's thoughts on the American recognition of Manchukuo, on American economic cooperation with Japan and Manchukuo, and on U.S.-Japan rapprochement were elaborated in discussions with William O. Inglis, a well-known American journalist and a Wilsonian. In March 1939, the Federation of Economic Organizations (Japan Economic Federation), the most influential Japanese business association, invited Inglis to visit Japan and Manchukuo as part of its attempt to reduce the political and economic tensions that had been growing between Japan and the United States since the Manchuria Incident.

Inglis, a native of New York City, had built his reputation as a reporter for the *New York Herald* and the *New York World*. His achievements in journalism were notable, and he worked on the personal staff of Joseph Pulitzer (1847–1911). Later, as a member of the editorial staff of *Harper's Weekly*, he wrote articles on social, political, and economic issues, including U.S.-Japan relations in February–March 1907, the Cuban revolution, President Theodore Roosevelt (1858–1919), and the Panama Canal. Inglis also served as an aide to George B. M. Harvey (1864–1928), president of Harper & Brothers, and aided in Harvey's efforts to elect Woodrow Wilson to the presidency.

Japanese business leaders may have opted for Inglis because of his reputation as a journalist and his strong connection with the Rockefellers. In 1917 John D. Rockefeller, Jr. (1874–1960), had hired Inglis to conduct interviews with his father, the transcriptions of which became the basis for the biography of John D. Rockefeller, Sr (1839–1937). Although the younger Rockefeller canceled the project in 1919, Inglis continued in charge of biographical materials relating to Rockefeller, Sr., and in 1940 Columbia University Professor Allan Nevins (1890–1971) published a biography of Rockefeller, Sr., using Inglis's transcribed conversations as one of his two major sources.[1]

On April 15, 1939, Ayukawa met Inglis in Hsinking, the capital of Manchukuo. Ayukawa was reluctant to grant Inglis's wish that the interview be made public and, off the record, stated his views on Sino-Japanese relations, President Roosevelt, and the potential benefits to Americans of participating in the economic development of Manchukuo. "China is now preparing for a long period of resistance, and Japan is ready to cope with that resistance with firm determination," said Ayukawa. He argued that many influential Chinese statesmen wanted peace with Japan. Japan, according to Ayukawa, had wanted to avoid expansion of the war, and American and British support for Chiang Kai-shek only enhanced Japan's resolve to fight to the last man.[2]

Because Ayukawa realized the situation in the Far East and in Europe was heading for another world war, he told Inglis that Roosevelt ought first to recognize Manchukuo and then mediate the Sino-Japanese war, and, through these means, achieve stability in the Far East. Ayukawa argued that Roosevelt had "a greater opportunity today than President Wilson had when he tried to bring peace to the world, in the fall of 1914." "America, though unwilling, was drawn into the World War, and there is danger of such a calamity again." Roosevelt could prevent "an even more horrible war" by recognizing Manchukuo. Ayukawa emphasized that "President Roosevelt is the one man in the world today" who can assist in quickly bringing about "a fair and just settlement carried out by Japan." Roosevelt should be interested in Ayukawa's proposal because "when . . . Roosevelt has established peace in the Far East, his prestige and influence will be enhanced, and he can go to the rescue of the European situation with far more assurance of preventing world disaster, to say nothing of the benefit achieved by stabilizing the Orient."

From Ayukawa's perspective, his proposal made economic sense because many Americans thought the New Deal relief projects were economically wasteful and demoralizing. Peace in the Far East would open an "outlet in Manchoukuo for American products," and "American industries can work up to their full capacity, with no unemployment, and Americans will be investing capital in a country where Japan's industrialists like [Ayukawa] are taking charge of operations." Ayukawa summed up by saying: "Peace can be established in the Far East by Japan alone, and Manchoukuo can be developed by Japan alone, but it would take time; . . . if . . . Roosevelt exerts his influence, peace and development can be expedited for the benefit not only of our two nations but of all the world." Because Ayukawa thought Roosevelt would not run for a third term in 1940 and his successor would not be as strong a leader, he wanted Roosevelt to act as soon as possible.

On economic issues, Ayukawa called for American investment in Japan and Manchukuo. He noted that the Japanese had "never defaulted on their obligations to pay foreign debts and that Japan [wa]s already one of the best customers of the United States." Ayukawa regretted the U.S. government's lack of cooperation in his investment schemes in Manchukuo and stated that "certain American industrial leaders . . . seem to be willing to extend credit to our people." On the other hand, he was aware that "the political element stands in the way—not by interposing any formal objection, but by implication." Ayukawa knew that some Americans argued that participation in the industrial development of Manchoukuo might lead to Japanese use of American productive power for "wanton purposes." But, Ayukawa stated, Japan had "never gone to war for the sake of fighting or for greed. We have been forced into wars, and we might be forced to war again to protect ourselves from Communistic aggression." Ayukawa emphasized the fact that "the five-year plan is [intended] to give a better life to Manchurian people, oppressed as they have been for centuries, and only in case of need to protect ourselves from Communist attack." (Ayukawa's mention of Communist attacks may refer to the border clashes with the Soviet Union in the 1930s, which ended in significant Japanese losses in the 1938 and 1939.)

Inglis was eager to publish an account of the interview in American papers. In an April 18, 1939, cable to Inglis in Peking, Ayukawa stated that circumstances were developing in a manner "very unfavorable to publication of the interview," and he regretted that he had to "cancel [his] consent to [Inglis's] request." Although Ayukawa was willing to discuss the matter when Inglis returned to Tokyo, in a May 1 cable to Inglis in Peking, Ayukawa informed him that it was "impossible . . . to consent to publication," and he again emphasized that he would "explain [the] circumstances upon meeting" Inglis in Tokyo. The two, however, could not meet when Inglis returned to Tokyo; in a June 20 cable, Ayukawa expressed his regret. Ayukawa's retrospective account implies that he would have told Inglis that he judged American public sentiment unfavorable to his proposals and hence felt reluctant to let Inglis publish an article before he met high-ranking U.S. government officials, including, if possible, President Roosevelt himself.[3]

Joseph Grew and Eugene Dooman

In the summer of 1939, however, it was difficult for Ayukawa to visit the United States with such an agenda because the Hiranuma cabinet (January–August 1939) was intensively debating whether to side with the Axis or with the Anglo-American camp. In July, a member of a right-wing organization that perceived Yuasa Kurahei (1874–1940), Lord Keeper of the Privy Seal and a man trusted by the emperor, as pro-Anglo-American attempted to assassinate him, and in early August it was rumored that the Army might topple the Hiranuma cabinet and impose martial law.[4]

After the signing of the non-aggression pact between Germany and the Soviet Union on August 23, 1939, and the downfall of the Hiranuma cabinet shortly thereafter, Japan began to reorient itself toward the Anglo-American camp, and Ayukawa tried to contribute to this shift. On November 27, U.S. Ambassador Joseph C. Grew sent a telegram to the secretary of state informing him of a four-hour meeting between Ayukawa and a member of his staff, Eugene H. Dooman. Dooman made disparaging remarks about Ayukawa's scheme for joint economic cooperation in China and Manchukuo since the United States was interested not only in the economic and cultural well-being of the Chinese but also in the establishment of a stable government capable of resisting foreign encroachment. Although Dooman was critical of Ayukawa's scheme as benefiting mostly, if not solely, Japanese economic interests and argued that Ayukawa's ideas had little or no chance of consideration, Ayukawa replied that "he might decide to visit the United States if such visit were not likely to be productive of harm."[5]

Ayukawa's idea was not well received by either the American or the Japanese government. In the State Department, Stanley Hornbeck kept a wary eye on Ayukawa's overtures. He knew of the existence of "various interests in New York and in some other of our financial (and industrial) [interests] favorably disposed toward the efforts which Mr. X [Ayukawa] presumably will make to obtain credits and to put over some 'big deals' for sale of American materials, especially in the heavy industry line, ostensibly for use in 'Manchukuo.'"[6] Hornbeck was not the only person to express concern about Ayukawa's efforts. In Japan, Ayukawa's friend, Ōhashi Chūichi (1893–1975), a high-ranking official in the Foreign Ministry, warned Ayukawa's secretary Tomoda Juichirō: "It seems Mr. Ayukawa is expending efforts to introduce American capital [into Manchukuo], but if he is not cautious he might encounter trouble with the German-Italian faction [in Japan]."[7]

After his meeting with Dooman, Ayukawa made two suggestions to Grew through a "trusted mutual American friend," probably Robert Moss. First, although "some people" in Japan were working to establish a Japanese-German-Soviet Axis, Ayukawa believed mutual friendship and confidence between Japan and Great Britain and between Japan and the United States could most practically be brought about through economic and financial cooperation. Second, Ayukawa believed that the Japanese Army was looking for ways to withdraw from China with a minimal loss of face. He thought that this could be achieved through economic cooperation with the United States in China. The Open Door policy could be firmly established by assuring the principle of equality and American financial support for the development of China. In response to these two points, Grew informed Ayukawa through their "mutual friend" that a "condition which would permit consideration of [Ayukawa's] view does not now exist; that [I] could not predict when such a condition would come about; and that [I] could not encourage any optimistic expectation with regard to character of my reply if and when made."[8]

Ayukawa's Trip to Europe and Plans to Visit the United States

Given the uncertain relations between the United States and Japan and Manchukuo's need for Western capital, equipment, and technology, it should come as no surprise that Ayukawa evinced interest in pursuing business with Germany. Although World War II had stalled German-Japanese and German-Manchukuo trade, Wagner, the German minister to Manchukuo, approached Ayukawa in late 1939 and proposed bartering Manchurian soybeans for German goods to be shipped over the Trans-Siberian Railway. Confident that the railway could haul a considerable amount of goods between Germany and Manchukuo, the German minister told Ayukawa that the German production capacity was high enough to spare some of the goods Japan desperately needed to boost its war production, and he invited Ayukawa to visit Germany. Ayukawa asked for an opinion from his aide Yamamoto Sōji, who was touring Italy and Germany as chairman of the Manchuria Automobile Company. Yamamoto agreed a trip to Germany might be worthwhile.[9]

Despite Ayukawa's interest in strengthening ties with Germany and Italy, his real motive for making a trip to Europe was to use it as a jumping-off point to visit the United States. He would visit Germany, conclude an agreement with the government to barter Manchurian soybeans for German machinery, and then try to visit the United States via Sweden. Ayukawa approached Manchukuo Secretary General Hoshino Naoki and told him confidentially of his plans to visit the United States. Hoshino did not oppose Ayukawa's schemes and granted him an allotment of 10,000 metric tons of soybeans. On December 22, 1939, Ayukawa and two aides, Kishimoto Kantarō and Miho Mikitarō, left Tokyo for Germany via Manchukuo and the Siberian Railway.[10] Both the Japanese Foreign Ministry and the Soviet government were unusually prompt in issuing visas for this trip. The Ayukawa mission left for Europe on the same train as the group led by Minister to Sweden, Norway, and Denmark Matsushima Shikao, who was on his way to assist Ambassador to the Soviet Union Tōgō Shigenori (1882–1950) in negotiating the Japanese-Soviet commerce treaty in Moscow.[11] In Moscow Ayukawa made arrangements with Soviet Trade Minister Anastas Mikoyan (1895–1978) to ship soybeans to Germany by the Trans-Siberian Railway.[12]

Ayukawa received royal treatment everywhere he went in Germany. The Japanese representatives of the Mitsubishi and Mitsui trading companies told the Ayukawa mission they had never seen such a welcome. Indeed, the factory tours were so extensive and detailed that Ayukawa felt he was seeing things that were irrelevant and unnecessary. But just as Japan and Manchukuo needed German machinery, the Germans were in desperate need of vegetable oil and animal feeds. Their sources of vegetable oils in the South Pacific and India had been shut off with the outbreak of the war, and imports of soybeans were dwindling since shipment by sea was increasingly difficult. Ayukawa and his group speculated that they were so well treated because Manchurian soybeans were an important source not only of vegetable oil but of cattle and chicken feed. The Germans wanted to impress Ayukawa that their mighty production was large enough to spare some for exports to Manchukuo and Japan in exchange for Manchurian soybeans. The closest source of soybeans was Romania, but it produced only meager amounts compared to Manchukuo. Another reason for the German fanfare over the Ayukawa mission was that German factory owners initially omitted from the list felt compelled to invite Ayukawa because of their perception that a visit from him symbolized prestige and importance.[13]

Because Hitler could not see Ayukawa immediately to finalize the barter arrangements, Ayukawa traveled in Italy from February 16 to March 1, where he contemplated his proposed trip to America. On the morning of February 20, Ayukawa met and talked for several hours with Shirasu Jirō, who had just returned from a business trip to the United States through London, where he had conferred with Miho. Shirasu gave his views on the current American attitude toward Japan on the same day that Yamamoto Sōji and his group left for the United States. Yamamoto had been negotiating business deals in the United States prior to meeting his boss in Italy, and Ayukawa wanted him to resume those after learning about the latest situation in the United States. In addition to receiving briefings from Shirasu and Yamamoto, Ayukawa contacted Miho in London and had him come to Italy to talk about Ayukawa's planned American trip. Ayukawa also solicited opinions on the American view of Japan from his nephew Kuhara Mitsuo in New York.

Shirasu, Yamamoto, and Kuhara told Ayukawa that given the surge of anti-Japanese sentiment in the United States, nothing concrete would materialize from a visit. Furthermore, Kishimoto indicated to Ayukawa that he had modified his view that Germany would lose a war against Britain and France and now thought that Germany might succeed in achieving a stalemate in its war with the Allies. Under Hitler's effective leadership, Germany might conquer the Balkans, Scandinavia, Eastern Europe, Middle Europe, and the Low Countries, which in turn would enable the Germans to boost their war production by exploiting the economic resources of those areas and by trading with the Soviets. If such a boost in production were possible, contrary to the view that a prolonged war would be disadvantageous to Germany, Kishimoto now thought that the situation might become more favorable than had been anticipated. Kishimoto suggested that Germany might be left in the more advantageous position if the two sides exhausted themselves. Although Kishimoto did not say the Germans would win a prolonged war with Britain and France, he shared Shirasu's opinion that even if Britain and France begin receiving needed economic resources from the United States, German submarines would render this supply line unstable and hence the Allies and Germany would likely fall into a stalemate. Kishimoto thought that the Germans believed a fight against Britain inevitable because the two nations were now contesting the future of the European economic order. In Kishimoto's opinion, the Germans might have an advantage if both sides faced exhaustion.[14]

In spite of these negative remarks from his aides, Ayukawa pursued his American contacts. On February 26, Ayukawa talked for an hour with Seymour Weller, who was working in the Paris office of the American investment bank Dillon, Read and Company, a firm owned by his uncle Clarence Dillon (1882–1979), an influential business leader who enjoyed amicable relations with President Roosevelt. Ayukawa discussed, "among other things," the international financial situation in Europe. Ayukawa was introduced to Weller by a Japanese man with the code name "Hagoromo," who had arrived the night before and talked with Ayukawa for about two and a half hours, until 2:00 in the morning.[15]

But Ayukawa's decision on his American trip had to be delayed when he was informed by Japanese Ambassador to Germany Kurusu Saburō that he had managed to schedule an appointment with Hitler on March 5. Kurusu suggested that Ayukawa postpone his American voyage at least until after meeting the dictator, and Ayukawa re-entered Germany. Prior to his meeting with Hitler, Ayukawa was told by Kurusu, a man Ayukawa had known for many years, that his idea of concentrating his efforts on securing American investments was a "shrewd tactic." Kurusu, however, believed that Ayukawa would have to be patient until a favorable diplomatic shift took place.

During his previous stay in Germany, Ayukawa had talked with Kurusu on many occasions and discovered that they shared a similar outlook on international affairs. Both men were aware that the United States was conducting diplomatic talks with Germany on the European war because of news reports about the official visit to Germany by Undersecretary of State Sumner Welles (1892–1961), who saw Hitler on March 2, but they were probably unaware of unofficial talks between James D. Mooney (1884–1957), executive vice president of General Motors Corporation, who served as President Franklin Roosevelt's secret envoy, and German officials including Hitler, whom Mooney met on March 4.[16] Kurusu sympathized with Ayukawa's desire to visit the United States and negotiate directly with the top officials, including President Roosevelt, in order to promote joint economic development of Manchukuo and U.S.-Japan rapprochement. Kurusu also liked Ayukawa's international relations strategy for Japan and Manchukuo; in 1934, as director of the Foreign Ministry's Commerce and Trade Bureau, he had recommended to Director of Military Affairs Colonel Nagata Tetsuzan that Japan should seek the cooperation of America and England in developing Manchukuo. Kurusu had argued that Great Britain and the United States would support Japan's China policies if their interests gained favorable access to the Manchurian market. This idea led to the Military Affairs Department's approval of a plan for SMR to purchase British steel products. However, this plan was canceled at the last moment because of opposition from SMR, which insisted on importing Japanese-made steel from Yawata. This ended Kurusu's idea of reviving Gotō Shinpei's idea of Great Britain and the United States joining Japan in the economic development of Manchuria. While Kurusu was the ambassador to Belgium from 1937 to 1939, he cooperated closely with Yoshida Shigeru (1878–1967), the Japanese ambassador to Britain until 1938, in trying to realign Japan with England; Kurusu felt it imperative to have both Great Britain and the United States on Japan's side in the Far East.

Kurusu thought that Ayukawa's attempt to visit the United States was not timely because of the diplomatic situation, and he persuaded Ayukawa to postpone the trip. Kurusu argued that (1) the Nazi-Soviet non-aggression pact would inevitably come to a quick end; (2) Japan should preserve peace in the Pacific; and (3) Japan should maintain friendly relations with the Soviet Union. If these three conditions were established, Japan's international position would be secure. Ayukawa agreed, and as he left for Japan, he thought his pursuit of American economic cooperation in Manchukuo should be based on this diplomatic strategy.[17]

Although Ayukawa was not thrilled about postponing his U.S. trip again, he was even less enthusiastic about cooperating with German propaganda. He refused to acquiesce to the German pressure to state during a March 16 recording for a German radio interview that the Germans would win the war because of their production capacities. Since Ayukawa had not seen the capabilities of the Allies, he was unwilling to boost German morale by serving German propaganda. He conceded only that German industries were far superior to Japan's and that only the strong would win.[18]

Ayukawa was also not thrilled by Hitler's March 5 decision not to strike a barter deal. During a forty-minute meeting between Ayukawa and Hitler, the Führer rejected Ayukawa's request to barter Manchurian soybeans for German goods:

There is no need to talk about that. Instead, listen to me. First, on the issue of politics and economics, contrary to the general belief that economics leads politics, politics leads economics. Problems such as those concerning soybeans and vegetable oil can be solved by politics. The current top priority for Germany is to beef up its military equipment. We do not have surplus machines to barter for soybeans. Second, as you and I know, everything about Germany is more advanced than Japan. But there is one thing Germany does not have that Japan has . . . *kokutai*, that is, the emperor system. This cannot be created overnight. It takes at least five hundred years to develop. This is Japan's greatest treasure, which no other country can imitate. The Japanese race should guard this system forever.

Ayukawa left the Führer's office puzzled. "He rejected an offer everybody else around him wanted. And he understood the value of the emperor system. He must not be an ordinary German. He must have Oriental blood running in him." Although the Japanese and Manchurian press described the Ayukawa-Hitler meeting as an acknowledgment of the need to strengthen economic relations between Japan and Germany and between Manchukuo and Germany, the media were unaware of the underlying tensions between Ayukawa and the German government.[19]

Both Ayukawa and Kishimoto were impressed by the level of German industrial production and felt that, contrary to the common Japanese perception, German industry was not in a bottleneck. They did not have much to say about the Italian economy and were disappointed by lack of business opportunity there because of the stagnant economic situation. Kishimoto speculated that the German economy had succeeded in maintaining adequate industrial production because, although providing strong leadership and believing that politics drove economics, Hitler did not intervene in the details of the working of the economy. After visiting over fifty German factories, most of them Germany's best, Ayukawa concluded that on top of a strong foundation in heavy industry, the Germans had further strengthened their industries by successfully "Germanizing" American technology. Ayukawa observed that under Hitler's leadership the Germans were effectively coordinating the production of various industries for the war effort. Ayukawa commented that Japan and Manchukuo had a lot to learn from Germany, given the weakness of their heavy industries and their poor coordination of production. As for Italy, Ayukawa remarked that the Italian industries were much more spontaneous and applied their ingenuity freely and appropriately.

Because Ayukawa thought Germany's expanded production capabilities would allow it to continue to fight Britain and France,[20] he could not afford to antagonize Germany. MIDC was in desperate need of machinery, and Ayukawa was willing to barter with the Germans because the United States had terminated the trade treaty with Japan. Although he could not make the American voyage, Ayukawa instructed Miho to stay in the United States until a shift in Japanese-American relations took place.

At the end of his visit to Germany, Ayukawa had concluded that because of its own war effort Germany could not spare machinery and other technological goods for Japan and Manchukuo. Ayukawa also felt the Siberian

Railway was not a reliable route to ship German goods even if that was possible. Even so, while in Germany, Ayukawa visited the Soviet ambassador with Kurusu, and after the Soviet ambassador stated that his country had no intention of exporting communism to a third country, Ayukawa asked that a meeting be arranged between himself and Josif V. Stalin (1879–1953) on his way back to Japan. He wanted to pursue Kurusu's strategy of establishing amicable relations with the Soviet Union by hearing from the Soviet dictator himself that his regime had no such intention so that Ayukawa could reassure the Japanese business community, who were fearful and suspicious of communism. Although the Soviet ambassador attempted to arrange a meeting, Stalin simply sent Ayukawa a polite letter, which was seen as a rare incident in itself by the Japanese embassy in Moscow.

After returning to Manchukuo on March 31, Ayukawa told news reporters that Germany's "abnormal [heavy industrial] development" resulted from the fusion of a strong, indigenous technological basis and American technology. Hitler was in full control of a country whose industries were horizontally and vertically integrated. Ayukawa probably envied the apparent efficiency of the German corporate state and commented that Japan's and Manchukuo's heavy industries were weak compared with Germany's. In Ayukawa's opinion, the Japanese corporate state lacked both vertical and horizontal coordination.

In the same interview, Ayukawa stated that Germany would continue to fight Britain and France and not compromise with them because the Germans trusted Hitler and had rallied around him; the German economy was strong; Germany was solving its energy problem by rapidly developing and exploiting the Polish liquefied coal industry; and relations between the Soviet Union and Germany were good.

Although impressed by German technology and Hitler's leadership, Ayukawa did not want to cooperate on a large scale with the Germans. His attraction to American capital, technology, and goods remained strong. He knew that the Soviet Union had achieved success in the production of automobiles and tanks after receiving assistance from Ford in building and running the assembly plants. During a brief trip on March 9–11 to Prague where he met business executives from Skoda and toured the company's factories, Ayukawa told a young Japanese diplomat in Berlin named Kamimura Shin'ichi (1896–1983) that German industry was too advanced for Japan to master and Italian industry was a better model for Japan. However, what

Ayukawa really had in mind was to take an accelerated approach to industrialization by following the Soviet model of using foreign technology and production methods; the difference would be that in Manchukuo market forces would create a horizontally and vertically coordinated economy centered around MIDC.

Following his return, Ayukawa discovered that Hoshino, contrary to his promise, had not secured the soybean quota to back Ayukawa's negotiations with Germany. Moreover, Hoshino knew that the Siberian Railway did not have the facilities to ship German machinery. Hoshino would later reveal in his autobiography, published in 1963, that, as a leading Japanese civilian policymaker in Manchukuo, he had decided to promote the policy of increased economic control in Japan. MIDC had become an obstacle in the path of Japan's exploitation of Manchukuo's raw materials for its own war efforts at the expense of Manchukuo's industrialization. He and Kishi Nobusuke (who had returned from his post in Manchukuo to lead his old organization, the MCI, as vice minister) had not only begun funding a secret project of the Japan Economic Federation to encourage American investment in Japan and Manchukuo (see below) but also were cultivating ties with other business leaders who wanted to break Ayukawa's monopolistic hold over Manchukuo for investment and business opportunities. They had begun to see Ayukawa as ineffective because he could not deliver the needed foreign capital. Realizing that he had been tricked by Hoshino about the soybean quota, Ayukawa was glad that the Führer had rejected the offer. In his autobiography, Ayukawa wrote: "[This] was this moment that I decided to withdraw from Manchuria."[21] Despite his personal feelings, he remained chairman of MIDC until the beginning of 1943, and he continued to strive for U.S.-Japan rapprochement until Japan's attack on Pearl Harbor in December 1941.

Dillon, Read and Company and the John F. O'Ryan Mission

Japan's signing of the Axis pact in September 1940 accelerated the deterioration in its relations with the United States, a downward spiral that had been quickening since the Marco Polo Bridge Incident in July 1937. But from May to July 16, 1940, when Admiral Yonai Mitsumasa was the Japanese prime minister, opportunities for improving relations existed, and Japan had a chance to gain American acknowledgment of its hegemony in the Far East, including U.S. recognition of Manchukuo. Because of Hitler's successes in Europe, President Roosevelt was willing to explore a settlement with the Japanese in the Pacific. From May to July, he permitted an official dialogue between American and Japanese diplomats to consider rapprochement.

During that time, the Japanese business community was orchestrating a major effort to improve relations with the United States and obtain U.S. economic assistance for the industrialization of Japan and Manchukuo. Two projects were being carried out at the time, one by the Japan Economic Federation and the other by Ayukawa and his aides. These efforts reflected strong support within the Japanese business community for a rapprochement with the United States by attracting American investments to Manchukuo. Many policymakers and leading businessmen in Japan thought that Americans were interested in the Far Eastern market[22] and thus in increasing exports and investments to the Japanese empire, particularly because the American economy, even with demand stimulated by the European war, was experiencing a slow and painful recovery from the Great Depression that, in retrospect, finally occurred only in the middle of 1941.[23] Of the two efforts, that of Ayukawa's group was more promising than the project pursued by the Japan Economic Federation.

On May 7, the day following the conclusion of the unsuccessful meetings between Japanese Foreign Minister Arita Hachirō and the new high commissioner to the Philippines, former Assistant Secretary of State Francis B. Sayre, Ayukawa's aide Miho Mikitarō contacted State Department officials in Washington. In the midst of the changing European war situation, Roosevelt had secretly instructed Sayre, who was on his way to Manila to take up his new appointment, to meet Arita and discuss U.S. relations with Japan.[24] Despite the failure of the talks, Sayre "believe[d] that the way is open for further developments if the President feels the time is ripe for pushing the matter further." Both Sayre and Ambassador Joseph C. Grew agreed that the State Department was pursuing the correct policy of using the threat of an embargo to encourage Japan to seek a compromise in China and that the United States should avoid a situation in which Japan would blame America for its behavior in the Far East.[25]

In this setting, Miho was introduced to Under Secretary of State Sumner Welles, a man instrumental in ending the Sayre-Arita talks, by an American businessman. On May 8, Miho officially met with Welles,

Stanley K. Hornbeck, advisor on political relations in the State Department's Far Eastern Affairs Division, and Maxwell Hamilton, chief of the Far Eastern Division. Hornbeck and Hamilton argued that "the system which had been set up in central China and in north China . . . resulted in Japanese trade and enterprise having a preferred position as compared with American and other third-country trade enterprise." Miho replied that "everyone made mistakes and that he was not so much interested in what had happened in the past." Both Hornbeck and Hamilton agreed with Miho on the importance of improving the situation. When Hornbeck and Hamilton argued that Japanese actions in China were not serving the "best interest of Japan, China, the United States, or other countries," Miho "indicated agreement" that Japanese actions in China were "not to Japan's own best interest." Finally, Hornbeck told Miho that Japan could not obtain credit from the United States for the "so-called reconstruction work in China . . . as long as the present situation attended as it was by fighting and military activities, continued."[26]

Although it is unclear whether Ayukawa learned about Miho's talk with State Department officials immediately, the sudden change in the military situation in Europe following Dunkirk and the imminent fall of France made him ambivalent about the future world order. If the Germans won, Japan and Manchukuo would have to rely on German capital and technology for their industrialization. On May 13, Ayukawa discussed his views on this scenario with House of Peers member Prince Konoe Fumimaro; Kido Kōichi (who was to become Lord Keeper of the Privy Seal in June); and Baron Itō Bunkichi (a House of Peers member and president of Ayukawa's Japan Mining Company) at Itō's residence.[27] Itō and Ayukawa were close friends, and Itō, who frequently met and played golf with Kido, had often helped Ayukawa in politics.[28] Ayukawa had met Kido to discuss MIDC's problems on January 27, 1938, and at Ito's residence, he had exchanged opinions with Kido, including the subjects of the U.S. view of Japan (December 9, 1938), international and domestic politics (December 25, 1938), and ways to settle the Sino-Japanese War (October 30, 1939).[29] In his meeting with Konoe and Kido, Ayukawa stated that Germany was probably going to win, and Japan should wait for an opportunity after the German victory to seek capital and technology from Germany. He thought Japan should extend its current economic plan for two more years to allow time for the delivery of German capital and technology. He also thought Germany would assist in

Manchukuo's industrialization after the war. Finally, friendly relations should be maintained with the Soviet Union so that it or China would buy Japan's surplus goods from Japan. Kido thought Ayukawa's opinions were worth considering.[30]

Meanwhile, leaders of the Japan Economic Federation hoped to improve relations by introducing American capital into Manchukuo and Japanese-occupied areas in China. They felt that this would not only relieve the capital-deficiency problem in those areas but also emphasize the common, rather than the conflicting, interests of both parties. In order to pursue this issue, the federation established the Foreign Relations Council and, under it, the Foreign Relations Bureau, as the administrative arm of the council, in April 1939. Because such an action might provoke nationalistic groups within the military and elsewhere in Japan, the Federation kept the project a secret. Kishi Nobusuke and Hoshino Naoki, the two leading civilian officials in the Manchukuo government, secretly approved ¥100,000 per year in funding for the federation's efforts.[31]

The council members quickly concluded that they should focus on attracting American investment to two or three mines in Manchukuo and to industrial development in North China. The council would invite an influential American business leader to the Japanese empire and show him the attractive business sights. Later, Sawada Setsuzō (1884–1976), the council's vice chairman, was to visit the United States and secretly negotiate American loans for these projects.

In response to the council's request, the Japanese financial commissioner in New York, Nishiyama Tsutomu (1885–1960), began to approach influential American business leaders in New York City. He used Ayukawa's acquaintance Maxwell Kleiman as an intermediary; at the time Kleiman was handling legal disputes for a Japanese trading company.[32] Nishiyama's search led him to Major General John F. O'Ryan, a lawyer and a World War I hero who had strong ties to the New York business world but was nevertheless generally unknown to the American public. As O'Ryan prepared for his visit to Japan, some American firms agreed to support his mission financially. Among them was the well-known New York investment bank Eastman Dillon and Company (unrelated to Dillon, Read and Company), which decided to send its representative, Simon N. Whitney of Lionel D. Eddie and Company, after Nishiyama's talks with Eastman Dillon had failed to conclude a loan to Japanese interests.[33]

As Hornbeck had commented to Miho, the State Department disapproved the provision of American credit to Japan. An argument by the American consul in Shanghai undoubtedly typified the department's view of the O'Ryan mission:

> It would seem quite safe to assume that the O'Ryan mission is an introductory feature in what may be regarded as a resumption or perhaps re-intensification of effort to achieve this long-cherished dream of securing American financial backing for exploitation of Manchuria and China by Japan, and to assume also that further "junkets" . . . as contributory to a "buildup" for Japan in this direction may be expected.[34]

Unwilling to support the O'Ryan mission, the State Department characterized it as a private event, a negative view that was further strengthened when O'Ryan met with President Roosevelt before his departure. In fact, the Japanese invited O'Ryan primarily because he was an old acquaintance of the president and political associate of Roosevelt's dating from the president's days as a New York state legislator. O'Ryan met with the president on June 3, and Roosevelt reacted positively to his planned visit to Japan. Hitler's European victories prompted the president and Secretary of State Hull to consider a rapprochement with Japan.[35] The Japanese were apparently unaware that O'Ryan had met with the president shortly before his departure, although the meeting was reported by *Time* magazine on July 29.

In meeting Roosevelt and gaining his unofficial approval, O'Ryan had hoped to receive a presidential letter of introduction to Ambassador Grew in Tokyo, but the State Department intervened. Maxwell Hamilton argued to the president that "under the circumstances, I suggest that I write Mr. Grew directly and inform him of General O'Ryan's forthcoming visit to Japan and of the circumstances relating thereto."[36] The State Department kept a close eye on the O'Ryan mission. It knew, for example, that the foreign minister of the puppet "National Government" in Nanking led by Wang Ching-wei (1885–1944) had welcomed the O'Ryan mission as a possible starting point for a U.S.-Japan rapprochement and eventually the settlement of what the Wang regime viewed as the war between the Chiang Kai-shek regime and Japan. The State Department informed Grew that O'Ryan had visited the president and that O'Ryan was a registered foreign agent; the department told Grew it "does not . . . desire that [he] give any official recognition to the mission" but he should do what was "appropriate and convenient toward making General O'Ryan's visit in Japan pleasant and instructive." The department also told the U.S. consulate in Shanghai and the embassies in Peking and Chungking on June 15 that O'Ryan was a registered foreign agent.[37]

In contrast to the State Department's view, journalist Walter Lippmann (1889–1974) wrote a letter of support for O'Ryan, as he was about to leave for Japan. Based on a request from a Mr. McKenna of Eastman Dillon, who had helped organize the O'Ryan mission, Lippmann enclosed "a few articles which I have written on the subject of Japan during the past year" so that O'Ryan could inform the Japanese "there is a school of American opinion which has sought to avoid irreconcilable conflict." Lippmann argued in his letter that "a conflict" between the two nations "must be avoided at all cost" because American interests in the Far East were secondary to its interests in the Western Hemisphere and the Atlantic. O'Ryan had been advocating an American declaration of war on Germany and collecting money to help the Finns buy arms to fight the Soviet Union. Lippmann believed that Germany, after emerging victorious in Europe, would threaten the political and economic independence of the Western Hemisphere, whereas Japan could not. He thought that cooperation with Japan would enable the United States to transfer the Pacific fleet to the Atlantic. Enthusiastic about O'Ryan's trip, Lippmann stated: "If there is anything that can be done through the newspapers here which would help matters, I should be only too glad to do what I can if you will call upon me."[38]

Miho, who at the time was in New York City, learned of the O'Ryan mission only slightly before its departure. He immediately wrote to Ayukawa that O'Ryan was "now a forgotten man." Although Miho thought O'Ryan's status as a general made him credible, he was "worried about the fact that Kleiman may later cause problems," an opinion shared by Nishiyama. Miho informed Ayukawa of the "top-secret" information that "the diplomats Mr. Inoue and Consul General Wakasugi [Kaname; 1883–1943] oppose this ongoing project." Miho had learned of the project's existence from an American acquaintance and thought that Ayukawa was involved in the creation of this mission. He worried that it could potentially conflict with the existing diplomatic channels. In addition, Miho informed Ayukawa about his meetings with officials in Washington in May and touched on the current political climate in the United States as it affected relations with Japan, his meeting with Herbert Hoover, and the general mood of the American public.

At this point the current President is expected to be the next President. The atmosphere in Washington these days has changed quite a bit, and I no longer see much of the news about Japan and China in big letters. Mr. Lippmann's column in the *New York Herald Tribune* on the sixth [of June] seems to have stated for the most part what we want to say. His views are closely read by intellectuals and are respected.

As for the problems concerning the Dutch East Indies, there are many people, including those in the government, who are thinking about protecting it against Japan. When I saw Mr. [Herbert] Hoover the other day [May 31], he was particularly worried on this point. I talked to Mr. Sumner Welles . . . without being too formal. The Under Secretary of Treasury told me that after the election, [U.S.-Japan relations] may improve. Depending on how the diplomatic relations between the two countries is handled and depending on how the wind blows, the President may respond favorably. . . . I have talked to Ambassador Horinouchi [Kensuke; 1886–1979], who had greeted me in Washington D.C.

Miho was headed for Detroit to discuss a business deal with Ford Motors. Because Ayukawa probably wanted to keep the facts that the federation was seeking American credits and was attempting to distance Japan from the Axis powers as secret as possible, even from Miho, he provided Miho with only a partial picture of the O'Ryan mission. Thus, Miho was unaware of the indirect involvement of the Japanese and Manchukuo governments in the mission.[39]

At the same time, although Ayukawa was cooperating with the federation, he seemed to have been displeased about the O'Ryan mission, perhaps because he had not been instrumental in realizing this project. In a June 6 telegram to Miho, Ayukawa said that he had handed over to the Army the cables exchanged with Miho about the O'Ryan mission and was going to warn them about the mission. Ayukawa promised to contact Miho if further developments took place. Ayukawa probably would have reacted positively to the O'Ryan mission had he known that O'Ryan had conferred with President Roosevelt about his trip.

In a June 21 cable to Ayukawa, Miho opined that "U.S.-Japan relations have entered . . . a very important phase" and informed Ayukawa that "according to my sources in the American business and political community who are close to the President, they believe the best policy the president could adopt right now is to send a personal envoy to Japan."[40] Although the Japanese and most Americans were unaware of it, O'Ryan's meeting with Roosevelt opened the possibility his mission might serve that function.

Ayukawa, however, sensed a diplomatic opportunity. At about the same time that Ayukawa received this telegram from Miho, he changed his mind and supported the federation's push for the O'Ryan mission. He informed

Miho that his goals for U.S.-Japan relations were finally on the verge of realization. Ayukawa felt that the Japanese, instead of taking the first initiative, should this time respond to Roosevelt's overture.[41]

The State Department, despite its misgivings about the O'Ryan mission, resumed official talks with the Japanese government because of the European situation. The Allies had lost the battle of Dunkirk, and France seemed about to endure the same fate as Holland and Belgium as the German war machine plowed through western Europe. On June 10, Ambassador Grew resumed discussions with Japanese Foreign Minister Arita on a Pacific non-aggression pact, an issue discussed during Sayre's visit. In order to minimize the disruptive effects of the European war in the Pacific, the department proposed that the two countries agree that changes in the status of the European colonies in the Pacific would be effected only through peaceful means. The department also demanded that Japan agree to an international trade order based on equal economic opportunities as a prerequisite for reviving the abrogated bilateral trade treaty. Arita responded with the Japanese demands: mutual recognition of established spheres of influence in the Pacific; U.S. cessation of material and economic assistance to Chiang Kai-shek's regime and cooperation with Japan in reordering China; and, above all, a trade treaty between the two countries. Arita told Grew on June 28 that although his government was committed to a policy of non-involvement in the European war, it nonetheless wanted to avoid making a commitment to the American proposal for a modus vivendi. Arita also said that the Japanese government was willing to discuss American protests against Japan's closed economic policy in its empire and the exclusion of U.S. economic interests in China. But before reaching an agreement on these issues, Arita demanded the United States sign a new trade treaty.

On July 6, the Grew-Arita talks received a boost when President Roosevelt endorsed the idea of extending the Monroe Doctrine from the Western Hemisphere to Europe and Asia. Perhaps he was responding to Arita's radio broadcast of June 29, in which Arita had called for an American sphere of influence in the Western Hemisphere, a Japanese sphere of influence in Asia, and non-intervention among the United States, Germany, and Japan. Roosevelt's announcement implied a possible recognition of Germany and Japan as the leaders of their respective blocs. However, when this remark drew fire from the press and China, the president retracted his statement.[42]

After O'Ryan's arrival in Tokyo on June 26, Grew met him several times and told him cordially and frankly the American government's views regarding some of the political and economic questions with which his mission was concerned. Grew observed that "O'Ryan has been careful in his views and speeches, and taking his illustration from preventive medicine, placed the emphasis of his words upon the desirability of attacking the problem of war also by advance preventive methods."[43] In meeting Japanese business leaders, O'Ryan was assisted by Sawada, who in turn was helped by Kleiman, whom O'Ryan distrusted and kept out of his American group.[44]

On July 13, O'Ryan wrote President Roosevelt from Nara, arguing that Japan was much more important for American interests in the Far East than was China and that Japan and the United States should cooperate to maintain peace in the Pacific. O'Ryan argued that "unless for momentous and paramount reasons to the contrary and which to me are unknown, the United States and Japan, separately facing the unprecedented world conditions of the hour, have become logical allies in the interest of their own national security." He believed that "our interests in China and the benevolent aims we have proclaimed in aid of the Chinese people are clearly secondary to this paramount obligation of safeguarding the national security" and "similar comment applies to the Japanese in their consideration of the state of their Empire." O'Ryan emphasized that "the educated, traveled, experienced and able banking and business men of Japan and their loyal supporters constitute a class who discern in any war, major elements of waste, irrelevant and vainglorious distractions, economically demoralizing taxation and political dangers which disturb the steadiness of sound economic progress." O'Ryan characterized the Japanese business leaders as "friendly to the American viewpoint of world relations." In contrast, army officers were "somewhat out of hand" and "unhampered by the hard logic of experience, fiercely confident of their actions, virtues and its military power, [and] stimulated by those leaders in the field (probably of similar background)."[45]

As the O'Ryan mission toured the Japanese empire and talks continued between Grew and Arita, an even more promising event was unfolding. On July 1, Grew dispatched a telegram to the secretary of state, informing him that a "completely trustworthy American citizen [Robert Moss, Republic Steel's representative in Japan and a president of a local company in Tokyo] . . . recently had an interview with 'Mr. X' [Ayukawa] in Hsinking, Manchuria" and reported Ayukawa's comments and offers. Ayukawa felt glad his previous attempts to go to the United States had failed because he had been able to get the latest insights about Germany during his European tour by meeting with Hitler, Göring, and the other principal Nazis. He expressed his wish to visit the United States immediately if he could receive American government assurance that he could meet with President Roosevelt both to discuss rapprochement and to provide the president with "valuable firsthand information regarding conditions in Germany."

Ayukawa was confident that "much good" would come from their discussion. At Hitler's instructions, he had been "shown everything," including the principal industrial plants and the most important munitions factories, where he had seen the secret manufacture of "two-ton bombs." Hitler wanted an alliance with Japan and had wanted to use Ayukawa to influence Japanese business leaders who opposed the alliance. Ayukawa argued that England would probably soon lose the war. He argued that this end would be followed by a German-American war because the Americans would refuse the German demand to transfer the U.S. assets of conquered European areas. Meanwhile, Japan would fight Germany, since it would refuse the German attempt to secure the Dutch East Indies and French Indochina. These comments hinted that both countries faced grave security threats, but it was still possible to establish mutual security in the Far East. Ayukawa suggested that peace in the Far East could be maintained by broad U.S.-Japan economic cooperation such as the provision of an American credit worth a few million dollars.[46]

Ayukawa's lobbying effort was enhanced by Miho's telegrams from New York City. On June 27, Ayukawa received two cables from Miho. The first cable stated that Minister to China Katō Sotomatsu (1890–1942) was leaving for Japan on July 2 and arriving in Tokyo on July 15. Miho told Ayukawa to meet the minister as soon as he arrived in Japan and requested that the outcome of that discussion be cabled to him immediately so that he could inform his American contacts. Although both Miho and Ayukawa were disappointed that Miho's negotiations with Ford had failed, Ayukawa must have agreed with Miho that Japan was now "at a diplomatic crossroad." Miho believed now was the time for Japan both to secure its position in Asia and to reach a diplomatic settlement with the United States, a settlement that in his mind should resolve the following issues concerning Japan's interests in Asia: (1) the independence of north China; (2) the opening of central and south China; (3) French Indo-China; (4) realistic ways to obtain oil and other raw materials from the Dutch East Indies; and (5) a U.S.-Japan commercial treaty.

Miho thought that the United States, to contain Hitler's expansion in Europe, had to support Britain, and therefore Japan should take advantage of the situation by demanding American economic cooperation in Japan's reconstruction of the Far Eastern order. Miho considered it essential that the war minister agree to a policy that called for both U.S.-Japan economic cooperation and the prosperity of the Far East and the Western Hemisphere. Such cooperation would also permit Japan to take a strong stand against the Soviet Union, which Miho described as "an obstacle in the future." Miho suggested to Ayukawa that if an agreement with the United States were reached, it should be kept secret until after the November presidential elections. But, he added, this scheme also depended on whether the Japanese military was preparing a new campaign in Asia and how long Britain could withstand Germany.

After receiving these messages from Miho, Ayukawa moved quickly. On June 29, he sent a request to Kwantung Army Commander Umezu Yoshijirō. Arguing that the present European situation was encouraging the United States to adopt a conciliatory stance against Japan, Ayukawa said that now was the time to make demands about Manchukuo. When the United States and Japan began negotiations, he wanted the Kwantung Army to back his request that the agenda include a discussion of economic cooperation between the two countries in Manchukuo. Ayukawa wanted the United States to recognize Manchukuo and to underwrite $1 billion worth of Manchukuo government bonds so that Manchukuo could finance the purchase of American machinery and technology for its industrialization and war efforts.[47]

As Ayukawa talked to Grew through Moss, he received additional coded telegrams from Miho who, in a July 1 cable, emphasized again the need to secure the Army's backing because "the people I have contacted in the American government in Washington and the banking community do not feel satisfied with remarks by the Foreign Ministry" unless the Army had indicated its support. Miho stated that we "need to strive to create a situation in which the president or his confidants can have an opportunity to make a gesture to us," and Ayukawa "should be sent as an envoy from the Japanese military to one of the President's Brain Trusts." Miho thought that after this meeting "it will not be difficult to meet the president." Although

Miho thought that his scheme could not bypass the State Department (that is, Hull and Welles), "if the limits of the demands under Asian Monroeism c[ould] be stated [to the United States], particularly if the opinions about this in the military c[ould] be brought to a conclusion," he believed the two countries could achieve a diplomatic settlement.[48]

In sum, Miho was asking his boss to persuade the military to reach a consensus on both the content of an Asian Monroe Doctrine and a general outline of demands toward the United States and Britain. He also wanted Ayukawa to act as an envoy on behalf of the Japanese military, whom American policymakers and the business community correctly identified as the most powerful group in Japan. As soon as Japan decided to side with the United States, Miho thought, Washington would send a secret envoy to Japan.

While Ayukawa lobbied in Japan for a rapprochement with the United States, on July 3 Miho cabled the results of his meeting with Clarence Dillon, head of Dillon, Read and Company and one of Wall Street's most influential investment bankers. Miho reported that in Dillon's opinion "the China issue, as far as the U.S., Britain, and Vichy France [we]re concerned, could be permanently resolved with Japan if Japan decide[d] to take the same position as the U.S. on the European war." In that case, Dillon could persuade the American government to support massive investment in Japan, Manchuria, and China and also arrange satisfactory business deals for Japan in Hong Kong, French Indochina, and the Dutch East Indies. Dillon argued that Britain's dependence on America for its war efforts permitted the United States to dictate London's policy toward China. He assured Miho "that he will personally carry out these propositions because he felt the ordinary channels between the U.S. State Department and the Japanese Foreign Ministry were useless."

Based on his discussions with Dillon, Miho recommended that Ayukawa not get deeply involved with O'Ryan, because the mission was ineffective compared to the Dillon connection. Miho also stated that he had not told anyone, including Nishiyama and Ambassador Horinouchi Kensuke, of this ongoing discussion with Dillon. Miho was optimistic that Ayukawa's meeting with Roosevelt could soon be arranged through Dillon. He urged Ayukawa to strive for an alliance with the United States because Miho felt Japan was at a crossroads. Playing the American card would be the most effective means of solving the China issue and would contribute to the economic development of China in the future and hence more business opportunities. He also believed that if Japan decided to side with the United States right now, America could become more friendly toward Japan. Miho told Ayukawa not to divulge the information about Dillon, who was helping Miho contact James V. Forrestal, the former president of Dillon, Read and Company, who had recently joined the White House as an aide to Roosevelt. Miho stressed to Ayukawa that Dillon was the right man because his company was just as powerful as the House of Morgan. Furthermore, unlike J. P. Morgan and Company, which he thought was pro-British and anti-Japanese, Miho argued that Dillon was sympathetic to Japan and that his firm would serve Japan's interest because it would maintain political influence regardless of the outcome of the fall presidential election because of its friendly ties with both Roosevelt and the Republican candidate for president, Wendell Willkie (1892–1944).[49]

While Miho was making his arrangements, the State Department evinced some—lukewarm—interest in Ayukawa's effort. On July 3, Secretary of State Hull sent a telegram to Ambassador Grew, informing him that Ayukawa's views had been studied with interest and Washington appreciated his persistent attempts to discuss problems in the Far East directly with American government officials. Although the department's attitude toward economic cooperation with Japan, Japanese-controlled areas of China, and Manchukuo remained negative, Hull stated that he concurred with Ayukawa's call for U.S.-Japan cooperation, an idea Hull wanted Ayukawa to pursue by organizing an influential support group in Japanese ruling circles. Hull informed Grew that if Ayukawa wished to visit the United States, it would have to be "upon his own initiative and responsibility and not upon the initiative and responsibility of the [State] Department or of . . . [the American] Embassy [in Tokyo] or . . . any person or group connected with either." And if he did visit, "appropriate officers of [the U.S.] Government [would] be glad to talk with him on the subjects indicated." As for meeting with the president, Hull stated that although no prior commitment could be made, an appointment was possible provided that the Japanese ambassador requested such an appointment after Ayukawa arrived and provided that Roosevelt was available.[50]

On July 8, 1940, Grew informed Hull that Ayukawa had contacted him through Moss and was convinced that "with one bold stroke" the problems in the Far East could be settled between the United States and Japan. Ayukawa claimed he was the only Japanese industrialist who possessed such extensive contacts and unique influence that he could "bring the army into line." In Ayukawa's opinion "neither Mitsui nor Mitsubishi could accomplish this nor could the Foreign Office persuade the army to accept a reasonable settlement." Grew informed Hull that Ayukawa wanted "a very large credit to extend over a period of years to be used for the purchase from the United States of machinery for manufacturing, . . . mining, bridges, railroad rolling stock, steel and various other materials." Ayukawa emphasized not only "the important effect which such orders would exert on the economic life of the United States" but also the fact that "broad economic cooperation will pave the way for Japan's alignment with the democratic powers, the creation of [a] China which would be satisfactory to American and Japanese criteria, and lead to the settlement of all outstanding problems between the U.S. and Japan." Although Grew could not estimate Ayukawa's "apparently genuine conviction [in his unique influence over Japanese leaders]," "if it were quietly made known to military leaders that he had been encouraged to come to the United States to discuss economic and financial problems, even without any commitment, . . . a pause might . . . be given to whatever extremist plans are now under consideration." Based on discussions with Moss, Grew thought that Ayukawa would consider visiting America if he was encouraged to do so by the State Department.[51]

As Grew conveyed these ideas to Hull, Miho urged Ayukawa to keep pushing for the military to endorse his peace efforts and Washington visit, an endeavor that, in Miho's mind, might necessitate a representative from the military. Miho informed his boss that he was attempting to bypass the State Department and inform Roosevelt to deal directly with Ayukawa. Miho had been lobbying the White House, through Clarence Dillon and James V. Forrestal,[52] and perhaps through Bernard M. Baruch, who had been Dillon's boss in the War Industries Board during World War I and exerted considerable political influence on Roosevelt, to convince the president that Ayukawa was the most qualified person to represent Japan in discussions of the reactivation of the U.S.-Japan trade treaty and Japan's purchase of needed America goods, such as machinery. Miho believed his and Ayukawa's efforts were gaining momentum. Although Ayukawa was probably unaware of the contact between Miho and Baruch, the two men had agreed to continue their discussion of U.S.-Japan economic cooperation.[53]

Even though Miho could not realize his wish to bypass the State Department completely, the department decided to send Ayukawa a somewhat more favorable message. On July 10, Maxwell Hamilton of the Division of Far Eastern Affairs wrote a memorandum on the department's "wish to explore all constructive possibilities" and to prevent Japan from "aligning itself with the Axis powers." In Hamilton's opinion, Ayukawa "could prevail upon the Japanese military group to hold off committing Japan to align itself with the Axis powers pending the outcome of a visit such as he is desirous of making to the United States to put his views before officials of the American Government."[54] On the same day that Hamilton issued this memorandum, Secretary of State Hull instructed Grew to send Ayukawa a memorandum, which Ayukawa received on July 12, and which incorporated Grew's suggestions of July 8. In this message, Hull informed Ayukawa that "in the event that you should decide to undertake . . . a trip [to America,] American officials will be glad to discuss with you such problems as have been the subject of our conversations here." Hull also stated that "it would be impossible for [him] in advance of fuller information to offer an opinion on what would be the reaction [of his] Government with regard to the attitude which the American Government would adopt toward the suggestions [that Ayukawa will make]."[55]

Although Grew's note to Ayukawa was not an explicit American invitation to Ayukawa, it was a gesture that allowed Ayukawa to avoid the appearance of being the one making an overture and enabled him to approach the Japanese Foreign Ministry and Army for support. As part of this lobbying effort, Ayukawa told Kido that there now was a chance to improve U.S.-Japan relations because it seemed Roosevelt was willing to facilitate a $1 billion loan to Japan in exchange for a report from Ayukawa on what he had learned about developments in Germany during his visit there.[56]

But shortly before receiving Hull's message from Grew, Ayukawa encountered a huge political stumbling block, the imminent collapse of the Yonai cabinet. Before receiving Grew's memorandum, Ayukawa was thinking of going to Manchukuo to enlist the support of the Kwantung Army, which would in turn influence the War Ministry. In Manchukuo, Ayukawa planned to convey his ideas to his aide Kishimoto Kantarō, who was to inform Minister to China Katō Sotomatsu, who would then tell Baron Itō Bunkichi. Itō and Katō were supposed to "carefully think and survey with all information available." Ayukawa felt that due to the "delicate situation" he had to adopt this "round-about" way despite the urgency of the situation. Furthermore, he still hoped that President Roosevelt would send for him. An hour before Ayukawa's scheduled departure for Manchukuo, he received the Hull memorandum from Grew. Ayukawa canceled his trip and began getting in touch with his contacts.[57]

Meanwhile, Miho expressed confidence that the scheme he had been working on with Roosevelt's confidants (Dillon, Forrestal, and probably Baruch) had suddenly become an important issue among people close to the president. He encouraged his boss to fight harder for a favorable outcome and told Ayukawa he could tell important policymakers such as Prime Minister Yonai and Foreign Minister Arita that he had found a satisfactory communications channel to Roosevelt, a recommendation that Ayukawa followed by talking to them and Konoe. Miho also recommended that because Katō enjoyed an even better reputation in Washington than the late ambassador Saitō Hiroshi (1886–1939), who had been widely respected in Washington, Ayukawa should arrange for Katō to assist him on issues such as China and the bilateral trade treaty upon his arrival in Washington.[58]

Unfortunately, Ayukawa's private diplomacy ceased to be promising when the Army ended the Yonai cabinet on July 16 and agreed to the creation of the less moderate cabinet under Konoe Fumimaro. In retrospect, Ayukawa thought that the domestic political situation in Japan had worked against him. Threats from right-wing organizations made it hard for him to move quickly in his pursuit of U.S. recognition of Manchukuo. He thought Miho's efforts indicated that powerful American business executives would facilitate an agreement once he reached the United States and that this would lead to American investment in Manchukuo and a channel for the settlement of the Sino-Japanese War. Ayukawa believed that the American provision of a half-billion or a billion dollars to Manchukuo would lead to U.S.-Japan rapprochement, which in turn would help realize world peace centered around U.S.-Japan cooperation.[59]

If Ayukawa had possessed the capacity to influence the military to the extent he claimed, Japan's foreign policy might have taken a more moderate trajectory if he had been appointed foreign minister by Konoe, who was aware of Ayukawa's clandestine negotiations with the American government. On July 16, Baron Itō Bunkichi recommended to Konoe that he appoint Ayukawa foreign minister. Although Ayukawa had refused a cabinet position on three occasions in the past, for the first time, he wanted a post so that he could continue his negotiations with the American government. Konoe, however, informed Itō that he had already offered the post to Matsuoka Yōsuke, who had accepted it. Matsuoka had been a rival of Ayukawa since the days when they fought over the transfer of SMR's subsidiary companies to Ayukawa's MIDC. Although Ayukawa won no official position to carry out Japan's foreign policy, in late July the *Wall Street Journal*, along with some Japanese newspapers such as *Yomiuri*, incorrectly reported that he was slated to become the next ambassador to the United States.[60]

Because of the political turmoil in Japan resulting from the cabinet change, Ayukawa could not greet O'Ryan personally in Hsinking during the American's tour of Manchukuo.[61] Even though Ayukawa could not keep an eye on O'Ryan, State Department officials carefully monitored him. Press reports on O'Ryan's favorable comments regarding the economic development of Manchukuo must have made them nervous. On August 3, the State Department told United Press International that O'Ryan had registered with the department, with reservations, as a foreign agent representative of the Japan Economic Federation. The department also disclosed the information that O'Ryan had "receive[d] an advance honorarium of $15,000 which implied no obligation." As for his assessment of the economy of the Japanese empire, O'Ryan declared there was no prior obligation to have the conclusion conform to the views of the federation. Still, concerns about O'Ryan's possible bias ensured that the mission was treated unfavorably among the American public.

On August 15 O'Ryan made the following remarks during a speech over Japanese radio JOAK:

International trade tends to thrive when built upon relations that are harmonious, while that trade tends to drift toward disruption when ill will or misunderstanding [are] substituted for the harmony. . . . People who are widely separated by distance as well as the language barrier, are both largely and unconsciously influenced in their views, each of the other, by propaganda which they do not regard as such. . . . It would seem clear that Americans and Japanese should be vigilant and energetic to visit each other more frequently than has been the custom in the past, to become better acquainted, to give sympathetic attention to the problems and purposes of the other, and to develop that form of cooperation which is mutual and not expected to be one sided. . . . Perhaps the time is ripe for [Japanese and Americans] to sit down together and . . . confide to each other mistakes they have made, adjust their remaining difficulties, and together face a world which is in effect destroying its civilization through the waste and destruction of war.[62]

In retrospect, O'Ryan's call for a greater exchange of people between the two countries was not realized until the termination of the Pacific war exactly five years later. O'Ryan made this speech the day after he learned that Japan would sign the Axis Pact. According to Sawada, on hearing this bad news, O'Ryan pounded his fist on a desk and stated that his efforts were now futile. He had just finished a report that included some concrete proposals to submit to Roosevelt, but he thought it would be useless now that Japan was siding with the Axis. After the O'Ryan mission, the federation's Foreign Relations Council became defunct. When O'Ryan returned to the United States in September, he announced that the report was handed to the Japanese and the content of it was disclosed only to the federation. (O'Ryan later served as an advisor to his acquaintance Secretary of War Henry Stimson.)[63]

Japan's signing of the Axis Pact also ended Ayukawa's hope for American recognition of Manchukuo and a U.S.-Japan rapprochement. These efforts marked the last year in the prewar years when Ayukawa played an active role in private diplomacy between Japan and the United States.

SEVEN

Efforts for Peace: Ayukawa
and Hoover in 1941

Although by 1941 Ayukawa's role in U.S.-Japan relations had become peripheral, he continued his efforts to avoid war between the two nations. Although his activities were ineffective at the time, he and like-minded persons on both sides of the Pacific foreshadow the types of people who played important roles in nurturing strong bilateral relations during the immediate postwar years. In the years right before the Pacific War, the activities and thinking of people around Ayukawa—Takasaki Tatsunosuke, Kurusu Saburō, and Miho Mikitarō—intersected and paralleled in significant ways the activities and thinking of people around Herbert Hoover—Raoul E. Desvernine, William R. Castle, Jr., Lewis Strauss, and H. Foster Bain. Both Ayukawa and Hoover wanted to avoid war between the two countries.

Ayukawa, Bain, Takasaki, and Hoover

The geologist H. Foster Bain, who was hired in 1938 by Ayukawa to survey the mineral resources of Manchuria (see Chapter 3), probably made his greatest contribution to Ayukawa's efforts by putting him into indirect contact with former president Herbert Hoover. Ayukawa reminded Bain of Hoover because, like Hoover, Ayukawa had "a view to results [rather] than to building up a further fortune, much as Hoover felt" during his London

years, when he was a leading businessman in mining. Bain believed Ayukawa had "reached about the same stage of development that Hoover had
then." Ayukawa had "a high admiration for Hoover" and wanted Hoover "to
come over here and help straighten things out."[1] Furthermore, Hoover's
world trade strategy for the United States resembled that of Japan; he, too,
advocated maximum benefits from world trade through high tariffs at home
and maximum local market access (most-favored-nation treatment) overseas.[2] Hoover's view of U.S.-Japan relations centered around economic interdependence, which is precisely what Ayukawa hoped to achieve through
a U.S.-Japan rapprochement after 1937.

Bain met Hoover in New York City on May 9, 1938; by that time Hoover
had already received and read Bain's letters from Manchuria,[3] which described Ayukawa in a positive way:

Aikawa [Ayukawa] is one of the most interesting men I have ever met and one
of the ablest. He is a business man with vision and is very practical . . . though of
course achievement usually falls far short of the objective and this is a most difficult
situation.

The real objective is to bring about as nearly as that is ever possible permanent
peace in the Far East by producing the conditions under which the economic condition of the people will be bettered. [Ayukawa] has captured the imagination of the
'young officer' group who distrusted the old houses of Japan but feel the need of
business leadership.[4]

In a long conversation with Hoover, Bain explained what Ayukawa had
in mind. Bain reported to Ayukawa that he found Hoover "keenly interested in the Far Eastern situation and well informed." On the other hand,
"whether or not he would care to take any part in Far Eastern matters
would . . . depend very largely on the exact nature of the particular project
and how it came up." The good news was that "at least he did not tell me to
take steps to kill the whole possibility." Bain encouraged Ayukawa to meet
Hoover if he had a chance to visit the United States because "each of you
will meet an interesting man, and I think you will like each other."[5]

Although one may question the wisdom of approaching a leading figure
in the anti–New Deal camp to solicit American economic cooperation in
Manchukuo, it did make sense that Ayukawa wanted to communicate with
Hoover because the former president not only had lived for several years in
China at the turn of the twentieth century as director of the Kaiping coal

mines but also, in Frank Ninkovich's words, "had a deeper understanding of the relationship between business and politics in that region than any American statesman before or since."[6]

Hoover shared the Wilsonian belief in the inevitability of global economic integration and "a world society bound together by the cords of commerce and an increasingly specialized division of labor."[7] In 1927, writing for *Jitsugyō no sekai*, a popular Japanese business magazine for young men, then–Secretary of Commerce Hoover expressed his views on maintaining peace between the two countries:

It is worthy of note that in 1926 the United States held first place in both the export and import trade of Japan, a position which we hope we shall be able to occupy indefinitely.

There is no more powerful a factor in the maintenance of friendship between peoples than that of trade relations. The larger they are and the more mutually dependent they are, the more likely it is that their course will not be broken through misunderstanding or a failure to overlook shortcomings. There is every prospect that the volume of trade between the United States and Japan will develop even more rapidly in the years to come than in the years behind, and the maintenance of peace on both sides of the Pacific, in order that these relations may remain undisturbed, has come to be regarded among both peoples as their mutual responsibility. I look forward with confidence to a day when the lines of commerce and travel and communications across the Pacific will be as abundant and as busy as the lines that cross the Atlantic. [Italics added]

Like Ayukawa in his 1936 essay (see Introduction), Hoover believed in the attainment of peace between the two nations through trade. He was satisfied that Japan and the United States would not compete in the world market since their respective major trading partners did not overlap and Japan imported American goods it did not produce.

Even in those rare instances where the two countries attempt to sell similar commodities in the same market, there is enough difference in the character of the products to make them each appeal to different classes of trade.

Finally, Hoover believed that

American capital and engineering talent are being utilized to an ever increasing degree, particularly in the development of Japanese waterpower resources and in the electrical industry. . . . Japan's achievement of a stable economic condition is bound to open up to us many new opportunities for services.[8]

At the same time, like Ayukawa in his 1936 essay, "Hoover understood that the realities of interdependence cut both ways, that the compression of space and time that brought people closer together in enforced contact was not necessarily conducive to harmony, and that global modernization contained within itself the potential for economic chaos and social revolution."[9]

Yet, unlike Ayukawa, Hoover looked at the impact of global economic interdependence on Americans' sense of cultural uniqueness, and he feared "the division of labor, domestic and foreign, by virtue of its power to effect radical social change, seemed more likely to generate a crisis of cultural values" in American society. In other words, he perceived that economic interdependence would inevitably entail the clash of civilizations. "Cultural and racial differences could not be bridged by appealing to a universal conscience." The global economy was an arena in which civilizations clashed with one another for domination, and America had to shield itself from outside cultural and racial influences to preserve Americanness. Hoover sensed an "international society pulled together by growing functional interdependence" even as it was pulled apart by a "growing sense of cultural distinctiveness."[10]

Given his reluctance to countenance racial and cultural influences on American society and his pessimism about the ability of non-Europeans to Westernize, Hoover's Lamarkianism, though racially progressive for his time, led him to advocate a ban on Japanese immigration into the United States.[11] In a letter dated April 21, 1924, Hoover wrote: "There can be no question of the high esteem and appreciation of our own people for the greatness of Japan, her civilization and genuine purpose of world advancement. A building up of common purpose of advancing peace, good will, commerce, and security in the Pacific is the great service that the citizens of both countries need." On the other hand, he argued that the exclusionist 1924 immigration law was a "minor question" and on April 18, 1924, told President Calvin Coolidge that the law was needed because the people on the West Coast would continue to press for this issue by "creat[ing] one disagreeable incident after another which [will] undermine . . . good will" between the two nations. Furthermore, Hoover believed, as many other Americans, including Franklin D. Roosevelt, did at the time, that "the biological fact makes mixture of blood disadvantageous in Japan if it occurred there and to us if it occurs here, and no population can be included by emigration in another without contemplation of eventual mixture."[12]

Hoover's ambivalence did not lead him to advocate economic isolation from the rest of the world economy. To the contrary, he believed that the United States' well-being depended on the international economy; hence economic isolation from the rest of the world was not a serious option as long as the world economic system functioned. Hoover, however, did not oppose high tariffs at home, and because he saw no trade opportunities for American business within the foreseeable future in China, he rejected the Open Door policy in the Far East. In the 1920s Hoover shared the views of J. P. Morgan partner Thomas W. Lamont that the peaceful economic development of China had to be achieved through economic cooperation between Japanese and American business interests. After the Japanese invaded Manchuria in September 1931, Hoover argued against the Wilsonian notion that "local conflicts had the potential for spreading into global war."[13] Hoover supported the non-recognition of Manchukuo, but he opposed further pressures, such as the embargoes that Secretary of State Henry L. Stimson (1867–1950) privately wanted.[14]

Hoover was also contacted by Ayukawa's business colleague Takasaki Tatsunosuke, who had deeply respected and admired Hoover since they first met in the spring of 1912 through the introduction of President David Starr Jordan (1851–1931) of Stanford University. Hoover, an alumnus of the first class to graduate from Stanford and by then a millionaire mining engineer, joined Jordan in helping Takasaki in the spring of 1912 fight the accusation of the *San Francisco Examiner*, a Hearst newspaper, that Takasaki was a spy for the Japanese Navy in Mexico. To fight off the unjust Hearst reports, Takasaki, who was working for a fish-canning factory in Mexico, appealed to Jordan, whom he knew from Jordan's trip in 1911 to investigate the Japanese fishing industry.[15]

Even after his return to Japan in 1915, Takasaki remained an admirer of Hoover. In a pamphlet published some time in 1928 called "Herbert Hoover and Our Corporate Policy," Takasaki, as managing director of the Oriental Can Company, reprinted a letter he had sent to Hoover in 1927 to thank him for his contribution to the success of the Oriental Can Company since its founding a decade earlier. Through Hoover's introduction, the Oriental Can Company had benefited from the generous provision of machinery and technical assistance by American Can, and the company's excellent performance owed much to Hoover's managerial and organizational principles. For example, Takasaki had successfully applied Hoover's idea of standardizing products to the Japanese canning industry. In a reply dated October 7, 1927, Hoover acknowledged receiving a booklet entitled the "History of Can Making Industry in Japan." Another pamphlet called the "Mission of the Oriental Can Company," which was published in July 1933, began by introducing the previous pamphlet and the company's principles based on Hoover's teachings.[16]

In fall 1939, undoubtedly because of Ayukawa's request for help in finding a new basis for U.S.-Japan trade relations following the recent American decision to abrogate the 1911 bilateral trade treaty, Takasaki sent a letter to Hoover asking for advice on ways to secure the cooperation of American businesses and financial interests in the joint economic development of China and Manchukuo. Takasaki also asked Hoover to head and choose the staff for a commission that would formulate recommendations for the economic reconstruction of China and Manchukuo, provided that the "governments and interests concerned" approved the formation of such a committee. Takasaki pointed out that the Sino-Japanese War had disrupted peaceful commercial and industrial development in the Far East. Since he viewed Hoover as a humanitarian and an engineer, a man who espoused efficiency and loathed waste, Takasaki described the problem in the Far East as a "subject for thought from a practical businessman's view." Although Takasaki acknowledged that a peace settlement remained uncertain, he proposed that the United States and Japan start planning the postwar reconstruction of the economies of Manchuria and China. Like Ayukawa, Takasaki emphasized Manchukuo's need for the American assistance for its industrialization.

When time comes I feel that in the actual planning of stupendous hydro-electric [*sic*], irrigation, transportation, mining industrial and agricultural projects on a vast scale (they must be gigantic or they will prove entirely inadequate to recover the enormous losses sustained, or to carry in their stride the burden of the rehabilitation of a quarter of the human family.) [*sic*], it is above all essential to enlist in their conception the genius which in the past half century has tamed and developed the resources of a mighty continent—the American Vision, for breathtaking enterprises. And no less in the task of working out the plans, it is necessary that American factors shall be given scope and encouragement for willing participation (dare I say partnership?)[17]

Although Hoover apparently did not respond to this letter, in early 1940 Takasaki sent his close friend Nakamura Kaju, president of the Oriental Culture Society of Tokyo and an alumnus of New York University, as a personal envoy to discuss the matter. Takasaki pleaded with Hoover to "graciously grant [Nakamura] an interview concerning the matter which he and I talked over before his departure for the United States." Takasaki assured Hoover that Nakamura could "entirely be depended upon in any matter which [Hoover] may be inclined to talk over with him." The only reply Takasaki received from Hoover was that he had had a meeting with Nakamura.[18]

Ayukawa's and Hoover's Efforts to Avoid War

After fall 1940, Ayukawa's and Hoover's paths crossed in behind-the-scenes efforts to bring about a U.S.-Japan rapprochement. Even following his defeat in the 1932 presidential elections, Hoover had continued to oppose retaliatory actions against the Japanese for the invasion of Manchuria and China, a policy that the Roosevelt administration followed until the abrogation of the 1911 commercial treaty. Hoover thought economic sanctions would lead to war with Japan, and he opposed Roosevelt's move to impose them on Japan in summer 1940. Hoover was active behind the scenes in opposing American interventions in Europe and Asia, and President Roosevelt, even after his victory for the third term in 1940, had to be careful about assisting Great Britain because public opinion was still deeply divided over the issue of U.S. intervention against the Axis. Representatives of the two sides in the debate were Kansas journalist William Allen White's (1868–1944) Committee to Defend America by Aiding the Allies, which advocated intervention, and Sears, Roebuck chairman General Robert Wood's (1879–1969) America First Committee, which argued against intervention. Hoover and Wood were friends and political allies, and through William R. Castle, Jr. (1878–1958), a leading America Firster and a Hoover confidant, Hoover was a silent partner of the committee.

One of the major tenets of the America First Committee was that trade with Japan was the main national interest of the United States in the Far East, a conviction Hoover shared. For example, at a forum sponsored by the *New York Post* on November 18, 1940, Castle argued that Japan and United States should reach an understanding since in the event of war between the two countries, the United States would not be able to help Britain, and would lose trading opportunities in the Orient, including Japan, "the most highly industrialized and most progressive nation in the Far East" and the last remaining large-scale purchaser of America's cotton. (Castle had been ambassador to Japan and, later, an undersecretary of state during Hoover's presidency.)[19] A month earlier, Robert Wood had also argued for continuing trade with Japan, because the trade between America and Japan was five to six times larger than the Sino-American trade. Even if Japan were to control the Dutch East Indies, its severe foreign exchange shortages would induce it to sell tin and rubber to the United States from those islands. Although Wood emphasized that "Japan needs us far more than we need her . . . and if war with Japan comes, we can get Bolivian tin and develop our synthetic rubber," he nonetheless favored avoiding war with Japan by continuing to trade with it.[20]

The Roosevelt administration, however, did not want the Japanese to control strategic raw materials in Southeast Asia, such as tin, tungsten, manganese, and rubber, because it viewed Japan as unwilling to export them to either the United States or England. Data on the volume of trade between America and Manchuria to the contrary, Hornbeck argued in December 1940 that just as Japan had done when it occupied Manchuria and North China, it would discriminate against American and British trade if it came to control Southeast Asia.[21] As Ninkovich argues, Roosevelt saw neither world public opinion nor the balance of power as answers to solving the international situation because "modernity had changed reality to the point that . . . [the] contemporary international environment required a reorientation of the basic perceptual forms of space, time, and velocity upon which people depended to gauge international change." Hence, Roosevelt made foreign policies based on worst-case scenarios and believed that the United States had to prevent the Axis from gaining control of raw materials in Europe, Africa, Asia, and Oceania, which would lead to an interruption in American access to them. The encirclement of the United States by authoritarian systems and planned economies would seriously challenge American capitalism and democracy.[22] In the Pacific, in order to deter Japan's southward expansion, the United States was not only willing to continue diplomatic talks with Japan but also prepared to use embargoes against Japan and to keep Japan militarily occupied in China by providing China with economic support.[23]

An influential portion of American public opinion disagreed, however, with the Roosevelt administration's policy. In a book published in 1940, GM executive Graemer K. Howard argued for an idea that resonated with the worldview of Japanese business leaders such as Ayukawa and conflicted with the worst-case scenario of Roosevelt. Howard, who had negotiated with Ayukawa in the Nissan-GM talks in the mid-1930s (see Chapter 1), stated that although the United States should not permit aggression against Australia and New Zealand, it should recognize "Japan's moral right to, and economic need for, a preferred position among the nonoccidental nations in the Orient." Howard's framework for a new world order was cooperative regionalism among "Continental Europe, a British Empire, a Union of Soviet Republics, a Latin-Mediterranean Federation, an American Federation, and a New Order of Asia," with Germany, Britain, the U.S.S.R, Italy, the United States, and Japan being the respective regional hegemons. Unlike Hull's free trade policy, Howard argued against "adherence to the 'most-favored-nation clause'" because this "can lead only to the economic disturbance of the world, to the breakdown of trade, and to failure to realize a better international order." Instead of this trade policy, Howard suggested "that the immediate execution of commercial agreements be on a new basis of individual circumstances and bilateral requirements with full recognition of the changing character of international trade." American tariffs should be based on the "aggregate interests of the American people."[24]

Howard was but one of many Americans trying to head off war. In November 1940, Hoover loyalist Lewis Strauss, the de facto head of Kuhn, Loeb, began helping a private diplomatic initiative started by two Maryknoll priests, Bishop James E. Walsh (1891–1981) and Father James M. Drought (1896–1943). This effort led to indirect negotiations between the United States and Japan through a group known as the John Doe Associates, whose four members were, on the American side, Drought and Walsh and, on the Japanese side, Wikawa Tadao, an acquaintance of Hoover, and Colonel Iwakuro Hideo. Strauss was instrumental in Drought's rapprochement scheme and wrote letters of introduction for the Maryknoll priest to prominent Japanese acquaintances.[25]

In Japan, Wikawa became the point man for the priests, because he was a close friend of Strauss. As a young Finance Ministry official, Wikawa had worked for several years at the Japanese Financial Commission in New York City in the 1920s and he had established his ties with Strauss because his mentors told him to cultivate ties with Kuhn, Loeb. As Wikawa was leaving for America, two leading politicians and former finance ministers, Wakatsuki Reijirō (1866–1949) and Takahashi Korekiyo, stressed to Wikawa the importance of maintaining equidistance between J. P. Morgan, a firm they perceived as pro-English, and Kuhn, Loeb and Company, which they saw as pro-German. Although Japan relied more on Morgan than on Kuhn, Loeb for floating bonds in the United States, the uncertainty in international relations dictated constant preparation for contingencies. The British had won the war, but Japan might in the future establish close relations with Germany, and then Kuhn, Loeb might end up playing an important role for Japan. In 1940–41, Wikawa still believed that Strauss was inherently anti-British and would have maintained that position had it not been for the anti-Semitic ideology of the Nazi regime; all the main partners at the company were Americans of German-Jewish ancestry.

Hoover was aware of the developments in the John Doe project from its early stages through Strauss, who frequently contacted him on questions concerning international and domestic political economies. When Drought and Walsh returned from a seven-week stay in Japan in early January 1941, Drought called Strauss from San Francisco. Strauss advised Drought to contact Hoover, who in turn told Drought to contact the White House immediately. Hoover declined to be an intermediary because of the animosities between Roosevelt and himself, but he suggested that Drought solicit help from Frank Walker, U.S. postmaster general and a close ally of Roosevelt.[26]

While Hoover and Strauss quietly supported and advised the American half of the John Doe Associates, Ayukawa actively but quietly supported the efforts by the Japanese side. Before leaving Japan in March to join Wikawa in America, Colonel Iwakuro, whom Wikawa had approached to gain the Army's support for the John Doe project, met as many people as possible in an effort to gain support for the John Doe project. Ayukawa invited Iwakuro for a chat with him, Miho Mikitarō, and Itō Bunkichi. Ayukawa and Colonel Iwakuro undoubtedly knew of each other since Iwakuro was part of the reformist wing of the Japanese military and had been a major player in policymaking in Manchukuo from 1932 to 1934.[27]

In cooperating with the John Doe project, the Army was, in effect, following the strategy toward the United States that Ayukawa had been pursuing for several years (although their intentions were far more aggressive): achieve peace through U.S.-Japan economic interdependence centered around a joint venture scheme with the Ford Motor Company and, based on this, accelerate production and technological innovation for the war effort. In securing scarce foreign exchange for Wikawa's trip to America, Iwakuro had been helped by President Suzuki Shigeru of the Japan-America Trading Company (Nichibei shōkai), a company that was

Trading Company (Nichibei shōkai), a company that was negotiating a joint venture between Ford-Japan and Japan High Frequency, a company with which Nissan Motors had close business dealings (see Chapter 8). The purpose of Wikawa's trip was to negotiate with the Ford Motor Company's head office about this merger.[28] The contract for the proposed merger stated that the two companies would establish "a manufacturing plant in Japan to make automobiles, trucks and tractors, and their components and accessories," with Ford having majority control, to be marketed in "Japan, Manchukuo and such parts of China as may be under Japanese control." Ford further agreed to participate indirectly in "the manufacture of military tanks and aeroplanes parts . . . after the factory for making automobiles, trucks and tractors is in regular production."[29]

Ayukawa recommended to Iwakuro that he see Kurusu Saburō, who was returning to Japan via the United States from his assignment as ambassador to Germany. If Kurusu could be persuaded to stay in the United States and assist Japanese ambassador Nomura Kichisaburō (1877–1964) and the John Doe Associates, Ayukawa believed he would make a big difference.[30] Ayukawa told Iwakuro that Kurusu's successor in Berlin, General Ōshima Hiroshi (1886–1975), was not serving Japan's national interest; as a military attaché in Berlin in 1935–36, Ōshima had been instrumental in realizing the anti-Comintern pact. Ayukawa thought Ōshima, unlike Kurusu, who was critical and mistrustful of Hitler and his foreign minister, was open to manipulation by the two Germans because he was too blind in his pro-Axis faith. Ayukawa said Hitler and his men disliked Kurusu, who did not serve their purpose. Iwakuro had supported strengthening the anti-Comintern pact during the debates over it in 1938–39,[31] and he stated only that the Japanese government ought to keep Ōshima under control. On the other hand, he believed that Kurusu would serve as an excellent intermediary between the Foreign Ministry and the Japanese embassy in Washington, and he accepted Ayukawa's suggestion that he meet Kurusu and attempt to persuade him to stay in the United States.

In addition to recommending a meeting with Kurusu, Ayukawa offered Miho Mikitarō's service as Iwakuro's interpreter during his trip to Washington. Miho, a former businessman at the Mitsui Trading Company, was fluent in English and had traveled extensively in America and Europe on behalf of Ayukawa's efforts to attract foreign capital, technology, and machinery to Manchukuo. Ayukawa thought Miho's extensive connections would aid Wikawa in his negotiations with both Ford and the American government.

Iwakuro suspected that Ayukawa had an ulterior motive in recommending Miho and that Miho would use this opportunity to entice the Ford Motor Company to invest in Manchukuo. The severe foreign exchange shortage prevented people from traveling overseas, and Iwakuro thought Ayukawa was using his mission to carry out his own business. Iwakuro replied that he would decide whether to ask Miho to be his interpreter after he arrived in Washington. Although Ayukawa probably did have a business stake in the upcoming round of negotiations, Iwakuro felt obligated to help Japan High Frequency in its merger talks with Ford.

Ayukawa was also backing another secret mission to the United States. Hashimoto Tetsuma (1890–1990), editor of the nationalist publication *Shiunsō*, had been working for U.S.-Japan rapprochement since around the time of the O'Ryan mission in the summer of 1940. Ayukawa became acquainted with Hashimoto in the 1920s when Kuhara asked him to help Hashimoto financially. Later, Ayukawa himself began to support Hashimoto because he was attracted to the integrity of the man. Ayukawa never demanded that Hashimoto do favors for him and never intervened or involved himself in Hashimoto's activities. In 1939, Hashimoto had helped Ayukawa by quieting scathing criticism of Akyukawa's efforts to cooperate economically with the United States in Manchukuo in 1938. Hashimoto frequently sought Ayukawa's advice on U.S.-Japan rapprochement.[32]

Hashimoto's efforts began in spring 1940 and continued until November 1941.[33] Overall, his activities had a marginal effect, but his mission did demonstrate to State Department officials that some Japanese leaders were trying to tip the political balance in favor of those who wanted cooperation with the United States and Britain rather than with the Axis, especially since his efforts were succeeded by those of the John Doe Associates, a project Hashimoto was unaware of. Because the Konoe cabinet perceived the John Doe project as more promising than the Hashimoto mission and because of interference from Axis supporters, the Japanese government ignored Hashimoto on his return to Japan. This treatment was a complete surprise to Hashimoto because Prime Minister Konoe Fumimaro and Director of Military Affairs Mutō Akira had asked him in early November 1940 to visit the United States, and he did so with the support of chief cabinet members—War Minister Tōjō Hideki, Navy Minister Oikawa Koshirō

(1883–1958), Interior Minister Hiranuma Kiichirō (1867–1952), and Justice Minister Yanagawa. The only exception was Foreign Minister Matsuoka, who was not informed of the Hashimoto mission and opposed it when he found out.[34] However, although Prime Minister Konoe, War Minister Tōjō, and Navy Minister Oikawa refused to see him, Hashimoto managed to meet Interior Minister Hiranuma and Lord Keeper of the Privy Seal Kido Kōichi[35] shortly after his return. The following day, Kido met Ayukawa for four hours at Baron Itō's house, and he undoubtedly talked about Hashimoto.[36] Although Hashimoto continued his efforts to better U.S.-Japan relations by periodically meeting with Eugene Dooman at the American embassy, who along with Ambassador Grew had helped arrange Hashimoto's meetings with State Department officials, and by lecturing and writing newspaper articles, politicians in Japan saw him as a liability. Without any formal charge, the military police incarcerated him from June 30 to August 22, 1941.[37] During his troubles with the authorities, Hashimoto was politically and financially assisted by Ayukawa.[38] After his release, Hashimoto was prohibited from any political activities for six months and confined to internal exile on his home island of Shikoku.[39]

While Iwakuro was on his way to America to participate in the John Doe project, Kurusu was returning to Japan through the United States instead of the usual trans-Siberia route. Like Nomura, Kurusu favored the United States over the Axis powers, and he wanted to exchange opinions with Nomura. He also wanted to see the situation in Washington for himself. The Foreign Ministry in Tokyo gave him permission for this trip. Shortly before leaving Berlin, Kurusu told the U.S. chargé in Berlin, Leland Morris, that although U.S.-Japan relations had deteriorated "too far," he thought it important to "explore every possible peaceful solution of the problem."[40] Morris reported to Secretary of State Hull that "Kurusu very clearly indicated without definitely so saying, that one of his main motives . . . would be to endeavor through conversations with officials of the Department to explore the possibility of solving or at least arresting the decline in relations between the two countries." Although Morris and his embassy had "no knowledge of . . . Kurusu's attitude . . . toward Japan's relations with Asia and the United States," Kurusu had "given his American acquaintances the impression that he personally is opposed to the extremes of Japanese policy in recent years and particularly its lineup with the Axis powers."[41] In Washington, Nomura informed Kurusu that the informal talks between himself and Hull were going well and that the talks were strongly supported by Postmaster General Frank Walker, President Roosevelt's close political ally. Kurusu also received a telegram at the embassy from Ayukawa, urging him to meet Iwakuro in San Francisco.[42]

Meanwhile, Secretary of State Hull and Hornbeck learned of Kurusu's thoughts on the international situation following Kurusu's March 17 meeting with his friend from their years as ambassadors to Belgium, Joseph E. Davies (1876–1958). Kurusu told Davies that once the "military clique . . . prevailed, the whole matter had been taken out of his hands in Berlin, and had been transferred to Tokyo." On the order of his government and against his own wishes, he had signed the Axis Pact. His preference was for a U.S.-Japan rapprochement. He informed Davies that although Japan had no desire of militarily absorbing Singapore and other parts of South Pacific, American economic sanctions could leave the economically desperate Japan "no other recourse" but to fight "even though it meant defeat." Kurusu shared Davies's belief that the American people and government officials "would not tolerate appeasement" of the Japanese and that the opportunity that had existed for Japan to break from the Axis would soon end, since "within the next four or five months, in all probability, events of a military character would determine that either one side or the other" would gain considerable advantage. Japan by then would not be "a contributing factor to permanent world order and possibly world peace." Kurusu said he expected Matsuoka to bring "something back" from his trip to the Soviet Union and Germany, but "he had been 'riding' . . . too hard" by "using the military clique politically" and "the steed had gotten out of control." Kurusu thought that "Stalin was 'sitting tight' biding his time and watching his opponents trying to outbid each other to secure his support." Although the Germans "were very confident of ultimate victory," "Italy . . . had become a joke thr[o]u[ghout] Europe as well as Germany," and Germany had taken control of the Balkans, Kurusu thought that "barring some accident," U.S. economic aid would in the long run allow Britain to "win the war." In concluding his remarks, Kurusu said "he was going back to Japan [to] make some inquiries and investigat[e] on his own and that if he came back, which he might do, on a special mission, [Davies] would then know that he came with authority and something definite."[43]

At this time, Hull also learned from Drought and Walker that Ayukawa's telegram had been delivered to Kurusu at the Japanese Embassy.

Even though Hull probably was aware that Ayukawa belonged to the moderate wing of the Japanese establishment, because of Ambassador Grew's presentation of Ayukawa's proposal in June and July 1940, Drought and Walker gave Hull a negative picture of Ayukawa. They described Ayukawa as "a cousin of Matsuoka," a "pro-Axis businessman," and suspicious of the "current conversation" because "an agreement with America would destroy the virtual business monopoly of Ayukawa in Manchukuo." They thought "it would be better, in the public agreement, to announce the application of the Open Door to Manchukuo as well as China, but to say nothing probably concerning the use of American mechanized products for the development of Manchukuo."[44]

In San Francisco, Iwakuro was joined by Wikawa on March 20. When Kurusu arrived from Washington, he told them that Britain's capacity to resist the Germans should not be underestimated and that it would be difficult for Hitler to triumph over them. Kurusu predicted that Hitler would soon attack the Soviet Union; the Germans could not win a two-front war, and Stalin would probably enmesh the Germans in a protracted struggle. For Japan, the best thing would be to side with the United States and avoid its full commitment to the Axis Pact. He encouraged Iwakuro and Wikawa to pursue U.S.-Japan negotiations since Walker's backing was a great opportunity for Japan. During this long conversation, the two men urged Kurusu to accompany them and said they would ask Ambassador Nomura to seek the Foreign Ministry's permission. Kurusu, however, was reluctant; he thought it was better to return to Tokyo first and then be sent to Washington. In retrospect, Kurusu, Iwakuro, and Wikawa regretted that they had not sought the Foreign Ministry's permission for Kurusu to stay. Iwakuro thought that Kurusu could have mediated the trouble between him and the embassy staff during Iwakuro's involvement in the U.S.-Japan negotiations; Iwakuro told Kurusu during their meeting that except for Ambassador Nomura, the other Japanese diplomats in Washington opposed Wikawa's efforts.[45]

On April 16, Nomura cabled his government about the progress of the U.S.-Japan negotiations and introduced the content of the April 9 "Draft Understanding," which was the work of Iwakuro, Drought, and Wikawa. The proposal focused on Japan's relations to the Axis, the independence of China, the withdrawal of Japanese troops from China, the observance of the Open Door in China, the creation of a coalition government between

Chiang Kai-shek and Wang Ching-wei, restrictions on large-scale Japanese collective migration to China, and the recognition of Manchukuo. In discussing this proposal Japan hoped for American mediation to end the Sino-Japanese War. Although Secretary of State Hull had indicated to Nomura only that he was willing to discuss the proposals in the April 9 "Draft Understanding" as a basis for negotiation, Nomura not only failed to inform Tokyo that this proposal was the work of Iwakuro, Drought, and Wikawa but also gave the Japanese government the impression that the American government had initiated this proposal. Furthermore, neither Nomura nor the Japanese government understood the importance Hull placed on Japanese acceptance of his four principles (territorial integrity and respect for the sovereignty of all nations, nonintervention in internal affairs, equal opportunity in international commerce, and changes in the status quo in the Pacific only through peaceful means) as a precondition for further discussions. Finally, when Foreign Minister Matsuoka read Nomura's April 16 telegram upon his triumphant return from Europe on April 22, a trip in which he and the Soviet Union signed a treaty of neutrality, he thought this proposal was an attempt by the American government not only to undermine his own attempts in March and April to contact President Roosevelt through American Ambassador to the Soviet Union Laurence Steindhart (1892–1950), newspaper mogul Roy Howard (1883–1964), who was anti-Roosevelt and sympathetic to the idea of the U.S. recognition of Manchukuo, and Japanese Minister in Washington Wakasugi Kaname but also to neutralize Japan in the Pacific. (Matsuoka was unaware that Secretary of State Hull had in early March become suspicious of the efforts of the John Doe Associates because of an abrupt proposal brought to his attention by Howard, suspicion that was quelled by Postmaster General Walker.) Even if Matsuoka had known that the April 9 draft was for the most part the work of the three men, he would have nonetheless concluded that the efforts of the John Doe Associates and Nomura were an obstacle to his attempt to use the Axis to maintain Japanese security.[46]

By late April, the John Doe project seemed to have failed. Iwakuro and Wikawa headed for New York City on April 28 to make a direct international phonecall to Foreign Minister Matsuoka because they feared American wiretapping of the embassy phonelines.[47] On the following day, the two men sent Konoe a telegram that read "Decisive decision urgently requested before we all fall to hell by inability to support the rolling stone in middle of

a cliff." They became even more discouraged when Matsuoka neither supported nor opposed their initiative.

On April 28, Iwakuro and Wikawa visited Hoover at his residence in the
Waldorf Astoria Hotel.[48] Wikawa and Hoover had known each other since
1920 when Hoover had been commerce secretary in the Harding administration and Wikawa was a Finance Ministry official at the Japanese Financial Commission in New York. In 1927 Wikawa translated Hoover's *American Individualism* with Hoover's approval and had kept in touch with Hoover
since returning to Japan in 1928.

Despite his friendship with Hoover, Wikawa was cautious about approaching him since he knew that the White House had reacted badly to
the foreign minister's overture to Roosevelt through Roy Howard, a critic of
the Roosevelt administration. Like Howard, Hoover was also critical of the
Roosevelt administration. After Wikawa and Hoover talked about the old
days, Hoover suggested that Nomura, whom Americans liked, pursue a
U.S.-Japan rapprochement. To achieve this, Hoover suggested a meeting of
high-ranking politicians and businessmen for a frank and free exchange of
opinions without the presence of stenographers. This would serve not only
to create a positive atmosphere for rapprochement with Japan but also to
find effective ways to avoid war. Such a meeting of this sort was necessary to
break the deadlock in normal diplomatic channels. Hoover told the two he
regretted that he could not openly support them because he belonged to a
party out of power and thus was not in a position to help.

Although no mention was made of the John Doe project, Hoover was
well aware of the developments in it.[49] He was willing to support the rapprochement between the two nations from behind the scenes, and he indicated that the Republican party would support the Roosevelt administration if it pursued rapprochement. He commented it would be a tragedy for
the two nations to go to war. Although in this meeting Hoover described
Hull as "fair and sincere" and encouraged Iwakuro and Wikawa to pursue a
U.S.-Japan meeting, Hoover privately thought the State Department and
Hull were undermining their efforts.

Hoover's advice on U.S.-Japan affairs was also sought by Americans. On
the same day that Wikawa and Iwakuro saw Hoover, Admiral William V.
Pratt (1869–1957), chief of naval operations in the Hoover administration
and a journalist for *Newsweek*, wrote a letter to Hoover. He had seen Nomura Kichisaburō the day before at the Plaza Hotel in New York and

wanted to find a way to avoid a war in the Pacific. Pratt thought Hitler was trying to spread the war in the Atlantic to the Pacific, and he wanted to keep that from happening. He felt that "if things move in the right way, your influence would be invaluable!"

After their visit to Hoover, Wikawa and Iwakuro went to the residence of Lewis Strauss for lunch. Since Strauss was Hoover's confidant, Wikawa had been cautious about meeting his old friend. Even though the two priests had told Strauss about Iwakuro and Wikawa's mission, Strauss and Wikawa deliberately avoided discussing the U.S.-Japan negotiations. Instead, the talk centered around Strauss's son and Wikawa's daughter from his previous marriage to an American woman, who was studying at Barnard College. Strauss and his wife told Wikawa that the State Department was anti-Japanese, and Mrs. Strauss advised him to watch out for the "undersecretary" (probably a reference to Sumner Welles) and Hornbeck. It was not until a meeting that summer that Wikawa discovered Strauss had known about his mission. By that time, Strauss was back on active duty in the Navy.

On August 1, the day their ship *Tatsuta maru* was departing for Japan, Wikawa and Iwakuro tried to see Hoover in Palo Alto. Because Hoover was away when they visited, the two could only leave their name cards. The John Doe project failed because of Matsuoka's intransigence, because of mishandled negotiations in Washington, and because of Japan's invasion of southern Indochina on July 26. On July 24, Roosevelt had proposed that Japan, the United States, Great Britain, China, and the Netherlands declare Indochina neutral and that the other four countries guarantee Japan's access to raw materials in Indochina. The invasion prompted the Roosevelt administration to freeze Japanese assets on July 27 and later revoke export licenses for petroleum products destined for Japan.[50]

By this time, in addition to their concern over Japan's penetration into Southeast Asia, American policymakers were worried about the fate of the far eastern portion of the Soviet Union. Although Foreign Minister Matsuoka Yōsuke had advocated that Japan attack the Soviet Union after the outbreak of the German-Soviet war on June 22, Konoe dissolved the cabinet to remove him, a removal prompted by American mistrust of Matsuoka.[51] But American policymakers were concerned with the bigger picture. In order to support Soviet resistance to the Germans and prevent Japan's southward expansion, American policymakers were willing to buy time to contain Japan, as long as the outcome of German-Soviet struggle was in doubt. (In retrospect, American policymakers did not seriously entertain an agreement with Japan until early November, when it became clear that the Soviet Union would survive.)[52]

The Japanese government was, of course, unaware of this American perception of the Far East, and on August 6 it tried to improve relations by asking the United States to hold a summit meeting. Ayukawa welcomed this development. He met Kido and Itō on August 1 and probably agreed with Kido's assessment of the proper course for Japan in its foreign relations. Kido thought it impossible for Japan to conduct, on top of fighting the Chinese, a two-front war against the Soviets and the Americans. If Japan went to war against the United States, Kido estimated that the Navy would use up its current oil reserves in a year and a half and the Army in a year. Japan could try to boost its oil reserves by taking over the Dutch East Indies. But this would necessitate the occupation of other areas in the region, such as the Philippines and Singapore, because Britain and America would certainly contest Japan's conquest of the Dutch East Indies. Kido also thought that the Allies would destroy the Indonesian oilfields before Japan could occupy them and that the time necessary to get them operating again would confound the Navy's optimistic projections. He also pointed out the difficulty of running a long supply line that could be interdicted by American and British submarines and air attacks.

Given these harsh realities, Kido thought Japan faced a situation similar to the intervention in 1895 by France, Germany, and Russia right after the Sino-Japanese war of 1894–95. These powers had forced Japan to relinquish the Liaotung peninsula, but their pressure had also caused Japan to pursue industrialization and militarization based on the slogan *gashin shōtan* (withstand hardship in achieving an objective). Kido suggested that Japan should persevere and reach a rapprochement with the United States to obtain the necessary materials. Japan should set a ten-year goal of expanding southward and build its power by establishing its capacity for long-distance shipping and heavy industries, such as machine tools and synthetic fuels.[53]

At a meeting on September 14, Ayukawa learned from Baron Itō that Grew and Prime Minister Konoe had secretly met at Itō's residence on the evening of September 6. It was around this time that Ayukawa approached Commander Umezu Yoshijirō of the Kwantung Army and suggested that one of the issues Konoe should discuss with Roosevelt was the issuance of

$1 billion worth of dollar-denominated Manchukuo government bonds (see Chapter 6). Ayukawa was hopeful about this scheme since Miho had reported that Bernard Baruch supported it. During a secret meeting in summer 1940, Miho and Baruch agreed to pursue the matter on their respective sides. When Ayukawa asked Umezu to recommend this proposal to Prime Minister Konoe in Tokyo, Umezu informed Ayukawa that in the event that a summit conference took place he would ask that Ayukawa participate. The diplomatic talks, however, dragged on into October without progress.[54]

That fall witnessed the end of Ayukawa's long-cherished dream of attracting American investment in Manchukuo. On September 20, 1941, the *New York Times* reported a speech in which Ayukawa expressed his disappointment that "because of the international situation the plan for introducing foreign capital into Manchukuo for industrializing the country has become impossible." "Where the land is vast and the population small it is necessary to use big machinery, as is used in the United States, or else it will never pay. Particularly when the people's intelligence is low and they do not use the same language it is necessary to have modern equipment that can be operated by merely pushing a button."[55]

Despite the worsening relations between the United States and Japan, two prominent Americans whom Ayukawa had previously contacted helped Nishiyama Tsutomu, Japanese financial commissioner in New York, and Ambassador Nomura Kichisaburō in their efforts to avoid a Japan-America war. They were Herbert Hoover and Raoul E. Desvernine.

Desvernine was a Catholic, a Wall Street lawyer and businessman, and an opponent of the New Deal who maintained a friendly view toward Japan. Upon receiving his law degree from New York University in 1914, Desvernine began practicing law in New York City. His legal experience included extensive international involvement, such as special counsel to the Mexican government and Mexican embassy in Washington (1918–19), counsel to the Cuban embassy in Washington and Cuban Commercial Committee in the United States (1920–21), New York counsel for the Cuban Banking Liquidation Commission (1924–25), and counsel for American bankers negotiating foreign loans in Europe and South America (1926–29). He was well connected in the New York business and social community and frequently discussed public policy issues, often at his residence in the Hotel Pierre, with former governors of New York Alfred E. Smith (1873–1944) and Nathan L. Miller (1868–1953), *Wall Street Journal* journalist Thomas Woodlock, *Newsweek* journalist Raymond Moley (1886–1975), former president of U.S. Steel Irwin, president of U.S. Steel Edward R. Stettinius (1900–1949), Pierre Du Pont (1870–1954), Walter Lippmann (1889–1974), and Wendell Willkie.[56] Smith and Moley were famous anti–New Deal and anti-Roosevelt figures, and Moley and Lippmann were moderates on the issue of American policy toward Japan.[57] Desvernine's moderate position on Japan is exemplified by the fact that as president of Crucible Steel Corporation, he had evinced strong interest in exporting steel to Manchukuo in the winter of 1938–39 as Ayukawa proposed. Desvernine was also a board member of an anti–New Deal organization founded by influential political and business leaders, the American Liberty League.

Desvernine and Hoover thus had much in common. The two became acquainted when Desvernine wrote Hoover in May 1936 that he shared Hoover's critical view of the New Deal and that it was "fundamentally totalitarian in its conception and tendency."[58] At this time Desvernine was a partner in the law firm of Miller, Owen, Otis and Bailly (Miller being former New York governor Nathan Miller).[59] After eighteen years with this firm, Desvernine served as president of the Crucible Steel Company of America from 1938 to the spring of 1941.[60] At this time, he also chaired the Committee on Problems of Industrial Mobilization of the National Industrial Conference Board.[61] After spring 1941, Desvernine resumed his law career as a partner at the firm of Garey, Desvernine, and Garey. Among his clients were Japanese firms in New York City, the Mitsui Trading Company, and the Yokohama Specie Bank.[62]

In late 1940, Desvernine became better acquainted with Hoover,[63] and after mid-October 1941, Hoover became aware of Desvernine's Japan-related activities. Desvernine informed Hoover that he had been serving as an advisor since that summer on the U.S.-Japan negotiations,[64] and he expressed a wish to introduce Hoover to Japanese financial representative Nishiyama, whom Desvernine described as "the dominating factor in the present negotiations." According to Desvernine, Nishiyama was "anxious to meet" Hoover.[65] Nishiyama had been instrumental in bringing about the O'Ryan mission in June 1940, had assisted Wikawa Tadao in transmitting many important messages to Tokyo during the first few weeks of Wikawa's activities in February and March 1941, and, with the assistance of Max Kleiman, had tried to send an unofficial American emissary to Japan in January 1941.

Hoover met with the two men at his residence at the Waldorf Astoria Hotel on October 27.[66]

From this point on, Hoover became Desvernine's chief advisor for the U.S.-Japan negotiations. Desvernine informed Hoover that Ambassador Nomura had asked him to be his legal advisor because Judge Frederick Moore, counselor to the Japanese Embassy for fourteen years and a cousin of High Commissioner to the Philippines Francis B. Sayre, was old and feeble. (Nomura was probably reluctant to use Moore on sensitive issues because of Moore's seemingly close affiliation with the State Department.) Desvernine decided he would give the Japanese ambassador "sound and frank advice" without charging him, but he wanted Hoover's advice about what he should say to the Japanese officials.[67] Perhaps being modest about his background as an international lawyer, Desvernine "had been reluctant, as he had little experience in international affairs" but "thought war could be avoided with a common sense approach from both sides." Upon hearing this, Hoover answered that "war with Japan would be the wildest folly." Hoover thought that "might mean the defeat of Great Britain." Hoover said he "would be glad to make any suggestions [he] could, of course not putting [him]self in opposition to [his] own Government, for every citizen should promote peace on proper terms." Hoover argued that "the problem was to get our Administration to understand that they could not bluff, pinch, or stick pins in this tiger without getting bit." American economic sanctions had propelled Japan into Southeast Asia, and "she would fight even if she knew it was suicide in the end."[68] From time to time, Desvernine complained to Hoover that "Hornbeck was so violently anti-Japanese that discussion with him was almost impossible. He was positively discourteous. Mr. Hull also . . . was strongly anti-Japanese and discussions with him tended to be lectures by him on international morality."[69]

Desvernine was supposed to see Hoover for dinner on November 21, but he canceled because he had to leave for Washington suddenly. Two days later, Desvernine called Hoover and told him that

the Japanese situation had become very dangerous. . . . He insisted that the Ambassador and Kurusu, the recently arrived special Ambassador, were personally absolutely genuine in seeking a solution; that they represented the naval and civilian elements; that these elements strenuously wished to avoid war; that they realized the future of Japan lay in cooperation with the great naval powers; that they had a most difficult corner to turn and save national face and dignity; that their thesis was that it was urgent action should be taken at once to ease the situation; that Hull was driving absolutely to war; that Roosevelt was apparently hanging back.

After Desvernine "repeated in detail the interviews they had had with Hull and Roosevelt where he had been present, ... [Hoover] suggested that he find out if the Japanese would agree to a six-months' standstill agreement on all military action, they to have civilian supplies through the sanctions, a Five-Power Conference to be called at Honolulu or somewhere for the purpose of finding a formula for peace in the Pacific." Hoover argued these five powers should be the United States, Japan, the Netherlands, Britain, and the Chiang regime in China. Hoover thought if Japan agreed to hold this conference, then he or his friend would see "Roosevelt and suggest to Roosevelt that he propose it and take the glory." Hoover also wanted the current U.S.-Japan negotiations to be carried out by Roosevelt and not by the State Department. He believed that Britain wanted to avoid war with Japan and would pressure Roosevelt for a rapprochement with Tokyo.[70]

Meanwhile, in Japan, on November 16, Wikawa had conveyed his idea of *gashin shōtan* to Director of Military Affairs Mutō Akira, an idea shared by Ayukawa. Wikawa argued that "in an era of total war, our industries and industrial power are clearly inferior to those of countries like Germany and the United States, and given this situation we should, instead of fighting, seek to reorganize our industries and think in longer terms as we will be improved in terms of our industry five or ten years down the road." Wikawa suggested Japan "for the next few years should use American credit and materials as much as possible so as to develop the Far East, and thereby achieve in form and in reality a co-prosperity sphere. It will be abundantly clear by then that we will not have to fear countries like Britain and the United States since our economic powers and other national powers will be fulfilled." Wikawa claimed that "the Europeans and Americans, including Germans and Italians, will not respect our warrior mentality [which places so much emphasis on honor]; instead they will insult us." Therefore, "without becoming vulgar by international standards we should behave based on calculation and manipulation."[71]

At around the same time, Ayukawa was asking the Army to give peace a chance. His efforts were being seconded by Miho Mikitarō and former chairman of the Planning Board Aoki Kazuo, who had been a supporter of Ayukawa's industrialization scheme in Manchuria as deputy director of the

Steering Committee on Manchurian Affairs in 1937 and Nissan's merger talks with GM in the mid-1930s. Aoki was the chief economic advisor to the "Nationalist government" in Nanking as well as an advisor to the Japanese Foreign Ministry. He had been telling his Japanese colleagues in Nanking, including Ambassador Shigemitsu Mamoru (1887–1957), that if Japan and the United States went to war, the United States would win because of its greater economic power. When he returned to Tokyo in mid-November, Aoki told Foreign Minister Tōgō Shigenori that Japan should solve its problems with the United States and China by diplomatic means; he was acutely aware that England and America possessed far greater economic power than Japan, based on his days as an officer of the Japanese Finance Commission in London and his trips to Europe and the United States. In 1940 he thought Japan should negotiate with Washington and withdraw from China as well as from the Axis pact while trying to establish a coalition government between Chiang Kai-shek and Wang Ching-wei. Ayukawa, Aoki, and Miho drafted the following proposal:

1. The U.S. will recognize Japanese dominance (*shijōshidōken*) in Manchukuo and Mongolia.

2. In China, the Open Door will be maintained by strictly applying the principle of equal opportunity in trade and industry. Therefore, all foreign-leased territories will be abolished and none will be established in the future.

3. In order to eliminate anti-Japanese activities, all railroads in China will be supervised and managed by the Japanese, and the Japanese will have the right to deploy troops along the railroads. As the situation improves, Japan will gradually withdraw its troops and transfer the rights back to China.

4. The United States will promise to stop all activities that invite anti-Japanese activities by China and will help mediate the creation of the Chiang-Wang coalition government. In cooperation with Japan, the United States will help bring about the full political independence of China.

5. A neutral state will be created in the Soviet Far East, whose territory will include Sakhalin, Kamchatka, the Maritime Provinces and the territory adjacent to Manchukuo.

6. The Philippines, French Indochina, and other territories in Southeast Asia will gain their independence. They will be demilitarized, and the principle of equal economic opportunity will be applied.

7. Once these proposals have been agreed, Japan will withdraw from the Axis pact. At that point the United States will revive the commercial treaty with Japan, and it will provide a $5 billion credit to Japan for the economic development of Manchuria, Mongolia, and China.

8. Once U.S.-Japan friendship has been rebuilt on these proposals, the two countries will be the center of the Pacific League, serving as a savior to achieve world peace. By eliminating war on earth, the idea of *hakkō ichiu* (universal brotherhood) will be realized.[72]

This proposal, unrealistic and naïve as it looks today, was probably formulated out of desperation. Ayukawa, Aoki, and Miho had to entice the military away from war. Most of the ideas in the first, second, seventh, and eighth clauses reflected issues Ayukawa had been pursuing since 1937.

On November 23, the same day that Hoover conveyed his proposals to Desvernine, Ayukawa submitted this outline to Mutō Akira and brought it to the attention of Prime Minister Tōjō, whom Ayukawa lobbied several times. Ayukawa told Mutō that Japan should try just once more to avoid war with Britain and America by negotiating through the Jewish conglomerates.

Coincidentally, on November 23, the Jews of Shanghai, many of them refugees from the European war and Nazi persecutions, sent a cable calling for peace between the United States and Japan, partly because of prodding from the local Japanese army, to the major Jewish organizations in America, as well as to President Roosevelt's secretary of the treasury, Henry Morgenthau, Jr. (1891–1967), himself a Jew:

This day when the fate of Pacific is in balance we voicing opinion of a large community deem it necessary to emphasize that irrespective of the fact that Japan is allied to the Axis its people are against national hatred and oppression stop War in Pacific would bring untold hardships to many millions and in the interest of humanity we hope a peaceful mutual understanding will be reached stop convey this sincere unsolicited opinion all influential organizations.[73]

Ayukawa was undoubtedly aware of this cable because of Aoki's connections in China. It is also plausible that Ayukawa and Aoki had been receiving information from Japanese Finance Commissioner Nishiyama in New York; Miho had kept in touch with that office during his stay in the United States in 1940 and, as mentioned above, had met Jewish businessman Bernard Baruch in summer 1940 to discuss American loans to Japan. In addition, as a former high-ranking Finance Ministry official, Aoki retained a considerable influence in that ministry, to which Nishiyama's office belonged. Probably Ayukawa and Aoki were not only lobbying in Japan to further the negotiations in Washington but also assisting Nishiyama's efforts, although they probably were unaware of the efforts by Hoover and

Desvernine. Although some say Mutō privately preferred to avoid war with the United States, he informed Ayukawa it was too late, and Prime Minister Tōjō flatly rejected the proposal.[74] Ayukawa, probably after receiving these responses, expressed his concern to Kido Kōichi about the seemingly irreconcilable differences between the two countries.[75]

Around this same time, Hoover told *Newsweek* journalist William V. Pratt about his proposal to Desvernine. On November 25, Hoover told Pratt "to urge this formula to Pratt's old friend, the Japanese Ambassador." Pratt "readily agreed to do so because he considered war in the Pacific was senseless, would accomplish nothing, and would seriously endanger the British." He told Hoover "it would take anything from three to five years to defeat Japan."[76]

On November 26, the crisis worsened. On that day Ambassadors Nomura and Kurusu cabled Japan the text of the Hull note, which they had received in a meeting with Hull earlier. The Hull note not only called for Japan's adherence to the four principles Hull had stated during his talks with the John Doe Associates but also demanded the complete withdrawal of Japanese troops from China and Indochina, Japan's withdrawal from the Axis, and an agreement that Japan and the United States would not recognize regimes in China other than that of Chiang Kai-shek. As Butow points out, although "the terms contained in the Hull note of November 26 were stiff, the Secretary of State was not asking Japan to take unilateral action in a vacuum. He was prepared to reciprocate in various ways," including a multilateral treaty for equal economic opportunity in French Indochina, reviving a commercial treaty with a most-favored-nation clause, financial cooperation, and the unfreezing of Japanese assets.[77]

Later that same day, the two ambassadors sent their own government their proposal for peace. The two ambassadors proposed that President Roosevelt and Emperor Hirohito exchange telegrams aimed at averting war. Kurusu originally got the idea for this exchange of telegrams from a rumor he had heard that some quarters in Washington wanted to prevent the fall of the Konoe cabinet in October 1941 by sending a telegram of goodwill from the president to the Japanese emperor. Upon his arrival in Washington, Kurusu had heard from his subordinate Terasaki Hidenari (1900–1951) that Reverend E. Stanley Jones, an influential minister, had been lobbying the president to send a telegram to the Japanese emperor calling for peace and that Senator Elbert D. Thomas had made a similar suggestion.[78] This idea was risky since if Tokyo accepted his proposal but the president refused to send a cable or if the content of the U.S. cable were contrary to Kurusu's wishes, it not only would be a major embarrassment but also result in a severe reprimand to the two ambassadors. Kurusu intended to lobby the president to send a cable to the emperor indicating his wish to maintain peace in the Pacific through U.S.-Japan cooperation. Then, Kurusu wanted the emperor to send a friendly and positive response, thereby creating an opportunity for renewed discussions.

However, as he mentioned in a November 26 telegram to Tōgō, the American government had publicly announced its decision to land U.S. troops in Dutch Guyana in South America to protect the bauxite resources there. Kurusu thought it possible that the Americans might take similar action in the Dutch East Indies, on which the United States depended for its tin and rubber for the current war preparedness program. Occupation of the Dutch East Indies by American and British troops would trigger war between Japan and the Allies. Nevertheless, Kurusu thought it would be wiser to continue the diplomatic talks and for Japan to take the initiative in calling for the formation of a neutral territory that included Indochina, Thailand, and the Dutch East Indies, a proposition similar to the one Roosevelt had made in July for a neutral area that included Thailand and Indochina. Kurusu expressed doubt that the Germans would declare war on the United States if Japan went to war with America. (According to the terms of the Axis Pact, Germany was obliged to declare war on the United States if the latter attacked Japan first but was not obliged to do so if Japan attacked the United States first.) He also believed that the Sino-Japanese quagmire would not be settled until the termination of the current world war.[79]

Although "the Ambassadors requested that their plan be made known at least as far as to Lord Keeper of the Privy Seal Kido, and that they then be instructed immediately," Foreign Minister Tōgō thought the suggestion "superficial" and was once again upset about the fact that the two ambassadors were not doing their best to persuade the other party "on the basis of instructions received" from Tokyo. After he brought this cable and the Hull note to Prime Minister Tōjō, Navy Minister Shimada Shigetarō (1883–1976), and Kido, the four men agreed it was "utterly impossible to achieve a solution through any such scheme," particularly when the United States gave no assurances if Japan tied its own hands. Kido even said that "such plan would result in a rebellion." Therefore, on November 28, Tōgō sent a cable to the two ambassadors stating "that their plan had been made known in the quarters concerned, including that mentioned by them, but that none found it appropriate at the moment."[80]

Despite Tokyo's rejection of their proposal, Kurusu and Nomura decided to negotiate by themselves with the American government because a diplomatic breakdown would probably lead to war. The clandestine effort involved Kurusu, Nomura, and, to a lesser extent, Terasaki Hidenari. For Kurusu and Terasaki, the consequences of the diplomatic breakdown meant not only war but also emotional torment for their American wives and children in a Japanese society that perceived Americans as enemies. Nomura's and Kurusu's behavior was not unusual in an emergency situation, as exemplified by Nomura's unauthorized acts during the John Doe project. Moreover, although the two ambassadors were unaware that Americans had decoded Japanese diplomatic cables, neither they nor the Americans knew about the decision of the December 1 Imperial Conference for war. The two ambassadors saw President Roosevelt and Hull on November 27, but the discussions between the two sides went nowhere. Even so, at the end of the meeting, Roosevelt replied in the affirmative when Nomura asked if he would still act as an "introducer" for China and Japan.[81]

By the time Roosevelt returned to Washington on the morning of December 1 from a vacation in Warm Springs, Kurusu had contacted two persons who had access to the president, Reverend E. Stanley Jones and Bernard M. Baruch, to suggest the exchange of telegrams between Roosevelt and the Japanese emperor. Hoover played an instrumental role in arranging Kusuru's meeting with Baruch, although in his memoirs Kurusu mentions only that Japanese Finance Commissioner Nishiyama had assisted him in getting in touch with Baruch.[82] Hoover suggested that Desvernine contact Roosevelt by calling not only Roosevelt's aide in Warm Springs Basil O'Connor but also Baruch. According to a memorandum written on April 10, 1942, Desvernine called O'Connor from Hoover's office in the Waldorf. Unaware of other possible reasons for Roosevelt's early return, Hoover thought that Roosevelt "cut short his visit [to Warm Springs] and returned to Washington" because of this call.[83] According to Hoover, on November 30, "Desvernine, knowing [Raymond] Moley to be a great friend of Baruch, asked Moley to call at his apartment and he explained to Moley the whole Japanese situation and asked if he would take it up with Baruch." From Desvernine's apartment, Moley contacted Baruch, who was at his residence in South Carolina. Upon hearing Moley's request, Baruch told Moley "he was leaving for Washington that night and would meet Desvernine on Monday morning [December 1] in Washington." That night Desvernine took the train for Washington.

Although the recollections of Hoover, Baruch, and Kurusu as to the place, date, and list of participants differ, Kurusu, Desvernine and Baruch did meet. Hoover was informed by Desvernine that on December 1 Baruch, Desvernine, and Kurusu drew up a proposal that Baruch agreed to present to the president. On December 2, "Desvernine gave Baruch the memorandum in two copies—one without initials and one initialed by Kurusu for Baruch's own personal keeping for his own protection."[84]

Roosevelt had been entertaining the idea of sending a direct appeal to the emperor. Even though the emperor had no real power, some thought his support for peace negotiations would serve to prevent war. This idea had been advocated since the fall by not only Jones and Senator Thomas but also Langdon Warner (1881–1955), a specialist in ancient Japanese arts and culture at the Fogg Museum at Harvard, and Asakawa Kan'ichi (1873–1948), a professor of history at Yale University. Before he left for Warm Springs, on November 28, Roosevelt had instructed Secretary of State Hull and his staff to draft messages over the weekend to both the emperor and Congress. The message to Congress was intended to warn of the impend-ing danger to the United States. The message to Hirohito seemed politically more plausible to Roosevelt, because of his reluctance to present the issue to Congress until he knew which eventuality he faced. When Roosevelt came back to Washington from Warm Springs, he conferred about the two draft messages with Hull, who had just talked with the two Japanese ambassadors.[85]

On the same day of Roosevelt's return to Washington, the two ambassadors cabled Foreign Minister Tōgō, recommending the revival of the idea of a mid-Pacific conference, last floated in September, between the Japanese prime minister and the president of the United States. They recommended the discussions be based on Foreign Minister Tōgō's Plan B (a modus vivendi in which the United States would resume shipments of oil to Japan in return for a Japanese withdrawal from southern to northern Indochina) and the Hull note; in this case they suggested a meeting between Konoe Fumimaro or Ishii Kikujirō (1866–1945), a Privy Council advisor, on the Japanese side and Vice President Henry A. Wallace (1888–1965) or Harry

Hopkins (1890–1946) on the American side. The Japanese government ignored this suggestion.[86]

Could Baruch exert the kind of influence on Roosevelt that Kurusu hoped? As Jordan A. Schwarz points out, "Roosevelt could not repress a Baruch opinion on policy and organization; so it was evidently in the president's best interest that Baruch have access to the White House for venting his judgments."[87] Roosevelt, however, was suspicious about Japanese intentions in meeting Baruch. According to Henry Morgenthau's diary entry for December 3, 1941, Roosevelt told Morgenthau "he had the Japanese running around like a lot of wet hens. After he asked them the question [on December 2 through Undersecretary of State Sumner Welles] as to why they were sending so many military, naval and air forces into Indo-China. He said that Kurusu asked Barnie Baruch and a number of other people to try to bring influence to bear on the President." Roosevelt thought "the Japanese are doing everything they can to stall until they are ready." In the meantime, Roosevelt was "talking with the English about war plans as to when and where the USA and Great Britain should strike."[88]

Baruch's "conferences with . . . Kurusu were held with the full consent of . . . President Roosevelt." Afterward, Baruch "dictated a full report of the conversations to the President—including a request that Mr. Roosevelt send a personal appeal direct to Emperor Hirohito." Both men were well aware of the grim situation confronting the two countries, and Kurusu agreed with Baruch's warning "that in the event of a war between the two countries that Japan 'will be completely crushed by the U.S. because of its industrial might.'"[89]

Although Baruch had "no recollection" of suggesting a $1 billion loan to Japan,"[90] Kurusu later claimed this had been discussed (during a meeting on November 30 according to Kurusu's recollection and·on December 3 according to Baruch).[91] According to Kurusu, Baruch told him that he was worried about the slow progress of America's preparedness program. He saw no reason for Japan and the United States to go to war; Baruch had been advocating war preparedness and industrial mobilization since 1938, but he wanted America to avoid entering a war, particularly on two fronts. Like many other American policymakers, Baruch's primary concern was the European theater. In order to realize America's world strategy, by which he presumably meant Wilsonianism, he thought it necessary for America to use Japan in the Far East and Germany in Europe to achieve that objective, however distasteful the present regimes in those countries were. On the European front, however, based on a balance-of-power perspective, Baruch preferred the survival of Britain over German military expansion. Baruch saw an underlying insecurity in the psyche of the Japanese military since their loss to the Soviet Army at Nomohan in 1939. They realized their limits and were nervous. In order to remove the "Inferiority Complex" of the Japanese military, Baruch argued that Roosevelt's "arsenal of democracy" idea should be applied to Japan in a way that would help build Japanese industries and boost production. Baruch suggested to Kurusu that America should lend Japan $1 billion for its industrial development.[92] After his meeting with the Japanese, Baruch "immediately telephoned General Watson, who came over with a White House stenographer to whom [he] dictated a summary of [his] conversations with Kurusu." According to Kurusu, after this meeting, Baruch sensed a positive reaction from the president and told Kurusu that he and the president were planning to meet for the second time regarding this matter on December 10.[93]

Meanwhile, at 12:15 P.M. on December 3, Reverend Jones saw the president at an "off the record" meeting (Jones and the White House arranged to have "[some]one" greet him at the East Gate so he could avoid reporters).[94] During the meeting, Jones emphasized the need to send a telegram appealing for peace to the Japanese emperor. Initially Roosevelt told Jones he had been entertaining the same idea, but he felt reluctant "to hurt the Japanese here at Washington by going over their heads to the Emperor." Upon learning from Jones that Nomura wanted to bypass his own government, Roosevelt replied in relief, "That wipes my slate clean; I can send the cable." Roosevelt would send the cable to Ambassador Grew in Tokyo, who had the right to audience with the emperor. He also added, "I've learned how to do some things, so if I don't get an answer in twenty-four hours I will give it to the newspapers and force a reply." According to Kurusu, that same evening the president and Baruch had dinner together. Baruch told Kurusu that he received some positive hints from Roosevelt and that the two agreed to meet again on December 10.[95]

In Tokyo, Wikawa continued his attempt to assuage the explosive situation. Wikawa was aware that Nishiyama, who had assisted him in the John Doe Project, had been meeting with Baruch, probably through his access to Nishiyama's cables to the Finance Ministry. Furthermore, because Bishop Walsh, who had been in Japan from June to October 1941, and Nishiyama knew each other through Wikawa and both men worked in the New York City area, Nishiyama had undoubtedly kept in touch with Walsh, who advised Wikawa in a cable on November 27 that Hull's proposals of November 26 were meant to be a friendly gesture leading to complete understanding. Walsh, who undoubtedly kept in close touch with Father James Drought, who in turn was in contact with the two Japanese ambassadors, asked Wikawa to inform the highest authorities about the intent of the note and to warn that Japan's response would determine everything. On December 1, Wikawa received a cable from Walsh that read: "Federals Great Statesmanship concentrating North Carolina only can prevent worst. Recommend Tournament for relaxation." This cable refers to the efforts of Nishiyama, Kurusu, Nomura, Desvernine, and Hoover around this time to lobby for the assistance of Baruch, who normally resided in South Carolina when he was not serving as an elder statesman in Washington. Wikawa undoubtedly was aware of Nishiyama's and Kurusu's efforts to avoid war.[96] (Whether Ayukawa knew about this message is unknown.)

At 6:00 P.M. on December 6, Roosevelt received information that the Japanese were on the verge of starting a war with the United States.[97] In order to make sure the message would not be held up in the Foreign Ministry, Roosevelt sent the cable to Ambassador Grew with the message for Hirohito. Roosevelt instructed Hull to send it by gray code to save time and stated he was willing to risk an interception. Since the message arrived at noon in Tokyo, the cable was deliberately delayed for ten hours because of a recent general directive of the Japanese government. Even though aware that such a message was coming because he heard a report about it on a San Francisco radio broadcast, Grew did not receive the coded triple-priority message until 10:30 P.M., and the telegram reached Emperor Hirohito after the attack had started.[98] Upon their return to Japan in 1942, Nomura and Kurusu learned from Prime Minister Tōjō that he felt Japan probably would not have started the war had the December 5 cable from the president been sent a few days earlier and had the Hull note been a little more conciliatory.[99]

After Pearl Harbor, although Hoover publicly called for unity in the war effort, he remained critical of Roosevelt's policy toward Japan before Pearl Harbor.[100] Meanwhile, Desvernine ran into trouble, as the Justice Department considered prosecuting him because of his involvement in the clandestine effort at the eleventh hour. This charge was dropped when Baruch told

Attorney General Francis Biddle (1886–1968) that "he would appear as the first witness for the defense."[101]

As Kurusu wrote to Ayukawa on September 6, 1946, he was "filled with deep emotion" when he compared Japan's "numerous economic difficulties up ahead with [his] negotiation with Bernard Baruch over a billion-dollar loan to Japan, a subject matter having close relations with [Ayukawa's] activities before the war; [Kurusu] really regret[ted] the fact that that one-in-a-million opportunity slipped through [his] hands [because of Pearl Harbor]."[102]

EIGHT

MIDC's Downfall and Ayukawa's Activities During the Pacific War

On January 18, 1939, with an eye on the growing support for economic regulation (*tōseishugi*) and totalitarianism, Ayukawa told Japanese college students enrolled in engineering programs and interested in finding a job in Manchukuo (where Japanese civilians and bureaucrats generally earned more than their counterparts in Japan) that Manchukuo espoused totalitarianism—"the regulation of the whole [system]" (*zentai no tōsei*)—as a goal. For Ayukawa, totalitarianism was a system in which the economy and individualism were regulated for the well-being of the entire society. Ayukawa indicated that he disliked the autarkic aspects of this trend, but he told the students that whether the trend was good or bad, Japan would increasingly resemble Manchukuo. He also said, however, that totalitarianism might lead to bankruptcy some day. In the meantime, his managerial experience had only very limited applicability to Manchukuo's economy. The lessons of what he described "as the previous period of individualism and economic liberalism" were no longer useful in Manchukuo. Students interested in building a career in Manchukuo had to prepare themselves psychologically for the fact that the individualism and economic liberalism that they had learned in school did not exist in Manchukuo. If they wanted to base their careers on these outmoded ideas, they should remain in Japan and cling to what Ayukawa described as the segment in that society that still had them.[1]

This chapter examines Ayukawa's fruitless battles between 1938 and 1945 to limit state intervention in the economy and to maintain MIDC's central role in Manchukuo as well as the failure of Manchukuo's economic programs as illustrated by the attempts to establish automobile and aircraft industries. Until the end of World War II, Ayukawa continued to argue for a business-led approach to running the economies of Manchukuo and Japan.

Changing Tides in Manchukuo's Economy

In the late 1930s, both Japan and Manchukuo pursued conflicting economic policies toward each other and toward the United States. They wanted more economic interdependence within the Japanese empire, as well as stronger relations with the United States, ideas espoused by Ayukawa. These ideas increasingly fell out of favor, however, and wartime imperatives bolstered economic regulation.

Ayukawa's activities and both the original and the revised Five-Year Plan for Manchukuo assumed (erroneously) that the new state could easily acquire material resources, capital, labor, and technology from Japan and the West. Furthermore, the original plan, despite its goal of creating a self-sufficient military industry in Manchukuo, did not include a section on building a machine tools industry. In fact, the two plans incorporated Ayukawa's major assumption that machine tools would be imported from Japan and Western countries, mainly America and Germany. (Although the revised plan did include a section on establishing a machine tools industry, it was not considered seriously until after the outbreak of the Pacific War.)

Both Japan and Manchukuo depended heavily on sophisticated technology, including machine tools, from Europe and the United States, and Japan's imports of machine tools from Western countries, mainly Germany and America, increased steadily after 1931, jumping from ¥153.1 million in 1936 to ¥242.2 million in 1937, and remained high until 1940. Japan depended more on American, rather than German, machine tools. Its imports of German machine tools dropped significantly after 1939 because of the war in Europe, and, of course, its imports of American machine tools ceased in 1941 with the outbreak of the Pacific War. Between 1939 and 1941, Japan and its formal and informal empires became more dependent on American capital and technology than on those of any other Western country.

Manchukuo depended as well on imports of machine tools from Japan. After 1934, Japan increased its export of machine tools, including those imported from the West, to its formal and informal empires. This trend peaked between 1939 and 1941 and ended with a dramatic drop between 1944 and 1945. Manchukuo absorbed 30–40 percent of the machine tools exported by Japan between 1939 and 1943 and 37–46 percent of the industrial machinery exported by Japan between 1938 and 1942. Japan's exports of machine tools to Manchukuo dropped after 1942 because of Japan's domestic imperatives and the difficulties in shipping caused by Japan's loss of air and naval supremacy.[2]

The outbreak of the Sino-Japanese War in 1937 worsened Japan's trade deficit, accelerating a trend that had begun in 1931, and prompted the passage in September 1937 of two regulatory laws that aimed, along with the 1918 Munitions Industries Mobilization Law, to ease foreign exchange shortages and trade deficits and increase military-related production.[3] In October 1937, the newly created Planning Board drafted a proposal for the National Mobilization Law and the Material Resources Mobilization Plan. The Mobilization Law, which went into effect in May 1938, gave the government much broader powers than had the 1918 law over military-related industries in Japan. For example, as long as the government considered it necessary to mobilize the nation for war, it could allocate resources and labor to military industries through imperial ordinances, rather than through laws passed by the Diet.

Despite these regulatory measures, after September 1937, Japan experienced not only increasing shortages of material resources due to the ever-increasing demand from Japan's military industries but also worsening foreign-exchange shortages. Although Japan experienced trade surpluses after 1938 because of increased trade within the yen bloc, its trade deficit with the West, particularly the United States, worsened after 1937. While cutting back on domestic consumption, Japan also decreased exports to the yen bloc and demanded that Manchukuo increase its exports of natural resources and semi-finished industrial products to Japan.

In January 1939, the cabinet approved the "Outline for the Cabinet Planning Board Plan to Expand Production Capacity," which had been drafted by the Army in 1937 and proposed by the Planning Board in 1938. This four-year economic plan concentrated on strengthening basic industries vital to the military. For Manchukuo, the plan justified subordinating the establishment of a self-sufficient military industry to the provision of natural resources and semi-finished industrial products to Japan. The plan called for the coordinated expansion of productivity in Japan, Manchukuo, Taiwan, Korea, and the Japanese-occupied areas in China, with the goal of ending economic dependence on the West and establishing autarky in the Far East. However, this plan assumed no enlargement of the war effort. Unfortunately for the success of the plan, the prolonging of the Sino-Japanese War increasingly thrust Japan toward total war.

These negative economic changes in Japan and a slowdown in capital inflows from Japan after 1940 contributed to a decline in Manchukuo's economy. The situation was aggravated by a bad harvest in 1939 and the slump in the Japanese capital markets that made it difficult for Manchukuo to raise money by issuing bonds to finance industrial activities.[4] These trends also affected MIDC. The initial enthusiasm for MIDC among the reformist civil servants and Army officers faded quickly because of the short-term imperatives of the Sino-Japanese War and, later, the war in Europe, the deterioration in U.S.-Japan relations, and Ayukawa's inability to secure American capital.

Moreover, Ishiwara Kanji's loss of influence in Japan and Manchukuo because of his opposition to the Sino-Japanese War meant that he no longer had a voice as the main figure in Japanese policymaking circles who wanted to eliminate exclusive Japanese economic privileges in Manchukuo, curtail the Kwantung Army's power in favor of a truly independent Manchukuo government, and create greater economic interdependence between America and Manchukuo. Ishiwara wanted to win the trust of the Chinese people so that Japan could exploit the rich natural resources of China to prepare for the "Final War" (see Chapter 2), a showdown with the Soviet Union and, later, the United States.[5] By the spring of 1936, Ishiwara had concluded that natural resources of northern China were not essential for his industrialization scheme. He argued for the avoidance of conflict with the Chiang Kai-shek regime because the real enemy was the West and Japan should preserve its military capabilities for its war with the Soviet Union.[6] By fall 1937, however, Ishiwara found himself in a less influential position, working as vice chief of staff from September 1937 to August 1938 under Chief of Staff Tōjō Hideki, with whom he did not get along.[7]

By May 1938, the Sino-Japanese War had prompted the Kwantung Army to revise the original five-year plan for Manchuria. The original plan, initiated in April 1937, allocated ¥1.39 billion out of ¥2.58 billion of capital to mining and industry over five years. The revised plan, which continued in effect until 1941, increased the total capital between 1937 and 1941 from ¥2.58 billion to ¥4.80 billion. Of this total, ¥3.80 billion was earmarked for mining and industry. The revised plan dramatically raised the targets for the production of iron and steel, coal, light metals, synthetic fuel, electric power, and ammonium sulfate. It also called for substantial investments in the manufacture of trucks, automobiles, and aircraft and decreased capital allocations and production figures for agriculture, dairy farming, communications, and transportation slightly.

The Revised Plan made it mandatory for Manchukuo for the first time to fulfill specific quotas of natural resources and semi-finished industrial products to Japan's heavy and chemical industries and transportation system. For example, Manchuria now had to export to Japan the following proportions of its annual production: pig iron, 33.8 percent; steel ingots, 35.5 percent; coal, 17.2 percent; naphtha, 83.4 percent; heavy oil, 94.6 percent; aluminum, 38.7 percent; lead, 69.0 percent; salt, 49.5 percent; soda ash, 34.8 percent; and wood pulp, 75.0 percent. The emphasis thus shifted away from creating a self-sufficient military industry to supplying Japan's industries.

This shift of emphasis, however, did not signal the end of the idea of achieving a self-sufficient Manchukuo in the long run. Policymakers in Japan planned to coordinate economic development in the yen bloc so as to create and strengthen the basic industries on which heavy and chemical industries could flourish in Japan and Manchukuo. They believed this was possible because, at the time they formulated the revised plan, they did not believe the Sino-Japanese War would turn into a total war.

The revised plan incorporated the plan to borrow foreign capital, but not as much as Ayukawa envisioned. For the mining and industrial sectors, the revised plan sought to acquire 37.4 percent of the capital necessary from Manchukuo, 43.6 percent from Japan, and the remaining 19 percent from other countries; the figures for all sectors combined were 38.5, 46.5, and 15 percent, respectively. On the other hand, Manchukuo planned to spend more capital on its own goods and goods from foreign countries other than Japan. The figures for the mining and industrial sectors were 35 percent for domestic payments, 33 percent for payments to Japan, and 32 percent for payments to foreign countries. For all sectors combined, these figures were 43, 30, and 27 percent, respectively.[8]

Ayukawa and the Automobile Industry in Japan and Manchukuo

From the late 1930s to 1940, amid these changes in Japan's and Manchukuo's economic policies, Ayukawa tried to use the state and the market to achieve his aspirations to dominate the Japanese automobile industry and to help create automobile and aircraft industries in Manchukuo. On November 11, 1937, Ayukawa told Asakura Tsuneto, director of Nissan Motors, that he still hoped to merge all Japanese car companies into a single corporation. He believed such a unification would boost productivity through the integration of resources, technology, and production, and he tried to use the military and the market to achieve this end. In April 1938, Nissan Motors gained majority control of Tōkyō Gas and Electric by purchasing 124,700 of this company's 240,000 shares from the Fifteen Bank. That same month, in order to secure raw materials for its production of autos, MIDC and Japan High Frequency Heavy Industry took equal portions of the 270,000 shares of the Tōkyō Automobile Industry Company held by Tōkyō Gas and Electric, through the mediation of the Army's director of munitions. MCI was not informed of this development, and on April 19, the day before these changes were publicly announced, Minobe Yōji (1900–1953), section chief for Industrial Policy and Industrial Business in MCI's Industrial Affairs Bureau, complained to Asakura that neither the Army nor the car companies had notified the ministry about this reorganization in the automobile industry. Ayukawa's next target for a complete takeover was the Tōkyō Automobile Industry Company. In July, Ayukawa hurried to achieve this aim because he wanted to meet the rising demand for vehicles. MCI was opposed to Ayukawa's desire to merge all automobile companies, and even within the military, some groups, including the Economic Regulation and Mobilization Bureau, shared MCI's opinion.

Some events in 1939 and at the beginning of 1940 satisfied Ayukawa's desire for a grand merger. In May 1939, Hitachi, which through Nissan was a majority shareholder in Tōkyō Gas and Electric Company, acquired the firm completely and divided it into Hitachi Aircraft, Hitachi Munitions, and Hitachi Machine Tools. On November 11, Asakura, now the managing director of Nissan Motors Sales Company, learned from Vice War Minister Anami Korechika (1887–1945) that the Army supported the eventual merger of all Japanese car companies, but, for the time being, it wanted to maintain the status quo to avoid "confusion." Nissan Motors prepared for this eventual goal, and at the end of 1939 and the beginning of 1940, Asakura spoke with Managing Director Takahashi Shōzō of Japan High Frequency regarding Nissan Motors' interest in merging with the Tōkyō Automobile Industry Company. On January 22, 1940, Takahashi informed Asakura that he had obtained approval from the Army and executives at Tōkyō Automobile Industry for the merger of Nissan and the car company. Takahashi, however, said that, for the time being, Nissan and Japan High Frequency were to support the expansion of Tōkyō Automobile's operations and retain the existing top management. Nissan executives opposed the latter point, and the merger talks apparently ended.[9]

Even as Ayukawa worked on dominating the Japanese automobile industry and striking a joint venture with Ford (see Chapter 4), he tried to fulfill his obligations in Manchukuo because the Japanese and Manchukuo governments were pressuring him to invest in the establishment of Manchukuo's automobile and aircraft industries. On March 24, 1939, Manchukuo and MIDC decided to establish the Manchuria Automobile Manufacturing Company; the necessary law was promulgated on May 5. On June 15, Asakura heard from Asahara Genshichi, a Nissan Motors director who had just returned from Manchukuo, that Ayukawa was having managerial difficulties. The Manchukuo government was moving to take the coal and steel operations away from MIDC and make the holding company concentrate on producing automobiles and airplanes. Nissan executives seemed inclined to support their boss's move to have Nissan Motors invest directly in Manchukuo, as did MCI. Meanwhile, MIDC sent Yamamoto Sōji, president of the newly established Manchuria Automobile Manufacturing Company, on a mission to the United States to purchase large amounts of equipment and machinery for manufacturing automobiles. The Manchukuo government backed this project fully and granted Yamamoto authority to use up to U.S.$15 million of its scarce foreign reserves.[10] The war in Europe, however, put an end to this project, when it became impossible to export Manchukuo's soybeans, the primary source of foreign exchange earnings. Ayukawa phoned Yamamoto to stop the project and cancel any contract he had signed.[11] The sudden surge in European demand for American machines induced a rapid rise in prices, and Yamamoto ended up not having to pay penalty fees for the canceled purchases and even obtained blueprints free.[12]

Although Nissan's talks with Ford kept alive the possibility that Manchukuo might obtain American capital and technology for its automobile industry, it could no longer count on Yamamoto's mission. On November 21, Ayukawa told Asakura about the plans for starting automobile and aircraft industries in Manchukuo. The Manchukuo government, the Kwantung Army, and MIDC had decided to build a new industrial city in Antung that would eventually produce 50,000 vehicles and 600 airplanes a year. Subcontractors and auto parts industries, including machine tool manufacturers and foundries, were to be located in this new area. The complex would not be dependent on subcontractors and parts from Japan and would have a workforce of 70,000 and an overall population of 200,000, including families. The estimated cost for building the entire complex was ¥1.7 billion yen.[13]

While Ayukawa was considering this grand scheme in Antung, Yamamoto managed to strike a bargain at the Lycoming Company, a manufacturer of automobile engines in Pennsylvania that was replacing its production line with new machines. Yamamoto paid $2.7 million for the used equipment, one-third the price of new machinery; the Japanese Army granted this amount from its account in the United States to the Manchukuo government. At the time, the machines and equipment purchased from Lycoming were the most advanced in the Japanese automobile industry; until then, Nissan Motors had been using a 1927 production facility to manufacture engines. Although the Lycoming machines reached Japan in 1940, delays there made it impossible to ship them to Manchukuo once war with the United States broke out. Instead of providing state-of-the-art technology for Manchukuo, they were used in Nissan's Yoshihara factory to produce airplane engines during the war.[14]

As with the Lycoming machines and equipment, the automobile industry in Manchukuo never received significant direct investments from Nissan Motors. Although Ayukawa planned to move the center of Nissan Motors' activities to Antung in spring 1940, Nissan executives, including Asakura, opposed the project. They did not mind cooperating to some extent in Manchukuo's automobile project, but not to the degree that Ayukawa had in mind. The executives thought it almost impossible to move manpower and subcontractors to an as yet undeveloped location and stated that the project would not contribute to national defense. Asakura was aware that although the Army was behind this project, the Cabinet Planning Board and MCI opposed it and wanted to maintain the status quo. Asakura expressed his frustration when Army officers told him on April 11 that this was now a matter of national policy. That same day, he read an article in *Yomiuri shimbun* and learned that Nissan Motors was moving to Antung to establish Manchukuo's automobile industry and that the move would be completed in three years. Because Ayukawa had been obliged since the founding of MIDC to start an automobile industry in Manchukuo, he told his top executives at Nissan Motors on May 16 that he had to follow national policy and that diesel cars were going to be built in Manchukuo, possibly with the help of Daimler-Benz. On May 24, Asakura wrote in his diary that he thought the whole scheme was a coincidence of interests between the Army, which wanted to establish an automobile industry in Manchuria, and those groups in Japan that wanted to push Nissan Motors out of the Japanese market. On June 14, Nissan president Murakami Masasuke stated at a board meeting that the scheme was good neither for the country nor for Nissan Motors nor for his boss.[15] Thus, Ayukawa, founder and chairman of Nissan Motors, encountered another revolt by his top lieutenant shortly after the Nissan-Toyota-Ford episode (see Chapter 4).

Fortunately for Ayukawa and his men, the pressure on Nissan Motors to move to Manchukuo weakened after the fundamental change in Manchukuo's economic policies after mid-1940. On May 8, 1940, Hoshino Naoki, secretary general of Manchukuo's General Affairs Agency, announced that the agency would place an increased priority on the development of iron and steel, coal, nonferrous metal, and important agricultural products and would focus solely on increasing production each year in these four areas. It would abandon the idea of expanding productive capacities for comprehensive economic development and terminate, de-emphasize, or defer development in other industries and sectors.

In response to the Japanese demands for more coal, iron, and steel from Manchuria, the Manchukuo government instituted administrative reforms and austerity measures. Although there had been signs of an increased emphasis on supplying natural resources and semi-finished industrial products to Japan over the development of heavy and chemical industries in Manchukuo, it now became clear that the latter was being abandoned for the sake of the former. This policy became official after December 22, 1941, under the Second Five-Year Plan.[16] In addition to this major policy change, when Konoe formed his second cabinet in July 1940, Japan was swept by the "new order" movement to reform domestic political and economic arrangements. As a result, the priorities of Japanese policymakers shifted even more to boosting industrial production in Japan rather than in Manchukuo.

One of the major debates during this time was the move to form industrial control associations, and Ayukawa indicated his opinions of this issue for the automobile organization on September 22, 1940. To develop the automobile industry in Japan and Manchukuo, Ayukawa proposed the formation of a control company capitalized by four automobile manufacturers: Nissan, Manchuria Automobile Manufacturing, Toyota, and Tokyo Automobile. The control company would supervise the production of vehicles, and a marketing company would be established under the four companies. This proposed company would not only fulfill Ayukawa's long-cherished scheme of merging the major automobile companies but also create a desirable alternative to an industrial control association. Ayukawa wanted to maintain more market incentive than the reformist bureaucrats envisioned. In addition, to avoid a repeat of his Manchukuo experience, he wanted to minimize government and military intervention in the management of companies. It should come as no surprise that Ayukawa's scheme failed and an automobile industry control association was formed. As Ayukawa pointed out after the war, the association did not serve the purpose of effectively allocating resources for war production; the Japanese conglomerates dominated the control associations and expanded their control of the economy by maintaining self-regulation of these associations.[17]

Because MIDC failed to acquire foreign and Japanese technologies adequate to start automobile and aircraft industries, the most it accomplished was to manufacture automobile parts and to produce a few cars. The aircraft industry did better; MIDC produced high-quality practice planes, which Manchukuo used in actual combat during the Nomonhan Incident in 1939,[18] and toward the end of the war it was manufacturing bombers.[19]

Bureaucratic Nightmare in Manchukuo

According to Takasaki Tatsunosuke, who became the chairman of MIDC after Ayukawa's departure in 1943, the original plan would have been realized for the most part had the Sino-Japanese War ended quickly and the U.S.-Japan war been avoided. He, however, believed that capital was needed at the level specified in the revised plan. In Manchukuo, according to Takasaki, five major constraints paralyzed Ayukawa's scheme for comprehensive industrial development: (1) intervention by the Manchukuo government, (2) meddling by the Kwantung Army, (3) control of the distribution channels for the allocation of resources by the Japan-Manchuria (Nichiman) Trading Company, (4) managerial problems concerning the Manchuria Coal Mining Company (Mantan), and (5) lower than predicted mineral resources at Tungpientao.

Although Ayukawa was supposed to lead Manchukuo's industrialization, both the Manchukuo government and the Kwantung Army continued to intervene in MIDC's operations. The government maintained the legal right to intervene because the Law on the Control of Key Industries, passed in May 1937, stipulated that special and semi-special companies fell under government regulation. MIDC and all of its subsidiaries were either special or semi-special companies. Within the Manchukuo government, the Kwantung Army's Fourth Section was the most powerful voice in economic issues.[20]

The regulatory situation in Manchukuo increasingly disadvantaged Ayukawa's MIDC. Japan's increased orientation toward a controlled economy in 1938 prompted Manchukuo to establish, in May 1938, a Planning Committee chaired by the secretary general of the General Affairs Agency and consisting of seven committee members, seven secretaries, a special committee member, and a special secretary. The head of the Planning Bureau in the General Affairs Agency served as the committee's secretary general. The committee was supposed to function in the same way as Japan's Planning Board and formulate important economic policies through discussions involving the various organs of the Manchukuo government, the military, and the special companies; through cooperation between the private and public sectors; and through unified control of industries, the economy, and the administration of economic regulations. In August, the committee inaugurated the Committee on Prices and Material Resources (CPMR), which took charge of the mobilization of material resources in Manchukuo.[21]

After the Manchukuo government established the Planning Committee and the CPMR, it decided to increase and strengthen the power of the Japan-Manchuria Trading Company significantly. When the government had transferred the stocks of SMR subsidiaries to MIDC in March 1938, it did not transfer the shares of the Japan-Manchuria Trading Company. Formed during the reorganization of SMR in September 1936, this company resented MIDC, the newcomer, and gradually gained control over the distribution of important material resources, such as coal, iron and steel, nonferrous metals, and chemicals. The Planning Committee and CPMR supported the Trading Company over MIDC because of MIDC's failure to attract foreign investments.

On December 26, 1939, while Ayukawa was in Europe, the government changed the status of the Trading Company from a semi-special to a special company. The government's enhanced control gave the Trading Company an overwhelmingly important role since it now monopolized the distribution, as well as the import and export, of material resources such as coal, iron and steel, nonferrous metals, chemicals, fuel, and minerals. Thereafter the Planning Committee and the Trading Company played a central role in the control of material resources.[22]

Because of the Trading Company's role, MIDC could not freely transfer coal from Mantan to the Shōwa Steelworks; all materials necessary for production had to go through the Trading Company.[23] Because the Manchukuo government failed to coordinate distribution plans through the Trading Company effectively, many material resources were underutilized, and construction of production facilities and the manufacture of goods were delayed and sometimes even canceled. As early as August 1938, even before the reorganization of the Trading Company, MIDC complained to the government about its activities and demanded that it stop interfering with the distribution of material resources among MIDC subsidiaries, particularly those producing gold, iron ore, aluminum, airplanes, and automobiles. However, the deputy director of the Industry Bureau Shiina Etsusaburō, who had been seconded to the Manchukuo government by MCI, rejected the demand; Shiina had never really supported MIDC.[24]

Nor could MIDC push its subsidiary Mantan, which controlled most of the coal supplies in Manchukuo, the main exception being SMR-owned Fushun, to achieve the goals for coal production. Coal was a key natural resource for heavy industrialization, and coal and iron processing had to be coordinated in producing steel. Manchukuo's failure to reach the target figures in its industrialization plan owed much to the failures of its coal mines, its dependence on coking coal from north China, and its inability to meet the heating requirements of the new factories. According to the revised plan, Mantan was supposed to produce 70.3 percent of all coal in Manchukuo (the Fushun and Penshiu collieries were to produce 3.9 percent and 8.7 percent, respectively). Mantan achieved 66 percent of the targeted output for 1937, 68 percent for 1938, and 77 percent for 1939. In comparison, Fushun achieved 93, 95, and 102 percent of its quotas for the same years, and Penshiu achieved 95, 110, and 90 percent. Because Mantan required new investment—and therefore time—for its coal mines to achieve the projected production goals, MIDC had to rely increasingly on the more costly, less productive, older coal mines at Fushun. Under the circumstances, the decision in May 1938 to set Fushun's total output over the next five years at 10 million tons and Mantan's at 18 million tons was unreasonable. Mantan failed for many reasons: labor shortages; insufficient electricity and frequent blackouts; difficulties in acquiring machinery from Japan, the United States, and Germany; flooding of the mine shafts because of heavy rainfall; transportation delays; atrocious working conditions, particularly for Manchu, Chinese, and Korean workers; and antagonism between MIDC and Mantan, which was run by Kōmoto Daisaku, the man responsible for Chang Tso-lin's assassination in 1928.

Yet another reason for the failure of Manchukuo's industrialization was the disappointing findings at Tungpientao. Optimistic assumptions about that area's mineral resources were one cause for the high production targets set for iron and steel in the original and the revised plans. MIDC had hoped to create major coal, iron, and steel operations in the area. The Tungpientao Development Company was established in May 1938 to exploit these resources, but because of poor quality of the ore, inadequate transportation, shortages of labor and resources, and guerrilla activities, the company produced only insignificant amounts. As a result, MIDC had to continue to rely on the Shōwa Steelworks, which produced 82 percent to 87 percent of the pig iron, 92 percent to 100 percent of the steel, and 63 percent to 91 percent of the rolled steel in Manchukuo between 1937 and 1942.[25]

In confronting the five problems pointed out by Takasaki, Ayukawa did try to absorb Mantan and the Japan-Manchuria Trading Company. In the fall of 1938, he asked his close friend Baron Itō Bunkichi to recruit Itō's protégé at MCI, Yoshino Shinji, to join MIDC as its vice chairman.[26] Yoshino, who considered himself a competent administrator, had been disappointed in May 1938 by Prime Minister Konoe's decision to drop him as minister of commerce and industry and fill this position and that of minister of finance by a Harvard-educated leader of the Mitsui group, Ikeda Seihin, who had briefly served as governor of the Bank of Japan. Yoshino thought that his knowledge of how other countries had mobilized for World War I and demobilized after peace would help Japan. In fall 1938, with travel expenses paid by Baron Itō and a letter of introduction to President Roosevelt from Asano Ryōzō, vice president of the steel firm Nihon kōkan, who had known Roosevelt since their Harvard years, Yoshino was ready to travel to the United States in December to study the New Deal economic programs. Then came MIDC's offer, which he felt reluctant to accept. In the end, Yoshino was persuaded by his protégé Kishi Nobusuke, deputy director of the Industry Department of Manchukuo; Isogai Rensuke, chief of staff of the Kwantung Army; and Itagaki Seishirō, minister of the Army. Baron Itō had apparently staged these meetings, presumably at Ayukawa's request. (When Yoshino paid a courtesy call on Ikeda Seihin, Ikeda indicated his disgust that Yoshino was joining Ayukawa's group. Ikeda was probably upset by the fact that the Kwantung Army had picked Ayukawa's group for monopolistic projects in Manchukuo over Mitsui and by the fact that Yoshino had declined Ikeda's and Konoe's offer of a post in the North China Development Corporation.)[27]

After Yoshino joined MIDC, Ayukawa asked him to find ways to absorb Mantan and the Japan-Manchuria Trading Company. After looking into the matter, Yoshino told Ayukawa that nothing could be done without changing the laws concerning those two companies. Aside from this legal obstacle, Yoshino also failed because, unlike Ayukawa, he neglected to pay frequent visits to the colonel in charge of the Kwantung Army's Fourth Section. Yoshino's unpopularity among Kwantung Army officers owed much to his failure to cultivate them. Despite the military's dislike of Yoshino, Ayukawa tried to trade positions with him in the spring of 1940, so that in his new position as chairman, Yoshino could help MIDC absorb the two companies. In January 1941, Ayukawa gave up the idea, and Yoshino became an advisor to MIDC and an economic advisor to Manchukuo. Takasaki Tatsunosuke succeeded Yoshino as vice chairman.[28]

With the backing of the Kwantung Army, Ayukawa finally managed to oust Kōmoto and his cronies from Mantan's Board of Directors in September 1940. He, in turn, became its chairman. He then formulated an idea to split Mantan into smaller companies so as to make them compete and achieve efficiency in management, an idea realized after Ayukawa left MIDC.[29]

After mid-1941, MIDC focused primarily on raising capital for the industrialization of Manchukuo because both Ayukawa and Takasaki concluded that they could not solve MIDC's managerial problems, including the lack of communication not only between MIDC and its subsidiaries but also among the chairmen of MIDC's subsidiaries, as well as the rivalry between chairmen from Nissan and chairmen from the SMR. Because of these circumstances, it was impossible to manage projects to promote Manchukuo's comprehensive industrial development. Takasaki was shocked to find out during an inspection tour that a furnace at the Shōwa Steelworks was not running because it could not secure enough coal. Takasaki attributed the problem to animosity toward MIDC on the part of Shōwa Steelworks and Mantan. Employees in both companies felt bitter about being "taken over" by MIDC, and Mantan resented having to supply coal to a steel company that enjoyed strong ties to the SMR-owned Fushun Coal Mining Company, the rival of Mantan.[30]

In May 1941, Ayukawa founded the Manchuria Investment Securities Company (Manshū tōshi shōken kabushiki kaisha, or Mantō) to invest in Manchuria by issuing stock with a 5 percent annual return guaranteed by the Manchukuo government. Ayukawa issued the stock by using ¥400 million worth of stocks in Nissan subsidiaries owned by MIDC as collateral for investments by Japanese life insurance companies, which sought alternatives to government bonds, which yielded only a 3 percent annual return. In addition, Ayukawa secured an exemption from taxes for selling the stocks of Nissan subsidiaries that Mantō had inherited from MIDC. Finally, under a Japanese law, Mantō managed to guarantee an 8 percent return on its stock for six years. Despite these favorable conditions, Mantō could not invest much in Manchukuo; between 1943 and 1945, the military ordered Mantō to invest ¥650 million out of ¥700 million in Japan. Only ¥30 million was invested in Manchukuo. All profits went for dividend payments to the life insurance companies, and Mantō acquired capital only from Japan. This situation, however, did not prevent increases in the targeted figures for capital under the revised five-year plan and the subsequent 1941–45 plan. Although only an insignificant amount of capital was raised from foreign countries and capital inflow from Japan slowed after 1942, the amount of capital raised in Manchuria was more than enough to offset these two setbacks. Between 1937 and 1945, capital investment in Manchukuo reached 167.7 percent of the target figure of ¥6.06 billion.[31]

In February 1941, MIDC announced a reorganization of its corporate structure, to take effect in August. August 1, 1941, officially marked the end of MIDC's position as the central organization in Manchukuo's comprehensive industrial development. The reorganization narrowed MIDC's responsibilities primarily to making important personnel decisions, providing technical guidance, and raising capital. Since technical guidance was the least important factor and the government, contrary to Takasaki's hopes, goaded MIDC to raise capital, the sole power that remained in MIDC's hands was the right to make personnel decisions. However, the Manchukuo government and the Kwantung Army continued to meddle in this area.[32]

Ayukawa failed in his endeavors to lead Manchukuo's industrialization programs and to implement his ideas on the management of the political economy of Manchukuo and Japan because his ideas conflicted with the thinking of civilian and military bureaucrats on managing the economy to meet the imperatives of the changing war situation. For Ayukawa, the war years were a time when he tried to formulate better and more efficient methods for managing the Japanese economy. But, in attempting to carry out his ideas, he again ran into bureaucratic opposition and experienced failures and frustrations.

On May 6, 1942, Ayukawa delivered a speech on the subject of the future pattern of economic policy based on the nation's wartime experiences to MIDC's Wednesday Meeting group. Ayukawa argued that whereas economics had tended to drive politics in the market-oriented economy in Japan before the war worsened, the wartime experience would lead to a mixture of regulated and market-oriented economic practices after the war. He thought that even the Germans, whose economic policies he described as "[economic] regulations based on totalitarianism" (*zentaishugi tōsei*), might switch to such practices.[33]

On January 7, 1943, at an MIDC stockholders' meeting, Ayukawa announced his retirement as chairman and from the front lines of business. Ayukawa expressed his regret that the international situation had proved unfavorable to his plans to bring direct and indirect foreign investments to Manchuria. At the time he had become the chairman of MIDC, he thought it would take at least ten years, if not twenty, under ordinary circumstances, to determine the failure or success of Manchukuo's industrialization program. Because he could not claim that he managed the company effectively under the system of heavy economic regulation then in force, he thought it wise to pass the baton to Takasaki at the end of his first term; Ayukawa served as counselor to MIDC until the end of the war and continued to confer with Takasaki on MIDC's personnel decisions. Ayukawa told the audience that henceforth he would concentrate on being the chairman of a research institute, Giseikai, which he had created in September 1942.

The Giseikai's mission was to conduct scientific research on ameliorating the pitfalls in the transition from a laissez-faire economy to a command economy so as to better manage the economics of the Great East Asia Coprosperity Sphere. It also promoted Ayukawa's continuing agenda of allowing businessmen, rather than bureaucrats, to run the economy. At the time Yoshino Shinji became MIDC's vice chairman in 1938, Ayukawa had been lobbying the Manchukuo government to implement his remedies for the problems of running a planned economy. Ayukawa had been arguing since 1936 that the government's economic plans failed to give adequate consideration to the time factor in coordinating all the elements underlying the management of the economy.

In 1938, Ayukawa had proposed the establishment of an "economic general staff" in Manchukuo, The most qualified Japanese businessmen and academics were to be invited to help run Manchukuo's planned economy by forming a council with representatives from the Manchukuo government and the Kwantung Army to review all administrative proposals for economic regulation before presenting them to the General Affairs Agency, the most powerful body in Manchukuo on economic matters after the Kwantung Army's Fourth Section. During his tenure at MIDC, Ayukawa's proposal did not win the approval of the General Affairs Agency's secretary general, probably because the agency already had its own Planning Committee. What Ayukawa wanted was to realize his vision of businessmen efficiently managing the Manchukuo economy, rather than bureaucrats or military officers, whom he saw as impediments to that endeavor. At the time General Ishiwara Kanji had recruited Ayukawa to Manchukuo, he had told Ayukawa to make this happen as soon as possible, and Ayukawa had wanted to achieve this goal. To Ayukawa's dismay, the closest he got was the Council of Economic Advisors, which consisted of Ayukawa himself, SMR president Ōmura Takuichi (1872–1946), and Yoshino Shinji and served as the nominal body to save Ayukawa's face.

Ayukawa had some successes with the Giseikai to the extent that it organized research activities. Business executives such as Nagasaki Eizō, president of Shōwa Oil Company, and Kobiyama Naoto, chairman of the iron and steel industry control association, former MIDC board member, and ex-president of Shōwa Steelworks, participated in its research projects, which ultimately sought to make the regulated economy run more efficiently through radical administrative reorganization. As part of his Giseikai activities, Ayukawa also arranged financial support for other think tanks that were conducting scientific studies of economic issues. Without attaching strings, he financed the Labor Science Research Institute (Rōdō kagaku kenkyūjo) and labor union expert Takano Iwasaburō's (1871–1949) Ōhara Social Problems Research Institute (Ōhara shakai mondai kenkyūjo), which, as a result, was saved from bankruptcy. Ayukawa supported Takano, Morito Tatsuo (1888–1984), and Ōuchi Hyoe (1888–1980), who was a famous Marxist economist at the University of Tokyo. Ōuchi also helped with much of the economic and industrial research at the Giseikai. Ayukawa hoped that Giseikai's projects would lead to the organization of a study group consisting of academics, businessmen, military officers, and civil servants to model the administration of state economic policies. According to Ayukawa, like mass production, economic policies had to be formulated by trial and error. Even though Ayukawa expressed the fear, during his retirement speech, that government economic statistics, on which Giseikai based its research, were full of errors (a fear he later confirmed), he emphasized that if the implementation of economic policies by technocrats could somehow be rehearsed at a research institute by incorporating the time factor into coordinating and managing regulated economic policies, these technocrats could evaluate the policies' effectiveness before their actual implementation. Administering these policies thus might be rationalized and simplified.

Upon returning to Japan, Ayukawa was nominated as a member of the House of Peers in January 1943. In November, he assented to Cabinet Secretary Hoshino Naoki's request that he join the Tōjō cabinet as economic advisor. He served in two other cabinets in this capacity before the Japanese surrender, one headed by Koiso Kuniaki (1880–1950) and the other by Suzuki Kantarō (1867–1948). He lobbied each cabinet to back his projects, but the only time that he thought he might be successful was when the Tōjō Cabinet decided on July 14, 1944, to establish the Economic Policy Evaluation Organization (Keizai enren shisaku kikan), an organization that seemed to him a possible first step toward realizing the goals sought in his Giseikai activities. This decision was never implemented because two weeks later, on July 18, the Tōjō cabinet collapsed after a successful and fierce political maneuvering to oust Tōjō against Emperor Hirohito's wish by such influential people as Lord Keeper of Privy Seal Kido, Prince Konoe Fumimaro, and former prime ministers and top naval officers Okada Keisuke (1868–1952) and Yonai Mitsumasa, top business executives such as Ikeda Shigeaki and Fujiyama Aiichirō (1897–1985), and Tōjō cabinet member Kishi Nobusuke, who was then a cabinet minister, vice minister of munitions, and a Lower House member. These men were critical of Tōjō, who was gaining dictatorial power, and of Japan's devastating losses in its war against the Allies.[34] At the time of the Japanese surrender on August 15, 1945, Ayukawa and Fujiyama Aiichirō represented the business community as advisors to the government in a meeting with the members of the Suzuki cabinet; they learned that the emperor was about to announce Japan's surrender. According to Fujiyama, Ayukawa turned to him and said: "From now on, it is going to be a time when real industrialists are to work. I am very happy that I am going to be busy. From now on, it is going to be our era, and we must work hard."[35] Because Ayukawa had resumed his job as chairman of Nissan Motors (a position that he last held in 1941) in September 1944 when it had been renamed Nissan Heavy Industries Company (Nissan jyūkōgyō kabushikigaisha), Ayukawa may have been looking forward to renewing his efforts to manufacture automobiles for the peacetime economy.

History did not smile on Ayukawa, however. He could not resume his activities for U.S.-Japan economic cooperation as a means of achieving economic rehabilitation until the spring of 1948. As a suspected war criminal, he was held for 21 months in Sugamo prison for interrogation and possibly for trial. In January 1947, during his incarceration, he learned that Miho Mikitarō, his confidant of many years, had passed away. Miho's death was a huge shock for Ayukawa. Even though Ayukawa was cleared of the charges and released at the end of August 1947 (see Chapter 9 for details), as the founder of Nissan Holding Company he was barred from returning to his companies because the Supreme Commander for the Allied Powers (SCAP) had designated the holding company a zaibatsu.

NINE

Re-creating a
Common Interest: U.S.-Japan
Relations, 1945–1948

Shortly after the Japanese surrender, Yoshida Shigeru, who later became foreign minister and then prime minister, wrote to Kurusu Saburō, a good friend from their years in the Foreign Service, that he hoped Japan would achieve its economic recovery through technological and scientific research as well as the introduction of American capital.[1] How was this to be achieved? Would Japan continue to follow the neo-mercantilist strategy it had pursued since the 1930s, or would it revive the relatively open trade policy that it had followed for much of the 1920s? As would become apparent later, Kurusu favored a liberal trade policy and an approach similar to Ayukawa's for reconstructing Japan's industries. Much as in the prewar period, Ayukawa and Kurusu, who were good friends, hoped to establish and stabilize bilateral relations with the United States based on commerce and Japan's economic recovery. Their views gained momentum as policymakers in Washington began to support the idea of giving Japan's economic recovery priority over the occupation's economic reforms, an idea represented and promoted by, among others, Herbert Hoover and former executives of Dillon, Read and Company such as James V. Forrestal and William H. Draper, Jr.

Thoughts and Activities of Ayukawa's Friends, 1945–1947

In September 1946, during his imprisonment in Sugamo prison as a war crimes suspect, Ayukawa received a letter from Kurusu Saburō, who was living in his mountain villa in Karuizawa with his American wife, to whom he had been married for over thirty years. Kurusu had withdrawn from public life over the death of his son, a pilot who died when he single-handedly confronted a squadron of American planes over Chiba prefecture shortly before the Japanese surrender. After hearing about Ayukawa from Miho Mikitarō, however, Kurusu felt he had to come forward. As he wrote to Ayukawa, "My discussions with Mr. Miho reminded me of my resistance to the direction of the domestic 'driving force,' the attempt and failure in Berlin [in early 1940] by you and me to move Japan away from the Axis and align ourselves with the United States, and the final defeat after flying to Washington."[2]

Around the time Ayukawa went to Sugamo prison in December 1945, Kurusu had come up with an idea similar to what Secretary of Commerce W. Averell Harriman (1891–1986) would later suggest to the American government. He advised Prime Minister Shidehara Kijūrō (1872–1951), who was in office from October 1945 to April 1946, to ask the General Headquarters of the Allied Powers (GHQ) to invite prominent American businessmen to serve as economic advisors to the occupation forces and prevent the military officers from tinkering with the Japanese economy. Shidehara, however, said that it was too early to make such a suggestion.[3] Kurusu's recommendations for achieving Japan's postwar economic recovery paralleled the arguments Hoover and Ayukawa had been making since the prewar years. He wanted to re-establish and stabilize bilateral relations centering around commerce. On the political front, Kurusu wanted Japan to stir the American sense of justice as the United States considered the new order in the Far East. On the economic front, he wanted Japan to use America's enlightened self-interest to promote Japan's industrial recovery.

Kurusu thought the United States should allow Japan to pay war reparations gradually rather than require the immediate liquidation of Japanese assets, and he wanted Tokyo to appeal to Washington to agree to this. The two countries should avoid the kind of reparations imposed on Germany after World War I. Japan should argue for separate consideration of the issues of reparations and the re-establishment of international trade and make Japan's economic recovery a prerequisite for the complete payment of reparations.

Kurusu shared Ayukawa's aversion to allowing bureaucrats to be responsible for Japanese initiatives on economic issues and proposed the establishment of JATRA (Japan-American Trade and Rehabilitation Administration), an organization headquartered in the United States, with an office in Japan. The Japanese side of JATRA would consist of representatives from the Mitsui, Mitsubishi, Sumitomo, and Yokohama Specie banks, major trading companies in the import-export business, and import-export trade organizations for important materials and merchandise. If one or more of the banks could not serve as a facilitator, then organizations such as the Japan Economic Federation or the World Economic Research Council, a group affiliated with the federation, could serve this purpose. Although a government representative would head the Japanese side, Kurusu wanted to minimize the involvement of bureaucrats. He wanted skillful Japanese negotiators to win U.S. support for Japan's economic recovery, but these negotiators had to overcome the slow, bureaucratized style of prewar negotiations. He thought Japanese businessmen more qualified than the bureaucrats to work on economic matters since they were more sensitive to the needs of the Japanese economy.[4]

In seeking American economic assistance, Kurusu thought that dumping Japanese products to earn foreign exchange would not be profitable for Japan. He was deeply aware that Japanese dumping had been a source of trade friction before the war. He proposed that JATRA be in charge of the funding of trade with the United States so that dumping could be prevented by exchange licenses and other measures. While securing the necessary foreign exchange, Japan should first strive for the recovery of light industries and then the heavy and chemical industries. Like Ayukawa before the war, Kurusu wanted joint U.S.-Japanese management of Japan's heavy and chemical industries. Japan should argue to the Americans that since the United States enjoyed supremacy in the air, had demilitarized Japan, and possessed the atomic bomb, it should not fear the possible re-creation of Japan as a military power based on its heavy and chemical industries.

Ayukawa undoubtedly agreed with Kurusu's approach to reconstructing Japan's industries; Kurusu was clearly seeking to rebuild bilateral relations through Japanese business leadership, not through Japanese bureaucrats. While Kurusu busied himself with realizing these plans, Ayukawa received help from an old American friend, Robert Moss, whose assistance was reinforced by the emerging American preference for a "reverse course" in Japan. Moss's brother-in-law Burton Crane was a *New York Times* correspondent in Tokyo, and, like Harry F. Kern (1911–96) and Compton Packenham of *Newsweek*, he viewed the purges of the Japanese business community as a major factor in the postwar economic havoc in Japan. Because of his views, he was considered by leftists to be a right-wing journalist. Moss had worked in Tokyo as a business executive for many years before Pearl Harbor. As a result of his ties to Moss and his firsthand observation of the economic chaos in Japan, Crane was aware of the questionable treatment of businessmen, including Ayukawa, who were being interrogated as possible war criminals. In fall 1946, Crane received a letter dated October 21, 1946, from Moss, who stated that "in November, 1939 and again in June and July, 1940, I acted as an intermediary in protracted negotiations between Mr. Yoshisuke Aikawa and Mr. Joseph C. Grew, then U.S. Ambassador in Tokyo relating to plans proposed by Mr. Aikawa for the purpose of avoiding hostilities between Japan and the United States." Because Moss heard that Ayukawa was "now on trial for his life, and as these negotiations disclosed much information regarding his attitudes and his thinking at that time, I feel that I should offer to reveal such information as I possess on this subject to the proper authorities." Crane brought Moss's letter to SCAP, and although the interrogators at SCAP did not ask Moss for further information, the letter without doubt helped to clear Ayukawa's name.[5]

In January and February 1946, Ayukawa had talked about his diplomatic efforts to avoid war with the United States, including the episode in which Moss had rendered his assistance (see Chapters 6 and 7) during his interrogations by Solis Horwitz, staff member of the International Prosecution Section (IPS), in preparation for the International Military Tribunal for the Far East (IMTFE).[6] The direct and indirect charges against Ayukawa were:

He planned, prepared, initiated and waged aggressive warfare and was a member of a conspiracy in relation thereto in that:

1. He was an ardent militarist and as such conspired with the Kwangtung [*sic*] Army and other militarists to execute plans and preparations for aggressive wars.

2. He was largely responsible for the economic exploitation of Manchuria and in particular for the development of war industries in Manchuria.

3. He was materially responsible for the development of war industries in Japan and for the carrying out of the industrial expansion plans which had as their object the urging of aggressive wars.

4. During the war he acted as an adviser to the Government in connection with the industrial measures necessary for the conduct of the war.[7]

On March 7, 1946, Henry A. Hauxhurst, IPS attorney, and Horwitz reported to Chief Prosecutor for the IMTFE Joseph B. Keenan (1888–1954) that IPS could not justify treating Ayukawa as a war criminal. However, a week later both men recommended to Keenan that Ayukawa's "case be left open as it is believed that evidence which is produced in connection with the preparation for the Trial may develop additional facts in reference to [Ayukawa's] activities in [Manchukuo] which may prove him to be a war criminal."[8] On August 1, Keenan, in a memorandum to the Legal Section of GHQ's G-2 (intelligence) unit, concluded that the investigation of Ayukawa had failed "to reveal at this time evidence sufficient to warrant charging him with any offense recognizable before the International Military Tribunal for the Far East" and recommended Ayukawa's "release from Sugamo Prison at this time subject to his reincarceration in the event additional evidence is discovered, unless the Legal Section recommends to the contrary."[9] Finally, on May 14, 1947, the Legal Section of G-2 concluded, "it would be very difficult to prove that [Ayukawa] was a party to the planning and/or execution of aggressive war. Unless it is decided to indict him on the prima facie evidence of having made business profits in wartime G-2 strongly recommends his release without preference of charges."[10] By the end of August 1947 Ayukawa was again a free man.

In summer 1947, the increasing trend toward a "reverse course" in Japan enabled Kurusu to write a letter of appeal to Bernard M. Baruch, who had negotiated with him shortly before Pearl Harbor, for American economic assistance to Japan. The fact that Major General Charles A. Willoughby (1892–1972), director of G-2, supported Kurusu in sending this letter on July 7, 1947, indicates the changing trend in American policy toward Japan. Kurusu wrote that "if all leading banks in Japan get together and organize a syndicate and succeed in soliciting the participation of some powerful American banks which are now preparing to operate in this part of the world, it will certainly go a long way towards the reestablishment of the public confidence." He also thought that "if this syndicate . . . announce[d that it would] . . . accept long term deposits in Yen, which, through some necessary arrangement with our government, may enjoy a certain priority in being converted into U.S. dollars in future by depositor's choice, a considerable amount of our currency which is now hoarded by the people will rapidly be accumulated into the hands of this new international organization." Furthermore, Kurusu argued that "the syndicate will serve as an excellent intermediary for American trade and investment." He emphasized that "the effect of such a cooperation will be very farreaching in regaining a popular sense of security and in checking [Japan's] present inflationary trend." Finally, Kurusu "earnestly pray[ed] for at this juncture . . . some practical suggestion along this line may be forthcoming from a personage of international renown like your good self, and may render its powerful contribution in restoring public confidence and elsewhere."[11] Kurusu's appeal, however, did not produce any results.

In addition to Kurusu, another friend of Ayukawa and his successor as head of MIDC since December 1942, Takasaki Tatsunosuke, sent a plea for American economic assistance to another prominent American statesman. On December 7, 1947, at a time when the Diet was intensively discussing the Deconcentration Bill, an antimonopoly law to dissolve the large combines, Takasaki wrote Herbert Hoover that he believed "the rehabilitation of industry in Japan entirely depends upon the technical and financial assistance of the U.S.A. Japan will never be reconstructed unless sympathetic aid of your country is extended to her." He appealed for Hoover's assistance for the two companies he had been instrumental in establishing, the Oriental Can Company and the Oriental Steel Company, so that these companies could get back on their feet.[12] Until October, Takasaki had been forced to stay in Manchuria as an economic and technical advisor to the Chinese Nationalist government and as the chief supervisor of the repatriation of Japanese civilians. The Soviets, the Chinese Communists, and the Nationalist Chinese came in successive waves to Manchuria, and Takasaki was busy negotiating and cooperating with these groups, particularly with the Soviets and the Nationalist Chinese, in liquidating the assets of the MIDC. Toward the end of 1945, Takasaki also helped write economic reports for the Reparations Mission, headed by Edwin W. Pauley (1903–81), a California oil entrepreneur and an antimonopolist who believed in demanding heavy reparations from Germany and Japan (but not pastoralizing them), breaking the power of German and Japanese combines, and transferring Japanese reparations, mainly plants and equipment owned by the zaibatsu, to neighboring

Asian countries so as to achieve a more balanced regional economic growth much less dependent on the Japanese economy. Takasaki was well aware of the mounting tensions between the Nationalist regime and the Soviets over who ultimately would control the economic resources and industries of Manchuria, a region described by Steven Levine as "the largest and most industrialized region in Asia," in the immediate postwar years. He also had a firsthand view of the mounting tensions between the United States and the Soviet Union.[13]

Hoover's Political Comeback After May 1945

Although Hoover apparently ignored Takasaki's plea, he had been a leading advocate of a lenient policy toward Japan since the closing of the Pacific War because of his concerns about Soviet expansionism in Asia. After Japan's surrender, Hoover was active behind the scenes in promoting milder occupation policies toward Japan and Germany in order to contain the spread of communism.

Toward the end of the Pacific War, a conservative political trend and the death of President Roosevelt on April 12, 1945, thrust Herbert Hoover, the most knowledgeable statesman in America about the Far East, back into the political limelight. During the war, President Roosevelt adamantly opposed advice by various leading public figures, including Columbia University President Nicholas Murray Butler, Adlai Stevenson, Secretary of the Navy Frank Knox, and Director James F. Byrnes (1879–1972) of the Office of Economic Stabilization, that a new food administration be established and headed by Hoover. In June 1943, Bernard Baruch informed Hoover about an episode in which Roosevelt got upset after receiving such advice from Knox, Stevenson, and Byrnes. Ten days after Roosevelt's death, Secretary of War Stimson asked Hoover to come to his home for a discussion, but nothing developed (Stimson had been Hoover's secretary of state). But during a May 1 meeting attended by Stimson, Secretary of the Navy James V. Forrestal, who had assumed Knox's position on the latter's death in April 1944, and Undersecretary of State Joseph Grew, who was also serving as acting secretary of state, recommended to President Harry S Truman (1884–1972) that Hoover become an informal advisor. Hoover had been a hero in orchestrating the American famine relief in Europe following World War I, and both Stimson and Grew agreed with Forrestal that the U.S. government needed Hoover for such a project as the war was coming to an end in Europe. Forrestal opposed the approach advocated by Secretary of Treasury Henry Morgenthau to create a pastoral Germany and argued for the need to dismantle Germany's war machines but to retain its industrial capability. Forrestal had the same views on the issue of Japan's postwar economic recovery. He was already concerned about the spread of Soviet communism in the postwar era and wanted to use Germany and Japan in containing the Soviet expansion.

But how could the United States get Japan to surrender sooner rather than later? Grew's answer was to modify the demand for unconditional surrender by indicating to the Japanese that the imperial throne would be preserved; Grew felt that this guarantee would lead to Japan's early surrender and save many American lives. Furthermore, the issue of the throne could be revisited after it had been used to expedite reform measures during the occupation of Japan. Grew was a relatively close friend of William Castle, Hoover's confidant, who, as Hoover's undersecretary of state, had been instrumental in choosing Grew as ambassador to Japan in 1932.[14]

In May 1945, Truman brought Hoover back to Washington to advise on famine relief in war-ravaged areas. Before meeting the president, Hoover told Stimson that the United States should seek ways to negotiate a peace with Japan without having to land on Japan's main islands, since the continuation of the war in Asia would come at the expense of a half-million to a million American casualties and only profit the Soviet Union's territorial ambitions in Asia (the Soviet Union had informed Japan in April that it would not renew the bilateral neutrality pact due to expire in April 1946). Hoover considered the new Japanese prime minister, Suzuki Kantarō, who was appointed on April 7, 1945, a moderate, and he had thought all along that the Japanese emperor was a reasonable man. Like Forrestal, Stimson, and Grew, Hoover agreed that although the military industries of Japan and Germany had to be destroyed, the other industries were vital to the recovery of the world economy. Hoover emphasized that Suzuki was a moderate and suggested an early peace with Japan, a possibility that he thought had a slight chance of succeeding if it were based on a joint declaration with England and, if possible, China. Hoover thought the Japanese emperor and the Suzuki cabinet might acquiesce to a joint declaration to surrender if the terms of surrender indicated, on the one hand, unconditional surrender of all Japanese military forces and the complete disarmament of Japan for a generation and, on the other hand, no desire on the Allies' part to destroy the imperial throne. Hoover also wanted the United States both to prevent a Soviet penetration into the Far East and to continue peaceful relations with Moscow. Hoover told Truman that the Russians would declare war on Japan only at the very last moment and cautioned the president to avoid war with the Soviet Union because that would mean the end of Western civilization.

Hoover also suggested to Truman that this joint declaration should indicate that although the Japanese-occupied territories in China, including Manchuria, should be restored to China, Korea and Formosa should be placed under a Japanese trusteeship. Hoover believed that the Koreans and Formosans were incapable of governing themselves. At the same time, he praised Japanese civilian leaders "who are liberal-minded, who have in certain periods governed Japan and in these periods they gave full cooperation in [sic] peaceful forces of the world." He believed that "the only hope of stable and progressive government" in Japan was to have "this group" restored to power. (In making this statement, Hoover probably had in mind the Japanese political and business leaders who were close to American business leaders.)

Three of Hoover's suggestions ran counter to the common positions of Truman, Stimson, Forrestal, and Grew. First, Hoover emphasized the need to achieve peace with Japan by making a joint declaration with Great Britain and possibly China before the Russians intervened in Japan. Second, Taiwan and Korea should continue to be part of Japan. And third, the longer the war with Japan, the greater the possibility of American postwar economic stagnation and hence shrinking of American ability to supply resources for postwar world recovery. Although both Forrestal and Grew were concerned about Russian expansionism in Europe and Asia, both were willing to go along with Truman's and Stimson's reluctant support of the Yalta agreements of February 1945, although, as Walter LaFeber argues, Truman wanted to dismantle the Yalta agreement once he learned all its provisions. Hoover was unaware of the secret agreements in the Yalta accord.

In the afternoon of the same day he saw Hoover, Truman met with Grew, who argued the need to indicate to the Japanese that the United States had no intention of destroying the imperial throne. From this point until Truman's departure for the Potsdam Conference, this idea was pushed by Grew, Grew's subordinates Eugene Dooman and Joseph Ballantine, Secretary of War Stimson, and Assistant Secretary of War John J. McCloy (1895–1989) despite the harsh views on the treatment of the Japanese emperor and the imperial throne that dominated American public opinion at the time and despite fierce opposition from two assistant secretaries of state, Dean G. Acheson (1893–1971), who in the postwar years admitted he had been wrong on this point, and Archibald MacLeish. But the idea of allowing the retention of the imperial throne stalled not only because of the divisions among American policymakers over internal political conditions in Japan as well as progress in the development of the atomic bomb but also because of the divisions among Japanese policymakers over the issue of surrender or fight to the bitter end. Although on May 28 Truman commented to Grew that he shared Grew's view on the imperial throne, on the following day when seven policymakers met at the Pentagon to discuss this issue at the president's request, although Forrestal, Stimson, and Army Chief of Staff George C. Marshall (1880–1959) agreed with Grew, they opposed Grew's recommendation that the president make a public statement to this effect for military reasons. Truman, Stimson, Forrestal, Grew, and Marshall knew that this reason was the atomic bomb, but Grew and Forrestal shared the view of Hoover, who was unaware of the program, that in the near future an exhausted Japan would surrender if the United States promised to preserve the imperial throne. In the end, after attempting to persuade the Japanese to surrender by indirectly indicating in the Potsdam Declaration the retention of the imperial throne, two atomic bombs were dropped on Japan at the decision of top American policymakers led by Truman, Stimson, Marshall, and James F. Byrnes, who had replaced Stettinius as secretary of state on July 3. The Soviet Union declared war on Japan shortly before the second bomb was dropped. Ironically, Hoover's estimates of a half-million to a million American casualties became Truman's and Stimson's rationale for dropping the atomic bomb. With the Japanese surrender, Grew resigned as undersecretary of state. Byrnes chose as his successor Dean G. Acheson, who until the start of the Cold War was sympathetic to the idea of using China rather than Japan for advancing American interests in the Far East.[15]

In the immediate aftermath of World War II, Hoover was the spokesperson in Washington for the argument that the United States had to contain the Soviet Union's expansionistic tendencies. As he had done while in charge of food relief operations in Europe after World War I, he argued for using food and other economic means to curtail the threat of worldwide communist expansion. When, at President Truman's request, he toured the world in spring 1946 to survey famine conditions, he made this argument privately and publicly, both in Washington and abroad.[16]

In the immediate postwar period, Hoover was concerned with restoring economic order in Japan. On November 12, 1945, he handed Lieutenant General Robert C. Richardson in New York a memorandum for the latter's friend since West Point, General Douglas MacArthur (1880–1964), who had been Hoover's chief of staff during his years in the White House. Hoover worried that "all reports . . . indicate an impending food shortage in Japan which may amount to death for from three to ten million people." Hoover praised MacArthur's policy of "gradually dissolv[ing] the Bismarckian government and social structure which the Japanese adapted to their own ideas many years ago." He predicted "General MacArthur's second great triumph and service to the world" if the Japanese, whom Hoover perceived as "an imitative people," could accept a peaceful and democratic state by "what liberal elements there are in Jpan [sic]." To achieve this goal, Hoover stressed "productivity and ability to build a self-supporting economic state." For the United States to realize its long-term objective of democracy in Japan, it had to prevent "a cesspool of poverty, starvation and its consequent constant breeding of hate and antagonisms."[17]

Hoover saw Japan as a bulwark against the advancement of communism. His idea was to contain the communist advance more through economic than through military means. Hoover began advocating the containment of communism a year before George F. Kennan (1904–) wrote his famous policy paper on that topic. Furthermore, by May 1946, Hoover had concluded that the Chiang regime was not an effective bulwark against communism. During his trip around the world for emergency food relief, he visited China from April 30 to May 3, before he went to Japan. Hoover criticized the Nationalist regime as incompetent and corrupt.[18] In addition, Hoover felt that the Chiang regime was ineffective against the Soviet Union.[19] In fact, he was aware that the regime was losing to both the Chinese and the Soviet communists.[20] When he met General George C. Marshall, who was attempting to mediate the Chinese civil war, Hoover argued that a Communist-Nationalist coalition government was an impossibility, and even if it became possible, the Chinese Communists would take over the government, as their colleagues had the coalition governments of Eastern Europe. Hoover wrote scathingly about Marshall's comment that most of the Chinese Communists were not ideologues and were, in fact, liberal.[21]

During his trip to Japan, Hoover had three private conversations with General MacArthur: on May 4 for three hours, on May 5 for an hour, and on May 6 for an hour. MacArthur was grateful for Hoover's support of the food program for the Japanese and shared Hoover's animosity toward Roosevelt and his belief in the need to make Japan an ideological dam against the spread of communism in Asia. MacArthur agreed with what Hoover had suggested to Truman during their meeting in May 1945; "MacArthur said . . . we would have avoided all of the losses, the Atomic bomb, and the entry of Russia into Manchuria." Both men thought the American war with Japan reflected "a madman's [i.e., Roosevelt's] desire to get into war." The financial sanctions in July 1941 were "provocative," and "Japan was bound to fight even if it were suicide unless they could be removed, as the sanctions carried every penalty of war except killing and destruction, and . . . no nation of dignity would take them for long." MacArthur thought "Roosevelt could have made peace with Konoye [Konoe] in September 1941 and could have obtained all of the American objectives in the Pacific and the freedom of China and probably Manchuria" because "Konoye [Konoe] was authorized by the Emperor to agree to complete withdrawal."

Hoover was struck by the feeling among MacArthur and his staff that Soviet communism posed a real threat in Japan and in the Far East. MacArthur told Hoover "that he thought the chances were 2000 to one against Marshall's succeeding in China" and thought "that [the Soviets] were steadily propagandizing the Japs; that they were conducting Communist schools among their Japanese prisoners and infiltrating them into Japan." MacArthur also told Hoover "that if the Japanese standard of living were lowered and heavy indemnities imposed upon them that they . . . would go Communist, both to get free and to secure Russian protection." Like Hoover, MacArthur wanted to contain communism by economic means.[22]

In thinking about American policy toward Japan during the early stages of the Cold War, Hoover kept a watchful eye on the Reparations Mission, headed by Edwin Pauley. The Pauley mission visited Japan and Manchuria in November 1945 and submitted its report, which reflected Pauley's views, to President Truman in December. This mission was immediately followed by another, headed by Northwestern University economics professor Corwin D. Edwards (1901–79), which visited Japan in early 1946 and argued that dissolving the zaibatsu into small, competitive units would permit the growth of labor unions, higher wages, a middle class, higher domestic consumption, and less dependence on external trade.[23]

The two reparations missions considered the large industrial combines just as guilty as the militarists for Japanese aggression overseas. The Pauley mission argued for moving a significant portion of plants and equipment from Japanese industries to the Asian countries that had suffered from Japanese aggression. Japan would be allowed to make an economic recovery but not to achieve economic domination of the region again. This would be accomplished by moving industrial facilities from Japan to other Asian countries so that their economies would become strong enough to compete against the Japanese economy and thus ensure balanced economic growth in the region. The Pauley mission viewed the zaibatsu as a major factor behind Japanese "economic aggression," hand in hand with Japanese militarism; during Japan's expansion to the Asian continent in the 1930s and during World War II, the combines' heavy industries had grown by using raw materials from conquered areas and by exporting goods to these areas. Furthermore, the combines possessed most of the leading industrial facilities. Therefore, given the criteria used for selecting the industrial plants and equipment to be moved, the zaibatsu were chosen as major targets. On December 8, 1945, as an interim measure, Pauley recommended taking away the "excess capacity" of the heavy industries of the zaibatsu that had grown under the war economy. He then formulated a comprehensive removal plan in April 1946, which, after a long delay, he submitted to President Truman on November 12, 1946.

Despite these reports and Truman's initial endorsement of them, both Truman and MacArthur opposed their implementation. Truman, his political aides, and the U.S. Army showed little interest in reforming Japan in the way the reports advocated. MacArthur and the conservative wing within SCAP, such as Generals William F. Marquat (1894–1960) and Charles A. Willoughby, considered the reports' calls for reparations and dissolution of the zaibatsu as unrealistic and too radical.[24] The War Department, which had gained more power than the State Department in formulating foreign policy during the war and the immediate postwar years, wanted to change Pauley's recommendations, and its opinion was shared by General MacArthur and by powerful Japanese and American business interests. The department argued that if Pauley's recommendations were executed, the cost of the occupation would rise because the extensive removal of industrial facilities would create economic uncertainties in Japan. The fear of this outcome and the ambiguity over the extent of the proposed removals was hampering the economic recovery of Japan.[25]

Truman asked Hoover, who all along had opposed radical measures against the established Japanese economic system, to persuade Pauley to change his views on reparations. Truman had been interested in removing Pauley from a leading role in the reparations issue by giving his close political friend and Democratic fund-raiser a new job as undersecretary of the Navy, an attempt that was torpedoed during the Senate confirmation hearings in February. When Hoover saw MacArthur in May, "MacArthur said that Pauley, the F.E.C. [Far Eastern Commission] and the vindictive 'liberals' were attempting to destroy Japan." MacArthur thought of "the Potsdam Agreement as being in spirit entirely contrary to a constructive program" and stressed "that all that was needed was to destroy munitions works, disarm the Japanese, and to keep a commission there to watch, and to have an airfield on some island an hour away." MacArthur did not want to put "restraints on the Japanese heavy or light industry of any kind" and expressed his frustration that he "could do nothing towards recovery now because of the threats to remove the plants."[26]

On his way back from Tokyo, Hoover met Pauley in Hawaii by having the latter's flight to Japan delayed by a day. Truman wanted Hoover to advise Pauley about his "impressions and views on Asiatic questions." For three hours, Hoover "took a strong line against the destruction and limitations on Japanese economy, pointing to their necessity to export to buy food or that we should be perpetually saving them from famine and especially that here we had an opportunity to develop a protection against the spread of Communism over the whole of Asia, etc." According to Hoover, Pauley "finally . . . came to my view and said that the proposals and plans of his commission must be greatly modified." When Pauley asked whether MacArthur would agree to this reversal, Hoover "suggested that with [Pauley's] own powers of persuasion, [Pauley] ought to be able to accomplish that, especially if Truman backed [Pauley]." On May 9, 1946, Hoover telegraphed MacArthur that he had "convinced [Pauley] of the need of entire reversal of policy in order to build an idealogical [sic] dam." Hoover thought he had managed to open Pauley's mind but that Pauley needed a "push from [MacArthur]." He implicitly suggested that "[MacArthur] should take the attitude that Pauley had converted him." Ultimately, Pauley ignored Hoover's advice and stuck to his policy recommendations after his arrival in

Tokyo. (However, in 1953, Pauley wrote to Hoover that he was "particularly grateful for the fine advice" he had received from Hoover in Hawaii and stated he had "never forgotten [his] admonitions concerning the Soviet Union and they have certainly proved to be true.")[27]

As Daniel Yergin has pointed out, "the postwar anti-communist consensus existed first in the center, in the policy elite, before it spread out to the nation."[28] Within the administration, five men spearheaded the move to contain Soviet penetration into Japan: Secretary of the Navy (Secretary of Defense after 1947) James V. Forrestal, a former president of Dillon, Read and Company; advisor to the American Occupation Government in Germany and later (after August 1947) Undersecretary of the Army William H. Draper, Jr., who, like Forrestal, was a former partner at Dillon, Read and Company; George F. Kennan, a Sovietologist in the State Department, who was chargé d'affaires in Moscow and the head of the Policy Planning Staff; Secretary of the Army Kenneth Royall (1894–1971), a former New York business executive; and Secretary of Commerce W. Averell Harriman, the oldest son of E. H. Harriman and a prominent New York business executive.

These men, along with other high-ranking government officials, however, were initially willing to cooperate with the Soviet Union in the postwar reconstruction of the world. For example, Assistant Secretary of War John J. McCloy visited Japan in October 1945 to persuade MacArthur to allow the Soviet Union and other Allied countries to participate in the governing of occupied Japan.[29] After a few days of argument, MacArthur agreed to allow them nominal, nonbinding advisory roles. McCloy shared MacArthur's suspicion of the Soviet Union, but he made MacArthur comply with Washington's policy at the time. Furthermore, unlike MacArthur, who gave little thought to the European situation, McCloy, along with other high-ranking officials, saw the need to solve problems globally rather than locally in order to spread democracy and free markets.[30]

But as tensions mounted between the United States and the Soviet Union, these men and other high-ranking officials became convinced of the need to contain the Soviet threat. Although Hoover was the chief spokesperson for this argument, the man who initiated the American reversal of policy toward Japan was Secretary of the Navy James V. Forrestal. In a letter written in April 1946 to General MacArthur, Forrestal expressed his worry about "a vacuum of power into which influences other than ours are bound to be attracted as much by internal suctions as by external pressures."[31] Just as he had concluded by V-E Day that Germany had to be restored as the engine of European economic recovery to serve as an anti-communist bulwark, Forrestal had adopted the same views toward Japan by 1946.

Forrestal was the godfather of the containment policy. After Kennan transmitted the now-famous Long Telegram from Moscow on Washington's Birthday, 1946, Forrestal used it during 1946 in his arguments regarding the Iran and Trieste crises and the British request for a $5 billion loan. Kennan later commented that policymakers in Washington viewed his telegram as timely. The response was "sensational" and "changed my career and my life in very basic ways." Forrestal persuaded Secretary of State Byrnes to bring Kennan back as deputy head of the National War College. After his return, Kennan (under the pseudonym "X") published "The Sources of Soviet Conduct" in the July 1947 issue of *Foreign Affairs*. The article was based on a paper called "Psychological Background of Soviet Foreign Policy" that Kennan had written for Forrestal's "private and personal edification." By May 1947, Kennan was back in the State Department, working under the new secretary of state, George C. Marshall, in the newly established Policy Planning Staff. As Kennan later stated, "It was, I suspect, due to [Forrestal's] influence."[32]

By March 1946, almost all the elite foreign-policy thinkers in the Truman administration had concluded that the intention of the Soviet Union was expansionist and evil, the one major exception being former vice-president Henry A. Wallace, who was Truman's secretary of commerce until September 1946, when the president forced him to resign. In the midst of growing suspicion toward the Soviet Union, and because of General Marshall's failure to stop the Chinese civil war, American policymakers began to see Japan as a regional power, like Germany in Europe, whose industries could serve as an anti-communist economic and military bulwark. With regard to Japan, these policymakers unanimously perceived the reparations and zaibatsu-dissolution proposals by Pauley and Edwards as irrelevant to containment, a consensus that culminated in the declaration of the Truman Doctrine on March 12, 1947. On the following day, both Hoover and Forrestal argued, in a meeting attended by Secretary of Commerce Harriman, Secretary of Agriculture Clinton P. Anderson (1895–1975), Secretary of War Robert P. Patterson (1891–1952), and Undersecretary of State Acheson, that restrictions on the Japanese and German economies be removed both to contain communism and to reduce the costs of the occupations; both men also argued in favor of removing the sanctions on Japanese businessmen.

As part of this anti-Soviet consensus, the Strike mission, headed by McGraw-Hill president Clifford Strike, submitted its report to the War Department in May 1947. Subsequently, the mission's document was discussed among policymakers, including representatives from the Army, Navy, State Department, and SCAP. Although Pauley, who was part of the mission, still argued for his position and even though the State-War-Navy Coordinating Committee (SWNCC) in Washington had transferred some 16,000 Japanese machine tools to Japan's Asian neighbors, the policy current in Washington regarding the Japanese economy now favored the Strike report, which argued against Pauley's previous recommendations. In February 1948, the second Strike report (also known as the Overseas Consultants, Inc., or OCI report) expanded on this argument by suggesting that the heavy industries, such as iron and steel, shipbuilding, oil refining, and synthetic rubber, were now necessary for rebuilding the Japanese economy.

The American foreign policy elite agreed with Hoover's argument that Germany and Japan should serve as the engines for economic recovery in their respective regions. To achieve this aim, it was imperative that they themselves recover economically, although the State Department did not abandon the idea of a regionally balanced approach to economic growth in Western Europe and Asia. This idea was pursued in Europe under the Marshall Plan, and in Asia after the department dovetailed its policy with the policies of the Defense Department in the fall of 1947. With this evolving consensus in the background, Dean Acheson made his now-famous speech on May 8, 1947. Through Acheson, the United States unilaterally declared, without the consent of the Four Powers, that it was going to reconstruct Japan and Germany economically as the "workshops" of Europe and Asia.[33]

On May 7, 1947, the day before Acheson's speech, Hoover wrote to Secretary of War Robert Patterson and argued for an end to repressive measures against Japanese industries; supervision of, instead of intervention in, Japanese economic affairs, except in bringing about some "de-monopolized" measures for orderly competition; and the recovery of Japan's productivity for nonmilitary purposes and exports as part of reviving productivity worldwide to achieve global peace. Hoover wanted "de-monopolized" measures because they provided "the only hope of increasing the standards of living in Japan" and of making Japan "a bulwark against the Communist invasion of Asia." Hoover stressed that "chains on any productive area are chains on the whole world." He wanted "a larger vision of the primary basis of world peace which is productivity" because "otherwise there will be a disintegration of Western Civilization everywhere." Although Hoover "sympathize[d] emotionally with Draconic measures of punishment" when he thought "of the white crosses over tens of thousands of American boys in the Pacific and the millions of butchered Chinese," based on "the real interest of the United States and the future peace of the world," Hoover argued that Americans "must confine punishment to the war leaders and realize that we must live with this 80,000,000 people."

Although Hoover thought "the 'new level' of industry . . . d[id] not fulfill the urgent Strike recommendations," he also thought "the Strike recommendations did not go nearly far enough." Hoover argued for "a revolutionary change in the whole concept of 'levels of industry', 'plant removals' for reparations and destruction of peace industry plants," because Japan had "to produce enough exports to pay for their food and other necessary imports" and to become "a stable and peaceable state." He thought his view was valid because of "the fact that the American taxpayer is called upon to furnish upwards of $400,000,000 in the next fiscal year to keep the people barely alive; and unless there are revolutionary changes, it will continue indefinitely." He wanted to remove Japan as the tax burden on Americans. Hoover pointed out that "the food deficiency in Japan was under-estimated" and "the estimate of Japan's foreign trade deficit under these regulations showed a deficit for 1947 of under $20,000,000, whereas experience proves the deficit to be over $400,000,000." Hoover wanted to "do away with the whole concept of 'level of industry', both 'original' and 'new'" and "establish a few absolute prohibitions such as monopolies, arms manufacture, aircraft construction, speed (but not size) of ships, and install a general watch to see that industry is devoted to peace-time production." He had reached these conclusions because the American government "cannot find competent American men over the years to competently direct the kind of planned economy for Japan which either the 'original' and 'new' limit of industry plus the export controls amount to," although America "could find the minor inspection staff to see that Japanese industry does no evil." He agreed to "the removal to claimants of machine tools and equipment from such munitions factories as cannot be converted into peacetime production," but Hoover wanted "independent engineers" to "assess . . . the actual value to any proposed recipient of the peace-time plants, deducting cost of removal and shipment, and then call upon Japan to pay such a sum over the years and to retain the plants." Hoover argued "no further industrial repressions are necessary to preserve peace in a perpetually demilitarized country," and "the continued uncertainty of plant removals and the present proposed levels of industry are bound to continue the paralysis of export industry." Furthermore, "Japan's full productivity (except arms) aide [sic] in the recovery of her neighbors."[34] A week after he wrote to Patterson, Hoover sent Secretary of State Marshall a similar message.[35]

In sending these letters, Hoover wanted to persuade the State and War departments of the utmost need to raise Japan's productivity by creating a market-based economy with a degree of zaibatsu dissolution, an approach he had taken to the American economy as secretary of commerce in the 1920s. Hoover wanted regulated competition. The only restrictions on industry that he advocated were those on industries that had engaged in manufacturing weapons; as he and the policy elite in the administration had known all along, in the age of total war, no industry could avoid contributing, at least indirectly, to a country's war-making capabilities, particularly the heavy industries. Judging from his economic reform activities as the secretary of commerce in the 1920s, Hoover was not opposed to big business as long as it cut costs (and hence prices) and boosted productivity. He supported the formation of informal cartels through voluntary arrangements, provided that expenses were reduced and productivity improved. In fact, as both Jordan A. Schwarz and Alan Brinkley point out, the New Dealers applied antitrust laws to cut prices and raise productivity, not to atomize industries.[36]

Hoover was careful to avoid public criticism of MacArthur's economic programs because he wanted to use the general's charismatic image to further the resurgence of the Republican party. But unlike those who pushed MacArthur as the party's presidential candidate, Hoover seemed lukewarm toward that idea. His first choice was Ohio Senator Robert A. Taft (1889–1953), who considered Hoover one of his two greatest mentors, the other being his father, former President William H. Taft (1857–1930). In considering the future of the Japanese economy, Hoover became a silent partner in efforts to lobby the policymakers in Washington who wanted to prioritize Japan's economic recovery, efforts led by William R. Castle, Joseph Grew, Eugene Dooman, and *Newsweek* journalist Harry F. Kern. Castle served as the point man for the members of this movement who wanted to contact Hoover; Hoover's indirect affiliation with this group through Castle resembled his role as a silent partner of the America First Committee through Castle in the prewar years. In June 1948 this group formed the American Council on Japan, a lobbying organization that promoted Japan's economic recovery and U.S.-Japan economic interdependence. By this time, Hoover was busy as the chairman of the bipartisan Committee on the Reorganization of the Executive Branch, better known as the Hoover Commission, a committee consisting of twelve members, four each from the Democrats and Republicans in Congress, two from the private sector, and two public officials. Speaker of the House Joseph Martin (R, Mass.) had appointed Hoover a member of the committee, which in turn chose Hoover as its chair. The Hoover Commission included Secretary of Defense James V. Forrestal and Undersecretary of State Dean Acheson. One of its task forces addressed the reorganization of the national security apparatus, and this task force included Hoover's political allies, Rear Admiral Lewis L. Strauss (a member of the Atomic Energy Commission, a partner at Kuhn, Loeb and Company until 1941, and an extremely capable administrator in the Navy Department during the war) and Sears Roebuck chairman and former chairman of the America First Committee Robert Wood (a retired brigadier general of the Army). Castle kept Hoover informed of his colleagues' lobbying efforts for Japan's economic recovery, and Hoover continued to maintain support.[37]

Given this reversal of policy toward Japan among the American foreign-policy elite, the big question was whether or not SCAP would comply. The American commanders in charge of the occupation enjoyed near autonomy in making decisions. They could argue against and delay, if not ignore, policies formulated in Washington with which they disagreed by stating that they represented the Allies and opposed Washington's unilateral measures. As a result, even the War Department and the president had only partial control over the commanders. As Kennan points out, because the State Department was virtually eliminated "as a factor in policy-making . . . in favor of the military" during the war, this situation was "carried over into the postwar period insofar as the military still had forces and occupational responsibilities abroad." The State Department was further disadvantaged by the fact that it and the War Department were not cooperating very well on occupation policies.[38]

In Japan, MacArthur seemed to be trying to turn the content of the Edwards report to his political advantage in 1947 and 1948 by using it to show the American public that he was fighting for reforms in Japan. He also seemed to have tried to resist Washington's reversal on the issue of zaibatsu dissolution because of his perception that policymakers in Washington were trying to take away his authority in Japan. In 1946 MacArthur was just as opposed to the Edwards report as the Pauley report because economic chaos would be created by implementing some of the Edwards report's policy recommendations, which were, in his overall view, unrealistic and excessive. Despite MacArthur's opposition, the Edwards report became an interim directive in October 1946. This was later renamed SWNCC 302/4, and in May 1947 SWNCC forwarded it to the highest nominal policymaking body for the Allies, the Far Eastern Commission (FEC), which renamed it FEC 230. Because FEC 230 neither prioritized its recommendations nor discussed procedures for implementation, MacArthur's SCAP was left with considerable power to determine its realization or demise.[39]

In spite of MacArthur's intransigence during 1947–48, Hoover's call to reverse economic reforms in favor of economic recovery in Japan (an opinion shared by Hoover's associates, such as Harry Kern, Joseph Grew, Eugene Dooman, and, above all, William R. Castle) was strongly supported in Washington by Undersecretary of the Army Draper and Policy Planning Staff head Kennan. Draper, as an official in the occupation government in Germany, had opposed decartelization and the purge of managers in these combines because these measures would hamper German economic recovery. In the midst of the reorganization of the War and Navy departments into the Defense Department in 1947, President Truman appointed Draper undersecretary of the Army in August, accepting Draper's precondition that he be allowed to return to Dillon, Read and Company in March 1949.[40]

By spring 1948, Draper had managed to win the State Department's support for his policy unilaterally to bypass the FEC, cut reparation removals, and stop dissolution measures. Although MacArthur had managed to defy Washington's demands and pushed the Deconcentration Bill through the Diet on December 8, Draper sought to delay the implementation of the law until Washington had settled all questions regarding FEC 230. On January

6, 1948, his boss, Army Secretary Kenneth Royall, spoke in San Francisco, hinting at reversal of reparations, deconcentration, and purges; although these measures contributed to the destruction of Japan's ability to wage war, he said, they were harming Japan's peacetime potential. This speech was followed by an announcement at the FEC meeting on January 21 of a compromise version of SWNCC 384, whose content differed from the original SWNCC 384 only by stating "more emphasis" on economic recovery than economic reform instead of "shift of emphasis" from economic reform to economic recovery to indicate the unilateral American decision to reverse the economic reforms and emphasize Japan's economic recovery rather than reparations and dissolutions. This situation reflected the further gaining of power within the State Department of those who shared Draper's view, such as Undersecretary of State Robert A. Lovett (1895–1986), a former Wall Street Banker, and Kennan. The need for more lenient reparation policies was confirmed in late February by the second Strike report on reparation policies for Japan, a follow-up to Strike's May 1947 report, which argued for the further delay in the removal of facilities from Japan to FEC claimants.[41]

After Kennan visited Japan in March 1948 and exchanged opinions with MacArthur and other SCAP members, he wrote and submitted Policy Planning Staff (PPS) Report no. 28 to Secretary of State Marshall on March 25. In this document, Kennan articulated his opposition to further reforms in Japan and argued for delaying a peace treaty until Japanese institutions had been strengthened by reversals of deconcentration and purges, by transferring more authority to the Japanese government from SCAP, and by centralizing the police force or even creating a small army. Kennan argued that these measures were necessary to combat possible communist subversion.

Kennan extended his stay to meet Draper and his economic mission, a mission chaired by Percy Johnston, chairman of Chemical Bank and Trust. Draper wanted to bring SCAP in line with Washington's policy reversal. MacArthur had continued to resist and had approved the formation of the Holding Company Liquidation Commission (HCLC) in February, a commission in the Japanese government, which identified 325 companies, representing 75 percent of Japanese industry and commerce, as possible targets for dissolution. As a countermeasure to further zaibatsu dissolution, Draper moved to create the Deconcentration Review Board (DRB), after arguments with SCAP over the nominees for dissolution. Although the mission's stated task was to make recommendations to the Army regarding Japan's economic problems, its real objective was to gather evidence to present to Congress to win appropriations for economic aid to Japan. To convince Congress to approve economic aid, it was also imperative that Draper show that an agreement now existed among SCAP, the FEC, the State Department, and the Japanese government for the reversal of economic reforms.[42]

American economic policy toward Japan had finally caught up with the ideas Hoover had been advocating since 1945. After MacArthur lost the Wisconsin primary on April 6, 1948, in a bid for the Republican presidential nomination, he increasingly lost his hold over SCAP's economic policies. On April 26, the Johnston report predictably called for a virtual end to FEC 230 and supported even more lenient reparation policies than had the second Strike report. This was followed by "a procession of advisers and consultants" who were "regularly sent to Tokyo to oversee the implementation of highly technical matters of foreign exchange, tax policy, currency, export and import controls, and the Japanese government's budget." In June, Draper's continued effort finally led to congressional approval of a somewhat smaller amount than he had proposed in economic aid to Japan. In October 1948, Kennan's PPS 28 was incorporated into National Security Council 13/2. In December, the DRB reduced the initial list of 325 companies to be dissolved to nine, and SCAP announced the satisfactory completion of deconcentration. Finally, in late 1948, the State Department withdrew FEC 230. In December 1948, Detroit banker Joseph M. Dodge (1890–1964) agreed, thanks to Draper's insistence, to supervise Japan's economic stabilization plan; for two years, Dodge would act with almost dictatorial power to fight inflation and pursue rationalization of the Japanese economy. Draper returned to Dillon, Read and Company in March 1949. His relations with Japan continued as he lobbied agencies, including the International Monetary Fund and the World Bank, in support of the economic recovery of Japan.[43] To the Japanese political and business leaders, including Ayukawa, Draper and Dillon, Read must have appeared to be the Kuhn, Loeb & Company and J. P. Morgan and Company of the Cold War era.

Ayukawa's Postwar Activities, 1947–1948

In the Cold War era, Ayukawa's wish for peaceful U.S.-Japan relations through economic interdependence was being fulfilled. Ayukawa, however, had to tread carefully in his attempts to promote international trade and to

attract American investment in the reindustrialization of Japan because, as a
purgee, he had to constantly seek prior approval of the authorities for his
lobbying efforts. In February 1948, five months after his release on August
30, 1947, Ayukawa sent a letter to James W. Murray, then a vice president in
the Record Department of Radio Corporation of America. In sending this
letter, Ayukawa received the assistance of GHQ in Tokyo, Colonel J. H.
Lowell in Washington, and George Yamaoka, counsel at the International
Military Tribunal and formerly a lawyer at the New York law firm of Hunt,
Hill & Betts, a law firm whose partner Kenneth Simpson, until shortly before his untimely death in 1941, had been a rising political figure in New
York City as a Republican internationalist.[44] Ayukawa asked Murray
whether Murray could return to Japan to help in his postwar efforts to
promote U.S.-Japanese economic cooperation. Murray's response was that
he would be interested in returning, provided that Ayukawa's financial offer
was as good as his current one at RCA Victor—a condition that Ayukawa
was unable to meet.

After his letter to Murray, Ayukawa attempted to recultivate his American business contacts with a circular letter dated May 12 to corporate executives, including James D. Mooney, president of Willys-Overland Motors
and former executive vice president of General Motors, and C. F. Cress, executive manager of Chrysler Corporation's Far Eastern Division. In the letter, Ayukawa expressed his optimism about the changes in Japan since the
surrender. Despite the chaos in the Japanese economy and psyche, "the
Japanese people will settle down sooner or later and will strive to build up a
new Japan along the lines defined by the Allied countries." He was waiting
for that time to use his past experience and connections with the United
States for bilateral economic cooperation.

In the middle of 1948, despite the favorable atmosphere cultivated by the
Johnston mission, Ayukawa agreed with George Yamaoka's June report
from New York that U.S. trade with Japan would not "open up" until after
the following spring. The prospects for renewed trade were helped, in part,
by the American consumer goods industries, which were looking for new
markets such as Japan because they were beginning to overstock their inven-
tories, a trend that ended with a recession in 1949. As for American investments in Japan, Yamaoka argued that "until the foreign exchange and reparations questions can be solved and unless and until SCAP permits
conversions of yen to dollars and unless the Japanese laws are amended giv-

ing more security to foreign capital, [he did] not see how any large amounts of American capital can be brought into Japan." In the American heavy in-dustries, because of the excess domestic demand for goods produced by these industries, Yamaoka told Ayukawa that "many important [American] bankers and industrialists" thought "it will be some time before American captains of industry will feel that heavy investments are justified or attrac-tive enough in Japan."[45]

While in prison Ayukawa had concluded that, if and when he got out, he would tackle three economic issues—modernization of small and medium-sized firms, construction of hydroelectric power plants, and building of roads—and he wanted to use American capital for these projects. First, Ayukawa wanted to modernize small and medium-sized businesses by pro-viding government subsidies and long-term, low-interest loans so that they could equip themselves with better machines to increase their efficiency and productivity and hence their international competitiveness. These firms ac-counted for a major portion of employment and, in the prewar years, had earned the bulk of Japanese foreign exchange; in fact, Ayukawa himself had started as an owner of a medium-sized business. Furthermore, Ayukawa, in-fluenced by his friend and leading businessman Ōkouchi Masatoshi (1878–1952), had promoted rural cottage industries from right after the Japanese surrender until the GHQ sent him to Sugamo. The majority of Japanese re-turning from overseas went back to rural areas, where they needed jobs.

Second, Ayukawa wanted to utilize rainwater, one of Japan's few re-sources, and build hydroelectric power plants all over Japan to foster regional economic development; these plants would help rebuild and enlarge Japan's industries. In summer and fall 1949, his business collaborator Kudō Kōki formulated such a plan for Ayukawa; Kudō had been a leading executive at Noguchi Shitagau (Jun)'s conglomerate and had played an instrumental role in creating a huge hydroelectric dam on the Yalu River between Korea and Manchuria. Finally, Ayukawa wanted Japan to have an adequate paved road system for transportation and for nationwide development.

On the issue of attracting American capital, in summer 1948 Ayukawa established the Foreign Capital Research Association. With the help of Ayukawa's aide, the Harvard-educated advisor to the Industrial Bank of Ja-pan (IBJ) Shudō Yasuto, who had negotiated with GHQ between April and August, the association received the blessing of SCAP. From 1920 until 1941, Shudō had been a commercial attaché in New York, Washington,

D.C., Berlin, and London, and from 1946 to 1948, he worked as an advisor to the Ministry of Finance, a job that frustrated him because neither the Finance Ministry nor any other government agency made a serious effort to attract foreign investment. As Miyazaki Masayasu points out, between November 1947 and January 1948, officials in the Japanese government (namely, the Finance Ministry) and SCAP discussed the treatment of foreign government loans and private foreign investment. The Japanese government much preferred government loans, and SCAP generally agreed with this stance. The two sides did disagree on the extent to which, in a regulated manner, private foreign investments could be introduced on an equal basis with Japanese capital in the Japanese market. SCAP showed more enthusiasm for this than the Japanese government did, but this debate was postponed because of power struggles over occupation policies between the American government and SCAP, the need to change various domestic laws to encourage foreign investment, and splits among and within SCAP, Japanese government officials, and business leaders on the issue of foreign investments.

In searching for American capital, Ayukawa, who acted as advisor to the Foreign Capital Research Association, ran afoul of the complicated politics surrounding the introduction of foreign capital. Despite this situation, his efforts complemented a trend within the Japanese government to seek foreign capital for Japan's economic recovery. Ever since March 17, 1947, when MacArthur had indicated during a rare public appearance at the Foreign Press Club a need for an early peace treaty with Japan as a necessary condition for helping Japan's economic recovery, debates had occurred within the government and in business circles on ways to achieve economic recovery through the introduction of foreign capital; the possible ending of the occupation meant that Japan could no longer rely on economic assistance from the American military. The introduction of foreign capital, mainly in the form of government loans, had been sought by the Socialist-led government and by the Ashida Hitoshi cabinet, led by the Democratic party. Because of the high expectations created by the Draper-Johnston mission in spring 1948, and because of increased expectations for economic assistance from the American government to Japan, the Ashida cabinet looked at foreign capital, including private capital, with greater enthusiasm than had previous postwar regimes. Until shortly before its downfall because of a major political scandal in summer 1948, the Ashida cabinet wanted to introduce large amounts of foreign capital, mainly government loans, to fight inflation, impose wage controls, and promote Japan's economic recovery. The Draper-Johnston mission told Prime Minister Ashida (1887–1959) that although U.S. aid was forthcoming, the Japanese government and SCAP had to dismantle regulations impeding foreign trade before a peace treaty could be reached. Inflation also had to be stabilized in order to arrange a fixed exchange rate system to replace the current system of multiple rates. Regulations on property holding and repatriation of profits, tax laws, and other measures were necessary to encourage American private investment in Japan. American investments, the members of the mission argued, would help Japan earn dollars, enhance export competitiveness, provide profits, and, above all, gain congressional approval for economic aid as an interim measure until private capital could take over the rebuilding of the Japanese economy. Such progress toward a solution to Japan's economic problems might help attract American capital to this market.

Under a political climate favorably disposed to importing foreign capital, business leaders also supported Ayukawa's project. The association's first meeting on August 5, 1948, was attended by Nagasaki Eizō, chairman of the Reconstruction Agency (Fukkō kōdan), who had participated in projects initiated by Giseikai, the think tank founded and headed by Ayukawa between 1943 and 1945; Ishikawa Ichirō (1885–1970), who had been a leading executive at Nissan Chemicals and was now chairman of both the Japan Economic Federation and the Japan Industry Council (Nihon sangyō kyōgikai); Bank of Japan (BOJ, Japan's central bank) governor Ichimada Hisato; Kobayashi Ataru (1899–1981), president of Fukoku Life Insurance Company; Kawakami Kōichi (1886–1957), former IBJ president; Ishizaka Taizō (1886–1975), who had worked with Ayukawa as president of Daiichi Life Insurance Company (a major shareholder of Nissan Motors since 1937) and who later became president of the Tōshiba Corporation and chairman of the Japan Economic Federation; Kishimoto Kantarō, Ayukawa's top aide; and Shudō Yasuoto. Ishikawa and his federation colleague Satō Kiichirō (1894–1974), president of the Teikoku (Mitsui) Bank, had been campaigning since March 20, 1948, to change the law and promote private foreign capital even if that meant allowing foreigners to own a majority share in a Japanese firm. In early April, Nagasaki had formulated a proposal that called for preferential treatment of private foreign capital in applying Japan's unfriendly laws on managerial participation, corporate profits, raw materials, and remittance of profits. In other words, Nagasaki thought that economic recovery would be achieved through the introduction of large amounts of both foreign aid and private foreign capital, and the regulations that hindered the inflow of foreign investments needed to be amended. Nagasaki's proposal was adopted as the official recommendation of the Permanent Committee on Foreign Investment of the Japan Industry Council; this committee consisted of leading businessmen such as Ishikawa, Nagasaki, Satō, and Kurata Chikara (1889–1969), Ayukawa's former employee and now president of Hitachi, a company controlled by Ayukawa before the zaibatsu dissolution.[46]

From the spring to the summer of 1948, Japanese business leaders perceived private foreign capital to be as important as foreign government aid. Although this consensus among business leaders fell apart with the demise of the Ashida cabinet, strong voices persisted within the business community that argued for the need to attract foreign capital. For example, in the October 1948 issue of the Japan Industry Council's monthly report, Ishikawa, although not as enthusiastic as Nagasaki or Ayukawa on this issue, supported foreign capital inflows to Japan under certain conditions. Shortly afterwards, he helped organize the Foreign Investment Research Society with BOJ Governor Ichimada, who chaired the group and had argued in mid-January that the government should enlist the help of businessmen in considering ways to attract foreign capital; chairman of the Japan Chamber of Commerce Takahashi Ryūtarō; and former ambassador to the United States Horinouchi Kensuke, who served as an advisor. In February this group submitted a report to the GHQ that argued for actively introducing foreign capital, including private capital, to Japan and proposed the following: (1) change the laws and tax codes to encourage foreign capital inflow; (2) nurture industries that could most effectively earn foreign exchange (which probably meant light industries); (3) attract foreign capital in the forms of machinery and technology, direct investment (with foreign ownership of over 50 percent of Japanese companies permitted), and indirect investments so as to develop coal fields, hydroelectric plants, roads, and a merchant navy; (4) reintegrate Japan into the American-led free trade system, including the International Monetary Fund; and (5) permit Japanese businessmen to travel overseas to conduct business.

Ayukawa continued to emphasize private foreign capital as being just as important as, if not preferable to, economic aid from foreign governments.

The breakdown in consensus did not necessarily mean an end to Ayukawa's ideas about linking foreign capital and modernizing Japan's small and me-dium-sized firms as a serious policy option among Japanese business and political leaders. For example, from the late 1940s to the early 1950s, the Bank of Japan under Governor Ichimada favored labor-intensive light in-dustry, which accounted for the bulk of small and medium-sized firms, rather than heavy and chemical industries. This bias was shared by Ayu-kawa, who had been advocating the promotion of these firms because their production of textiles and other cheap domestic goods better suited Japan's factor endowment, and their products were economically competitive enough to earn foreign exchange, in contrast to the goods produced in the heavy and chemical industries. Ayukawa's and Ichimada's policy preference was shared by the second Yoshida cabinet, formed after the Ashida cabinet in October 1948, because Prime Minister Yoshida also believed that light industries had a better chance of earning foreign exchange. This represented a major change in Japan's immediate postwar recovery program, which had been focusing on the state-led restoration of heavy and chemical industries. Yoshida pushed for the establishment of the Ministry of International Trade and Industry (MITI) in 1949, in opposition to the views of MCI bu-reaucrats who preferred to promote Japan's economic recovery by revitaliz-ing Japan's heavy and chemical industries through neo-mercantilist means (ironically MITI came to be dominated by MCI bureaucrats). Yoshida in-tended MITI to serve as an export-promoting government organization, be-cause Joseph Dodge's austerity measures assumed that Japan would be ex-porting while it was restructuring its domestic economy and because Yoshida's political party had been advocating Japan's participation in the American-led free trade system.[47]

TEN

Old Ideas Persist:
Ayukawa and Foreign Capital and Technology, 1949–1953

Since his prewar American business contacts still occupied influential business and political positions, Ayukawa thought he could revive his campaign to attract direct and indirect American investment. Although he was aware that economic assistance could be obtained from foreign governments in the form of aid, Ayukawa and his Foreign Capital Research Association concerned themselves primarily with private capital from foreign countries, particularly the United States.

The first challenge for Ayukawa's group was to prepare to use foreign capital effectively in Japan's economic reconstruction. The association had to collect accurate data on the state of the Japanese economy to assess which industries Japan should foster in the postwar economy; in addition, Ayukawa thought, these industries not only had to promote Japan's economic recovery but also had to be welcomed by the rest of the world. He wanted government funding to support the association's programs to run pilot projects in industries the association thought worth the risk of starting. If these experiments indicated that these industries would provide business opportunities, the knowledge would be disseminated among the business community.

Ayukawa also wanted to promote modernization among small and medium-sized businesses and bring order to that sector so as to obtain foreign investment. Although he thought some protectionist measures were necessary for these businesses, he also wanted cutthroat competition to be regulated to avoid overseas dumping of products by these industries, a frequent accusation from British and American businesses in the prewar years. Such regulation would help prevent friction with countries that might consider investing in Japan.[1]

Even as Ayukawa's was laboring to attract American investment in 1949–50, Joseph Dodge was implementing his austerity measures. Japanese business leaders in the heavy and chemical industries felt a sense of grave crisis, and Prime Minister Yoshida Shigeru and Finance Minister Ikeda Hayato were gradually disavowing the Dodge Plan. Although William Borden argues that the significance of the Dodge Plan has been exaggerated because it was not as deflationary as has been conventionally thought and because inflation had for the most part been curbed by the time of Dodge's arrival,[2] Dodge's program did stabilize wages and prices.[3] This stabilization, however, came at the cost of massive layoffs and bankruptcies and a major stock market crash.[4] Although economic indicators improved in early 1950, Japan had not progressed very far toward the goal of economic modernization and recovery because the world economy failed to absorb adequate amounts of Japanese exports, exports that were supposed to expand under the Dodge Plan. As a result, businessmen in the heavy and chemical industries became pessimistic about the outlook for their industries. On the eve of the Korean War, Toyota Motors was on the verge of folding,[5] and in a revival of its late 1930s negotiations with Ford, it was seriously considering a joint venture with the American firm. The onset of the Korean War finally turned the situation around.

How did Japanese political and business leaders like Ayukawa respond to the shifts in the United States' economic and political policies on reforms in Japan? This chapter examines Ayukawa's efforts from 1949 to 1953 to introduce American capital and technology to Japan for economic reconstruction. Particularly noteworthy are Ayukawa's efforts to revitalize direct financing of companies by establishing an investment banking firm in conjunction with Dillon, Read and Company, and his endeavors to introduce Tennessee Valley Authority (TVA)–style economic projects through his talks with David E. Lilienthal (1899–1981), the former chairman of the TVA. Ayukawa's actions were a resumption of his similar efforts in the prewar era, again based on the assumption that Japanese industries would benefit more from U.S.-Japan economic interdependence than from economic nationalism. As in the prewar years, his attempts to attract American investment were at times almost successful.

Ayukawa's Negotiations with Dillon, Read and Company

In mid-December 1949, Prime Minister Yoshida commented in an interview with *Mainichi shimbun* that he welcomed private foreign capital and expressed his optimism regarding the possibility of a fair amount of private capital inflows to Japan in the near future. Immediately after this statement, William H. Draper, Jr., who only nine months earlier had retired from his job as undersecretary of the army to rejoin Dillon, Read and Company as a senior partner, made another visit to Japan. Draper's visit had originally been scheduled to take place earlier at the request of Lieutenant General Edward M. Almond, who was MacArthur's chief of staff and who probably acted on MacArthur's wish. Before leaving the United States, Draper consulted with Undersecretary of the Army Tracy S. Voorhees. When Draper saw Prime Minister Yoshida in Tokyo, Yoshida asked him if Dillon, Read could officially represent the Japanese government in promoting Japan's economic recovery. On December 14, *Nikkei shimbun* reported that Draper intended to establish an investment company jointly managed and financed by Japanese and American interests. Although Voorhees advised Draper on the latter's return that Dillon, Read should limit itself to acting as an unofficial advisor to the Japanese government, the following spring Ayukawa and Shudō Yasuto secretly pursued their project, which resembled the rumored investment company with Dillon, Read.[6]

In the midst of the Dodge Plan, Ayukawa formulated two plans to attract American capital and technology to help in Japan's economic recovery: the establishment of an American-type investment banking firm and the implementation of TVA-style hydroelectric projects. Although one wonders whether there was secret coordination between Ayukawa's support of Shudō's negotiations with Dillon, Read and the dialogues between Japanese government officials and Draper from the end of 1949 to the first half of 1950, the former should be understood in the context of the latter. In spring

1949, Ayukawa prodded Shudō to request SCAP to permit Shudō to visit the United States "to study and investigate the long-term financing and securities markets . . . with special regard to the technique and practice of investment banking, with a view to setting up the investment banking mechanism in Japan in order to assure the supply of long-term or capital requirements on a sound economic basis for Japan's industry."[7] The postwar reconstruction necessitated this move. In a document submitted in English to SCAP, Shudō stated:

While Japan's financial structure is now undergoing the reorganization according to the latest American pattern, . . . due to the non-existence of investment banking firms in Japan up to now, the underwriting and issue business which had been carried on to a certain extent by the Industrial Bank of Japan and a few others, mostly semi-governmental institutions, are now left to securities companies. But they are essentially dealers and brokerage houses specialized in selling and buying already issued securities. At least up to now, they are not qualified to act as investment bankers nor equipped with requisite facilities. If Japan's industries is [sic] to be rehabilitated, Japan must have powerful investment houses which will help them in long-term financing and sometimes in management, technical and otherwise. Such investment houses, it is hoped, might become one of the channels for induction of foreign, especially American capital, through close contact with a few important investment bankers in the United States of America.[8]

Both Shudō and Ayukawa wanted this firm to be a major channel for introducing foreign capital; their tactic for accomplishing this was to gain market credibility by obtaining the backing of influential American businessmen and bankers. In May 1949, Shudō informed a friend from his Harvard years, Earl B. Schwulst, president of the Bowery Savings Bank in New York and an advisor to Ecuador's central bank in the 1920s, that the proposed firm was to be a joint stock company with Japanese and foreign financial institutions operating in Japan as stockholders. The firm was to have either a direct or an indirect connection with an American investment banking firm, preferably through managerial and capital participation. Shudō hoped that Schwulst would introduce him to influential Wall Street bankers.

Ayukawa and Shudō took pains to keep SCAP and influential figures in the Japanese financial world informed about this project in order to gain their support. SCAP looked favorably on this scheme, and Shudō informed Schwulst in his May 1949 letter that he was "receiving good understanding and support from competent authorities in SCAP," including General William F. Marquat, chief of the Economic and Scientific Section (ESS), which supervised financial issues; Walter K. Le Count, chief of the Finance Division in ESS, who had worked for J. P. Morgan and Company and the law office of J. W. Davis and who knew Schwulst; John R. Allison, assistant chief of the Finance Division; Frayne Baker, an advisor to ESS; and Colonel Lawrence E. Bunker, aide-de-camp to MacArthur. It was Bunker, one of the strongest supporters of the plan, who originally suggested that Shudō visit America to consult with investment bankers.[9]

In addition, Marquat chaired the Foreign Investment Board, a committee established by GHQ in January 1949 and consisting of American officers, including Baker and Le Count, who was a member until October 1949. This organization consulted with Japanese government officials in the Ministry of Finance, the Foreign Investment Commission, and the Foreign Exchange Control Board on the regulation of foreign investments. Until October 1949, this board had seven officers, six of whom were from the ESS; the remaining four were William Vaughn, member of the ESS Industrial Division, Edward G. Welsh, head of the ESS Antitrust and Cartel Division, Frank Pickelle, chief of the ESS Foreign Trade Division, and Charles S. Gregory, special assistant in the Legal Section. After October, the board consisted of Marquat, Baker, and Gregory, and by December 20, Baker, who was the *de facto* chair of the board, thought that the board's authority to regulate foreign capital should be delegated to the Japanese government, and the latter should formulate a law on foreign investments. In January 1950, ESS recommended that GHQ and the Japanese government start a joint working group to draft such a law. SCAP's representatives consisted of five individuals: Allison, who was designated the coordinator, and four officers selected from the Diplomatic Section, ESS Science and Technology Division, the Foreign Investment Board, and the Foreign Property Division of the Civilian Property Custodian. The Japanese representatives consisted of Chairman Kiuchi Nobutane (1899–1993) of the Foreign Exchange Control Board, Secretary General Kaya Masao of the Foreign Investment Commission, Director Ihara Takashi (1908–76) of the MOF Finance Bureau, Director K. Hirata of the MOF Tax Bureau, Director F. Kubota of the MOF Control Bureau, Director T. Ishihara of the MITI Enterprise Bureau, and Director H. Shimazu of the Foreign Ministry's Political Affairs Bureau.[10]

In summer 1949, Schwulst wrote a letter to MacArthur, whom he knew from his days as a financial advisor to Henry L. Stimson, governor of the Philippines in the late 1920s, to check on Shudō's bona fides and decide whether to sponsor Shudō's trip, a sponsorship that Shudō needed because of travel and foreign exchange restrictions placed on Japanese. MacArthur wrote Schwulst in September that within SCAP Shudō enjoyed "the reputation of being an extremely competent individual" and indicated that he would approve Schwulst's sponsorship of Shudō. Most important, MacArthur wrote Schwulst that "the introduction of foreign capital for investment purposes is recognized as a most vital factor in the accomplishment of economic recovery and self-sufficiency for Japan. You may be assured that your expression of interest in this regard is most welcome to Japanese financial circles and that full cooperation will be extended to your efforts to finalize your plans."[11]

Within the Japanese financial world, Shudō contacted and gained the support of Finance Minister Ikeda Hayato; MOF Finance Department Director Ihara Takashi, who, as noted above, was deeply involved in drafting a law governing foreign capital; the director of the MOF Banking Department; officials in the Securities and Exchange Commission; BOJ Governor Ichimada Hisato; IBJ Governor Kawakita Teiichi (1896–1981), who had worked under Ichimada as BOJ vice governor from 1947 to 1949; two former IBJ governors (Itō Kenji [1889–1970] and Kawakami Kōichi); and a number of prominent industrialists. Among these men, Shudō consulted frequently with Ichimada and Kawakita; Ichimada told Shudō that "he would give all possible assistance to the establishment of the corporation and to its future development," and Kawakita assured Shudō of "the full cooperation" of the IBJ.[12]

The IBJ was probably interested in becoming a shareholder in the proposed firm and cultivating ties with influential American businessmen. Along with the other large Japanese banks, the IBJ had been removed from the list of zaibatsu firms scheduled for dissolution because of the Draper-Johnston mission's recommendations to the Department of Defense in April 1948. The IBJ was now interested in playing a role in the postwar era.[13]

Until recent months, IBJ had been at the center of financing Japan's postwar reconstruction. In August 1946, IBJ established a Reconstruction

Finance Division after prodding from MOF and BOJ that originated from GHQ's wish to create an American-style Reconstruction Finance Corporation in order to deal with bank failures and economic depression. Although this division was separated from IBJ in 1947 and renamed the Reconstruction Finance Bank (RFB), the organization cooperated closely with IBJ in management and lending decisions. From 1947 until mid-1949, when it terminated lending activities as the result of the Dodge Plan, RFB monopolized loans to various public corporations. And the bank accounted for 60 to 90 percent of large, long-term loans (over ¥500 million for over a year) to finance investments by key industries such as coal, electricity, steel, shipbuilding, and fertilizers. (On April 25, 1950, changes in banking laws transformed IBJ from a state into a private bank, and in 1952 RFB, which had been limited to collecting and managing credits after the start of the Dodge Plan, was absorbed by the Japan Development Bank, a quasi-governmental bank established in April 1951 that assumed RFB's functions in dispersing credit to key industries under the leadership of its first president, Kobayashi Ataru.)[14]

Just before Shudō's New York visit, Ayukawa's scheme seemed to gain some momentum because of developments in the Japanese government's discussions with Dillon, Read and because of developments within the Japanese government itself. On January 8, MOF Financial Commissioner Watanabe Takeshi met Draper in New York, a conference at which the latter told the high-ranking MOF official, who spoke excellent English, that he was optimistic about Japan's future and its prospects for attracting foreign investments. At the same time, Draper advised that the next move regarding foreign investments should be made by Japan; it should avoid antagonizing GHQ and the U.S. government and promise that it would not nationalize foreign companies, that it would act favorably on the issue of taxing foreign investors, and that it would permit the export of foreign exchange by foreign investors. From late February to early March, both Prime Minister Yoshida and Finance Minister Ikeda considered a flexible approach similar to that Nagasaki had advocated to attract foreign investments, including private foreign capital. The approach was approved in a cabinet meeting on March 3, but this decision was immediately vetoed by MacArthur and GHQ. In retrospect, this was an ominous intervention.[15]

Although Shudō agreed with Schwulst's view that it was almost impossible to attract private American capital to occupied Japan because of political and economic uncertainties, he thought the investment banking project could contribute significantly to resolving these uncertainties by securing long-term capital for Japanese companies. If influential American businessmen and bankers supported this proposed firm, Shudō believed it would secure the confidence of investors inside and outside Japan.[16] When Shudō arrived in New York City on March 29, 1950, Schwulst had already started organizing a meeting with American bankers. On April 4, Shudō met more than two dozen bankers at a luncheon meeting; among those present were General William H. Draper, Jr., of Dillon, Read and Company; Chairman Monroe C. Gutman of the Lehman Corporation; Vice President William R. Strelow of the Guaranty Trust Company; Vice President Donald L. Ballantyne of the Chase National Bank; Senior Vice President Leo N. Shaw of the National City Bank; President Lawrence C. Marshall of the Bank of Manhattan; Vice President Arthur N. Jones of Morgan Stanley & Company; and Frederick M. Warburg of Kuhn, Loeb and Company.[17]

Shudō had already focused on Dillon, Read and Company. On March 31, Shudō met two of its partners, William Draper and a Mr. Wilkinson, at their office. Wilkinson had recently been to Japan, where he had been dismayed by the speculative behavior of Japanese securities companies, and hence he avoided answering their proposals for joint ventures. Wilkinson had confirmed SCAP's keen interest in establishing an American-style investment banking firm. Although Draper expressed concerns about the amount of stock still held by the Holding Company Liquidation Commission, the inconvertibility of yen to dollars, and the poor and speculative performance of the Japanese securities market and securities firms, he was willing to continue the discussion and stated, "I think the timing of American participation is very important." During the discussion, Shudō made the following proposal to Draper:

The plan I have in mind . . . has not been published in the paper[s] and, more important, it is not even known in financial circles [with the exception of the aforementioned people]. My plan is entirely open. The point of success or failure is whether or not we can get American participation. Should the latter be forthcoming, we are ready and will be delighted to accept. Regarding the question of capital, American interests could participate to the extent of 50 per cent or more, as you wish. It is felt that all details should be fixed through consultation with American investment bankers. After, we could come to some agreement as to principle. I hope the American interests could send their representatives to Japan. Based on this representative's advice and opinion, we would decide as to particulars.[18]

Prime Minister Yoshida was aware of this March 31 meeting because Kurusu, at Ayukawa's request, sent a letter, dated April 19, informing Yoshida about Shudō's meeting with Draper. In addition, Kurusu asked Yoshida to forward the letter to Finance Minister Ikeda, who was leaving for the United States on April 25, a mission whose official agenda was publicly stated as the observation of the American economy but was in reality a secret attempt to bypass GHQ and persuade Dodge to reverse his deflationary policy and to discuss with American officials the future of U.S.-Japan security arrangements and the peace treaty; this effort resulted not only in Dodge's rejections of the Japanese requests but also in MacArthur's anger toward Yoshida and Ikeda for attempting to circumvent him.[19]

Until mid-June, when he returned to Tokyo, Shudō consulted more than twenty times with Draper, Wilkinson, and C. Douglas Dillon (1909–2003), chairman of the Board of Directors of Dillon, Read and Company. These meetings would not have taken place without the approval of the firm's founder and Dillon's father, Clarence, because all important matters had to be discussed with him; Clarence Dillon at the time was in Europe, and he was very familiar with Ayukawa's efforts through Miho in 1940 (see Chapter 6). Shudō and the Americans discussed, among other things, capitalization, management, participation of other American firms, and prospective earnings.[20] Shortly before Shudō's return to Japan, Draper wrote a letter informing Shudō that Dillon, Read was interested in continuing the discussion. Draper's willingness to continue his talks with Shudō probably mirrored what he had told Prime Minister Yoshida's confidant Shirasu Jirō, Ayukawa's former top executive in the prewar years, some time between May 12, the day of Shirasu's arrival with Finance Minister Ikeda and his aide and MOF official Miyazawa Kiichi, and May 19, the day when Draper wrote a letter to MacArthur informing the general of his meeting with Shirasu. In meeting the Cambridge-educated Shirasu, who spoke impeccable English (and Japanese with an English accent), Draper stated that although Dillon, Read was unwilling to serve as an official representative for the Japanese government as had been requested by the prime minister, it was willing to advise the government informally without charge. One of the major points of contention between Dillon, Read and Ayukawa was the projected return on investments; Dillon, Read wanted over 10 percent per annum after all expenses and taxes had been paid, rather than Shudō's proposed 8 percent, because Dillon, Read enjoyed returns greater than 30 percent on its domestic investments.[21] After Ayukawa consulted with BOJ Governor Ichimada and IBJ Governor Kawakita, they proposed an annual return for Dillon, Read of 19.9 percent.[22]

The negotiations faced two other major obstacles: foreign exchange controls under the Foreign Investment Law (enacted in June 1950), which severely restricted foreign investment, and Japanese political and economic instability. Dillon, Read had been pressing since mid-April to place its capital in a dollar fund and avoid converting it into yen, but the Foreign Investment Law prohibited foreign investments unless such a conversion was made. Ayukawa suspected that Japan's political and economic uncertainties caused Dillon, Read to make this proposal.[23] Although the negotiations were gaining momentum, on the day Shudō returned to Japan, the Korean War broke out. In any case, Draper became occupied with the Long Island Railroad receivership in 1951, and Dillon, Read postponed any definite decision, in large part because of the volatile situation in Korea.[24]

Because the Foreign Investment Law was hastily approved without substantial examination or debate by the Diet at the end of its session in May and because the law resembled that formulated by the joint working group of Japanese and GHQ bureaucrats, the alliance of the Japanese and GHQ bureaucracies seemed to have prevailed over the Nagasaki approach, a situation that must have chagrined supporters of that approach, which included Prime Minister Yoshida, who was busy in May getting ready for the Upper House elections and preparing for the negotiations on Japan's peace treaty; Finance Minister Ikeda, who returned from the United States on May 22 and whose mission had angered MacArthur and the GHQ; Ayukawa; and Shudō.[25]

Ayukawa's Talks with David Lilienthal

Ayukawa at first did not anticipate that talks with Dillon, Read would lead to anything, and after mid-April he prodded Shudō to pursue the TVA scheme by approaching David Lilienthal. Ayukawa had been thinking about TVA-type hydroelectric power plant projects at least since November 1949. In summer and fall 1949, he had conducted a survey on the economic potential of constructing hydroelectric power plants throughout Japan based on comprehensive planning with Kudō Kōki of the Noguchi Research Institute, a former confidant of Noguchi Shitagau (Jun), the founder of the No-

guchi conglomerate, who had in the prewar years built Asia's largest hydroelectric dam on the Yalu River. After this survey, Ayukawa published a report from this institute in which he argued that rain was one of Japan's few
precious resources and that based on comprehensive planning financed by
domestic and foreign capital Japan should build hydroelectric power plants
with a total capacity of 15 million to 20 million kilowatts. A March 1950 report completed by Industrial Consultants, Inc., at Ayukawa's request projected that in order to build hydroelectric power plants with a total capacity
of 10 million kilowatts, construct roads, spread the electrification of railroads and households, and nurture light industries that were not of the cot-
tage-industry variety such as rayon, ceramics, glass, pulp, and aluminum
producers and electro-chemical industries such as nitrogen fertilizers, chlo-
rine, and ammonium chloride manufacturers within the coming decade, Japan would need $6 billion in the form of foreign capital. In spring 1951 Ayu-
kawa forecast that in order to construct hydroelectric power plants with a
total capacity of 15 million kilowatts and establish roads and electrification as
well as the industries mentioned in the March 1950 report, Japan would need
$20.7 billion from domestic sources and $7.5 billion from foreign capital.

An adequate supply of electricity is obviously necessary for industrialization. Although in the immediate postwar years Japan's main energy source
was coal, by 1950 the Japanese government began to emphasize the production of electricity. But, as indicated in Ayukawa's predictions, new power
plants require a large investment, and foreign capital was a prerequisite for
this endeavor. But before capital could be secured for power plant projects,
the power industry had to be reorganized and privatized. In February 1950,
in response to Prime Minster Yoshida's lobbying effort to electrify the
Tadami River area, General MacArthur informed Yoshida that such a project should be considered in the context of an overall plan for the development of the electric power industry in Japan and that the immediate task
facing Japan in this regard was the breakup and privatization of the electric
power companies, which had been under state control and supervision since
1939 when the Japanese government reorganized privately owned and managed electric power companies into ten publicly managed firms. Nine
months later, in November, GHQ privatized the electric power companies
into nine firms. Because of state-imposed ceilings on the price of electricity
and because of the economic surge caused by the Korean War, the demand
for electricity skyrocketed, and the surplus of electricity vanished. In 1951,

MITI's Public Utilities Bureau, which regulated the power companies, formulated a plan for Japan's electricity supply centered on the construction of hydroelectric power plants supplemented by thermal power plants. (As we shall see, the emphasis on hydroelectric and thermoelectric generation changed because of the weather and the World Bank's reaction to Japan's plan for securing electricity.)[26]

Ayukawa's TVA scheme coincided with a significant political realignment on March 1, 1950. The merger of Yoshida's Democratic-Liberal party and a Democratic party splinter group led to the creation of the Liberal party, which enjoyed greater control over the Diet. Since October 1948 Yoshida's Democratic-Liberal party had been promoting exports of light industry goods and imports of goods in the heavy and chemical industries. Yoshida now had to accommodate those within the Liberal party who advocated emphasizing the growth of heavy and chemical industries over light industries. By 1952, Yoshida's Liberal party, although somewhat wary of greater state control over the economy, shared MITI's view of promoting the heavy and chemical industries for both Japan's domestic economic development and exports. Such a shared perception reflected a major trend within the Japanese business and political community on the need to create internationally competitive heavy and chemical industries, a notion embodied in Kawasaki Steel's successful and ultimately profitable construction of a state-of-the-art steel mill in Chiba prefecture during the Korean War, a project seen as necessary by MITI and unnecessary and unfeasible by BOJ Governor Ichimada, the banks, and Kawasaki's competitors.[27] In this context, Ayukawa's TVA scheme could potentially provide support for this new policy. He, however, differed from those business, political, and government leaders who promoted the idea of using hydroelectric and thermal power plants to foster large firms in the heavy and chemical industries, because his emphasis lay on relying on hydroelectric power plants to nurture small and medium-sized firms in the light industries because of his pessimistic outlook about the future of the heavy and chemical industries, particularly the former.

Shudō met Lilienthal through Bernard Baruch, whom he had contacted at the suggestion of Kurusu. In pursuing the TVA scheme, Shudō also consulted Draper and Wilkinson at Dillon, Read. The consensus among Ayukawa, Shudō, Kurusu, Lilienthal, Draper, and Wilkinson was that, although the project needed the participation of investment banking firms, engineering consulting firms, and the World Bank (in which Japan was seeking membership and whose vice president, Robert L. Garner, Shudō met through Draper), initially the scheme had to be negotiated between the United States and Japan because only the American government possessed the economic resources to realize this project. The United States had recently started to promote the economic development of underdeveloped countries, and Ayukawa thought Japan could benefit from this program. Although Ayukawa wanted American private capital to finance TVA-type projects and road construction in Japan, he, Shudō, and Kurusu hoped for a Marshall Plan–type of aid, that is, a large, long-term loan from the U.S. government to build many hydroelectric dams and roads. Cheap electricity would help build chemical, steel, and light industries. They in turn could be used to manufacture cars, and more roads could carry more vehicles. In Ayukawa's view, the construction of dams and roads had to be planned from a comprehensive perspective; it should not be done in a piecemeal fashion. Here, his Manchukuo experience clearly influenced him.[28]

Lilienthal considered Ayukawa's idea "a matter of more than ordinary interest from the business viewpoint,"[29] but he considered himself an administrator and wanted to see more concrete plans and assessments by qualified engineers.[30] The Korean War seemed to provide an opportunity for Ayukawa to present his plan to the U.S. government as the way to stabilize and modernize Japan's economy. Ayukawa probably picked up an encouraging sign from the United States around February 1951 from his friend BOJ Governor Ichimada, who was told by Draper during a visit to Dillon, Read that although he understood the importance of securing adequate electricity in Japan and that it would take time to revise the rate structure and break up and privatize the Japanese power industry (the latter started in spring of that year), until Japan solved these problems, he found it inconceivable that funds would be forthcoming from either the U.S. Export-Import Bank or, if Japan was permitted to become a member, the World Bank. But as a financial measure to deal with this transition period in the Japanese power industry, Draper indicated that it might be possible to have American private capital help finance power plant projects whose construction was already under way. Although Draper's remarks did not indicate whether Japan should pursue the development of the power industry under a comprehensive plan or whether hydroelectric power plants were preferable to thermal power plants, it did show that private foreign capital might assist the development of Japan's power plants. Because Draper reported his statements to Ichimada to MacArthur, the general was probably aware of the Draper-Ichimada talks shortly after they took place.[31]

Ayukawa moved quickly after hearing that Lilienthal would visit Japan on March 8, 1951, on his way back to Washington from India and Pakistan.[32] Ayukawa and Shudō met Lilienthal at 5:00 A.M., two and a half hours after his plane arrived. Later that day, Ayukawa visited Lilienthal again and "repeated his wish that [Lilienthal] urge a huge American-financed hydro-scheme for Japan, linked up with industrial production, the former to be financed by 'state capital,' the latter to be private industry."[33]

Since the end of World War II, Lilienthal had been promoting the idea of exporting TVA-style programs for the economic development and democratization of underdeveloped countries. During his meetings with Ayukawa, Lilienthal stated that the development projects he had in mind for India and Pakistan were impossible, and the U.S. government could become interested in Ayukawa's proposal, particularly because of the Korean War and the need to have an economically and politically stable, anti-Communist Japan.[34]

Ayukawa's talks with Lilienthal were assisted by the positive impression he made on Lilienthal. Although Lilienthal thought Ayukawa "not long ago [had been] . . . a disturber of the peace of the world and security of the U.S.," he also thought Ayukawa was "almost a movie version (in appearance and manner) of a Japanese big shot," "a fabulous man," and "one of the greatest organizing brains I have ever known, beyond a doubt, astute, eloquent, resourceful—a very remarkable man."[35] Lilienthal's impression of Ayukawa was very similar to Bain's (see Chapters 3 and 7).

On March 9, Ayukawa secretly visited Prime Minister Yoshida to discuss Lilienthal's proposal. Yoshida was aware of Ayukawa's and Shudō's discussions with Lilienthal and with Dillon, Read because Kurusu, on Ayukawa's behalf, had sent the prime minister a letter in April 1950. Back then, Shudō had had an opportunity to meet Finance Minister Ikeda in New York City. Yoshida had not, however, bothered telling Ikeda of Ayukawa's TVA scheme. (The Ikeda mission was concerned primarily with Dodge's policy, future U.S.-Japan security arrangements, and the peace treaty.) The prime minister seemed to be interested solely in a hydroelectric project on the Tadami River in Fukushima prefecture in the Tōhoku region.

Although it is unclear whether Ayukawa visited Yoshida before or after Lilienthal, Ayukawa arranged for Lilienthal to see Yoshida on the same day. Unlike Ayukawa, Yoshida did not impress Lilienthal. The prime minister, the public utilities commissioner, and others "pumped [Lilienthal] on the hydroelectric prospects of Japan, asked a lot about TVA, and made [Lilienthal] feel, generally, like the freshman who is invited to the fraternity house and gets a pledge rush."[36]

Lilienthal, Ayukawa, and Yoshida were aware that any scheme for hydroelectric projects in Japan had to win the approval of General MacArthur. After he saw Yoshida, Lilienthal dined with MacArthur and managed to draw the general's attention to his argument for the need to boost Japan's electricity supply. Although unaware that Ayukawa was behind this scheme because Lilienthal did not mention his name, MacArthur expressed his support and recommended that Lilienthal see ESS Director General Marquat—advice that Lilienthal took.[37]

Upon his return from Asia, Lilienthal discussed his views on Ayukawa's proposed TVA-type program with Lazard Freres, an investment banking firm, and with John Foster Dulles (1888–1959) and Secretary of State Dean Acheson. Although Lilienthal and Dulles were supposed to meet for dinner shortly before the latter's departure for Japan as America's special envoy to help negotiate the peace treaty and Lilienthal had planned to discuss Ayukawa's scheme with him, Lilienthal had to cancel the appointment when his father became ill. Lilienthal instead wrote a letter on April 17 to Dulles about Ayukawa's proposal but the letter did not reach Dulles before his departure for Japan; he saw it upon his return.[38] Acheson told Lilienthal that "I can see nothing but [economic] disaster for us in Japan when the occupation is over," because it had become apparent in spring 1951 that the economic boom caused by the Korean War was fizzling. Lilienthal argued that, given Japan's future economic difficulties, large-scale hydroelectric plants might provide new hope for Japan's economy. He added that Ayukawa's "scheme was sensible and financially sound except for the political risk, which might be one this country would want to try to underwrite" because "it tied Japan into the U.S."[39] But with regard to private investments in Japan, Lilienthal, in contrast to Draper's indication to Ichimada in February, advised Lazard Freres that he could not encourage American firms to invest there for at least five years.[40] In fact, Lilienthal told Dulles that "until Japan was a member of the World Bank it might not be appropriate for a private individual to do anything over there." Although Dulles also thought "the hydro part was for the World Bank," he disagreed with Lilienthal's discouragement of American private investments in Japan and argued that he had been "trying to get the Japanese used to [the] idea" that "the U.S. Government should not loan or grant money to Japan in any large amounts." Dulles thought Ayukawa's "hydroelectric power scheme . . . should be encouraged because it would show ingenuity and inventiveness" on the part of the Japanese. Dulles believed that Japan could become self-supporting after the end of the occupation, even without substantial trade with China, and that "the Japanese ought to use their imagination and inventiveness" rather than "producing imitations of other people's products, making them cheaper and forcing them on already occupied markets."[41]

Based on his talks with American government officials, including Dulles, Lilienthal informed Ayukawa that they thought Ayukawa's plan, though worthy of attention, was too big and too expensive. Lilienthal indicated that the United States might support smaller and more piecemeal projects. Although Lilienthal declined Ayukawa's request that he direct the proposed enterprise, if it came about, because he preferred to live and work full time in America, he was nonetheless willing to assist Ayukawa.[42]

Ayukawa's Activities After 1952

Ayukawa's vision encountered as many obstacles in the postwar years as it had in the prewar period. In April 1951, Ayukawa wrote Yoshida urging the prime minister to demand Marshall Plan–type economic aid from the United States for the comprehensive planning and development of Japan's hydroelectric power plants. Yoshida even supported Ayukawa's going to America, but Ayukawa was not depurged until after the summer of 1952, a precondition for overseas travel.

Although Ayukawa wanted Yoshida to ask for Marshall Plan–type aid at the San Francisco Peace Conference (September 4–8, 1951), Yoshida ignored Ayukawa's suggestion. During the Korean War, Japan received a great amount of economic aid through military procurement, and Yoshida probably thought Ayukawa's approach was unnecessary.[43] As Lilienthal had predicted to Ayukawa in May 1951, in 1952 the Japanese government began to implement, with the U.S. government's economic support, piece-meal plans for the construction of hydroelectric and thermoelectric power plants under the supervision of the Electric Power Development Company, a public agency established in September 1952 and headed by Ayukawa's former MIDC colleague, Takasaki Tatsunosuke.

Ayukawa may have felt somewhat vindicated by Robert L. Garner, vice president of the World Bank, who visited Japan in December 1952, four months after Japan's admittance as a member of the bank. Garner's criticism of the Japanese government's request for World Bank loans was scathing—the amount requested was outrageous, and the "wish list" was not based on a comprehensive plan and did not list the industries seeking the World Bank loans in the order of importance. The World Bank rejected Japan's request for assistance in the construction of hydroelectric power plants and permitted lending only for construction of thermal power plants, loans that had been the subject of negotiations between Japan and the U.S. Export-Import Bank (the World Bank, through political maneuvering, had taken over the latter's talks with Japan). According to the bank, building hydroelectric power plants in Japan was expensive because of the costs of developing the limited areas in Japan's mountainous interior suitable for such plants. On the other hand, the bank argued that if provided with a steady supply of cheap oil and the most advanced machinery, Japan should be able to construct thermal power plants relatively cheaply. It was not until 1958 that the World Bank approved loans for building Japan's two major hydroelectric plants.

In addition to the World Bank's rationale for promoting thermal power plants, in fall 1951 a severe drought in Japan proved that relying heavily on hydroelectric power plants would be risky. Ayukawa, of course, probably did not deny the usefulness of thermal power plants in such a circumstance. Nonetheless he was displeased with the piecemeal approach. In fall 1953, as Japanese public opinion came to perceive the World Bank's lending conditions for the power plants as humiliating, he was also appalled by the fact that Japan was borrowing at unreasonable rates to build thermoelectric plants.[44]

Although Japan's dollar deficit continued to be a major problem in U.S.-Japan relations during the 1950s, Borden argues that American military procurement increased as the theme of American policy toward Japan shifted in 1951 from "self-support" to "economic cooperation," a shift that "enabled Japan to rebuild a highly competitive economy and at the same time, to retain the economic 'dualism' that continued the subsidization of heavy industry at the expense of the less fortunate workers not employed by the giant corporations."[45] American policy encouraged Japan to export, rather than develop its domestic market, and the policy led, contrary to the hopes of the U.S. government, to greater absorption by America than by Southeast Asia of Japanese products.[46]

After 1952, aside from a brief involvement in the oil industry, Ayukawa focused primarily on supporting and strengthening small and medium-sized firms. Ayukawa did not mind the resurgence of big businesses, as long as laws penalized them if they acted unruly in the market; in fact, he wanted the antitrust laws created by the GHQ changed, since he perceived their goal to be to weaken the Japanese economy. Ayukawa also felt that small and medium-sized firms had to organize themselves politically and lobby the Diet to address their concerns; he wanted to pass laws that would assist these firms in modernizing their facilities and strengthening their international competitiveness. In February 1952, Ayukawa founded the Small and Medium-Sized Firms Assistance Association as a step toward organizing these firms politically. And in August of that year, he founded the Small and Medium-Sized Firms Assistance Bank; this was the successor to the Atō Bank, which had been established by Ayukawa in 1951 and had been managed by leading businessmen Murata Shōzō (1878–1957) and Kodama Kenji (1871–1954). (Ayukawa hired them for their expertise in the China market, because he hoped to attract capital from overseas Chinese in Southeast Asia, who were looking for relatively safe places to invest, given the spread of communism. None of these talks produced results because the Chinese investors were unwilling to invest on a long-term basis.) To further promote the modernization of small and medium-sized firms, Ayukawa ran for election to the Upper House as an independent candidate and won a seat in May 1953.[47] In March 1956, he formed a political organization called the Political Federation of Small and Medium-Sized Businesses (Chūshō kigyō seiji renmei) as a lobbying organization. Ayukawa was pessimistic about the future of Japanese big business, since he was unsure that Japan could secure the raw materials big business needed or the capital to build enough power plants to supply cheap electricity for the heavy and chemical industries. In his view, Japan's small and medium-sized firms had more promise; their growth would be much faster because they required fewer raw materials and less capital than large companies in the heavy and chemical industries. Ayukawa particularly wanted to nurture small and medium-sized firms that were not dominated by large corporations. In other words, he preferred to foster the growth of labor-intensive industries rather than capital-intensive ones such as heavy and chemical industries.

Ayukawa also argued that Japan had benefited economically from war, and the current Cold War allowed Japan to obtain economic assistance from the American government. When the Cold War ended, however, Japan would face intense economic competition, and it had to be prepared for this eventuality. He thought the post–Cold War international economic competition would be the most deadly war Japan had ever faced, and Japanese companies had to prepare themselves to produce high-quality and price-competitive goods.

Kishi Nobusuke, whose postwar political comeback began with his election to the Lower House in April 1953 as a Liberal party member, agreed with Ayukawa that Japan's industrial structure was dualistic and unbalanced, but he was far more interested in centering Japan's economic growth around the heavy and chemical industries. Kishi based his views on his experiences in dealing with the issue as the director of the MCI's Industrial Bureau in the mid-1930s and as deputy director of the Industry Department of Manchukuo in the late 1930s, where industrialization programs had faced difficulties because Manchukuo lacked small and medium-sized firms. He agreed with Ayukawa's opinion that strong small and medium-sized firms were needed, but he believed that they were crucial not only for export earnings but also for the provision of parts and semi-finished goods to the heavy and chemical industries.

As for the issue of political leadership in Japan's economic recovery, Ayukawa thought that the Japanese prime minister was not acting like a CEO, an idea he had written about in his 1936 "New Era" essay. As a member of the Upper House, Ayukawa expressed his dissatisfaction with the lack of strong leadership in strengthening the Japanese economy; he anticipated another Meiji Restoration, in which the country would rejuvenate under strong leadership. Kishi, however, seemed more optimistic than Ayukawa that a way could be found to establish strong leadership before another "Meiji revolution" occurred. As Kishi rose through the ranks of the conservative party (he was successively chief secretary of the Democratic party after November 1954 and the Liberal party after November 1955, foreign minister in the Ishibashi cabinet, and prime minister from 1957 to

1960), he supported Ayukawa's call to bring in foreign, mainly American, capital and to strengthen Japan's small and medium-sized businesses. Ayukawa in turn supported Kishi.[48]

Despite Ayukawa's activities, the Japanese regulatory state was installed, and Japanese policy elites in the government and the private sector tended to oppose or maintain their distance from Ayukawa's call for developing Japan through direct American investment, labor-intensive industries, and the nurturing of independent small and medium-sized firms. As this chapter demonstrates, Ayukawa's postwar schemes should be understood in terms of shifts in domestic and international politics between 1948 and 1950.

In 1959, Ayukawa resigned from the Upper House because of a political scandal involving his son. Afterward, Ayukawa lost much of whatever political influence he had. It is not clear what Ayukawa thought of the Political Federation of Small and Medium-Sized Businesses as it became, in Karel van Wolferen's words, Kishi's "skeleton apparatus for top-level control of the subcontractors" and helped MITI by lobbying for the passage of a law in 1963 that was formulated by the ministry to "encourage further development of the *keiretsu* corporate groupings."[49]

Conclusion

Foreign direct and indirect investment never reached the levels that Ayukawa had hoped for in either the prewar or the postwar years. In both periods, Ayukawa's industrialization schemes conflicted with the agenda of the Japanese government, which sought greater state control over the economy and less foreign economic power in Japan. In the postwar years, as the Korean War led to increased American procurement of Japanese goods, Japanese government and corporate leaders grew more and more unwilling to listen to or pursue Ayukawa's approach to economic recovery, a formula based on direct and indirect foreign investment, the growth of relatively independent small and medium-sized firms, and the revitalization of direct financing. As John Dower argues, "much of what has been characterized as a 'postwar Japanese model' proves to be a hybrid Japanese-American model: forged in war, intensified through defeat and occupation, and maintained over the ensuing decades out of an abiding fear of national vulnerability and a widespread belief that Japan needed top-level planning and protection to achieve optimum economic growth."[1]

Japanese state regulation was not the sole factor in discouraging the inflow of foreign capital to Japan. Foreign capital inflow was also hampered by the Korean War, whose volatile situation reinforced the impression of domestic uncertainties in Japan, and by the opposition among British Commonwealth nations and Western Europe to granting Japan most-favored-nation status and membership in the General Agreement on Tariffs and Trade (GATT), a situation that the United States endeavored to overcome on Japan's behalf from the Havana Conference on Trade and Employment in 1947–48 to Japan's accession to GATT in 1955. These domestic and international factors helped solidify the highly regulated postwar economy of Japan.

Although SCAP approved the amendment of the Antimonopoly Law in June 1949 so that foreign corporations not only could buy Japanese corporate stock but also would feel that patent-licensing agreements would be honored in Japan, this measure was followed by the passage of the Foreign Investment Law, which severely restricted foreign direct investment.[2] Foreign technology was introduced mainly through licensing, and the regulations on direct foreign investment were not eased until the late 1960s.[3]

These regulations were designed to ameliorate the foreign exchange shortage, a problem dealt with by the Foreign Exchange and Foreign Trade Control Law of 1949, a law that almost completely replicated its predecessor, the Capital Flight Prevention Law enacted in 1932, and gave "the government the power to concentrate all foreign exchange earned from exports . . . , and this power made possible the control of imports through the use of a foreign exchange budget."[4] (It was not until December 1980 that the Foreign Exchange Law underwent major revision to permit the opening of Japan's foreign exchange market, a phase succeeded by another revision of this law in spring 1998 to launch Japan's Big Bang.) The law encouraged exports and discouraged imports of goods, services, and capital.[5] In addressing import restrictions, the Foreign Investment Law authorized MITI to restrict "the import of foreign technology to those cases deemed necessary for the development of Japanese industries." It also "separate[d] the foreign technology from its foreign ownership, patent rights, know-how agreements, proposals for joint ventures, capital participation, voting rights and foreign managers of boards of directors." This measure was a major factor in discouraging foreign direct investment.[6] Finally, the 1949 law made it hard for firms to secure capital in overseas markets and hence contributed not only to the prevention of capital flight but also to the dominance of indirect financing, because firms that disliked or could not receive bank loans in Japan were unable to secure capital in markets abroad.[7]

Even in the present age of mega-mergers of financial institutions in Japan, Europe, and the United States, Japan still lacks globally competitive investment banks of the European and American variety.[8] Calder argues that SCAP's failure to reorient the Japanese financial system from indirect to direct finance based on capital markets was "perhaps the Occupation's most portentous failure,"[9] a failure that was assisted by "internal SCAP divisions, MOF's internal cohesion (only nine of its officials had been purged), and the astuteness of MOF lobbying efforts by such experienced English-speaking financial diplomats as Takeshi Watanabe."[10] Ayukawa's idea of nurturing investment banking conflicted with the Ministry of Finance's policy of encouraging indirect financing as the main means of funding industry. After 1935, Japanese corporations increasingly relied on bank loans rather than on issuing stocks and bonds because the wartime environment created uncertainties in the capital markets and because the government's regulatory measures encouraged bank loans for corporate financng.[11] Even though Japanese corporations relied mainly on equity financing in the 1930s, this changed after 1939, and by 1945 bank loans provided 93.2 percent of external corporate funding.[12] The Finance Ministry's agenda was assisted by SCAP's continuation of the closure of the securities market, which had begun on August 10, 1945, shortly before the end of war, until May 1949, although it tacitly approved de facto over-the-counter dealings.

Although in 1947 and 1948 SCAP succeeded in two reform measures patterned after New Deal financial reforms—the establishment of a Securities Exchange Commission and the separation of banking and securities businesses[13]—it failed to create not only a market-oriented financial system but also a system centered around direct finance. The Draper-Johnston mission's recommendation to the War Department in April 1948 removed Japanese banks from the list of zaibatsu firms to be dissolved. Among the banks that was spared was the Industrial Bank of Japan, which was transformed from a governmental to a private bank in 1950 and played a crucial role in channeling long-term credit to the heavy and chemical industries.

The postwar inflation was another major obstacle to the reopening of the securities market.[14] Dodge's austerity measures, although bringing down inflation, also caused a depression in the recently reopened securities market. This depression continued until the short-lived boom of several months induced by the Korean War, a boom that was accompanied by further speculation and corruption in the securities market.[15]

Finally, smaller financial institutions, such as Ayukawa's Atō bank, could not lend as much as they wanted to startup firms because of severe interest rate regulation introduced by the Temporary Money Rates Adjustment Law, passed in 1947, which enabled the Ministry of Finance to regulate interest rates on loans and deposits. This law had the effect of encouraging the targeting of bank loans at large-scale and capital-intensive areas such as the heavy and chemical industries rather than at the often labor-intensive small and medium-sized firms.[16]

Ayukawa's approach was to encourage direct investments of foreign capital and to discourage the shielding of the Japanese financial and foreign exchange markets from overseas influences, which was the policy of the Ministry of Finance. If that ministry had adopted Ayukawa's approach, it would have allowed firms to secure capital from overseas, and the ministry would not have been able to continue the policy of keeping interest rates artificially low for as long as it did. That would have permitted banks to be more forthcoming in lending to small and medium-sized firms, a trend that would have tended to concentrate capital in the labor-intensive industries rather than the heavy and chemical industries. Japan's postwar industrialization would then have centered around labor-intensive small and medium-sized firms. On the other hand, deregulation of Japan's financial and foreign exchange markets in the 1950s, which seems to have been Ayukawa's preference, might have led to capital flight from Japan and thus to inadequate domestic capital accumulation. Furthermore, big business, manufacturers, and export industries probably could not have received the amount of capital they did under the Ministry of Finance's approach, and the high economic growth phase from the late 1950s to the early 1970s would not have occurred.[17] Yet, as Calder points out, the heavy and chemical industries became "far larger than either government or the leaders of private industry desired" and "had to be radically downsized after the Oil Shock of 1973."[18]

Epilogue

Japan is finally confronting the issues Ayukawa raised during the prewar immediate postwar years and in his essay introduced in the beginning of this book. New employment and business opportunities can be provided by small and medium-sized firms, but government regulations and the credit crunch brought about by the ailing financial system have severely hindered the unleashing of their creative energy. Under the indirect financing system, startup companies have severe difficulties in securing loans from banks because they are high risk and bankers are risk-averse by nature. These firms, however, could secure capital more easily if they had better access to the securities market, as do their counterparts in the United States.[1] (Stronger rules for financial disclosure are also needed in both countries and elsewhere in the post-Enron environment.) A front-page article in the August 15, 1998, issue of *Nikkei shimbun* argued that the knowledge provided by incoming foreign corporations is changing not only the financial system but also the system and policies that have dominated Japan.[2] An editorial in the same issue made the following point: "Many things must be reconsidered in the midst of this situation, which resembles the 'second defeat.' [The first was World War II.] In looking ahead into the next century, it seems increasingly important that we need to think how to deal with the issue of 'globalization' when we think about the relations between Japan and the rest of the world." The article admonished against excessive nationalism and argued that globalization is here to stay. Japan ought to engage in a dialogue with the rest of the world on what is valuable in globalization and what is not.[3]

As *Nikkei shimbun* commented in another front-page article on August 23, 1998, "What is certain is that Japan has entered an era when the private sector is pushing and leading the government to change the country." In addition to these articles, on August 5, 1998, *Nikkei shimbun*, in a front-page article, pointed out that only 35 large manufacturing corporations are responsible for over 50 percent of Japan's exports. These companies are increasingly shifting their production overseas, and the less competitive large manufacturing companies face the choice of retiring from the market or restructuring for survival. An example of the last point is Nissan Motors' desperate attempts, following the failure of its merger talks with Daimler-Chrysler and Ford, to revitalize its global competitiveness by allowing Renault to control 36.8 percent of its shares, an event that is part of the ongoing global reshaping of the automobile industry. But under the able leadership of Nissan Motors President Carlos Ghosn, who had been sent by Renault's chairman, the automaker underwent extraordinary managerial and financial reforms in one year, shakeups that resulted in a dramatic turnaround in Nissan's profitability by March 2001. Nissan's relations with Renault, then, demonstrate the benefits managerial participation of foreign multinationals brings to ailing Japanese corporations. But will Japan, after over a decade of economic slump and at least a decade of procrastination, further open up its doors to foreign investors and trade at this critical moment of a global economic slowdown?

On May 19, 2001, *Nikkei shimbun* admonished against the present protectionist mood in Japan, a mood represented by the emergency measures against the inundation of Chinese goods and agricultural products in the Japanese market. *Nikkei* argued that Japan should learn from the American efforts to restructure its economy in the 1970s and 1980s into an internationally competitive one, an effort that brought impressive economic prosperity to America after the early 1990s. The same article also argued that because many of the Asian economies had achieved their economic competitiveness through the introduction of foreign direct investments and because the most recent government white paper on international commerce and trade reveals the Japanese economy is in the lowest category among the advanced industrial nations in terms of the shares in production and employment provided by foreign companies in its own economy, Japan should strive to open its doors to the outside world through such measures as internationally acceptable financial disclosures, free trade agreements with Asian countries, and foreign direct investments.[4]

As Ayukawa had argued in the prewar years and in the immediate postwar years, the best prescription for Japan's economic survival, particularly in a free trade system, is to attract foreign direct and indirect investments by modifying Japan's xenophobic economic regulations so as to lure foreign capital inflows for mutual economic prosperity and for new innovations and industries. The odds were not on his side in the prewar years when, in the midst of a global economic collapse, Japan's adventurism in China brought economic, political, and military disasters to Japan, misery and tragedy to its people and those of its Asian neighbors, and isolation from the international community that ended with the ludicrous fight against most of the major powers. The odds were against Ayukawa's endeavors as well in the immediate postwar years. As Ayukawa had predicted in his prewar essay and his postwar discussions with Kishi, Japan now faces harsh global economic competition. In this competition China is emerging as a major economic and perhaps military power. In the late 1990s China emerged as the workshop of the world based on the authoritarian communist regime's drive since the late 1970s to restructure China's economy into a market-oriented one by attracting foreign direct and indirect investments from the United States, Asia, and Europe, investments that jumped exponentially in the 1990s. China was admitted to the World Trade Organization in November 2001, and the Beijing regime has so far been successful in reorienting the Chinese economy from one that relies heavily on state economic regulations and inefficient state-run companies to one that relies on deregulation, an open door to foreign capital, and indigenous and foreign entrepreneurs, economic strategies quite similar to those Ayukawa pursued unsuccessfully in the late 1930s and in the immediate postwar years. Just as in the 1930s American policymakers perceived Ayukawa's call for foreign investments in Manchukuo as an attempt to use foreign funds to underwrite Japan's military aggression in China, the United States now sees China as possibly using its economic gains for military expansionism and regional hegemony that will challenge the regional order secured by the American military presence in Asia, notably Japan. Will this American perception and the Chinese reactions to it based on its feelings of being contained by the United States contribute to undermining the economic interdependence between China and the rest of the world that has helped accelerate the globalizing trend in the international economy? How will Japan cope with its greater economic dependence on China at this critical moment when Japan is at a crossroads in formulating and making critical decisions for economic restructuring and for national security strategy centered on its alliance with the United States? This author hopes that all parties involved in this potentially unstable region will strive for peaceful economic expansion as well as the creation of a multilateral regional order that contributes to greater stability in the international political economy.[5] My hope remains strong even in the post–9-11 world and in facing the mounting crises concerning the Middle East and North Korea.

Reference Matter

Notes

For complete author names, titles, and publication data for the works cited here in short form, see the Bibliography, pp. 327–42.

Introduction

1. The other characteristics of "the 1940–era system" are the establishment of direct taxation as the main source of government revenues by such means as the world's first withholding tax on wages and the corporation tax, the centralization of tax collection, the dependence of prefectural and other local economies on central government funding, government subsidies for the production of rice, and the strengthening of the legal positions of tenants; see Noguchi, *1940 nen taisei*, 6–12. See also Nakamura Takafusa, "Gaisetsu, 1937–1954"; Hashimoto Jurō, "'1940 nen taisei' wa genzai to chokketsu shite inai," *Economist*, May 9, 1995; idem, "Kigyō shisutemu no 'hattsei,' 'senren,' 'seidoka' no ronri"; Okazaki Tetsuji and Okuno Masahiro, "Gendai Nihon no keizai shisutemu to sono rekishiteki genryū"; Okazaki Tetsuji, "Nihon gata kigyō shisutemu no genryū"; Dower, *Embracing Defeat*, 558; and Johnson, *MITI and the Japanese Miracle*, 155–56.

2. Ayukawa, *Searching for Truth*, 60–63; Ayukawa Yoshisuke Papers, Microfiche no. 912.62. The Ayukawa family has loaned this collection to the National Diet Library in Tokyo. For Japanese versions of this essay, see Ayukawa, *Watashi no kangaekata*, 207–8; and idem, *Mono no mikata kangaekata*, 67–76.

3. Ayukawa, *Searching for Truth*, 46–53 and 56–60; idem, *Mono no mikata kangaekata*, 52–59; Ayukawa Yoshisuke Papers, Microfiche no. 912.62.

4. Iriye, *Across the Pacific*, 80–81.

5. Ibid., 123.

6. Wilson, *American Business and Foreign Policy*, 21–22, 45.

7. Ibid., 9, 42; Hogan, *Informal Entente*, 10, 91.

8. Schulzinger, *U.S. Diplomacy Since 1900*, 156; Leffler, *The Specter of Communism*, 17.

9. Leuchtenburg, *Franklin D. Roosevelt and the New Deal*, 243–44.

10. See Brinkley, *The Unfinished Nation*, 699, 703, 729–30; idem, "The New Deal and the Idea of the State," 86–91, 91–99, 102, 108–12; Leuchtenburg, *Franklin D. Roosevelt and the New Deal*, 245–52, 256, 259, 263–66, 271–74, 290–94, 303, 307–24; and Schwarz, *The New Dealers*, xi–xii, xvi, 203–8, 297, 300–302, 306–13, 315–24, 344–45, for the significance of New Deal state capitalism and for the meaning of various public investment projects in the western and southern states during the New Deal.

11. See, e.g., Barnhart, *Japan Prepares for Total War*, 20, 272.

12. For other works on Ayukawa and the economy of Manchuria related to the subject of this book, see Hara Akira, "Manshū ni okeru keizai tōsei seisaku no tenkai"; Suzuki Takashi, "Manshū keizai kaihatsu to Manshū jūkōgyō no seiritsu"; Udagawa, "Nissan zaibatsu no jidōsha sangyō shinshutsu ni tsuite"; idem, "Nissan saibatsu no Manshū shinshutsu"; and Kojima Naoki, *Ayukawa Yoshisuke den*. In English, see Cusumano, *The Japanese Automobile Industry*.

Chapter 1

1. See Chō, "An Inquiry into the Problem of Importing American Capital into Manchuria," 381, 383; Kobayashi Michihiko, "Seitō seiji to Manshū keiei," 203–21; Rosenberg, *Spreading the American Dream*, 132, 148–52; and Lafeber, *The Clash*, 86–87, 95, 115–16. See *Shinmonkiroku (Interrogation Records)*, 1: 82–87, microfiche no. 163.1, Ayukawa Papers; and Awaya and Yoshida, *Kokusai kensatsukyoku (IPS) jinmonchōsho*, 272, for Ayukawa's discussion of his relations with Kuhara and Kuhara's proposed joint venture with U.S. Steel. The first document is a Japanese transcript (dated June 6, 1946) of Ayukawa's interrogations from Jan. 28 to May 22, 1946, by Solis Horwitz and Henry A. Hauxhurst in preparation for the International Prosecution Section of the International Military Tribunal for the Far East. The second document includes the English transcript of Ayukawa's interrogations by the two in January–February 1946.

2. Ayukawa's weakening relations with Kuhara and his own rise to prominence in business are based on Ayukawa, "Watakushi no rirekisho," 298–311, 316–20; Kojima Naoki, *Ayukawa Yoshisuke den*, 51–55; Cusumano, *The Japanese Automobile Industry*, 31; and Kobayashi, *Daitōa kyōeiken ho keisei to hōkai*, 170–71. For Kuhara's business and political activities from the 1910s until 1945, see Yonemoto, *Denki Kuhara Fusanosuke ou o kataru*, 18–19, 498, 501–5, 520–27, 531–35, 570, 572–73, 608–12, 655–1025 passim, 1082–1147 passim. See also Ayukawa's explanation of his relations with Kuhara during World War I in Awaya and Yoshida, *Kokusai kensatsukyoku (IPS) jinmonchōsho*, 256–57, 272. Although Ayukawa said in his interrogation record (*Shinmonkiroku 1*, 82–87, microfiche no. 163.1, Ayukawa Papers; Awaya and Yoshida, *Kokusai kensatsukyoku (IPS) jinmonchōsho*, 221–22) that he did not meddle in Kuhara's political affairs after he took

over Kuhara's firm, in the mid-1960s he stated ("Watashi no rirekisho," 321–22) that he had supported Kuhara's idea of a buffer state. Kuhara divorced Ayukawa's sister in 1942 (Yonemoto, *Denki Kuhara Fusanosuke ou o kataru*, 664, 1145–46). For the formation of the Imperial Rule Assistance Association, see Awaya, *Shōwa no rekishi*, 356–58, 366–73. For the grim social and political consequences of the movement, which some see as the Japanese version of fascism, see Eguchi, *Jūgonen sensō shōshi*, 218–22.

3. For Nissan's rise to prominence and its characteristics as a conglomerate, see Ayukawa, "Watakushi no rirekisho," 322–24; and Udagawa Masaru, "Nissan zaibatsu no Manshū shinshutsu," 49, 54–55. On Takahashi's economic policies, see Nakamura, *Shōwa keizaishi*, 72, 89–97.

4. *Jidōsha shiryō*, 1: 56–61, 64–65, 74–76; 2: 73–84, 95–105, 127–29, 187–202; see also NHK, *Dokyumentō Shōwashi*, 3: 27–40, 42–62, 84–91; William R. Gorham-shi kinenjigyō iinkai, *William R. Gorham den*, 164–180; and Halberstam, *The Reckoning*, 263–65. For Nissan's approach to GM for a merger, see Ayukawa Yoshisuke papers, microfiche no. 513.1; in addition, see nos. 512.1 and 512.2; and Udagawa, "Nissan zaibatsu no jidōsha sangyō shinshutsu ni tsuite," pt. II, 82–83. For Itō's report, see *Jidōsha shiryō*, 3: 12–20. Shinomiya, "Senzen no jidōsha sanhyō to 'Manshū,'" 16, 20, 28n42.

5. *Jidōsha shiryō*, 3: 12–20; Ayukawa Papers, microfiche nos. 512.1 and 513.1 (the latter includes Ayukawa's Jan. 9 cable to GM); and Udagawa, "Nissan zaibatsu no jidōsha sangyō shinshutsu ni tsuite," pt. II, 88–93. Microfiche no. 512.1 and Udagawa's article point to the fact that Ayukawa had to overcome opposition with Nissan board members such as Yamamoto Sōji, Asahara Genshichi, Kubota Tokujirō (who were also board members of Nissan Motors), and Odaira Namihei (president of Hitachi); his opponents preferred Nissan to develop Datsun and not rely on GM. Udagawa argues that this opposition and the interference by the Army led Ayukawa to abandon the Nissan-GM merger talks at the end of 1934. For Itō's recollection of Ayukawa's comment, see *Jidōsha shiryō*, 1: 68.

6. See *Jidōsha shiryō*, 3: 21–24, for Kogane's recollections in the policymaking process leading up to the Automobile Manufacturing Law of 1936. NHK, *Dokyumentō Shōwashi*, 3: 63–66. For Kishi's remark during an interview about his difficulty in deflecting the Army's intention to eliminate foreign car companies, see ibid., 72. Finally, see ibid., 98–99, 102–13, 120–22, 152–53, 162–66, on Ford's attempt to build this factory and the Japanese government's interference in this project.

7. For Miyata's remark, see *Jidōsha shiryō*, 3: 8–9. See ibid., 3: 17, for the text of the outline. In addition see NHK, *Dokyumento Shōwashi*, 3: 114–20.

8. On these talks, see Ayukawa Yoshisuke papers, microfiche no. 513.6; included with this handwritten memo by Kishimoto is a printed memorandum from MCI stipulating the four conditions for the merger. For Yoshino's later recollections, see Yoshino, *Omakaji torikaji*, 263–64. For Kurusu's and the Cabinet Legal Section's attitudes toward the Automobile Manufacturing Law, see *Jidōsha shiryō*, 1: 66–67, 69. For a

discussion of these points and the Navy's view of Ford-Japan, see Udagawa Masaru, "Kokusanka seisaku to gaishi: Jidōsha seizō jigyōhō to Ford, GM," 339–40; for the conversations between Phillips and Yoshino, see ibid., 334–36. For a discussion by Kogane of the disagreement between Kurusu and Matsushima, see *Jidōsha shiryō*, 3: 22–23. Ayukawa told Horwitz that the Army, although he had shown them the GM-Nissan agreement, was suspicious that the two parties had a secret agreement and twice burglarized Phillips's hotel room, once in Osaka, where nothing was taken, and once in Tokyo, where Phillips's briefcase containing all the important documents for this talks with Nissan, was stolen; see Awaya and Yoshida, *Kokusai kensatsukyoku (IPS) jinmonchōsho*, 282.

9. *Jidōsha shiryō*, 1: 62, 2: 105; Ayukawa Yoshisuke Papers, microfiche nos. 513.2–5.

10. See *Jidōsha shiryō*, 2: 68–71, 105–9, and 132–35, for Asahara's, Kubota's, and Hatakemura's recollections of their dealings with Graham-Paige. On the Graham-Paige engineers, see Cusamano, *The Japanese Automobile Industry*, 45.

11. Johnson, *MITI and the Japanese Miracle*, 132–33. Other laws passed during the late 1930s were the Artificial Petroleum Law (Aug. 10, 1937), the Steel Industry Law (Aug. 12, 1937), the Machine Tool Industry Law (Mar. 30, 1938), the Aircraft Manufacturing Law (Mar. 30, 1938), the Shipbuilding Industry Law (Apr. 5, 1939), the Light Metals Manufacturing Industry Law (May 1, 1939), and the Important Machines Manufacturing Law (May 3, 1941).

12. See NHK, *Dokyumento Shōwashi*, 3: 166–69. In addition, see Awaya and Yoshida, *Kokusai kensatsukyoku (IPS) jinmonchōsho*, 174, 186.

13. Asakura Tsuneto, *Nikki*, vol. 2, entry for Aug. 19, 1936. For Asakura's role as an advisor to Minister Ogawa, see, e.g., ibid., entries for Apr. 27, June 24 and 27, July 8 and 27, and Aug. 15, 20, and 22, 1936; and vol. 3, entry for Jan. 1, 1937.

14. Ibid., vol. 2, entries for Aug. 21, Nov. 3, 20, and 30, and Dec. 15, 1936; and vol. 3, entry for Jan. 29, 1937. Toyoda Automatic Loom Company's automobile section became Toyota Motors in August 1937.

15. On Ogawa's relations with Yoshino and Kishi, see Hara Yoshihisa, *Kishi Nobusuke*, 54; and Yoshino, *Omakaji torikaji*, 285–90.

16. Yoshino, *Omokaji torikaji*, 326, 342–43, 395–409, 419, and 421–22; and Barnhart, *Japan Prepares for Total War*, 68–69.

17. Kishi later confessed that when he arrived in Manchukuo in November 1936, he underestimated the difficulty of industrialization: "I believed all we needed was managerial skills of people from companies such as Mitsui and Mitsubishi" (Itō Takashi et al., *Kishi Nobusuke no kaiso*, 23). See also Hara Yoshihisa, *Kishi Nobusuke*, 54–59.

Chapter 2

1. Peattie, *Ishiwara Kanji*, 141.
2. Ibid., 50–52, 63.

3. Ibid., 68.

4. Ibid., 96–98, 166. For U. S.-Japan relations during the crisis in the Far East, see Iriye, *Across the Pacific*, 174–88.

5. Yamamuro Shin'ichi, *Kimera*, 16.

6. On the policy papers that developed into the outline, see Hara Akira, "Senkyūhyaku sanjūnendai no Manshū keizai tōsei seisaku," 19–34. For the Japanese military's views on the Open Door principle, see Chō Yukio, "Amerika shihon no Manshū dōnyū keikaku," 131–32. For the texts of policy papers issued by the military slightly before and a year after the Manchuria Incident that show support for the Open Door policy among the Japanese military such as Kwantung Army Chief of Staff Itagaki Seishirō's policy analysis written around April or May 1932, see *Gendaishi shiryō*, 7: 162, 167, 172–80, 228, 252, 342–44, 361–62, 494, and 636–39.

7. *Gendaishi shiryō*, 7: 156, 162, 167.

8. Ibid., 172–80.

9. Hara Akira, "Senkyūhyaku sanjūnendai," 31.

10. Suzuki Takashi, "Manshū," 99–100. Special companies and semi-special companies were founded on companies that had belonged to the Chang regime before the Japanese takeover by the Kwantung Army in 1931. With the announcement of the outline in 1933, Manchukuo established the Law on Special Companies. Companies in industries Manchukuo designated as "important" for the economic development of the new country became special companies. These companies enjoyed a monopoly based on the principle of one company per industry. Although they fell under government control in terms of personnel decisions regarding board members, management, allocation of profits, and the issue of making a profit, they received benefits such as tax exemptions, the right to issue bonds, and guaranteed returns; on the last point, the Kwantung Army remained vague during the initial years. Semi-special companies, although not as regulated as special companies, played a similar role. After 1933, special and semi-special companies took over the basic industries needed for heavy industrialization, and they controlled about 60 to 70 percent of capital in those industries even though the number of these companies constituted only 1–4 percent of all companies in Manchukuo. SMR and the Manchukuo government played the central role in financing these companies until MIDC came into existence in 1937. In addition to Suzuki's article, see also Kobayashi Hideo, *Daitōa kyōeiken no keisei to hōkai*, 51–52.

11. Hara Akira, "Senkyūhyaku sanjūnendai," 45, 51–57.

12. Suzuki, "Manshū," 102–3.

13. F. C. Jones, *Manchuria Since 1931*, 112. In the five years ending in 1938, SMR invested ¥0.8 million, half of which went for the building of new railroads.

14. On Aug. 28, 1935, the Army had addressed its concerns about the drying up of capital inflows into Manchukuo within a year or so (*Gendaishi shiryō*, 8: 802; Suzuki, "Manshū," 102–4). Japanese conglomerates feared excessive economic regulation in

Manchukuo and preferred to invest in Manchukuo by financing the SMR. In addition to Suzuki's article, see Hara Akira, "Senkyūhyaku sanjūnendai," 49–50. Before the outbreak of the Sino-Japanese War in 1937, Mitsui was interested chiefly in making indirect investments in Manchukuo. Afterward, it began to make more direct investments under the guidance of the Manchukuo government, which limited its direct investments to artificial fuel and munitions factories (Kasuga Yutaka, "Mitsui zaibatsu to Chūgoku/Manshū tōshi," 55–82). Japanese investment in Manchuria rebounded to ¥348 million in 1937 and by 1941 had reached ¥1,423 billion (Chō, "Amerika shihon no Manshū dōnyū keikaku," 139). For foreign trade figures in both absolute and percentage terms for Manchuria between 1931 and 1940, see Manshū teikoku seifu, *Manshū kenkoku jūnenshi*, 616–17. Although the shares of imports from and exports to Japan for Manchuria continued to increase from 1938 to 1940, exports to Japan from Manchuria dropped in absolute terms in 1940. For the shares of imports from and exports to Manchuria for Japan between 1928 and 1938, see Yamamoto Kazuto, "Bōeki no henka to kokusaitairitsu no gekika," 244–45.

15. Hara, "Senkyūhyaku sanjūnendai," 55–56.

16. Suzuki, *Nihon teikokushugi to Manshū*, 179–189. This book uses parts of Suzuki's 1963 article.

17. Suzuki, *Nihon teikokushugi to Manshū*, 216–26.

18. See Asakura, *Nikki*, "Introduction," 11, 12–13, and vol. 2: entries for Nov. 29 and Dec. 10, 1934. Asakura and Minami were from Ōita prefecture. Asakura's cousin, a famous sculptor and an organizer of a social club that Asakura frequently attended, invited Minami on many occasions as a guest of honor. Asakura was also a classmate of Minami's younger brother at Ōita Junior High School.

19. See Asakura Tsuneto's draft letter (probably to Minami Jirō), May 1935 in Asakura, *Nikki*, vol. 6. In a draft addressed to Minami, Asakura, although not touching on the second point mentioned in December, restated the first point. Furthermore, besides discussing the details of financing this joint Japanese-Manchukuo company, Asakura stated that both Japan and Manchukuo were going to export primarily raw materials to one another.

20. Asakura, *Nikki*, vol. 2, entry for Aug. 1, 1935. See also Asakura's draft letter to Minami, Aug. 3, 1935, in ibid., vol. 6. Asakura met Matsuoka through his artist-cousin's social gatherings (see ibid., "Introduction," 10; vol. 2, entry for Aug. 13, 1935).

21. Minami to Asakura, May 10, 1935, in ibid., vol. 6. Minami wrote a letter to Asakura on July 22, 1935, after receiving a letter from Asakura congratulating him on the establishment of the Japan-Manchukuo Economic Committee. Minami stated the country was working on becoming self-sufficient in textiles in several years. The committee was established on July 15, 1935, and it consisted of eight members: the Kwantung Army chief of staff, a counselor from the Japanese embassy, the chief advisor to the Kwantung Army, the president of the Kwantung Department (Kantōkyoku

sōchō), three Manchukuo ministers (Foreign, Finance, and Industry), and the secretary general of the Manchukuo General Affairs Agency (Suzuki, *Nihon teikokushugi to Manshū*, 225–26).

22. Matsuoka to Asakura, Apr. 13, 1936, in Asakura, *Nikki*, vol. 6. In this letter, Matsuoka regretted Minami's departure to become governor-general of Korea, succeeding Ugaki Kazushige (1868–1956), to whose faction Minami belonged in the Army. Later in the letter, Matsuoka stated he knew Ueda Kenkichi (1875–1962), Minami's successor, very well. As we shall see later, it was under Ueda's administration that Matsuoka faced the dismantling of the SMR.

23. Asakura, *Nikki*, vol. 2: entries for Apr. 16 and 18, May 4, and Sept. 8, 1936. See also Matsuoka to Asakura, in ibid., vol. 6, entry for Oct. 17, 1936. Asakura and Ayukawa belonged to the Chōsen Economic Research Committee (Chōsen sangyō keizai chōsakai), which consisted of prominent businessmen and served as an advisory group to Governor-General Minami Jirō on industrial development (see Mitarai, *Minami Juror*, 438–43). Asakura stated he met Ayukawa through Ogawa Gōtarō when Ogawa was minister of commerce and industry (Ayukawa Yoshisuke sensei henshū kankō kai, *Ayukawa sensei tsuisōroku*, 17).

24. Peattie, *Ishiwara Kanji*, 186, 197. For some of the policy papers that came out slightly before and after August 1935 that argued for increased and continued inflow of capital from Japan into Manchukuo and that discussed the future role of the SMR in Manchukuo, see *Gendaishi shiryō*, 8: 705, 785–96, 806–8, 814, and 818–19.

25. Ishiwara, however, differed from the State Control faction since he advocated the Shōwa Restoration: "the desire to reenact the Meiji Restoration, antagonism toward the privileged classes, professed anti-capitalism, concern for the rural population, fervent patriotism, and a mystical belief in Japan's unique destiny" (Peattie, *Ishiwara Kanji*, 201–2). However, he was different from the young officers who advocated this Shōwa Restoration. His idea was a revolution from above and not from below. Above all the restoration was necessary for preparing for the war with the Soviet Union and the Final War (see also Shillony, *Revolt in Japan*, 80).

26. *Gendaishi shiryō*, 8: 703.

27. Peattie, *Ishiwara Kanji*, 198, 205–6, 208; Hara Akira and Nakamura, "Kaidai," 1; Kojima Naoki, *Ayukawa Yoshisuke den*, 20–23. Miyazaki had studied in Russia at the time of the Bolshevik Revolution and had studied economic planning in the Soviet Union in the late 1920s. Although interested in Marxism, Miyazaki was never politically oriented in that direction. Miyazaki played a key role after the Manchuria Incident in overcoming those in the SMR antagonistic to the Kwantung Army and in economic planning in Manchuria from 1931 to 1936. For the General Staff's financing of Ishiwara's project, see Itō Takashi, *Shōwaki no seiji (zoku)*, 53. See Microfiche no. 941.2 in the Ayukawa Yoshisuke Papers, which discusses why Ayukawa ended up cooperating with the Army's Five-Year Plan in Manchukuo. This is a record of a discussion on

Oct. 26, 1951, among former ranking businessmen, government officials, and military officers who were involved in that program. Present were Ayukawa Yoshisuke, Aoki Kazuo, Asahara Kenzō, Katakura Tadashi, Kishi Nobusuke, Kishimoto Kantarō, Morita Hisashi, Suzuki Eiji, Uchida Tsuneo, and Tomoda Juichirō. This document reveals that at the time Minami Jirō was serving as Kwantung Army commander, Iwakuro Hideo, who will appear in Chapter 7, was actively involved with Ishiwara, Katakura, and Itagaki in finding ways to bring more private capital to Manchukuo.

28. Peattie, *Ishiwara Kanji*, 261–65. The fact that Ishiwara failed to completely influence the cabinet appointments of Prime Minister Hayashi Senjurō (1876–1943) bruised his prestige but not as gravely as Peattie claims. But as Peattie points out, Ishiwara became isolated in the Central Headquarters as many of his allies were reassigned to new posts during the March 1937 personnel change in which he was promoted to major general and made director of the Operations Bureau.

29. Ibid., 238–43.

30. Ibid., 243–45.

31. Although Chalmers Johnson (*MITI*, 129, 131) dramatizes the "economic general staff" and their planning of the entire Japanese economy under the Cabinet Planning Board, which was established in October 1937, economic plans for Japan and its empire were well under way in 1936. In addition, further discussion in this text will point out the fact that contrary to Kishi Nobusuke's comment, which Johnson used, that Shiina Etsusaburō was the central figure in the creation of the Five-Year Plan, a small group of army officers in the Japanese Army and the Kwantung Army and the people in the Miyazaki group were the central figures.

32. Kobayashi, *Dai Tōa kyōeiken no keisei to hōkai*, 66–68; Hara, "Senkyūhyaku sanjūnendai," 62. In addition, see the Oct. 26, 1951, discussion in Microfiche no. 941.2 in the Ayukawa Yoshisuke Papers.

33. Hara Akira, "Manshū ni okeru keizai tōsei seisaku no tenkai," 229–30; idem, "Senkyūhyaku sanjūnendai," 65–66.

34. Hara Akira and Nakamura, "Kaidai," 2; two top executives of the Mitsubishi Heavy Industry Company also saw the document. For the awareness of Kido, Konoe, Yūki, and Ikeda regarding the Ishiwara group's proposed five-year plan in Manchukuo and economic restructuring of Japan, see Kido, *Nikki*, vol. 1, entries for Feb 2, 5, 8, and 25, 1937, pp. 542–43, and 547; and Harada Kumao, *Saionji kō to seikyoku*, 5: 252–53.

35. Hara Akira, "Manshū ni okeru keizai tōsei seisaku no tenkai," 230. Aside from Ayukawa, Ishiwara had contacted top business executives Noguchi Jun (Shitagau) of the Japan Nitrogen Company, Kaneko Naokichi (1866–1944) of the House of Suzuki, Yasukawa Yūnoksuke (1870–1944) of the Oriental Development Company, Tsuda Shingo of the Kanebō Textile Company, and Mori Nobuteru of the Shōwa Fertilizer Company. See also note 39.

36. Hashimoto Jurō, *Daikyōkōki no Nihon shihonshugi*, 361–62.

37. See the figure taken from *Kōgyō tōkeishi shiryōhen*, 4–13, in Tatematsu Kiyoshi, "Dokusen." According to Nakamura Takafusa, *Economic Growth in Prewar Japan*, 23, heavy industries' share of manufacturing output increased from 43.5 percent in 1935 to 58.8 percent in 1940.

38. Tatematsu, "Dokusen," 206.

39. See the Oct. 26, 1951, discussion on how Ayukawa ended up cooperating with the Army's Manchukuo Five-Year Plan in Microfiche no. 941.2 in the Ayukawa Yoshisuke Papers; comment by Katakura in "Discussion" in Aug. 1, 1961, issue of *Zaikai*; Kojima Naoki, *Ayukawa Yoshisuke den*, 45–47; and Ayukawa, "Watashi no rirekisho," 283–90. In addition to Ayukawa and the businessmen mentioned in note 35, the Miyazaki group approached Isaka Takashi (1870–1949), president of Tokyo Gas Company; Matsukata Kōjirō (1865–1950), a prominent businessman and Lower House member; and Murata Shōzō (1878–1957), an influential maritime shipping business executive. Isaka rejected the request, and the rest seemed to have visited Manchukuo at the Kwantung Army's or the Manchukuo Government's invitation at one point or another. Asahara's father was an employee at a coalmine owned by Ayukawa's relatives, the Kaijimas; for Asahara's activities during the Yawata Steelmill strike and for a biographical sketch of his earlier life, see chap. 1 of Yatsugi, *Rōdōsōgi hiroku*. Awaya Kentarō (*Shōwa no rekishi*, 171–72) mentions Asahara as one of few men not affiliated with the two major parties who were elected after the implementation of the universal manhood suffrage. See Asahara's explanation at a meeting at Ayukawa's residence on Oct. 26, 1951, in Microfiche no. 941.2 of the Ayukawa Yoshisuke Papers. Ayukawa gave his opinion about Ishiwara and described Ishiwara's opinion about letting businessmen take over the management of the Manchurian economy in *Shinmonkiroku* (Interrogation records) 1, 80–81, Microfiche no. 163.1, Ayukawa Yoshisuke Papers; this is not mentioned in the English transcript in Awaya and Yoshida, *Kokusai kensatsukyoku (IPS) jinmonchōsho*, 208–83. In addition, see Ayukawa, *Zuihitsu gomokumeshi*, 116–17; and idem, "Watashi no rirekisho," 325. For Ikeda's skepticism about the feasibility of the Five-Year Plan, see Harada, *Saionji kō to seikyoku*, 253; and Kido, *Nikki*, entry for Feb. 5, 1937, p. 543. Regarding Yūki's and Konoe's skepticism, see Kido, *Nikki*, entries for Feb. 2 and 25, 1937, pp. 542 and 547, respectively.

40. Asakura, *Nikki*, vol. 2, entry for Nov. 2, 1936. Based on this diary entry, it is likely Ayukawa was in Manchukuo during November instead of October, although there is a possibility he went back and forth between Japan and Manchukuo starting in October.

41. Ayukawa speculated about Matsuoka's motives in inviting Ayukawa to Manchukuo during the Oct. 26, 1951, discussion; see Microfiche no. 941.2 in the Yoshisuke Ayukawa Papers. Matsuoka believed Ayukawa opposed the reorganization of the SMR and felt he would render Matsuoka assistance in managing SMR. See also

Ayukawa, "Manshū keizai shihai no kii pointo," 191; and Ayukawa, *Shinmonkiroku* 1, Ayukawa Yoshisuke Papers. Microfiche no. 163.1, 81–82.

42. For the places Ayukawa visited and the people he met, see Microfiche no. 182.2, Ayukawa Yoshisuke Papers.

43. Ayukawa, *Watashi no jinsei sekkei*, 80–82. In this essay, he misdates events that happened in 1936 as happening in 1937. See also Kobayashi, *Dai Tōa kyōeiken no keisei to hōkai*, 253–70; Hoshino, *Mihatenu yume*, 120; Kojima Naoki, *Ayukawa Yoshisuke den*, 5–6, 16, and 32; and Ayukawa, "Watashi no rirekisho," 325–26.

See Asahara's explanation during discussions at Ayukawa's residence on Oct. 26, 1951, in Microfiche no. 941.2 of the Ayukawa Yoshisuke Papers. Furthermore, see *Shinmonkiroku* 1, 2–7, Microfiche no. 163.1, Ayukawa Yoshisuke Papers; and Awaya and Yoshida, *Kokusai kensatsukyoku (IPS) jinmonchōsho*, 222–23, 228–34. Ayukawa incorrectly wrote in item 6 of this record that he did not know about the plan that was under way to implement a five-year economic plan in Manchukuo. Ayukawa stated in his retirement speech from MIDC and business on Jan. 7, 1943, that he thought at the time he got involved in Manchukuo's industrialization programs, it would take ten years for the economic development of Manchuria; see 257 in Microfiche no. 922.22 of the Ayukawa Yoshisuke Papers.

44. Around the same time, Ayukawa spoke to his aide Kishimoto Kantarō about his opinions on Manchukuo's industrialization. Ayukawa had hired this graduate of present-day Kobe University in 1932 because of his international business experience and fluency in English. (Kishimoto had worked for many years in London for the Kuhara Trading Company and had an English wife.) Ayukawa told Kishimoto that Japan's production capability, which he viewed as weaker than that of other industrialized countries, could not provide enough resources for Manchukuo's industrialization; Ayukawa recommended mobilizing foreign capital, including foreign technology, production facilities, and personnel. Ayukawa was well aware of the level of American production capabilities compared with Japan's based on his work experience in the United States, and he proposed Manchukuo's industrialization be based on joint ventures between the United States and Japan. See Kishimoto Kantarō's interrogation record, which is his recollection of what he had stated to Prosecutor Solis Horwitz on Jan. 30, 1946. He wrote down his recollections immediately after the interrogation in the presence of a Suzuki and Itō Bunkichi. See Microfiche no. 163.2, 7–8, Ayukawa Yoshisuke Papers. Kishimoto's biographical sketch appeared in an interview article in which Kishimoto talked about Ayukawa; see *Zaikai shisō zenshū*, 189.

45. Kojima Naoki, *Ayukawa Yoshisuke den*, 36; Suzuki, "Manshū keizai kaihatsu," 108; South Manchuria Railway Company, *Sixth Report on Progress in Manchuria to 1939*, 70; and Itagaki Seishirō to Ayukawa Yoshisuke, Nov. 30, 1936, and Ayukawa to Itagaki, Dec. 5, 1936, Microfiche no. 141.123, Ayukawa Yoshisuke Papers. Ayukawa

spoke about becoming an advisor to the Kwantung Army and about the Dōwa Automobile Company in *Shinmonkiroku* 1, 8–9, Microfiche no. 163.1, Ayukawa Yoshisuke Papers; and Awaya and Yoshida, *Kokusai kensatsukyoku (IPS) jinmonchōsho*, 235–36. The latter does not mention the two topics found in the former.

46. Tape recording of an interview with Ayukawa in 1964, Ayukawa Yoshisuke Papers; a transcript of this was made on May 8, 1990, by Nakamura Ryūji, a former associate of Ayukawa. Izumiyama Sanroku, *Tora daijin ni naru made*, 106–13. For the Army's discussions about Yasukawa, Mori, and Ayukawa regarding their qualifications to help industrialize Manchukuo, see the Oct. 26, 1951, discussion in Microfiche no. 941.2 of the Ayukawa Yoshisuke Papers.

47. Kishimoto, Ayukawa's aide, acknowledged Nissan's financial troubles during the Oct. 26, 1951, discussion; see Microfiche no. 941.2 of the Ayukawa Yoshisuke Papers. See also Udagawa Masaru, "Nissan zaibatsu no Manshū shinshutsu," 61–62.

48. Hara Akira, "Manshū ni okeru keizai tōsei seisaku no tenkai," 239–42; Suzuki, "Manshū keizai kaihatsu," 112; Nakamura, *Shōwa keizaishi*, 71, 90, 94–108; Kobayashi, *Daitōa kyōeiken no keisei to ōkai*, 171; Johnson, *MITI*, 120.

49. Asakura, *Nikki*, vol. 3. It was during this gloomy period that Ayukawa and Asakura established closer ties. In February 1937 Asakura joined Nissan Motors as a board member. By then Asakura had become sick of the vulgarity and the incompetence he had seen during the first year of his political career (Asakura, *Nikki*, vol. 3, entries for Jan. 1 and Dec. 31, 1937). Attracted by Ayukawa's philosophy of business and his personality and viewing Nissan Motors as the most promising Japanese manufacturer of passenger cars, Asakura by January 19, 1937, had indicated to Ayukawa that he wished to join the Nissan group. Although Ayukawa conveyed to Asakura through Minister of Commerce and Industry Ogawa that he could remain in politics and work as a board member for Nissan Motors, Asakura resigned not only from the Fuji Electric Power Company but also from the Diet (ibid., entries for Jan. 1, 9, 11, 13, 14, 19, 21, 22, 26, and 29; Feb. 2, 4, 5, 8, 9, 13, 14, 15, and 16; and Apr. 12 and 22, 1937).

50. Yoshino, "Mangyō jidai no omoide," 445–46. In his June 5, 1943, eulogy of Supreme Commander Yamamoto Isoroku, who had been shot down while inspecting the South Pacific theater, Ayukawa stated that Yamamoto had first approached him in the spring of 1937 regarding the aircraft project. Yamamoto had invited Ogura Masatsune, the top executive of the Sumitomo Holding Company and member of the House of Peers, a top Mitsui business executive, and Ayukawa to submit their opinions on ways to mass-produce airplanes. During the several meetings Yamamoto had with these men, he became attracted to Ayukawa's suggestion of mass-producing airplanes in a similar way as cars; in making this suggestion, Ayukawa also stated that Japan should mass-produce its technologically unsophisticated machine tools along with the aircraft and find ways to vertically integrate their production

with the production of materials needed for them (Microfiche no. 922.22, 272–73, Ayukawa Yoshisuke Papers).

51. For conditions in Manchuria, see F. C. Jones, *Manchuria Since 1931*, 119–20. See the Oct. 26, 1951, discussion in Microfiche no. 941.2 in the Ayukawa Yoshisuke Papers. In addition, see *Shinmonkiroku* 1, 9–10, Microfiche no. 163.1, Ayukawa Yoshisuke Papers. Ayukawa mistakenly recalled in this document that he had told these ideas to Hoshino shortly after the outbreak of the Sino-Japanese War; for the English transcript, see Awaya and Yoshida, *Kokusai kensatsukyoku (IPS) jinmonchōsho*, 235–38. For Hoshino's recollection of what Ayukawa had told him around this time, see the Japanese transcript of the official interrogation records of Hoshino Naoki in preparation for the International Military Tribunal, Microfiche no. 163.3, 8–11 and 1915–28, Ayukawa Yoshisuke Papers; see also Ayukawa's draft memoir edited by his aide Tomoda Jūchirō, 26–27, Microfiche no. 931.4, Ayukawa Yoshisuke Papers. Tomoda's November 1954 note explains that the memoir was not published because of a dispute with the publisher. In addition, see the Sept. 11, 1954, memorandum by Sakata, another of Ayukawa's aides, in the same microfiche.

52. Asakura, *Nikki*, vol. 3, entries for June 2 and 23. On June 24, the day after Ishiwara's visit, Asakura wrote about another visit by army officers to the Yokohama factory. Among them were Vice Minister of the Army Umeze Yoshijirō.

53. Hoshino Naoki, *Mihatenu yume*, 222–24, 286–87; "Mr. Ayukawa's Speech at MIDC Board Members Meeting, Aug. 26, 1941," in Hara Akira, "Manshū ni okeru keizai tōsei seisaku," 244; Kojima Naoki, *Ayukawa Yoshisuke den*, 67; and Katakura, "Ayukawa Yoshisuke-shi to Mangyō no omoide," 124. Ayukawa had told Asakura on Aug. 26, 1937, that he was willing to accept the responsibility for industrializing Manchuria if his views on bringing in American capital, equipment, and technology for the joint economic development of Manchukuo were accepted. Asakura participated in Nissan Motors' meetings on Aug. 13 and Sept. 9 concerning Nissan's participation in Manchukuo's industrialization programs; see the entries for these dates in Asakura, *Nikki*, vol. 3.

54. Johnson, *MITI*, 132. Johnson seems to have misunderstood Ayukawa's and Kishi's support for the principle of one company per industry. Although they may have agreed on the need for oligopolies in industries, they wanted a coordinated development of industries and were well aware of the need for foreign capital, technology, and equipment.

55. Hara Akira, "Manshū ni okeru keizai tōsei seisaku," 211–23; and Katakura, "Ayukawa Yoshisuke-shi," 125.

56. Asakura, *Nikki*, vol. 3. On Kishi's and Ayukawa's roles in the proposal for the MIDC, see the Oct. 26, 1951, discussion in Microfiche no. 941.2, 9–12, in the Ayukawa Yoshisuke Papers. According to this paper and Katakura, "Ayukawa

Yoshisuke-shi," 125–29, those who were instrumental in Manchukuo in bringing Nissan to Manchuria were Katakura Tadashi, members of the Kwantung Army General Staff, Hoshino Naoki, who was secretary of General Affairs Agency, and Kishi Nobusuke, who was deputy director of the Industry Bureau. Those in influential positions who opposed an arrangement with Nissan were, in addition to Ueda and Tōjō, Kuniwake Shinshichi, who was in charge of drafting the Kwantung Army's policy paper on the comprehensive economic plan for Manchukuo, Matsuda Reisuke, who was the head of the Planning Bureau, and Shiina Etsusaburō, who was the head of Mining and Industrial Affairs. In the end, through political maneuvering among those in the Army and Manchukuo who supported the comprehensive plan, they managed to persuade Ueda and Tōjō and overwhelm the opposition. (Ueda and his colleagues in the military were not aware of Nissan's tax problems at home.)

57. Hoshino, *Mihatenu yume*, 216–18; and the Japanese transcript of the official interrogation records of Hoshino Naoki in preparation for the International Military Tribunal, Microfiche no. 163.3, 1915–28, Ayukawa Yoshisuke Papers; and Katakura, "Ayukawa Yoshisuke-shi," 126.

58. See the Oct. 26, 1951, discussion in Microfiche no. 941.2 of the Ayukawa Yoshisuke Papers. This discusses the process leading to the cabinet approval of the MIDC between June and October 1937. Aoki Kazuo, deputy director of the Steering Committee on Manchurian Affairs, was the one who suggested inserting Ayukawa's proposal to bring foreign capital into Manchukuo at the cabinet meeting that approved the establishment of the MIDC. He stated the Army supported the idea, and the Kwantung Army had not raised any opposition before going into the cabinet meeting. According to Aoki's handwritten note describing his activities in Japanese foreign policy until 1945, probably to prepare for the war crimes investigation against him, he made his suggestion because he liked Ayukawa's ideas for attracting foreign capital. Aoki made this proposal after confirming the military's support for Ayukawa's proposal. He did this so that the Army would not change its policy after personnel changes. Aoki states that War Minister Sugiyama Hajime, who was also director of the Steering Committee on Manchurian Affairs, backed Ayukawa's idea. Aoki supported the reorganization of the SMR and the establishment of a new national policy company; he thought Ayukawa was the right man for the job partly because his company did not belong to the old zaibatsu. See Aoki's notes, Microfiche no. 163.3, 2–4, Ayukawa Yoshisuke Papers. For the text approved by the company, see *Gendaishi shiryō*, 8: 771–72. As his diary entry shows, Asakura (*Nikki*, vol. 3) learned of the establishment of the MIDC the day before the announcement. He also heard about a large iron ore deposit in Tungpientao from Ayukawa on the same day. To get an insight on the mood inside and surrounding Nissan before and after the announcement, see Yamazaki, *Fūunji Ayukawa Yoshisuke*, 1–86. For newspaper

articles at the time of MIDC's founding, see Microfiche no. 333.1 of the Ayukawa Yoshisuke Papers.

59. Asakura, *Nikki*, vol. 3: entries for Oct. 20 and 27, Nov. 1 and 14; and Ayukawa, "Manshū keizai shihai no kii pointo," 200.

60. "U.S. Financing for Manchukuo Reported, Ford and General Motors Linked to Plan," *New York Times*, Nov. 15, 1937, 1. Six days later, the *New York Times* reported skeptically about the new proposal by arguing that although American companies such as General Motors were profiting very well, "quotas and other restrictions" had discouraged the expansion of their sales, and they were being pushed out of the Japanese market. The article also argued that the return on investments in Manchuria seemed low and the new holding company probably could not take over all semi-public and private corporations operating in Manchurian heavy industries (see Burton Crane, "Japanese May Seek Aid Here in Growth," *New York Times*, Nov. 21, 1937, 1).

61. "Japan Seeking $50,000,000 Credit for U.S. Machinery," *New York Times*, Jan. 16, 1938, 1.

62. Ayukawa, "Manshū keizai shihai kii pointo," 200. Had Ayukawa's aide Kishimoto Kantarō not found a loophole in the commercial laws concerning the SMR zone, the moving of Nissan's head office would have been administratively complicated and financially costly (see Ayukawa, "Watashi no rirekisho," 326). According to Kishimoto, Ayukawa had asked him around September to find a way to avoid legal complications in moving Nissan's head office to a foreign country; in order to do this, Nissan would have had to dissolve itself, which meant the company would have had to break up and then reorganize under Manchukuo law. Ayukawa was sure that a large portion of the existing capital of over ¥210 million would not come back, since investors would put their money elsewhere. Ayukawa did not want to miss this economic opportunity. Kishimoto discovered that Japanese commercial laws applied in the Kwantung leased territory; this meant Nissan could move its head office as if it were moving to a different location in Japan and Nissan's transformation into a Manchukuo entity would be automatic when the extraterritorial law in the Kwantung leased territory expired and Manchukuo laws replaced Japanese laws there (see *Kishimoto Kantarō shinmonkiroku*, Microfiche no. 163.2, 11–12, Ayukawa Yoshisuke Papers). In another facet to this story, Ayukawa had to talk with MOF Director of Direct Taxation Ikeda Hayato (1899–1965), the future prime minister, about the fact that he was not going to pay taxes in Japan. Ikeda told Ayukawa: "Well, your company has been paying a lot until now, so don't worry about it. I thank you for that." Afterwards Ayukawa thought Ikeda would become a politician (see the Oct. 26, 1951, discussion in Microfiche no. 941.2 of the Ayukawa Yoshisuke Papers).

63. This was based on a treaty signed between the two countries on June 10, 1936. The abolition of extraterritorial rights in the SMR zone and the transfer of adminis-

trative authority over it to Manchukuo were approved by the Japanese cabinet on June 18, 1937 (*Gendaishi shiryō*, 8: 797).

64. For the content of the Law, see South Manchuria Railway Company, *Sixth Report on Progress in Manchuria*, 193–96. For Manchukuo's payment of its half of the capital, see *Kishimoto Kantarō Shinmonkiroku* 1, Microfiche no. 163.2, 13–14, Ayukawa Yoshisuke Papers.

65. *Manchuria Industrial Development Corporation*, 10, 13–14.

66. Matsuoka tried to calm the angered SMR employees by proposing a role for the SMR in Northern China. He agreed only because it was good for the country, although this change put him in a very difficult position; see the Oct. 26, 1951, discussion in Microfiche no. 941.2 of the Ayukawa Yoshisuke Papers.

67. Peattie, *Ishiwara Kanji*, 311–16; Katakura, "Ayukawa Yoshisuke-shi," 126–29; Hoshino, *Mihaatenu yume*, 27–28; Hara Akira, "Manshū ni okeru keizai tōshi seisaku," 233; Kojima Naoki, *Ayukawa Yoshisuke den*, 86; Harada, *Saionji kō to seikyoku*, 177–78; South Manchuria Railway Company, *Sixth Report on Progress in Manchuria*, 72–73.

68. Suzuki, "Manshū," 112–13; Hara Akira, "Manshū ni okeru keizai tōshi seisaku," 237–38; South Manchuria Railway Company, *Sixth Report on Progress in Manchuria*, 71.

69. See the Oct. 26, 1951, discussion in Microfiche no. 941.2 of the Ayukawa Yoshisuke Papers.

70. "The Significance of the Establishment of the 'Manchukuo Heavy Industries Development Company,'" Feb. 7, 1938, "Manchuria," Box 289, Stanley K. Hornbeck Papers, Hoover Institution on War, Revolution and Peace, Stanford University.

71. Hugh Byas, "Japan Offers U.S. Manchukuo Share," *New York Times*, Mar. 13, 1938, in Microfiche no. 130.2 of the Ayukawa Yoshisuke Papers.

72. Asakura, *Nikki*, vol. 3: entries for Oct. 7 and 30, Nov. 1, 4, 7, and 13, and Dec. 15, 1937.

73. Hara Akira, "Manshū ni okeru keizai tōshi seisaku," 235–36. Hara stated that the specific content of "preferential treatment" mentioned in the Oct. 22 document, which only vaguely talked about the issue, was relatively clearly stated in the suggestions in August.

74. Ibid., 277. For the texts of the "Outline for the Establishment of Heavy Industries in Manchuria" approved by the Konoe cabinet on Oct. 22, 1937, and approved by the Manchukuo government on Oct. 26, 1937, see Microfiche no. 333.1 of the Ayukawa Yoshisuke Papers. In addition, in the same microfiche, see a document on tax arrangements for MIDC between Japanese and Manchukuo officials on Dec. 4, 1937.

Chapter 3

1. Wilson, *American Business and Foreign Policy*, 223.

2. For foreign investment in Manchuria, see Amos, "American Commercial Interests in Manchuria Since the Japanese Occupation of 1931," 16–17.

3. Manshū teikoku seifu, *Manshū kenkoku jūnenshi*, 601–2, 607–14.

4. Ibid., 634.

5. F. C. Jones, *Manchuria Since 1931*, 194–95; Amos, "American Commercial Interests in Manchuria," 16.

6. For the texts of these laws, see South Manchuria Railway Company, *Sixth Report on Progress in Manchuria*, 72–75, 93–94, 103–6.

7. For U.S.-Manchukuo export statistics, see Manshū teikoku seifu, *Manshū kenkoku jūnenshi*, 599, 634–38.

8. Shinomiya, "Senzen no jidōsha sangyō to 'Manshū,'" 23. According to this survey, 63 percent of the 11,000-odd vehicles in Manchukuo were either Fords or Chevrolets. Other American cars present in Manchukuo included Dodges and Buicks.

9. See the two newspaper clippings in "Clipping Series: Scrap Book Clippings, Jan. 1939–April 26, 1939," Box 91, Gerald Nye Papers, Herbert C. Hoover Presidential Library: "Hull Ignores Big Manchuria Trade, Says Nye," Apr. 5, 1939; and "Manchukuo Buys for War Hull Tells Nye," Apr. 7, 1939. Both articles could only be identified as from the *Washington Post*. In addition, see "Side-lights on the Open Door Issue," *Far Eastern Review*, July 1939, in "Neutrality: Clippings and Printed Matter, 1939," Box 36, Gerald Nye Papers, Herbert C. Hoover Presidential Library.

10. U.S. Department of State, *Foreign Relations of the United States: Japan, 1931–1941*, 1: 156–57.

11. Clauss, "The Roosevelt Administration and Manchukuo, 1933–1941" 600. See also Hu, *Stanley K. Hornbeck*, 177–80.

12. Ibid., 610.

13. See John W. Masland, "Commercial Influence upon American Far Eastern Policy, 1937–1941," 296.

14. Ibid., 293–94.

15. Ibid., 286–97. See also "The *Fortune* Forum of Executive Opinion," *Fortune*, Sept. 1940, 72–73, 114. This poll was not based on a random sample since the magazine invited the executives to participate. Nor did the magazine indicate when the poll was taken, although it predates the Axis Pact of 1940. The majority of those who were surveyed thought presidential candidate Wendell Willkie would handle foreign policy, war preparedness, and industrial mobilization better than Roosevelt.

16. Looking back at his efforts to entice American investment to Manchukuo, Ayukawa in April 1939 told William O. Inglis, a journalist invited by the Japan Economic Federation:

At that time [late 1937] American trade was depressed so that, for example, the production of steel and automobiles in America was under one-third of their capacity, and I thought that if I called for the co-operation of American financiers and industrialists it would be forthcoming in a most willing way, because thereby the United States would be able to increase its industrial activities and employment through supplying the requirements of my corporation. If the goods were supplied on credit, Americans would have the best security in the fact that Manchukuo is full of valuable natural resources. . . . I was very anxious to get the co-operation of your countrymen without any loss of time, because I thought your people would not be so keen to supply goods on credit, once trade improved in your country by its own strength.

See William O. Inglis, "A Tip to Mr. Roosevelt: He Can Bring Peace to the Whole World by Acting on the Suggestion of the Greatest Industrial Magnate in the Orient," in Microfiche no. 517.1, 6–7, Ayukawa Yoshisuke Papers.

17. Hara Akira, "Manshū ni okeru keizai tōsei," 270. Nippon Victor began operating in 1927, and it accepted capital from Sumitomo and Mitsubishi in 1929. It became an affiliate of Nissan in 1935 and of Tōkyō denki in 1938; see Udagawa Masaru, "Business Management and Foreign-Affiliated Companies in Japan," 10–11.

18. "Japanese Seeking $50,000,000 Credit for U.S. Machinery," *New York Times*, Jan. 16, 1938, 1. Before 1937, International Business Machine had sold its products through Morimura shōji and then through Kurosawa shōten; see Udagawa, "Business Management and Foreign-Affiliated Companies in Japan," 12–13. For the Moss-Ayukawa discussions, see Microfiche no. 517.1, Ayukawa Papers.

19. See the following in "Houston, Herbert S., 1936–1945," Box 33, Thomas W. Lamont Papers, Baker Library, Harvard University: Houston to Lamont, Oct. 20, 1936; Lamont to Houston, Oct. 21, 1936; Houston to Lamont, Aug. 17, 1937; Lamont to Houston, Sept. 9, 1937; Houston to Lamont, Nov. 14, 1937; Houston to Thomas J. Watson, Oct. 26, 1937; May 26, 1943, memo; and Nov. 26, 1944 article. See also Watson to Lamont, Jan. 3, 1938, in "Watson, Thomas J., 1931–1947," Box 136, Thomas W. Lamont Papers, Baker Library, Harvard University. Watson in his January 3 letter informed Lamont that his new International Business Machine World Center was going to be dedicated to "World Peace through World Trade." According to Houston's letter of Oct. 20, 1936, to Lamont, many independent Republicans—such as Houston himself; William L. Clayton (1880–1966), a founder of the world's largest cotton-trading company; James P. Warburg (1896–1966), a Wall Street banker; and Thomas J. Watson—had decided to support Roosevelt instead of Alfred H. Landon (1887–1987).

20. For Hornbeck's scathing criticisms of Houston and his suspicions that the Japanese elites, including Matsuoka, were exploiting every opportunity to nurture American sympathy and support toward Japan through such events as the New York World's Fair and through the University of Oregon, to which Matsuoka had donated money prior to Houston's speech, see the following in the Stanley K. Hornbeck Papers, Hoover Institution on War, Revolution and Peace, Stanford University: Jan. 28,

1938, memorandum; and Herbert S. Houston, "Seeking a Way to Peace in Asia," in "Houston, Herbert S.," Box 207. For Hornbeck's observation regarding the influence of Matsuoka's upbringing in the United States on Matsuoka's personality and Matsuoka's view of Japan's position in the Far East and on U.S.-Japan relations, see the following in "Matsuoka, Yōsuke," Box 258, Stanley K. Hornbeck Papers: Hornbeck to Welles, Jan. 6, 1939; and Matsuoka Yōsuke, "Japan Puts Her Cards on the Table." For reports of Japanese war atrocities in Nanking in mid-December 1937 received by Hornbeck, see "Atrocities," Box 228, Stanley K. Hornbeck Papers.

For a biographical sketch of Matsuoka's early career and ten-year stay in the West Coast of the United States and the influence of that experience on his psychology and view of Americans, see Hosoya, *Nihon gaikō no zahyō*, 56–68. "Frank," as he was called by his classmates, graduated second in his class. Matsuoka very much appreciated his host mother in Portland, a Mrs. Beveridge, who treated him lovingly as if he were her own son. As he grew up, he saw life in America by working during his high school years as a dishwasher and a farmworker, and in college as a lawyer, newspaper reporter, construction company clerk, and a substitute Protestant preacher.

Compared to Ayukawa, who was born in the same year (1880) in the same province, Matsuoka's American experience started at age twelve and lasted ten years. With a cousin, in the spring of 1892, the young boy got on board a small freighter that took them to the West Coast. Matsuoka received his junior high school education in Portland, Oregon, and then attended a high school in Oakland, California. He left his high school before graduation and attended the University of Oregon in Eugene, where he earned a bachelor of law degree in two years at age twenty. The rising anti-Japanese immigration movement had a definite influence on him, and on top of the self-confidence he gained in this rough and tumble environment, Matsuoka was convinced by the time he returned to his native country in 1902 that the worst thing a Japanese could do in dealing with an American was to be servile. If an American hits you, hit him back. Only through this mentality would things work out with Americans and open up opportunities to make friends with them. Matsuoka's career in Japan began in 1904 as a young diplomat, and until 1912 he spent seven years in China and a year in Japan. He was stationed in Shanghai and Peking and worked for the Kwantung government during the years when the leading powers, including Japan, were penetrating China economically. While working in China, he became a protégé of Yamamoto Jōtarō, who at the time was head of the Mitsui Trading Company's Shanghai office and who later backed Matsuoka in switching from the Foreign Ministry to the SMR in 1921. He also began to receive advice from Gotō Shinpei (1857–1929), the first president of the SMR, and Yamagata Aritomo (1838–1922), one of the oligarchs from his home province. Matsuoka was probably influenced by Gotō's argument at the time that Japan should cooperate with Russia and Germany to counter American dollar diplomacy in Manchuria; Matsuoka, of course, was unaware that he would be doing this himself in 1940. This suspicion of American economic penetration into Manchuria, coupled with his conviction that Manchuria and Mongolia were Japan's lifeline, led him to advocate a unilateral Japanese intervention in Eastern Siberia after the Bolshevik Revolution without conducting this jointly with the United States, which he suspected of planning an economic expansion into the Far East. After he began his career in the SMR, he maintained a critical view of Shidehara diplomacy—Foreign Minister Shidehara Kijurō's (1872–1951) non-interventionist stance toward China and cooperative gestures toward the United States and Great Britain.

21. "Muraki Kenkichi-shi teian," Apr. 20, 1938; J. H. Anderton to Muraki, May 14, 1939; and Muraki to Ayukawa, July 4, 1938; Microfiche no. 517.1, Ayukawa Yoshisuke Papers.

22. Ayukawa, "Watashi no rirekisho," 328; Awaya and Yoshida, *Kokusai kensatsukyoku (IPS) jinmonchōsho*, 247; *Shinmonkiroku* 1, Microfiche no. 163.1, 30–31 and 41–44, Ayukawa Yoshisuke Papers. Kishimoto Kantarō's answers to his interrogators support Ayukawa's statements in Microfiche no. 163.1; see *Kishimoto Kantarō shinmonkiroku*, Microfiche no. 163.2, 15–16, Ayukawa Yoshisuke Papers.

23. Ishikawa Shigeru, "Shūsen ni itaru made no Manshū keizai kaihatsu," 742–43. In addition, see Hara Akira and Nakamura, "Kaidai," 10–14.

24. Murakami, "Ayukawa sensei no tsuisō," 389–94. Takasaki (*Manshū no shūen*, 18–24) recalled the amount as ¥100 million. Takasaki mentioned in his book that he had visited Ayukawa in Manchuria for the first time in May 1939 and then in late 1939. Actually his visits happened in 1938. Takasaki became chairman of the Manchuria Aviation Company, while the previous chairman, Maebara Kenji, was touring overseas. In Microfiche no. 331.7 of the Ayukawa Yoshisuke Papers, which consists of documents on the Maebara mission to the United States and Europe, the documents in the microfiche confirm that the Maebara mission occurred in 1938. Furthermore, Ayukawa mentioned that he had begun to think about focusing more on agricultural, instead of industrialization, issues after the discouraging findings by the world-famous American geologist H. Foster Bain and others, which took place in 1938; see Ayukawa, *Hyakumi dansu*, 140.

25. Takasaki's calculation of estimated agricultural production in Manchuria is confirmed only in Kojima Naoki, *Ayukawa Yoshisuke den*, 156. Ishiwara was reassigned from his post as vice chief of staff for the Kwantung Army to commander of the Maizuru Fortress area in Japan after August 1938. For Ayukawa's recollections of the mechanized farming episode, see Ayukawa, "Watashi no rirekisho," 329–30; idem, *Hyakumi dansu*, 140–42; Kojima Naoki, *Ayukawa Yoshisuke den*, 155–56; Takasaki, *Manshū no shūen*, 18–24; and Murakami, "Ayukawa sensei no tsuisō," 389–94. For the newspaper article regarding the Maebara mission, see Microfiche no. 331.7 in the Ayukawa Yoshisuke Papers. For a report on the amount of MIDC corporate

bonds Japanese Americans might be able to purchase, see Umimoto Tetsuo, "Zaibei dōhō no Mangyō shasai shōkaryoku no kōsatsu," April 1938, Microfiche no. 511.1, Ayukawa Yoshisuke Papers.

26. Ayukawa, "Watashi no rirekisho," 328–29.

27. Ibid., 329. See also H. Foster Bain to Herbert Hoover, Mar. 29, 1938, "H. Foster Bain," Post-Presidential Individual File, Herbert C. Hoover Papers, Herbert C. Hoover Presidential Library; as well as the following telegrams concerning the initial travel arrangements between Ayukawa and Bain in Microfiche no. 517.1 of the Ayukawa Yoshisuke Papers: Ayukawa to Bain, Mar. 1, 1938; Bain to Ayukawa, Mar. 4, 1938; Bain to Ayukawa, Mar. 7, 1938; and Ayukawa to Bain, Mar. 11, 1938. Bain described Miho and two other people with whom he had gone to Manchuria in a letter to his wife; see Bain to Mrs. Bain, Apr. 16, 1938, H. Foster Bain Papers, Nevada Historical Society. Aside from Miho, who accompanied Bain to Hsinking, there were two other men. One of them was identified as Kenekami, "one of the higher officials of the Columbia phonograph factory." The other person seemed to have acted solely as an attendant.

28. Frank W. De Wolf, "Memorial to H. Foster Bain," *Proceedings Volume of the Geological Society of America: Annual Report for 1948*, April 1949, 127–30, H. Foster Bain Papers, Nevada Historical Society. Bain in a letter to his wife wrote that he and Miho had met in the summer of 1937 and that after he arrived in Tokyo on his way to Manchukuo, he met Miho, his wife, and their six-year old daughter, whom he described as "one of the prettiest little . . . girls I have ever seen" (see Bain to Mrs. Bain, Apr. 16, 1938, H. Foster Bain Papers, Nevada Historical Society).

29. Apr. 8, 1938, H. Foster Bain Papers, Nevada Historical Society.

30. Bain to Mrs. Bain, Apr. 16, 1938, H. Foster Bain Papers, Nevada Historical Society.

31. For the quote, see Bain's letter to a family member on Apr. 8, 1938, H. Foster Bain Papers, Nevada Historical Society. As for his plans about home leave, see the Apr. 8 letter and the telegram Bain sent to Ayukawa on Mar. 2 in Microfiche no. 517.1 of the Ayukawa Yoshisuke Papers.

32. For the Apr. 9 Memorandum and Apr. 10 report, see Microfiche no. 517.1 of the Ayukawa Yoshisuke Papers. For Bain's May 1938 report, "Mineral Resources of Manchuria as a Basis for Industry," and its supplementary report that summarizes that report and makes recommendations based on it, see the H. Foster Bain Papers at the Nevada Historical Society.

33. Bain to Ayukawa, May 19, 1938, Microfiche no. 517.1, Ayukawa Yoshisuke Papers. Bain was aware the Japanese were becoming desperate to obtain foreign credits, equipment, and technology. This is reflected in his comment in a letter sent on Sept. 1, 1938, from Manila to C. A. Snider, president of Sulphur Export Corporation in New York City: "Japanese business is in a very tight corner indeed in nearly every

direction and that their difficulties as to foreign exchange are probably even greater than the world appreciates. They may pull through but it is at least possible that a change may come suddenly." See Bain to Snider, Sept. 1, 1938, H. Foster Bain Papers, Nevada Historical Society.

34. H. Foster Bain, "Problems of and Adjustment in the Mining Industry," National Research Council of the Philippines Bulletin no. 17, Sept. 1938, 10–11. This is found in both Microfiche no. 517.1 of the Ayukawa Yoshisuke Papers, and the H. Foster Bain Papers.

35. For coalfields, see H. Foster Bain, "Mineral Resources of Manchuria as a Basis for Industry," May 1938, 29–30, H. Foster Bain Papers, Nevada Historical Society. For Bain's idea for trading Manchurian coal for Philippine iron ore, see H. Foster Bain, "Supplementary Report: Mineral Resources of Manchuria as a Basis for Industry," May 1938, 7–8, H. Foster Bain Papers. For Bain's wish to drive down the price of the Japanese coal the Philippines imported, see Bain to Hoover, Mar. 29, 1938, "Bain," Post-Presidential Individual File, Herbert C. Hoover Papers, Herbert C. Hoover Presidential Library.

36. For Bain's letter to Miho of Apr. 10, 1940, see Microfiche no. 517.1 of the Ayukawa Yoshisuke Papers. For other materials used in this paragraph, see the following in the H. Foster Bain Papers, Nevada Historical Society: Joan Updegraff to Clyde E. Williams, Feb. 2, 1939; Bain to Clyde E. Williams, July 2, 1939; Bain to M. H. Caron, Apr. 10, 1940; M. H. Caron to Bain, Apr. 28, 1940; Bain to Caron, May 21, 1940; Bain to Joan Updegraff, June 21, 1940; Bain to A. Terry, Jr., July 1, 1940; Bain to Terry, July 27, 1940; Bain to Terry, Aug. 17, 1940; Terry to Bain, Aug. 29, 1940; Bain to Terry, Sept. 12, 1940; Bain to Terry, Oct. 5, 1940; and Bain to Ives, August 27, 1941.

37. Yoshino, *Omokaji torikaji*, 426–27.

Chapter 4

1. "Ford teikei'an ni tomonau doru sōkin mondai" (The dollar remittance problem that arises from a joint venture with Ford), Aug. 8, 1939, Microfiche no. 514.2, Ayukawa Yoshisuke Papers. See the specific terms for a joint venture stated by Ford-Japan to Nissan Motors in May 1937 in "Nihon Ford kaisha, 1937," Microfiche no. 514.2, Ayukawa Yoshisuke Papers; the last page has Miho Mikitarō's name stamp and the date, May 29, 1937. Ford Motor Company in Dearborn, Michigan, instructed Ford Motor Company of Japan, Ltd., to begin negotiations for a joint venture with a Japanese car company in a Jan. 27, 1937, letter; see Ford Motor Company to Ford Motor Company of Japan, Ltd., Dec. 30, 1938, Microfiche no. 514.1, Ayukawa Yoshisuke Papers. With regard to the freezing of Ford-Japan's assets by mid-1937, see Mason, *American Multinationals and Japan*, 93.

2. *Jidōsha shiryō*, 2: 111–14. As Ayukawa and Miho Mikitarō negotiated with Ford-Japan and Ford in Dearborn, other executives at Nissan Motors expressed displea-

sure. Asahara recalled that in addition to himself, President Murakami, Advisor Kudō Haruto, Nissan Motors director Kubota Tokujirō, and others disagreed with the merger. They argued that Nissan Motors could improve the Model 80. They also thought that, with the Automobile Manufacturing Law already in place, the military and MCI would not approve of the merger. The Nissan Motors board members unanimously decided to convey these thoughts to Ayukawa and Miho through Asahara. Although Ayukawa was displeased about this overwhelming opposition, he ordered the executives to start working immediately on improving the Model 80. The first Nissan Model 180 trucks, a cab-over type using the same engine as the Model 80, came off the assembly line on Jan. 6, 1941. Ogura made his remarks around October 1938 during a meeting with Foreign Minister Arita Hachirō (1884–1965) and Harada Kumao (1888–1946), secretary to and confidant of *genrō* (elder statesman) Saionji Kinmochi (1849–1940); see Harada, *Saionji kō to seikyoku*, 142–43.

3. This is my translation from "Ayukawa shachō to Kopf-shi kaiken yōryō" (The gist of the conversation during the meeting between President Ayukawa and Mr. Kopf), July 29, 1937, Microfiche no. 514.1, Ayukawa Yoshisuke Papers.

4. Nissan jidōsha kabushikigaisha, Sōmubu, Chōsaka, *Nissan jidōsha sanjūnenshi*, 77–78. Ayukawa mentioned the negotiations between MIDC and Ford in "Gaishi crejitto hōkokusho" (Report on foreign capital and credit), Jan. 30, 1939, and another report with the same title dated Mar. 7, 1939, Microfiche no. 516.3, Ayukawa Yoshisuke Papers. In addition, see the following agreements in Microfiche no. 514.1: "Memorandum of Agreement," Aug. 4, 1937 (in both English and Japanese), and the Sept. 20, 1937, contract, "Tsuika keiyakusho."

5. Mason, *American Multinationals and Japan*, 93.

6. Nissan jidōsha kabushikigaisha, Sōmubu, Chōsaka, *Nissan jidōsha sanjūnenshi*, 77–78; Miho Mikitarō to Ayukawa, Aug. 31, 1938, Microfiche no. 514.1, Ayukawa Yoshisuke Papers. In addition, see the following in the same microfiche: Ayukawa Yoshisuke to Tsurumi Yūsuke, Nov. 16, 1938; Ayukawa Yoshisuke's happy birthday message through Benjamin Kopf to Henry Ford including Ayukawa's wish to have Ford operate in Manchuria, Sept. 2, 1938; Kopf's message to Ayukawa conveying Henry Ford's thanks for the message, Sept. 9, 1938; "Suggestions for Cooperation Between MIDC and Ford M C"; Nov. 17, 1938, agreement between Dōwa Motors and Ford Motor Company of Japan, Ltd.; Kopf to Ayukawa, Sept. 13, 1938 (in Japanese); Kishimoto Kantarō to Director Murakami of Nissan Motors, Nov. 15, 1938 (in Japanese); Oct. 22, 1938, Ford-Japan proposal; and Oct. 26 Nissan Motors proposal. For the special report on U.S.-Manchukuo trade relations in the Nov. 30, 1938, edition of the *Journal of Commerce and Finance*, see Microfiche no. 333.4 of the Ayukawa Yoshisuke Papers.

7. Mason, *American Multinationals and Japan*, 92; Nissan jidōsha kabushikigaisha, Sōmubu, Chōsaka, *Nissan jidōsha sanjūnenshi*, 77–78. Ayukawa mentioned negotia-

tions between MIDC and Ford in "Gaishi crejitto hōkokusho," Jan. 30, 1939, and another report with the same title on Mar. 7, 1939, Microfiche no. 516.3, Ayukawa Yoshisuke Papers. In addition, see the following agreements in Microfiche no. 514.1: "Memorandum of Agreement," Aug. 4, 1937 (in both English and Japanese); and the Sept. 20, 1937, contract, "Tsuika keiyakusho." In addition, see the following documents in the same microfiche: Ford Motor Company, Dearborn, Michigan, Dec. 30, 1938; and Murray to Miho, Feb. 28, 1939. In his Feb. 28, 1939, letter to Miho, Murray mentions that Ayukawa's opponents or competitors were spreading rumors in the United States to prevent his talks with Ford from succeeding. He also stated that "the U.S. Government . . . have already opposed the idea" of Ford's "contributing any capital for the erection of a factory in Manchukuo."

A Mr. Okamoto, an executive from Dōwa Motors, had gone to Detroit to meet A. N. Little, an American engineer who had worked for several years in Japan for Nissan Motors who was now stationed in Detroit; they were probably the ones who had pursued the discussions with Ford. This talk was being held as Ayukawa pursued a joint venture between Ford's Japanese subsidiary and MIDC's subsidiary, Nissan Motors. Ayukawa was dependent on Ford products: between December 1937 and July 1939, MIDC purchased from Ford Motors cars and auto parts for $3,495,000; one-fifth of this was to be paid on a two-year credit and the remainder on a one-year credit.

Okamoto initially worked with Franze Moedlhammer before he went to Detroit to meet with Little; see MIDC to Moedlhammer, Oct. 29, 1938, Microfiche no. 516.1, Ayukawa Yoshisuke Papers. See also Microfiche no. 516.3 of the Ayukawa Yoshisuke Papers: Moedlhammer to MIDC, Jan. 7, 1939; and Moedlhammer to MIDC, Jan. 21, 1939 (see Chapter 5 for Moedlhammer). The Japanese translation of Moedlhammer's report refers to Ford as either "car company" or "F"; MIDC was obviously treating this in a highly sensitive way. For the Japanese translation of the cable on Jan. 7, see Microfiche no. 516.2 for the Japanese translation of a telegram dispatched from New York by Moedlhammer to MIDC on Jan. 6, 1939. For the Japanese translation of the Jan. 7 and Jan. 21 cables, see Microfiche no. 516.3. The fact that Okamoto was a Dōwa Motors executive is revealed in the aforementioned January progress report on foreign capital and credit. Okamoto and Asahara Genshichi, a top Nissan Motors executive, were also negotiating with a company called Emmerson, which supplied used machinery, to purchase equipment under a credit arrangement. They planned to use the machines at the Manchuria Aviation Company, Tungpientao, and Dōwa Motors.

See the following in Microfiche no. 514.2 of the Ayukawa Yoshisuke Papers: Ankeny's May 29 explanation to MIDC regarding Kopf's letter of May 2, 1939 to Ankeny (report in Japanese); Murray to Aikawa (Ayukawa), Sept. 27, 1939, regarding Ford and the State Department; and Murray to Ayukawa, Sept. 27, 1939 (Japanese translation). In addition, see "Kaidai," in Asakura, *Nikki*, vol. 3: entries for May 16 and 17, 1939. In addition, see Hill and Wilkins, *American Business Abroad*, 254–56.

8. "Proposed Basis for Merger Between Ford Japan and Nissan," Jan. 26, 1939; and "Memorandum of Agreement" between Nissan Motors and Ford-Japan, Feb. 23, 1939, Microfiche no. 514.1, Ayukawa Yoshisuke Papers. See also Kopf to Aikawa (Ayukawa), Mar. 28, 1939, Microfiche no. 514.2, Ayukawa Yoshisuke Papers.

9. Murray to Miho, Feb. 28, 1939, Microfiche no. 514.1, Ayukawa Yoshisuke Papers.

10. For GM's June 24, 1938, proposal for a merger with Toyota and a letter from Tsurumi Yūsuke to Baron Itō Bunkichi on Oct. 19, 1938, see Microfiche no. 514.1 of the Ayukawa Yoshisuke Papers. For MIDC's discussions with GM for Dōwa Motors' purchase of 1,000 Blitz trucks from Germany, see W. T. Lutz, managing director of GM-Japan, Ltd. to Aikawa (Ayukawa), Feb. 24, 1938, and "G.M. to no kōshō yōryō" (The gist of the negotiations with G.M.), Feb. 25, 1939, in Microfiche no. 517.2 of the Ayukawa Yoshisuke Papers. Itō, a son of Meiji oligarch Itō Hirobumi, was a friend and political ally of Ayukawa; they had known each other since childhood and became related when Itō's father adopted a nephew of his fellow oligarch, political ally, and friend Inoue Kaoru, who was Ayukawa's great-uncle. Their friendship became very close after Itō failed in his post–Ministry of Agriculture and Commerce career to manage the Manchuria Textile Company and became a board member of Kuhara Mining Company through the mediation of Gen. Miura Kanju (1846–1926), a powerful behind-the-scene politician from Itō and Ayukawa's home province; Itō sent a memorandum on Mar. 1, 1927, declaring his intention to do the utmost to assist Ayukawa and did so as he became influential in behind-the-scene politics. Whenever Ayukawa had to make important decisions, Itō was one of the persons with whom he conferred (see Ayukawa, *Hyakumi dansu*, 56–61).

11. Nissan jidōsha kabushikigaisha, Sōmubu, Chōsaka, *Nissan jidōsha sanjūnenshi*, 77–78. For the content of the negotiations between Toyota and Ford-Japan, see the following in Microfiche no. 514.2 of the Ayukawa Yoshisuke Papers: Ministry of Commerce and Industry, "Nihon kaisha to Ford to no teikei jōken hikaku an" (Comparison of conditions for a joint venture between Japanese companies [Toyota and Kokusan kaisha, probably referring to companies owned by Furukawa and Asano conglomerates respectively]), Aug. 11, 1939; Toyota Automobile Company, "Toyota, Ford teikei kōshō keika" (Report on joint venture talks between Toyota and Ford), Aug. 16, 1939; Director Kamiya Shōtarō of Toyota Motors to MCI Machine Industry Section Chief Hashii Makoto (1902–77), Mar. 6, 1939; Ford-Japan to Kamiya, May 22, 1939; and a Japanese cable from Ayukawa to Lt. Col. Akimaru, Apr. 19, 1938. The Aug. 16 Toyota report and Ayukawa's conversations with Kopf as recorded in "Kopf-shi to no kaidan yōryō," Mar. 27, 1939, show that MIDC and

Toyota learned of each other's negotiations with Ford-Japan in March 1939. For the latter document, see Microfiche no. 514.2 of the Ayukawa Yoshisuke Papers.

12. "Kopf-shi to no kaidan yōryō," Mar. 27, 1939, Microfiche no. 514.2, Ayukawa Yoshisuke Papers. Kopf also mentioned that in 1937 Ford-Japan had signed a joint venture agreement with a group led by an influential figure in the Japan Chamber of Commerce, but MCI had refused to approve the agreement based on the argument that Ford's partner had to be a licensed company, Nissan or Toyota.

13. "Ford teikei'an ni tomonau doru sōkin mondai," Aug. 8, 1939, Microfiche no. 514.2, Ayukawa Yoshisuke Papers. In addition, see the following in the same microfiche: Murray's two cables of May 18, written by Kuhara Mitsuo and dispatched from New York City to Tokyo; Miho to Ayukawa, June 5, 1939 (in Japanese); Murray to Miho, May 16, 1939; Miho to Aikawa (Ayukawa) in Hsinking, June 5, 1939 (in English); Ankeny to Aikawa (Ayukawa), June 19, 1939; Ankeny to Miho, July 14, 1939; July 31 memorandum (sent to Ayukawa, Miho, the Ministry of Commerce and Industry, the War Ministry, and the Ministry of Finance); and "Ankeny-shi kaidan yōten" (The main points discussed by Mr. Ankeny), May 29, 1939. In the last document, see in particular Ankeny's explanation of why Ford Motors wanted the 48.75-2.5-48.75 stockholding arrangement.

14. For the two MCI memoranda, see Microfiche no. 514.2, Ayukawa Yoshisuke Papers; and Asakura, *Nikki*, vol. 3: entry for Aug. 5, 1939.

15. Toyoda Risaburō to the Ministry of Commerce and Industry, Sept. 6, 1939, Microfiche no. 514.2, Ayukawa Yoshisuke Papers. On Toyoda Kiichirō and the origins of Toyota Motors, see Cusumano, *The Japanese Automobile Industry*, 58–72.

16. See the following documents in Microfiche no. 514.2 of the Ayukawa Yoshisuke Papers: "Nihon Ford no teian" (A proposal by Ford-Japan), Aug. 24, 1939; "Ford yori kaitō o motomeraretaru jikō" (Items requested for their reply by Ford), Aug. 26, 1939, "Ford kaisha to no teikei'an" (A proposal for a joint venture with Ford), Sept. 26, 1939; "Draft Agreement for a Merger," Oct. 24, 1939; Kopf to Aikawa (Ayukawa), Oct. 31, 1939; "Draft Agreement for a Merger," Nov. 1, 1939; Kopf to Aikawa (Ayukawa), Nov. 24, 1939; "Draft Agreement," Nov. 24, 1939; and Murray to Ayukawa, May 28, 1940 (Japanese translation). The May 28 cable informed Ayukawa that Count Kabayama Aysuke (1865–1953), whose son-in-law Shirasu Jirō (1902–1985) was one of Ayukawa's top executives, had tried without success to meet Ford directors. For the first and last pages of the Dec. 19, 1939, agreement, see NHK, *Dokyumento Shōwashi*, 3: 187. On the opposition from the Army and top Nissan Motors executives, see *Jidōsha shiryō*, 2: 111–13; and Mason, *American Multinationals and Japan*, 92.

17. Murray to Aikawa (Ayukawa), Sept. 27, 1939; and Murray to Ayukawa (Japanese translation), Sept. 27, 1939, Microfiche no. 514.2, Ayukawa Yoshisuke Papers.

Chapter 5

1. With regard to the views of Japanese authorities on European and American Jews, see Kranzler, *Japanese, Nazis & Jews*, 210–11, 222, 224, 609–19. For Ayukawa's dealings with Kuhn, Loeb in 1938–39, see the following in the Ayukawa Yoshisuke Papers: in Microfiche no. 516.3, Jan. 30, 1939, report on the Moedlhammer project, and the record of phone conversations between Ayukawa in Tokyo and Nissan Motors Director Asahara Genshichi in New York City, Feb. 3, 1939; and in Microfiche no. 922.22, "Gaishi mondai keika hōkoku" (Report on problems concerning foreign capital, equipment, and technology), July 20, 1939, 13. Asahara, Moedlhammer, and H. Otto Schundler were meeting somebody from Kuhn, Loeb about MIDC's business proposal. In addition, see the following in Microfiche no. 517.2: Parlophone Company to H. A. Straus, Oct. 21, 1938; a letter to the Japanese Ministry of Interior for permission to allow the entrance into Japan of a person's parents, who were Jewish, from Europe for an indefinite period, Nov. 26, 1938; and "Immigration of German Jews into Japan." See also Schonberger, *Japanese Connection*, 127–28. On relations between Japan and Jacob Schiff, see Iriye, *Pacific Estrangement*, 113, 203, 225. For Japan's idealistic view of its relations with the Jews, see Shillony, *The Jews and the Japanese*, 127–28.

2. Shillony, *The Jews and the Japanese*, 178–79; Goodman and Miyazawa, *Jews in the Japanese Mind*, 112–13; and Chūnichi shimbun, Shakaibu, *Jiyū e no tōsō*, 127–28, 200–201.

3. For the quotations, see Kranzler, *Japanese, Nazis & Jews*, 232–33. In addition, see Goodman and Miyazawa, *Jews in the Japanese Mind*, 111, 114.

4. See Goodman and Miyazawa, *Jews in the Japanese Mind*, 110–11, 113–14.

5. For MIDC's relations with Kleiman, see the following microfiches in the Ayukawa Papers: in Microfiche no. 922.22, 176, "Gaishi mondai keika hōkoku," July 20, 1939, 18; and in Microfiche no. 517.2, Kleiman to Kishimoto, Feb. 4, 1938, and Kleiman to Ishiwatari, Sept. 22, 1938 (including "Memorandum with Respect to Projected Credit Arrangements Between Japanese Industry and American Banks").

6. For Strauss's correspondences with Wikawa (Ikawa), see "Widk–Wilb: 1928–1938," Box 86, Lewis L. Strauss Papers, Herbert C. Hoover Presidential Library. Wikawa explained his friendship with Strauss from the 1920s to Pearl Harbor in Ikawa, *Nichibei kōshō shiryō*, 412–16.

7. For Wise's negative opinion of American-Jewish economic cooperation with Japan, see Kranzler, *Japanese, Nazis Jews*, 227–28, 244; and Shillony, *The Jews and the Japanese*, 184.

8. Strauss, who was very loyal to Herbert Hoover, became the youngest partner of the company in the late 1920s because of his ability and the fact that he had married a daughter of the company's senior partner, Jerome Hanauer. See the following

in the Strauss Papers: Keizō Obata to Strauss, Nov. 2 and 3, 1926, "Japan Trip of 1926: Masuda–Osborne," and "Japan: 1918–1938 & Undated," Box 44; and "Hanauer, Jerome J. and Mrs.: Death of Jerome, Estate etc.," Box 31. Ōkura owned a 50-50 joint venture company in Manchuria with the Chinese government called the Honkeiko baitetsu kōshi (Chinese: Penhsihu mei-t'ieh kung-ssu); after the Manchuria Incident in September 1931, that part of the company's stocks owned by Chinese were confiscated by the Kwantung Army, which in turn transferred these stocks to the Manchukuo government in 1935 under an arrangement in which Ōkura and Manchukuo controlled 60 percent and 40 percent, respectively, of the company. In 1939 a new arrangement allowed MIDC to control the same percentage (40) as Ōkura; the remaining 20 percent was held by Manchukuo. In February 1944, Honkeiko, the Shōwa Steel Mill, and the Tungpientao Development Company were merged into a company called Manshū seitetsu kabushikigaisha (Manchuria steelworks corporation); MIDC controlled about 80 percent of this new firm.

9. For Baruch's involvement in finding a safe haven for the European refugees, see Schwarz, *The Speculator*, 563–64. For Strauss's actions to save the European refugees, see Strauss, *Men and Decisions*, 109–20. The friendship between Hoover and Strauss is discussed in Smith, *An Uncommon Man*.

10. Kleiman to Ishiwatari, Sept. 22, 1938 (including "Memorandum with Respect to Projected Credit Arrangements Between Japanese Industry and American Banks"), in Microfiche no. 517.2, Ayukawa Papers.

11. See the following in Microfiche no. 517.2 of Ayukawa Papers: Kleiman to Kishimoto, Dec. 23, 1938; and MIDC to Ives, Dec. 23, 1938.

12. Kleiman to Aikawa (Ayukawa), Feb. 7, 1939, in Microfiche no. 517.2, Ayukawa Papers.

13. For MIDC's relations with Kleiman, see the following in Microfiche no. 517.2 of the Ayukawa Papers: MIDC to Kleiman, Apr. 20, 1939; Kleiman to Aikawa (Ayukawa), Apr. 20, 1939; and Kleiman to Aikawa (Ayukawa), Apr. 25, 1939. The quotations on Kleiman's activities in New York between March and August 1938 are from a memorandum attached to his Sept. 22 letter to Ishiwatari. For Kleiman, see also Schonberger, *Japanese Connection*, 132. For Arita's speech on Feb. 27, 1938, see Shillony, *The Jews and the Japanese*, 184.

14. See Moedlhammer to Ayukawa, May 11, 1938, in Microfiche no. 516.1 of the Ayukawa Papers. For Moedlhammer's German financial scheme, see the following in the Ayukawa Papers: on 168–70 in Microfiche no. 922.22, "Gaishi mondai keika hōkoku," July 20, 1939, 10–12; and in Microfiche no. 516.1, a May 28, 1938, memorandum in Japanese concerning Moedlhammer's proposed financial scheme, Moedlhammer to Aikawa, June 8, 1938; Moedlhammer to Kishimoto, June 28, 1938; Moedlhammer to Aikawa, June 28, 1938; and Moedlhammer to Aikawa, June 29, 1938; Moedlhammer to Aikawa, Aug. 17, 1938; Moedlhammer to Kishimoto, Aug. 13,

1938; Moedlhammer's Sept. 11, 1938; progress report to Aikawa, Moedlhammer to Aikawa, Sept. 15, 1938; Moedlhammer to Aikawa, Sept. 20, 1938; Ayukawa's cable to Oscar Henschel, Sept. 26, 1938; and Henschel's favorable reply regarding Moedlhammer, Sept. 28, 1938; Moedlhammer to Kishimoto, Sept. 26, 1938; Prince Urach to Moedlhammer, Sept. 25, 1938; Moedlhammer to Aguilar, Sept. 25, 1938; Memorandum in Japanese from Ayukawa to Assistant Director Sakomizu Hisatsune of the Japanese Finance Ministry regarding Moedlhammer's credibility and regarding Moedlhammer's plan to form a German financial syndicate, Sept. 23, 1938; Aikawa to Moedlhammer, Sept. 26, 1938 (longer version); Moedlhammer's own biographical sketch, Sept. 22, 1938; Moedlhammer to Aikawa, Sept. 27, 1938; negative credibility report regarding Moedlhammer's German credit syndicate from the deputy director of foreign exchange of the Yokohama Specie Bank to Assistant Director of Finance Sakomizu Hisatsune, Ministry of Finance, Sept. 30, 1938; Moedlhammer to Kishimoto and Moedlhammer to Aikawa, Sept. 29, 1938, Oct. 2, 1938; cable to Ayukawa from Germany, and Memorandum from MIDC to General Secretary Hoshino of Manchukuo's General Affairs Board, October 4, 1938, regarding Moedlhammer and his credibility. When Moedlhammer saw Ayukawa in May 1938, he was conducting business for Henschel & Sohn, a manufacturer of trucks; Deutsche Waffen & Maschinenfabrik A.G., an armament machinery and ammunition manufacturer; Wumag, Goerlitzer Waggon & Maschinenfabrik, a manufacturer of railway wagons, hydraulic presses, and marine engines; Carl Walther Waffenfabrik, a manufacturer of pistols; T. Bergman & Co., a manufacturer of submachine guns; and the American Armament Corporation of New York, a manufacturer of armament and ammunition.

15. Cumings, *The Origins of the Korean War*, 99, 141–45; and Kobayashi, *Dai Tōa kyōeiken no keisei to hōkai*, 253–60, 266–70. Kobayashi (p. 266) mentions that gold output in Korea in 1942 diminished as the result of the Pacific War; Japan no longer needed to export gold to buy imports from the United States. For Moedlhammer's negotiations to acquire Unsan gold mines from the Oriental Consolidated Mining Company, see the following in Microfiche no. 516.2 of the Ayukawa Papers: Mitsui & Co., Ltd., New York, "Re: Oriental Mining Company," Nov. 16, 1938, and its attached report about the Oriental Consolidated Mining Company copied from a report in Dun & Bradstreet. Although Cumings writes that this company sold its mines to Japanese interests in 1939, Kobayashi Hideo writes that Japan Mining Company purchased it in 1941. Although the Mitsui report indicates that this company had not yet exercised its right to extend the concession, the attached report copied from Dun & Bradstreet states that it had already exercised this option. An undated report whose author is unidentified in Microfiche no. 516.1 of the Ayukawa Papers said that the Oriental Consolidated Mining Company's concession expired on March 26, 1954, and afterwards the treatment of the mine would be subject to

Japanese laws. This report states that the American company approached the author's organization to sell the mining rights and that Unsan is the last, the largest, and the richest gold mine in Korea held by foreign interests; it speculates that since the American company had operated only a small part of the whole concession, at least three times the current annual production was possible with an additional investment of ¥10–20 million. The company was trying to sell the Unsan mines for ¥20–30 million yen (at $29/100 yen, between $5.8 and $8.5 million). Ayukawa in a cable to Moedlhammer on Oct. 31, 1938, instructed him to arrange a $6 million credit arrangement with his New York "finance group"; see MIDC to Moedlhammer, Oct. 31, 1938, 7.m. (Japanese trans.), Microfiche no. 516.1, the Ayukawa Papers. The report states that the Japan Mining Company had purchased the following foreign concessions by 1938: the Kapsan Copper Mine from the Colbran Bostwick Development Company (an American company under an Anglo-American joint venture) in 1916; the Suian Gold Mine from Fraser and Folks (an Anglo-American joint venture) in 1937; and the Taiyudō Gold Mine from Nurupi Mine Company (British) in 1938. See also the following in Microfiche no. 516.1: Moedlhammer to MIDC, Oct. 18, 1938; MIDC to Moedlhammer, Oct. 24, 1938; Moedlhammer to MIDC, Oct. 24, 1938 (Japanese trans.); Moedlhammer to MIDC, Nov. 1, 1938 (Japanese trans.); Memorandum on plans to purchase the Unsan Gold Mine (undated); Moedlhammer to MIDC, Nov. 7, 1938 (Japanese trans.); Moedlhammer to MIDC, Nov. 12, 1938; MIDC to Moedlhammer, Nov. 14, 1938; Moedlhammer to MIDC, Nov. 14, 1938 (Japanese trans.); and Moedlhammer to Ayukawa, Nov. 20, 1938 (Japanese trans.). MIDC sent a cable on Dec. 9 to Moedlhammer to pursue talks with the Oriental Consolidated Mining Company based on its Nov. 14 instructions; see the Japanese translation of the cable in Microfiche no. 516.2. MIDC initially planned for Moedlhammer to proceed immediately to Germany after the Mexican oil deal. Strauss met Schundler some time between 1917 and 1938; I found Schundler's name card in "Schn–Schurm, 1917–1938," Box 69, Lewis L. Strauss Papers. See note 18 to this chapter for other documents concerning Schundler.

16. See the Dec. 22, 1938, cable from Moedlhammer to MIDC and the Jan. 23, 1939, cable from MIDC to Moedlhammer in Microfiche no. 516.3, Ayukawa Papers.

17. In the fall of 1941 Desvernine played an important role in helping Ambassadors Nomura Kichisaburō and Kurusu Saburō negotiate with officials in Washington. He by then was in frequent contact with former president Herbert Hoover regarding this diplomacy; see Chapter 7; and Iguchi Haruo, "Herbert Hoover moto daitōryō to Nichibei sensō." With regard to American steel companies, see the following in the Ayukawa Papers: in Microfiche no. 922.22, 168–72 and 179, "Gaishi mondai keika hōkoku," July 20, 1939, 10–14 and 21; in Microfiche no. 516.2, MIDC to Moedlhammer, Nov. 25, 1938 (Japanese trans.); Moedlhammer to MIDC, Nov. 27, 1938 (Japanese trans.); Moedlhammer to MIDC, Nov. 29, 1938 (Japanese trans.);

Moedlhammer to MIDC, Dec. 2, 1938 (Japanese trans.); Moedlhammer to Mangyō, Dec. 8, 1938; Moedlhammer to MIDC, Dec. 10, 1938 (Japanese trans.); Moedlhammer to MIDC, Dec. 12, 1938 (Japanese trans.); Moedlhammer to MIDC, Dec. 18, 1938, and its Japanese translation; Moedlhammer to MIDC, Dec. 20, 1938; Moedlhammer, Dec. 28, 1938 (Japanese trans.); Moedlhammer to MIDC, Dec. 29, 1938 (Japanese trans.); Moedlhammer to MIDC, Jan. 6, 1939 (Japanese trans.); Moedlhammer to MIDC, Jan. 7, 1939 (Japanese trans.); Moedlhammer to MIDC, Jan. 11, 1939 (Japanese trans.); Moedlhammer to MIDC, Jan. 13, 1939 (Japanese trans.); Moedlhammer to MIDC, Jan. 15, 1939 (Japanese trans.); MIDC to Moedlhammer, Jan. 16, 1939 (Japanese trans.); and Moedlhammer to MIDC, Jan. 16, 1939 (Japanese trans.); in Microfiche no. 516.3, Moedlhammer to MIDC, Jan. 7, 1939; Moedlhammer to MIDC, Jan. 11, 1939 (Japanese trans.); Moedlhammer to MIDC, Jan. 16, 1939; Moedlhammer to MIDC, Jan. 21, 1939; a cable from New York to MIDC, Jan. 30, 1939 (Japanese trans.); and Asahara to MIDC, Feb. 1, 1939 (Japanese trans.).

18. See the following in Microfiche no. 516.3 of the Ayukawa Papers: J. & W. Seligman & Co. to Moedlhammer, Feb. 8, 1939; Moedlhammer to Aikawa, Feb. 10, 1939; H. O. Schundler to Moedlhammer, Feb. 11, 1939; the record of a phone conversation between Ayukawa in Tokyo and Asahara Genshichi in New York City, Feb. 3, 1939; and Moedlhammer to Aikawa, Feb. 10, 1939. See also the following in Microfiche no. 516.4: "Plan A and Plan B" attached in a letter from Schundler to Moedlhammer, Feb. 11, 1939; and in Microfiche no. 516.3: the record of a phone conversation between Ayukawa and Asahara, Mar. 14, 1939; and a telegram from Moedlhammer to Ayukawa, Mar. 27, 1939. Moedlhammer's letter to Ayukawa on Feb. 10 covers the major points up to then regarding Moedlhammer's pursuit of business talks on credit and on steel exports as revealed in the telegrams and their Japanese translations. Moedlhammer indicates in this letter the steel executives' interest in the business, provided that the U.S. government gives its tacit approval so that their business dealings with Manchukuo will not be a cause for denying them the much more lucrative defense contracts. During their phone conversation on Mar. 14, 1939, Asahara and Ayukawa reveal that Moedlhammer's "friend" who is serving as an intermediary with influential bankers and businessmen is H. O. Schundler; this is also confirmed by the Austrian's Mar. 27 cable to Ayukawa. Schundler claimed in his Feb. 11 letter to Moedlhammer that the financial consortium organized by Seligman had planned to finance $20 million for MIDC's planned purchase of iron and steel products from U.S. Steel and Bethlehem Steel. On the other hand, according to "Gaishi mondai keika hōkoku," July 20, 1939, 13–14, Microfiche no. 922.22, 171–72, the Seligman project and the steel project were separate business negotiations. With regard to Ayukawa's firing of Moedlhammer, see the following record, letters, and cables in Microfiche no. 516.4: MIDC to Moedlhammer, Mar. 3, 1939; and MIDC to Moedlhammer, Mar. 3, 1939. Finally, see the following in Microfiche no. 516.4: MIDC to

Moedlhammer, Mar. 6, 1939; Moedlhammer to MIDC, Mar. 6, 1939 (Japanese trans.); MIDC to Moedlhammer, Mar. 10, 1939; Moedlhammer to MIDC, Mar. 11, 1939 (Japanese trans.); and Moedlhammer to MIDC, Mar. 15, 1939 (Japanese trans.). Ayukawa's phone conversations with Asahara on Mar. 14, 1939; two cables from Moedlhammer to MIDC, Mar. 21, 1939 (Japanese trans.); Moedlhammer to MIDC, Mar. 23, 1939 (Japanese trans.); Moedlhammer to MIDC, Mar. 24, 1939 (Japanese trans.); two cables from MIDC, one to Moedlhammer and one to Asahara, Mar. 23, 1939 (Japanese trans.); Moedlhammer to MIDC, Mar. 25, 1939; Moedlhammer to MIDC, Mar. 27, 1939; MIDC to Moedlhammer, Mar. 28, 1939; Moedlhammer to MIDC, Apr. 6, 1939; Moedlhammer to Asahara, Mar. 28, 1939; Forrest F. Single to Asahara, Mar. 31, 1939; Schundler to Asahara, Mar. 30, 1939; National City Bank of New York to J. W. Murray, Apr. 4, 1939; Murray to Single, Apr. 12, 1939; and Murray to Schundler and Moedlhammer, Apr. 13, 1939. In addition, see the following in Microfiche no. 516.3: a cable to MIDC, Feb. 10, 1939 (Japanese trans.); MIDC to Moedlhammer, Feb. 10, 1939; MIDC to Moedlhammer, Feb. 12, 1939 (Japanese trans.); Moedlhammer to MIDC, Feb. 12, 1939 (Japanese trans.); and MIDC to Moedlhammer, Feb. 23, 1939 (these cables show the increasingly strained relations between Moedlhammer and MIDC). For the Seligman Company's view on MIDC's counterproposal, see Moedlhammer to MIDC, Jan. 22, 1939 (Japanese trans.); and MIDC to Moedlhammer, Feb. 13, 1939, in Microfiche no. 516.3, Ayukawa Papers. For the discussion between Breck and Hamilton, see U.S. Department of State, *Foreign Relations of the United States: The Far East, 1939*, 3: 494–95.

19. See the following in Microfiche no. 516.3 of the Ayukawa Papers: Asahara to Aikawa, Feb. 1, 1939; Moedlhammer to Aikawa, Feb. 10, 1939; and Schundler to Moedlhammer, Feb. 11, 1939.

20. See the following in "China and Japan Trip File," Box 17, John Foster Dulles Papers, Seeley G. Mudd Manuscript Library, Princeton University: James A. Mackay to Boies C. Hart, Feb. 10, 1938; John B. Grant to John Foster Dulles, Feb. 10, 1938; Mackay to Dulles, Feb. 28, 1938; and "Trip to Hankow," 13. For the National City Bank's support for the recognition of Manchukuo since 1933, see Wilkins, "The Role of U.S. Business," 360. For the State Department's view of the National City Bank's activities and the department's policy of requesting American banks in China to cooperate with British and French banks in opposing Japanese monetary and banking policy in North and Central China, and for Guy Holman's comment regarding China to State Department officials on Mar. 10, see U.S. Department of State, *Foreign Relations of the United States: The Far East, 1939*, 3: 376–81, 397–401, 404–5, 408–9, 412–15, 420–21, 424–25, 441–42.

21. Hornbeck to Hull, Aug. 1, 1939, and Hart to Hornbeck, Oct. 20, 1939, "Hart, Boies," Box 199; and Renschler to Hornbeck, Sept. 12, 1939, "National City Bank," Box 305, Stanley K. Hornbeck Papers, Hoover Institution on War, Revolution and

Peace, Stanford University. The National City's executives who met with Hornbeck and Grew were Joseph H. Durrell, senior vice president of overseas operations, John L. Curtis, supervisor of Japanese branches, John T. S. Reed, manager of the Shanghai branch, and Guy Holman, assistant vice president of the Far Eastern Division.

22. See U.S. Department of State, *Foreign Relations of the United States: The Far East, 1939*, 3: 482; and Memorandum for Mr. Lamont, Sept. 1, 1938, Lamont to Count Ayske Kabayama, Sept. 8, 1938, and Lamont to Richard J. Walsh, Oct. 16, 1939, Box 188, Thomas W. Lamont Papers, Baker Library, Harvard University.

23. Both Ayukawa and Asahara believed that American businessmen tended to view Japanese companies that sought large credits with skepticism since well-known leading companies such as the Mitsui Trading Company in New York tended to pay cash rather than buy on credit. Another factor was the growing resentment toward Japanese aggression in China among the American public, who might protest American companies' conducting business with Japan. Furthermore, the Federal Reserve Bank regulated the foreign lending of banks such as the National City Bank, an unfavorable situation since the government tended to view Japan with disfavor for its conduct in the Far East. Yet Schundler and Moedlhammer claimed that their group wanted to fulfill its ambition to dominate the American trade with Japan, Manchukuo, and Germany. They claimed a similar arrangement had been made with other countries. On Feb. 10, 1939, MIDC received a cable from New York that informed that Schundler's group had sent by registered mail proposals written by their lawyer and "the large industrial group," materials that could not be cabled for various reasons. Schundler's group requested that MIDC delegate it the authority to proceed with the negotiations and agree to commit to the outcome. MIDC responded immediately that it could not make commitments before reading the documents. After Ayukawa received "Plan A," which stipulated conditions for a $40 million credit, and "Plan B," which stipulated conditions for a $20 million credit, he sent a comment to Moedlhammer and Schundler that it might take some time to respond because he had to discuss the matter with government officials. Moedlhammer's telegram to MIDC, which arrived on Feb. 20, revealed that DuPont and the Bank of Manhattan were the companies willing to finance MIDC and facilitate its purchases of goods. He stated they would withdraw from the business negotiations if their names appeared openly before an agreement had been reached with MIDC. That was the reason why Moedlhammer and Schundler had not stated the names of companies involved. See Microfiche no. 516.3 in the Ayukawa Papers. This cable also stated that Moedlhammer was working on a steel deal with another "reliable finance group." Moedlhammer's and Schundler opinions about MIDC's credit needs and about their ambitions were reflected in two letters; see the following in Microfiche no. 516.3 of the Ayukawa Papers: Moedlhammer to Aikawa, Feb. 10, 1939; and Shundler to Moedlhammer, Feb. 11, 1939; in the latter, see the attached Plan A and Plan B.

Moedlhammer in his Feb. 10 letter described the new program as devised by "one of the largest industrial groups" in the United States, which was mediated by Schundler and his financial and industrial connections. Ayukawa initially learned about these new credit arrangements in a cable dispatched from New York on Feb. 5, 1939; see the Japanese translation of this in Microfiche no. 516.3. In the same microfiche, Ayukawa in his Mar. 7, 1939, progress report stated that he was going to discuss Plan A and Plan B and Schundler's Mar. 6 cable with government officials. For a summary of the developments concerning Schundler's two proposals, see "Gaishi mondai keika hōkoku," July 20, 1939, 14–18, in Microfiche no. 922.22, 172–76.

24. U.S. Department of State, *Foreign Relations of the United States: The Far East, 1939*, 3: 546–48.

25. See "Gaishi mondai keika hōkoku," Microfiche no. 922.22, Ayukawa Papers.

26. Ayukawa mentioned in his interrogation record during the preparation for the war crimes trial that MIDC's Manchuria Heavy Machinery and Mesta signed an agreement for a joint venture to which Mesta planned to contribute $1 million; see *Shimonkiroku* 1, 40–41, Microfiche no. 163.1, Ayukawa Papers; and Awaya and Yoshida, *Kokusai kensatsukyoku (IPS) jinmonchōsho*, 274. In addition, see "Gaishi mondai keika hōkoku," 4–7, Microfiche no. 922.22, 162–65, Ayukawa Papers. For Powell's talk with State Department officials, see U.S. Department of State, *Foreign Relations of the United States: The Far East, 1939*, 3: 488–89. For Yano's involvement in negotiations with Mesta, see Takasaki, *Manshū no shūen*, 132; and Hoshino, *Mihatenu yume*, 289. For the legal documents agreed between Mesta and MIDC, see Microfiche no. 511.2 of the Ayukawa Papers. For telegrams between MIDC and Mesta, see the following in Microfiche no. 517.2: Powell to Ives, Apr. 21, 1939; Kobiyama Naoto to Ayukawa, Apr. 22, 1939; and Fukutomi to Kobiyama, Apr. 22, 1939 (Japanese trans.). For the joint venture between United Engineering and Shibaura seisakusho, see Udagawa, "Business Management and Foreign-Affiliated Companies in Japan," 12–13.

27. Iriye, *Power and Culture*, 20.

28. U.S. Department of State, *Foreign Relations of the United States: The Far East, 1939*, 3: 550–58. The United States perceived that Japan had established a monopoly over occupied areas in four stages: (1) military occupation, (2) establishment of a Japanese-controlled regime, (3) the creation of new currency, and (4) the elimination of old currencies and the pegging of the new currency to the Japanese yen accompanied by trade and exchange controls that favored flows of capital and goods between the conquered areas and Japan over those between the conquered areas and other foreign countries.

29. U.S., Department of State, *Foreign Relations of the United States: Japan, 1931–1941*, 1: 789–90.

30. Ibid., 822.

Chapter 6

1. Horikoshi Teizō, *Keizai dantai rengōkai zenshi*, 336. Inglis's biographical sketch is taken from "William Inglis," in Microfiche no. 517.1, Ayukawa Papers. For Inglis's relations with the Rockefellers, see Marcus and Hall, *Lives in Trust*, 265–67, 269, 272–76.

2. All quotations and summaries of the conversation between Ayukawa and Inglis are taken from William O. Inglis, "A Tip to Mr. Roosevelt: He Can Bring Peace to the Whole World by Acting on the Suggestion of the Greatest Industrial Magnate in the Orient," 4, in Microfiche no. 517.1, Ayukawa Yoshisuke Papers; see also Kojima Naoki, *Ayukawa Yoshisuke den*, 120, 124–27.

3. Microfiche no. 517.1, Ayukawa Yoshisuke Papers. See also pp. 46–55 of Ayukawa's 1953 draft memoir in Microfiche no. 931.4 of the Ayukawa Papers.

4. Kido, *Nikki*, 2: 733, 737.

5. U.S. Department of State, *Foreign Relations of the United States* (hereafter cited as FRUS): *The Far East, 1939*, 3: 599–600.

6. Stanley Hornbeck's Dec. 13, 1939, memorandum, "Japanese Personages," Box 258, Stanley K. Hornbeck Papers, Hoover Institution on War, Revolution and Peace, Stanford University. As indicated in this memorandum, Hornbeck wrote this after he had heard about Ayukawa's planned trip from the U.S. embassy in Tokyo.

7. For Ōhashi's comment to Tomoda, see Kojima Naoki, *Ayukawa Yoshisuke den*, 130–31; it is also mentioned in Ayukawa's 1953 draft memoir, 71–72, in Microfiche no. 931.4, Ayukawa Papers. Ayukawa referred to this incident as an interference by the Foreign Ministry in *Shinmonkiroku* 1, 31, in Microfiche no. 163.1, Ayukawa Papers.

8. *FRUS: The Far East, 1939*, 3: 596–97.

9. Kishimoto Kantarō, "Oushū shisatsu sokumenkan" (My observations of President Ayukawa's European trip), May 11, 1940, 1–2, in Microfiche no. 182.3, Ayukawa Papers.

10. According to Microfiche no. 182.3 in the Ayukawa Papers, Miho Mikitarō was not a member of the group, but on p. 76 of the 1953 draft memoir that Tomoda Juichirō edited for Ayukawa, Miho was said to be part of the mission. See Microfiche no. 931.4 of the Ayukawa Papers. For Hoshino Naoki's report that Ayukawa had told him he might go to the United States via Europe, see Hoshino Naoki, "Ayukawa Yoshisuke," *Jiyū*, Dec. 1967, in Microfiche no. 913.3 of the Ayukawa Papers.

11. See the following in Microfiche no. 182.3 of the Ayukawa Papers: Kishimoto Kantarō, "Oushū shisatsu sokumenkan," May 11, 1940, 1–6; "Ayukawa sōsai hare no shuppatsu" (President Ayukawa leaves for Europe), *Manshū shimbun*, Dec. 27, 1939; and "Ayukawa, Matsushima ryōshi sakuya Manchuri hatsu Moskuwa e" (Mr. Ayukawa and Mr. Matsushima left last night for Moscow from Manchouli), *Manshū shimbun*, Dec. 29, 1939. Once they arrived in Moscow on Jan. 4, 1940, Miho, who was

not officially listed as part of Ayukawa's European tour group, left for London via a stopover in Sweden (where he visited the Swedish Match Company) to arrange for Ayukawa's visit to the United States by conferring with Kuhara Mitsuo, the eldest son of Kuhara Fusanosuke, who, as a business executive of MIDC, was working with James Murray in its New York office. Miho also contacted a former counselor and commercial attaché at the British embassy in Tokyo to discuss British investments in Manchukuo. Besides Kishimoto, Ayukawa listed, as members of the group, Asai Kazuhiko (another aide of Ayukawa's), Yamamoto Sōji, Director Kubota Tokujirō of the Manchuria Automobile Company, a Mr. Yonemoto Haruo, and Manchukuo Consul General to Hungary Ibuki, who joined the group as they passed through Bucharest. Yamamoto had abandoned a business trip to the United States to join the group. See Microfiche no. 182.3 of the Ayukawa Papers. On Yamamoto's joining Ayukawa's tour group, see Ayukawa, "Watashi no rirekisho." For Miho's mission in London, see 76–77 of Ayukawa's 1953 draft memoir in Microfiche no. 931.4 of the Ayukawa Papers; and Awaya and Yoshida, *Kokusai kensatsukyoku [IPS] jinmonchōsho*, 267. Although Ayukawa kept his plan to visit the United States secret, he did state in an interview with *Manshū shimbun* on Dec. 23, 1939, that although his main destinations were Germany and Italy, there was a possibility that he might go elsewhere; see Microfiche no. 182.3 of the Ayukawa Papers.

12. Ayukawa stated in his interrogation record (see Awaya and Yoshida, *Kokusai kensatsukyoku [IPS] jinmonchōsho*, 264) that he met Foreign Minister V. M. Molotov (1890–1986), but according to a travel diary that an aide made on his return from Europe, Ayukawa met with Mikoyan from 8:30 to 9:00 P.M. on Jan. 5. It does not indicate a meeting with Molotov. See "Ayukawa sōsai Oushū shisatsu ryokō" (President Ayukawa's European trip), in Microfiche no. 182.3, Ayukawa Yoshisuke Papers.

13. See Kishimoto Kantarō, "Oushū shisatsu sokumenkan," May 11, 1940, 5–7; *Manshū nichi nichi*, Apr. 3, 1940; and *Manshū shimbun*, Apr. 3, 1940, in Microfiche no. 182.3, Ayukawa Papers. For the factories Ayukawa visited and the names of people he met during his European trip, see the same microfiche. In Germany, Ayukawa visited, among others, the Fritz Werner machine tools factory outside Berlin, the Lindner precision machine factory outside Berlin, the Rheinmetall-Borsig weaponry and boiler factory outside Berlin, the Adam Opel transport cars factory in Brandenburg, the Daimler-Benz airplane factory in Gensehagen, two AEG factories (turbine and generator) in Berlin, three Junkers factories in Dessau, the Heinkel airplane factory in Oranienburg, two Vereinigte Leichtmetallwerke factories in Hanover, the Hansa Muhle oil and fat factory in Hamburg, the Brinckman & Mergell oil and fat factory in Hamburg, Krupp's low-temperature carbonization Fisher process plant and automobile factories in Essen, the G.H.H. metal-processing plant in Oberhausen, the Schiess machine tool factory in Dusseldorf, the I. G. Farben artificial

rubber-manufacturing factory in Leverkusen, the Fauth oil and fat factory in Wiesbaden, the Metalgesellsschaft factory in Frankfurt, the Adam Opel automobile plant in Russelsheim, the Bosch metal-molding factory in Stuttgart, the Daimler-Benz automobile factories in Unterturkheim and Sinderfingen, the diesel truck factory in Gaggener, the Siemens factory in Berlin, the Durener Metallwerke factory in Berlin, the Ammoniak Werke factory in Leuna, the Zeiss factory in Jena, the S.K.F. factory in Schweinfurt, the BMW airplane motors factory in Munich, the Rackwitz light metals factory in Leipzig, the I.G. Bitterfeld (magnesium alloys electron and hydronalium) factory in Leipzig, the Herman Göring iron works in Watenstadt, and the United Steel Works in Krefeld and Bochum. In Italy, Ayukawa visited the Fiat factories in Turin, the Villar Perosa ball bearings factory near Turin, the light metal foundry in Turin, the airplane factory near Turin, the Cantieri Reuniti dell'adriatic shipbuilding plants in Trieste and Monfalcone, and the Gaslini vegetable oil and fat factory in Trieste.

14. For Yamamoto's mission, see Hoshino Naoki, *Mihatenu yume*, 294. According to Ayukawa's travel report on Feb. 28, 1940, he spoke with Miho at a lunch meeting hosted by business executives and engineers of Cantieri, an Italian shipbuilding company, at its Monfalcone factory. For Kishimoto's remark, see Kishimoto Kantarō, "Oushū shisatsu sokumenkan," May 11, 1940, 26–33, in Microfiche no. 182.3, Ayukawa Papers. In contrast to Shirasu's remark about the European war situation as reported by Kishimoto, according to Ayukawa's post-1945 recollection, Shirasu remarked: "Both England and France will win since their spiritual strength is much stronger than we think. Compared with the English aristocrats who have a deep rooted Anglo-Saxon spirit, Hitler is a parvenu surrounded by a rabble"; see Ayukawa, "Watashi on rirekisho," 331; and Kojima Naoki, *Ayukawa Yoshisuke den*, 135. Perhaps this was not mentioned in Kishimoto's report because of the sensitivity of the topic at the time. For Yamamoto's opinion on Ayukawa's proposed trip to the United States, see Hoshino Naoki, *Mihatenu yume*, 294. For Shirasu's and Kuhara's opinions regarding this and Miho's preparation, see p. 77 of the 1953 draft memoir in Microfiche no. 931.4 of the Ayukawa Papers. Ayukawa also mentioned in the interrogation record that he had told Miho to carry out his business scheme in Britain and the United States (*Shinmonkiroku* 1, 32, in Microfiche no. 163.1, Ayukawa Papers; Ayawa and Yoshida, *Kokusai kensatsukyoku [IPS] jinminchōsho*, 267). Kishimoto Kantarō mentioned in his interrogation record that he had told Prosecutor Solis Horwitz that in 1940 Ayukawa had planned to visit the United States after his European trip but was told by his aides who joined him in Italy from London that a trip would be meaningless at that time. See Kishimoto Kantarō, *Shimonkiroku*, 18; and Microfiche no. 163.2, Ayukawa Papers. Finally, see the entries for Feb. 18–22, 25–27, 1940 in Ambassador Amau Eiji's diary, *Nikki shiryōshū* (Tokyo: Amau Eiji nikki Shiryōshū kankōkai, 1990), vol. 3.

15. See Microfiche no. 182.3 of the Ayukawa Papers for the meeting with Weller. For biographical information on Weller, see Perez and Willett, *Clarence Dillon*, 76, 108, 111–13. On the same day Ayukawa met Weller, he was introduced to the leading figure in the Italian textile industry, Angeli di Frua of the Breda Company. The two men discussed the possibility of a joint venture between Italy and Manchukuo.

16. Kojima Naoki, *Ayukawa Yoshisuke den*, 136, 140–41. According to Ayukawa's report on his European trip, he met Kurusu for discussions from 9:00 P.M. on Jan. 19 to 1:00 A.M. the morning of Jan. 20; at a dinner party hosted by Kurusu on the evening of Jan. 20; on the evening of Jan. 23; at a luncheon meeting hosted by Kurusu for Ayukawa and German officials including Economic Minister Walther Funk (1890–1960) on Feb. 4; on the evening of Mar. 2 (the day he arrived in Berlin from Munich); on the evening of Mar. 3; all day on Mar. 5 (see below); on the evening of Mar. 8 (the day before Ayukawa's group left for Prague); and in the afternoon and in the evening of Mar. 15 (see Microfiche no. 182.3 of the Ayukawa Papers). On Mar. 5, Ayukawa and Kurusu met with German Foreign Minister Joachim von Ribbentrop; the two men saw the Soviet ambassador to Germany to discuss Ayukawa's visa to the Soviet Union, which he needed for his return trip to Japan; and, starting around noon Ayukawa talked with Hitler for about forty minutes. That evening Ayukawa dined with Kurusu at the latter's residence. There, he also talked with a young diplomat named Kamimura Shin'ichi who had recently arrived from London. Ayukawa told his interrogators that he saw the German foreign minister and the German economic minister (Awaya and Yoshida, *Kokusai kensatsukyoku [IPS] jinminchōsho*, 266). With regard to the missions of Welles and Mooney to Germany, see Marks, *Wind over Sand*, 153–60. For the details of the Mooney mission, see Nishimuta Yūji, *Nachizumu to Doitsu jidōsha Kōgyō*, 228–40, and "Manuscript: 'Lessons on War and Peace,' Part III," Jan. 1, 1950, Box 4, Folder 5, James D. Mooney Papers.

17. For Kurusu's attempt to import British steel products to Manchukuo in 1934 and for his joint efforts with Yoshida, see Kurusu, *Nichibei gaikō hiwa*, 110–16. For Yoshida's efforts as ambassador to England to realign Japan with Britain, see Hosoya, *Nihon gaikō no zahyō*, 18–52. For Kurusu's comments to Ayukawa during the latter's visit to Germany, and Ayukawa's thoughts about Kurusu, see *Shinmonkiroku* 1, 32–33, Microfiche no. 163.1, Ayukawa Papers; and Awaya and Yoshida, *Kokusai kensatsukyoku (IPS) jinminchōsha*, 267–68. For Ayukawa's discussion of his efforts to attract foreign investments to Manchukuo, particularly from the United States, excerpts from this document exist in Microfiche nos. 163.2, 511.3, and 611.1. Ayukawa briefly discussed in his draft 1953 memoir Kurusu's comments about the poor prospects of the German-Soviet non-aggression pact. According to Ayukawa, among other things, Kurusu told him three things. First, in a conversation with Göring, Kurusu

described Germany, Japan, and the Soviet Union as three horses pulling a carriage. If the horses did not cooperate, the carriage would turn over. Asking what he thought of the analogy, Göring stated that Germany and Japan should put the Soviet Union in the middle and then take over. Second, the Soviet ambassador to Germany had told Kurusu that despite the German-Soviet pact, he did not hear much from the German government. Third, there was a military buildup along the Soviet-German border (see Ayukawa Papers, Microfiche no. 931.4, 77–79).

18. The German pressure was mentioned by Kishimoto during an interview in *Zaikaijin shisō zenshū*, 2: 191. It is also mentioned in *Shinmonkiroku* 1, 49–50, Microfiche no. 163.1, Ayukawa Papers; and Awaya and Yoshida, *Kokusai kensatsukyoku (IPS) jinminchōsha*, 272–73. Present on the day of the recording was Prince Urach of the German Foreign Ministry Information Bureau. According to Franz Moedlhammer, Urach was one of his German business contacts. The day before, Ayukawa had discussed the radio recording with an official of the Bureau, who had asked Ayukawa on Mar. 8 for a recorded interview for a radio broadcast (see Microfiche no. 182.3, Ayukawa Papers).

19. According to the Mar. 5 diary entry, the meeting lasted for forty minutes and took place during a snowstorm (see Microfiche no. 182.3, Ayukawa Papers). For newspaper reports, see in the same microfiche: *Shinkyō nichi nichi*, Apr. 2, 1940; *Manshū nichi nichi*, Apr. 3, 1940; and *Manshū shimbun*, Mar. 5, 1940. Ayukawa probably had this conversation in his mind when he described Hitler as a man who "in certain respects possessed an Oriental feeling" in *Manshū shimbun*, Apr. 3, 1940. *Manshū shimbun* in a report on Mar. 5 described Ayukawa's meeting with Hitler as confirming the strengthening of the relations between Manchukuo and Germany and hence promising satisfactory economic relations in the future. In addition, see Ayukawa, "Watashi no rirekisho," 331–32; and Ayukawa, *Hyakumi dansu*, 173–74. Ayukawa told his interrogator that in meeting Hitler, whom he described as giving him the impression of being a "special German," he had difficulty understanding what Hitler was saying because of a bad interpreter but he was surprised that Hitler made no mention of Manchukuo soybeans; see Awaya and Yoshida, *Kokusai kensatsukyoku (IPS) jinminchōsha*, 269.

20. Kishimoto Kantarō, "Oushū shisatsu sokumenkan" (My observations of President Ayukawa's European trip), May 11, 1940, in Ayukawa Papers, Microfiche no. 182.3, 22–23, and 29. In the same microfiche, see *Manshū nichi nichi*, Apr. 3, 1940.

21. *Manshū nichi nichi*, Apr. 3, 1940, in Microfiche no. 182.3, Ayukawa Papers. For Ayukawa's talk about his attempt to meet Stalin and his ideas about it, see pp. 46–48 of *Shimonkiroku* 1, Microfiche no. 163.1, Ayukawa Papers; and Awaya and Yoshida, *Kokusai kensatsukyoku (IPS) jinminchōsha*, 269–70. Kamimura's talk with Ayukawa as he escorted him to Prague is mentioned in Kojima Naoki, *Ayukawa Yoshisuke den*, 137–38. For a discussion of American economic assistance, such as the provision of

capital, technology, factories, and engineers through investments from the U.S. private sector to the Soviet Union after World War I, see Leffler, *The Specter of Communism*, 17. In addition, see Hoshino, *Mihatenu yume*, 294; and Ayukawa, "Watashi no rirekisho," 331–33. Finally, for the changes in the economic role of Manchukuo vis-à-vis Japan and the shift away from creating a self-sufficient economy in Manchukuo in 1937 to a dependent relationship because of Japan's military expansion in the Far East and because of the European war, see Hara Akira, "Senkyūhyaku sanjūnendai," 81–87, 107–9; and Kobayashi, *Daitōa kyōeiken no keisei to hōkai*, 346, 362. Hoshino Naoki, during his interrogation by the prosecutors in preparation for the war crimes trial, stated that the short-term imperatives of running the war economy in Japan undermined the long-term goal of creating a self-sufficient and highly industrialized state in Manchukuo (see p. 22 of the Japanese translation of the interrogation record of Hoshino Naoki in Microfiche no. 163.3 of the Ayukawa Papers).

22. Lafeber, *Cambridge History of American Foreign Relations*, 2: 169–77, 227–33; Williams, *Contours of American History*, 414–57; Iriye, *Pacific Estrangement*, 192–93, 207–9, 226–27; Perry, *Facing West*, 161–65; Chō, "An Inquiry into the Problem of Importing American Capital in Manchuria," 383–87, 691–92; *Gendaishi shiryō*, vol. 7, *Manshū jihen*, 156, 162, 167, 172–80.

23. On the state of the American economy between 1937 and 1941, see this book's Introduction.

24. Marks, *Wind over Sand*, 85–87.

25. Counselor to Hull, June 7, 1940, SD 711.94/1566, RG 59, National Archives, Washington, D.C. (hereafter cited as NA).

26. Memorandum of Miho-Welles-Hornbeck-Hamilton conversation, May 8, 1940, SD 711.94/1507, NA. This memorandum was sent to Grew in Tokyo on May 15.

27. Kido, *Kido Kōichi nikki*, 2: 784.

28. Kido's meetings with Itō for golf were numerous; see both volumes of *Kido Kōichi nikki*. For Itō's political assistance for Kido, see, e.g., ibid., 1: 568; and 2: 647, 682.

29. Ibid., 622, 687, 690, 754. Also present at the meeting were Foreign Minister Nomura Kichisaburō and Finance Minister Aoki Kazuo.

30. Ibid., 2: 784.

31. Chō, "Amerika shihon no Manshū dōnyū keikaku"; Horikoshi, *Keizai dantai rengōkai zenshi*, 336–38. The chief government officials who participated in this project were Sakomizu Hisatsune (1902–77), chief of the Finance Section of the MOF Finance Bureau; Minobe Yōji (1900–1953) of the MCI Price Bureau; Kishi Eiichi of the Foreign Ministry; Lt. Col. Shiba Katsuo (1901–70) of the First Section of the Naval Ministry's Naval Affairs Bureau; Lt. Col. Kageyama Seiichi (1899–1978) of the War Ministry's Military Affairs Section; Araki Eikichi (1891–1959) of the Bank of Japan; and the staff at the Manchukuo embassy. The main participants from the

business community were chairman of the Japan Economic Federation and of the Foreign Relations Council Gō Seinosuke; former ambassador to Brazil and vice chairman of the council Sawada Setsuzō (1884–1976); Takashima Seiichi, managing director of the Foreign Relations Bureau; Ayusawa Iwao, a friend of Sawada and a deputy director of the bureau; and Ashino Hiroshi, a deputy director of the bureau. At Gō's residence the following businessmen exchanged opinions regarding the economic problems Japan faced and the economic development of Manchukuo and North China with Sawada and Gō: Ayukawa, Ishizaka Taizō (1886–1975) of the Dai-ichi Life Insurance Company, President Akashi Teruo (1881–1956) of the Dai-ichi Bank, President Asano Ryōzō of the Tsurumi Steel and Shipbuilding Company, Ōkubo Toshikane of the Yokohama Specie Bank, Governor Yūki Toyotarō of the Bank of Japan, Yamashita Kamesaburō (1867–1944) of the Yamashita Shipping Company, Murata Shōzō (1878–1957) of the Osaka Merchant Shipping Company, President Hatta Yoshiaki (1879–1964) of the Tokyo Chamber of Commerce, Funata Kazuo of the Mitsubishi Holding Company, and Ikeda Shigeaki (Seihin), former head of the Mitsui Holding Company (see Sawada Setsuzō, *Sawada Setsuzō kaisōroku*, 221–22).

32. For details of relations between Kleiman and Ayukawa, see Chapter 5 of this book.

33. John F. O'Ryan received an LL.B. from New York University in 1898 and became a member of the New York State bar in 1898. At the time of his mission, O'Ryan was a partner in the New York law firm of Loucks, O'Ryan & Cullen. He became a major general in 1912, graduated from the Army War College in 1914, and served as a commander of the New York Division on the Mexican border in 1916. In 1917 he was appointed the commander of the 27th Division of the U.S. Army and served in Belgium and France from 1917 to 1919. He received numerous medals from the United States, Britain, Belgium, France, and Italy. In 1919 he received an LL.D. from New York University. O'Ryan opposed war with Japan until Pearl Harbor, shortly before which he became an advisor to Secretary of War Stimson. O'Ryan's public service centered around cutting waste and political red tape in order to achieve efficiency (see *Japan Times and Advertiser*, Aug. 13, 1940, SD 711.94/1717, RG 59, NA; Wilkins, "Kyōdōtōron," 3: 246; Microfiche no. 517.2, Ayukawa Papers; "O'Ryan's Job," *Time*, July 29, 1940, 15; "General O'Ryan Appointed Adviser to Stimson," *Washington Star*, Aug. 1, 1941; and "Major General John F. O'Ryan," box 324, Hornbeck Papers). Before he approached O'Ryan, Nishiyama had invited a dozen prominent businessmen, such as the presidents of the four largest American banks, including Guarantee Trust and the First National City Bank. The State Department, however, blocked these plans. As a result, none of the businessmen ended up accepting the invitation. Nishiyama and the federation then considered contacting Owen D. Young, a former top executive of General Electric who had retired from that firm in

1939, but the federation passed on this plan because Young would draw too much attention (Sawada, *Sawada Setsuzō kaisōroku*, 223–24).

34. Butrick to Hull, Aug. 8, 1940, SD 711.94/1664, RG 59, NA.

35. Memorandum of O'Ryan-Hamilton conversation, June 3, 1940, SD 711.94/1529, RG 59, NA. A copy of the report was sent to the American embassy in Tokyo on June 14. Hamilton wrote:

Major General O'Ryan was referred ... from the White House.... General O'Ryan said that he had just come from a talk with the President; that he had given the President a general outline of the facts relating to his prospective trip to Japan; that the President had expressed himself as very favorably disposed toward the idea and had said that he would write to Mr. Grew in regard to the matter. General O'Ryan then explained to me that he was going to Japan under arrangements made with the Japanese Economic Federation and Eastman Dillon and Company of New York City; and that he was to make a study of general economic, financial, and trade conditions in Japan, especially as they related to trade and commerce between Japan and the United States. He said that he expected to visit Japan and perhaps "Manchukuo."

In addition, see Dallek, *Franklin D. Roosevelt and American Foreign Policy*, 238.

36. Maxwell Hamilton, "Memorandum for the President," June 5, 1940, SD 711.94/1529, RG 59, NA. In addition, see "O'Ryan's Job," *Time*, July 29, 1940, 15.

37. Secretary of state to American embassy in Tokyo, June 13, 1940, SD 711.94/1528; Sumner Welles to Grew, June 14, 1940, SD 711.94/1529; State Department to the American consul, Shanghai, June, 15, 1940, SD 711.94/1533; and Plain, Nanking, to the secretary of state, June 14, 1940, SD 711.94/1534; all in RG 59, NA.

38. Lippmann to Major General John F. O'Ryan, June 10, 1940; and O'Ryan to Lippmann, June 14, 1940; "O'Ryan" folder, Lippmann Papers. *Time* reported that O'Ryan had been advocating war against Germany and supported campaigns to collect money for the Finns' resistance against Soviet aggression (see "O'Ryan's Job," *Time*, July 29, 1940, 15).

39. Miho to Ayukawa, n.d., 1940; Miho to Ayukawa, June 4, 1940; and Ayukawa to Miho, June 5, 1940, in Microfiche no. 517.2, Ayukawa Papers. Hoover's daily calendar confirms that he saw Miho on May 31 (www.ecommcode2.com/hoover/calendar/hoover.cfm).

40. For the June 6 and 26 cables, see Microfiche no. 611.1, Ayukawa Papers.

41. Ayukawa to Miho, June 22, 1940, Microfiche no. 517.2, Ayukawa Papers. The code name used to refer to the president in the telegram was "the stingy fool."

42. For a discussion of these events, see Marks, *Wind over Sand*, 85–87. For American documents that describe the Grew-Arita talks and the U.S. government's instructions to Grew regarding the American stance on those talks, see State Department to American embassy in Tokyo, June 15, 1940, and Grew to secretary of state, June 12, 1940, SD 711.94/1532; June 19, 1940, SD 711.94/1537; July 11, 1940, SD 711.94/1558; July 11, 1940, SD 711.94/1569; July 11, 1940, SD 711.94/1570; July 11, 1940, SD 711.94/1571; July 11, 1940, SD 711.94/1572; July 11, 1940, SD 711.94/1573; July 14,

1940, SD 711.94/1575; memorandum of conversation between the American ambassador and the Japanese minister for foreign affairs, June 19, 1940, SD 711.94/1599; June 10, 1940, SD 711.94/1603; June 28, 1940, 711.94/1628; and July 11, 1940, SD 711.94/1633. For Arita's talks with Sayre in May and with Grew in June and July, Arita's radio speech on June 29, and the domestic political situation leading to the downfall of the Yonai cabinet, see Takahashi Makiko, *Shizukanaru tate*, 1: 46–65.

43. Memorandum by the Department of State's Division of Far Eastern Affairs, Aug. 12, 1940, SD 711.94/1629, RG 59, NA.

44. Sawada, *Sawada Setsuzō kaisōroku*, 223; Schonberger, *Japanese Connection*, 133.

45. Memorandum for the State Department from the White House, Sept. 3, 1940, Hull to Watson, Sept. 9, 1940, and Watson to O'Ryan, Sept. 10, 1940, "PPF 1948," President's Personal File, Franklin D. Roosevelt Papers. As a way to bring about U.S.-Japan cooperation and to strengthen the political position of the business community and those who preferred to side with the United States in Japan, O'Ryan proposed a "corporate method" of administering the Netherlands East Indies by creating a trusteeship of those islands under the United States and Japan. This was to be arranged by having the Netherlands "request the United States and Japan to serve as joint trustees for the impartial administration of the economic affairs of the islands." After consulting with Secretary of State Hull, Roosevelt decided to respond through Edwin M. Watson, secretary to the president. Watson sent O'Ryan a perfunctory letter. The letter O'Ryan sent to Roosevelt on July 13, 1940, from the Nara Hotel can be found in SD 711.94/1670, RG 59, NA. Stanley Hornbeck wrote a memorandum that commented on the Sept. 9 letter, and he sent this to the secretary of state and the undersecretary of state (the State Department did not send the memorandum to the president, whom they considered busy with other matters). In this memorandum Hornbeck criticized all the suggestions that O'Ryan had made in his letter to the president (see Division of Far Eastern Affairs to Stanley Hornbeck, Sept. 11, 1940, SD 711.94/1769, RG 59, NA).

46. *FRUS: The Far East, 1940*, 4: 376–77, July 1, 1940. Moss was acting as Ayukawa's intermediary with Grew at the time. Grew described Mr. and Mrs. Moss as famous and widely respected figures in the American expatriate community in a recommendation letter for their son Richard to the personnel director of the National City Bank in New York. See Grew to Williams, July 10, 1940, Joseph Grew Letters, vol. 98. Ayukawa mentioned Moss as the acting intermediary (*Shinmon-kiroku*, 1: 33–34, Microfiche no. 163.1, Ayukawa Papers).

47. Microfiche no. 611.1, Ayukawa Papers.

48. Ibid.

49. Miho to Ayukawa, July 3, 1940, microfiche no. 517.2, Ayukawa Papers. See the copies of the telegrams between June 21 and July 3 from Miho to Ayukawa, Ayukawa's view of the O'Ryan mission, and Ayukawa's June 29 request to Umezu in Ayukawa's 1953 draft memoir, 81–86, 99–100, in Microfiche no. 931.4, Ayukawa Papers.

50. *FRUS: The Far East, 1940,* 4: 379–80.

51. Ibid., 390–91.

52. See the White House memorandum by Forrestal, which was read by Hornbeck, Hamilton, and Joseph Ballantine, entitled "More on Aikawa [Ayukawa]-Kato, M[iho]." It included Ayukawa's telegrams to Miho of July 11 about the delicate circumstance in Japan and of July 12 about the imminent cabinet change; see SD 711.94/1686, RG 59, NA.

53. On p. 336 of Ayukawa's "Watashi no rirekisho," the figure is given as $5 billion whereas it is $1 billion in Microfiche no. 163.1 of the Ayukawa Papers. Ayukawa mistakenly wrote in this memoir that Miho had such a discussion with Baruch in 1941, instead of 1940. Dillon had worked under Baruch at the War Industries Board during World War I; see Coit, *Mr. Baruch,* 165.

54. SD 711.94/1559, RG 59, NA.

55. *FRUS: The Far East, 1940,* 4: 397.

56. For a Japanese translation of Hull's message, see Microfiche no. 611.1, Ayukawa Papers. For Ayukawa's comment to Kido, see Kido, *Kido Kōichi nikki,* 2: 803.

57. Ayukawa to Miho, July 11 and 12, 1940, SD 711.94/1501 to 711.94/1669; Grew to Hull, July 13, 1940, SD 711.94/1574, RG 59, NA.

58. Microfiche no. 611.1, Ayukawa Papers; and memorandum of the Katō-Hamilton conversation, May 6, 1940, SD 711.94/1506, RG 59, NA. Hamilton stated: "I have known Mr. Katō well for a considerable no. of years, dating from the time when he served as Counselor of the Japanese Embassy here in Washington. Katō is, in my opinion, the best type of Japanese and I have always had very frank and friendly relations with him." Finally, the fact that Ayukawa had told Yonai, Arita, and Konoe about his clandestine negotiations with the United States is mentioned in *Shinmonkiroku,* 1: 37–38, Microfiche no. 163.1, Ayukawa Papers; and Awaya and Yoshida, *Kokusai kensatsukyoku (IPS) jinminchōsho,* 273.

59. *Shinmonkiroku,* 1: 33–37, Microfiche no. 163.1, and 1953 draft memoir, p. 93, Microfiche no. 931.4, Ayukawa Papers. On July 5, a group of right-wing men were apprehended and accused of attempting to overthrow the government; see Kido, *Kido Kōcihi nikki,* 2: 799–800.

60. Kojima Naoki, *Ayukawa Yoshisuke den,* 143–44. For consultations between Itō and Ayukawa and Ayukawa's desire to become foreign minister, see his 1953 draft memoir, pp. 101–3, Microfiche no. 931.4, Ayukawa Papers. For the rumor about his appointment, see "Tokyo Exchange Strong on Step Believed Aimed at New U.S. Trade Pact: Change in Ambassador to U.S. Reported Planned—1911 Treaty Abrogated One Year Ago," *Wall Street Journal,* July 31, 1940, Microfiche no. 130.2, Ayukawa Papers. Ayukawa stated that he had declined Prime Minister Konoe's offer to appoint him minister of commerce and industry on one or two occasions and that

the news reports regarding his appointment as the ambassador to the U.S. was only a rumor; see Awaya and Yoshida, *Kokusai kensatsukyoku (IPS) jinminchōsho,* 262, 274.

61. Ayukawa to O'Ryan, Aug. 1, 1940, Microfiche no. 517.2, Ayukawa Papers.

62. See Vice Consul J. Graham Parsons to secretary of state on July 26, 1940, SD 711.94/1667, RG 59, NA. See also *China Press,* Aug. 5, 1940, and *Shanghai Evening Post & Mercury,* Aug. 3 and 6, 1940, SD 711.94/1664, RG 59, NA. For the mission's tour of Manchukuo, see Parsons to Johnson and Hull, July 26, 1940, SD 711.94/1666, RG 59, NA. See also *Shanghai Post & Mercury,* Aug. 8, 1940, SD 711.94/1710; and *China Weekly Review,* Aug. 10, 1940, SD 711.94/1711; "Japan Wants U.S. Capital," Aug. 13, 1940, SD 711.94/1711; *Japan Times and Advertiser* editorial comment on Aug. 8, 1940, in Grew to Hull, Sept. 5, 1940, SD 711.94/1717; O'Ryan's speech on station JOAK on Aug. 15, 1940, SD 711.94/1878; all in RG 59, NA. Finally, see "O'Ryan's Job," *Time,* July 29, 1940; and "O'Ryan, on Mission for Japan Quoted as Blaming War on China," *New York Herald Tribune,* Aug. 3, 1940, in "Major General John F. O'Ryan" folder, box 324, Hornbeck Papers.

63. Wilkins, "Kyōdōtōron," 246; Horikoshi, *Keizai dantai rengōkai zenshi,* 338; and Grew to Hull, Sept. 5, 1940, SD 711.94/1717, RG 59, NA.

Chapter 7

1. Bain to Mrs. Bain, Apr. 16, 1938, H. Foster Bain Papers. Bain also wrote that he had met Hoshino Naoki and Kishi Nobusuke (whose name he misheard as "Keiji"). Bain was told by "one of the American counsels" that the two men "really run the country." After meeting the two, Bain wrote: "For the real ruler of a big country Hoshino is really remarkably well informed as to many things. . . . Both are modest, hard working and unassuming." Finally, Bain thought "the General, Ambassador and Chief of the Kwantung Army [had] quite a regal manner indeed."

2. Wilson, *Herbert Hoover,* 175–79.

3. Hoover to Bain, Apr. 26, 1938, Bain to Hoover, May 2, 1938, and Bain to Hoover, May 6, 1938, "H. Foster Bain," Post-Presidential Individual File, Herbert C. Hoover Papers.

4. Bain left this description of policymakers in Manchukuo and Ayukawa's view of them:

Those who ran Manchukuo are fascists in their faith for order and precision but are Bolshevists (or maybe New Dealers) in their belief that the common people have been needlessly exploited by business and their determination to do something about it. As individuals they are charming and friendly with certain deeply fixed limitations. Aikawa [Ayukawa] thinks [it] is possible by giving them sound advise [*sic*] and practical help, to assist in their purpose of making Manchukuo a center of peace rather than a 'land of conflict.' . . . To my surprise it seems there is a large measure [of independence] here but, primarily, as I see it, it is the independence of the Kwantung Army which feels it created this country and has more right than the Japanese Government per se to run it. . . . I have met a number of [Kwantung Army offi-

cers] and while they are . . . hellish fighters, which is the way of the Far East and you will re-
member of the Germans, they are also idealists.

See H. Foster Bain to Herbert Hoover, Mar. 29, 1938, "H. Foster Bain," Post-
Presidential Individual File, Herbert C. Hoover Papers.

5. Bain to Ayukawa, May 19, 1938, Microfiche no. 517.1, Ayukawa Papers.

6. Ninkovich, *Modernity and Power*, 89–90.

7. Ibid., 70, 80.

8. See "American-Japanese Commercial Relations for Jitsu-Gyo no Sekai," in "Japan, 1927–1928," Commerce Papers Series Subject File, Herbert C. Hoover Papers.

9. Ninkovich, *Modernity and Power*, 71.

10. Ibid., 71–72, 85–88.

11. Ibid., 72, 90, 344–45.

12. Herbert Hoover to Mark L. Requa, Apr. 21, 1924, "Japan, 1922–1926," Commerce Papers Series Subject File, Herbert C. Hoover Papers.

13. Ninkovich, *Modernity and Power*, 82, 90–92.

14. See Harold Phelps Stokes to T. Wikawa, June 26, 1924; "Wikawa, T. P.,"
1922–1927"; "Japanese-American Economic Relations" in "Japan, 1922–1926," Commerce Papers Series Subject File, Herbert C. Hoover Papers. For Hoover's views on
policy toward Japan in the 1920s to the 1930s, see Ninkovich, *Modernity and Power*,
92–97; and Wilson, *American Business and Foreign Policy*, 45, 228–30. For Franklin D.
Roosevelt's view of the Japanese race, see Marks, *Wind over Sand*, 8.

15. Takasaki, "Watashi no rirekisho."

16. "Tagg–Talb, 1921–1928," Commerce Papers Series Subject File, Herbert C.
Hoover Papers.

17. Takasaki to Hoover, Sept. 27, 1939, "SYCIP–TATE, H.," Herbert Hoover
Post-Presidential General File, Herbert C. Hoover Papers.

18. Takasaki to Hoover, Feb. 21, 1940, and Hoover to Takasaki, Apr. 7, 1940, in
ibid. According to Takasaki's autobiography, he seems to have made one last attempt
in 1941 in the hope of inviting Hoover to Manchuria and creating a momentum for the
joint economic development of Manchuria and China with the United States. Takasaki sent a letter soon after he agreed to succeed Yoshino Shinji as the vice chairman of
MIDC for three years beginning in 1941. Right before going to Manchukuo, Takasaki
invited Hoover to come and tour that country. Hoover sent a reply stating that given
the present international situation, Manchukuo could not be recognized as a country.
He, however, praised the vision Takasaki had in operating and managing the Manchurian economy and suggested introducing American consulting engineers to him
(see Takasaki, *Manshū no shūen*, 34–35). Since no records exist in the Hoover papers
regarding Takasaki's third attempt, his recollections may have been based on fuzzy
memory. The fact that he does not mention his letter to Hoover in 1939 and 1940 in his
book may be an indication that he confounded the dates.

19. "Castle Warns U.S. on Open Hostility in Stand on Japan," *Japan Times and Advertiser*, Nov. 18, 1940; entries for Nov. 13 and 14, 1940, in William R. Castle, Jr., Diaries, vol. 40; Castle to Hoover, Nov. 8, 1940, "Castle: 1940–1941," Post-Presidential Individual File, Herbert C. Hoover Papers; Smith, *An Uncommon Man*, 295, 301; and Doenecke, *In Danger Undaunted*, 8.

20. Wood made this argument at the Chicago Council on Foreign Relations on Oct. 4, 1940; see Marshall, *To Have and Have Not*, 183.

21. See ibid., 91–92; see also ibid., 10–12, 33–38, 41–42, 53, 70, 72, 76.

22. Ninkovich, *Modernity and Power*, 113–14, 116–17, 119.

23. Marshall, *To Have and Have Not*, 179–81.

24. Howard, *America and a New World Order*, 77, 101–2, 112. Howard wrote his author's note in Aug. 1940. Retired Major General James G. Harbord wrote a foreword to this book, and Howard submitted the manuscript for criticism and comments to opinion leaders including William Castle, who was an America Firster; James D. Mooney, the executive vice president of GM (see Chapter 6); Lionel D. Eddie, whose firm had supported the O'Ryan mission (see Chapter 6), and John Foster Dulles, the future secretary of state during the Eisenhower administration; see author's note. For Howard's negotiations with Nissan, see Mason, *American Multinationals and Japan*, 70–71, 74. Howard was born in Los Angeles on Mar. 4, 1896. He received a B.A. in economics from Stanford University in 1917 and served as captain in the 23rd Machine Gun Company from April 1917 to November 1919. After graduating from Harvard Graduate School of Business Administration in 1920, Howard joined General Motors; see Mooney Papers, Box 4, Folder 24. Howard was working on another manuscript co-authored by A. Whitney Griswold, E. A. J. Johnson, Harold H. Thurlby, and Paul Van Zeeland, tentatively entitled "After the Wars"; see Mooney Papers, Box 4, Folder 17. With regard to endorsements and criticisms of Howard's book and Howard's view on American foreign policy, see Doenecke, *Storm on the Horizon*, 130, 146–47, 411.

25. Chernow, *The Warburgs*, 110–11. Strauss became a good friend of Father Drought initially because Drought was in charge of budgets for the Maryknoll Society, and Strauss's company advised the society about its investments.

26. Butow, *The John Doe Associates*, 112, 375–76; and Strauss, *Men and Decisions*, 123. For events between Apr. 5 and 29, see Butow, *The John Doe Associates*, 155–74.

27. In addition to meeting the principal figures in this affair in the War, Naval, and Foreign ministries, all of them supporters of the idea of U.S.-Japan rapprochement, Iwakuro saw Foreign Minister Matsuoka Yōsuke, House of Peers member and former foreign minister Arita Hachirō, House of Peers member Aoki Kazuo, former finance minister Kaya Okinori, over a dozen right-wing fanatics including Inoue Nisshō (1886–1967) and Amano Tatsuo (1892–1974), and business executives Nagasaki Eizō (1881–1953), Nagano Mamoru (1890–1970), Mizuno Shigeo (1899–

1972), and Ayukawa Yoshisuke. Matsuoka was an advocate of U.S.-Japan rapprochement, but he emphasized the need to strengthen the Axis alliance in order to achieve this; Iwakuro instinctively questioned whether Matsuoka's upcoming European trip aimed first to strengthen the alliance and then to strike a neutrality pact with the Soviet Union, and Matsuoka frankly told him that this was so. He wanted Iwakuro to prepare for rapprochement while he carried out his European objectives. Arita told Iwakuro his mission would enable American policymakers to realize that the Japanese military wanted not war with the United States but rapprochement between the two countries. Iwakuro saw the right-wing fanatics, the Kaya-Nagasaki-Mizuno group, and Aoki separately. The fanatics told Iwakuro his job was to decide when to attack the United States so as to break the ABCD (America-British-China-Dutch) encirclement; Iwakuro replied perhaps the situation might turn out that way, but he preferred to put his efforts into reaching a compromise if that was possible. During this dinner gathering, Iwakuro could not forget Inoue's comment that there existed a perfect emperor inside his soul and he would act upon that emperor's order if there ever were to occur a contradiction with the real emperor; Iwakuro thought Inoue's idea potentially dangerous. Before he left Japan, he found these men to be the only ones who opposed compromise with the United States (see *Iwakuro Hideo-shi danwa sokkiroku*, 258). Ayukawa talks about his intention behind having Miho participate in the Iwakuro mission in his 1953 draft memoir, pp. 93–94, Microfiche no. 931.4, Ayukawa Papers. For Iwakuro's role in Manchuria, see Furukawa, *Shōwa senchūki no sōgō kokusaku kikan*, 39, 124.

28. Wikawa managed to receive a travel permit from the Foreign Ministry by explaining that he was negotiating the merger with Ford. The Army managed to dodge Matsuoka's opposition to Wikawa's travel and Matsuoka's accusation that the Army was financing Wikawa's voyage by saying it was financed by private interests (see *Iwakuro Hideo-shi danwa sokkiroku*, 258–59).

29. "Agreement Between Ford Motor Company of Japan, Ltd., and Nihon Kōshūha Jūkōgyō Kabushiki Kaisha (Japan High Frequency Heavy Industry)," in Wikawa Tadao (Ikawa) Papers.

30. See *Iwakuro Hideo-shi danwa sokkiroku*, 258–59. In January Ayukawa had secretly met Nomura just as Nomura was about to leave to take up his appointment in Washington. Clearly influenced by Kurusu's thinking, Ayukawa had argued that the Nazi-Soviet pact might end in the near future. Ayukawa remarked to Nomura that if this happened, Japan should switch sides and join the United States and Great Britain. Ayukawa emphasized to Nomura that this would be an opportunity for attracting American investment in Manchukuo. In his 1953 draft memoir, Ayukawa mentioned that he had met Nomura at Itō Bunkichi's house right before the admiral left for the United States (Microfiche no. 931.4, 101, Ayukawa Papers). In addition, see *Shinmonkiroku* 1: 32–33, Microfiche no. 163.1, Ayukawa Papers; Awaya and

Yoshida, *Kokusai kensatsukyoku (IPS) jinmonchōsho*, 273. The part in this record where Ayukawa describes his efforts to bring foreign investments to Manchukuo, particularly from the United States, exists as excerpts from this document in Microfiche nos. 163.2, 511.3, and 611.1. Ayukawa also briefly talked in his 1953 draft memoir about why Kurusu thought the German-Soviet non-aggression pact would not last long (see Chapter 6 of this book).

31. Furukawa, *Shōwa senchūki no sōgō kokusaku kikan*, 124.

32. Hashimoto Tetsuma, "Makoto ni aikoku no Kyojin Nariki," 307–14; *Shinmonkiroku* 1: 96–98, Microfiche no. 163.1, Ayukawa Papers. In this interrogation record, Ayukawa stated he did not say to the prosecutors he had given Hashimoto a severance payment of five times the annual contribution he had been giving him. Ayukawa answered in the negative to the prosecutors' question whether or not Hashimoto reported to him about his activities. Ayukawa denied he had asked Hashimoto for such information. He also told the prosecutors he knew nothing about Hashimoto's relations with Konoe, Kuhara, or General Yanagawa. These remarks were probably Ayukawa's way of keeping Hashimoto out of trouble with the prosecutors. Even though Ayukawa may not have actually asked Hashimoto to do certain things for him, because they shared a similar outlook on U.S.-Japan relations, it was not necessary for Ayukawa to say such things.

33. Hashimoto Tetsuma, *Nihon no haisen kōfuku rimenshi*, 85–305.

34. Hashimoto Tetsuma, *Nichibei kōshō hiwa*, 90–91.

35. Hashimoto saw Kido at Kido's residence on Mar. 19, five days after his return to Japan (Kido, *Kido Kōichi nikki*, 2: 863). In addition, see Hashimoto Tetsuma, *Nihon no haisen kōfuku rimenshi*, 271–91.

36. See entry for Mar. 20, 1941, in ibid., 863.

37. Hashimoto, *Nichibei kōshō hiwa*, 102–8; idem, *Nihon no haisen kōfuku rimenshi*, 289–305.

38. See footnote 32.

39. Hashimoto, *Nichibei kōshō hiwa*, 108; idem, *Nihon no haisen kōfuku rimenshi*, 304–5.

40. *FRUS: The Far East, 1941*, 4: 30–31.

41. Ibid., 2–3.

42. Kurusu, *Nichibei gaikō hiwa*, 77.

43. *FRUS: The Far East, 1941*, 4: 108–11. Davies was also the first U.S. ambassador to the Soviet Union.

44. Ibid., 108–11.

45. Kurusu, *Nichibei gaikō hiwa*, 66–67, 71–73, 76–77, 110–17. See the following in Ikawa, *Nichibei kōshō shiryō*: Iwakuro Hideo, "Amerika ni okeru nichibei kōshō no keika (A Report on U.S.-Japan Negotiations), May 10, 1946," 493–94; and Drought to Wikawa, Nov. 29, 1940, and Strauss to Wikawa, Dec. 8, 1940, 70–71. See also Kurusu

Saburō, "Ikawa Tadao kun," in Ikawa Tadao, *"Nichibei kōshō hiwa*—hōi no misshi," pt. 1, 83; idem, *"Nichibei kōshō hiwa*—hōi no misshi," pt. 2, 55–56; Butow, *The John Doe Associates*, 8–10, 61, 75–76, 80–85, 112, 118–20, 145, 375–76, 382–83; *Iwakuro Hideo-shi danwa sokkiroku*, 256–71; and Microfiche nos. 163.1 and 163.2, Ayukawa Papers.

46. Shiozaki, *Nichibei sensō no kiro*, 230, 263–64, 277; Marks, *Wind over Sand*, 47; Butow, *John Doe Associates*, 172, 390–91. Howard's thoughts about Matsuoka, Japan, and the American national interest can be found in the following letters in the Roy Howard Papers: Howard to High Commissioner of the Philippines Paul V. McNutt, Nov. 2, 1937, "1937 Foreign File: Asia," Box 133; Ambassador Grew to Howard, Nov. 8, 1940, Howard to Hoshio Mitsunaga, Oct. 25, 1940, S. Sheba to Howard, Oct. 26, 1940, Howard to Foreign Minister Matsuoka, Sept. 11, 1940, and Howard to Shingorō Takaishi, May 14, 1940, "1940 Foreign File: Japan," Box 170; and Minister Wakasugi to Howard, Mar. 6, 1940, Howard to Takaishi, Mar. 31, 1941, and Howard to Obata Shigeyoshi, Apr. 28, 1941, "1941 Foreign File: Japan," Box 180. Howard thought Matsuoka was level-headed enough to make a realistic settlement with Roosevelt. He was worried about the Japanese lack of understanding of American public opinion in domestic politics and sensed it had shifted against Japan when Japan joined the Axis. Howard's view of the Japanese Monroe Doctrine shows that he shared the same opinion as Secretary of State Hull: that Japan's "new order" and its Monroe Doctrine violated American rights in the Far East and excluded the United States from economic opportunities there; and that the American Monroe Doctrine did not exercise exclusionist and military practices. Furthermore, like Hull, Howard thought Japan should seek expansion in the Far East through peaceful means and abide with established international rules and obligations. Howard definitely did not think the United States should be intimidated into a compromise with Japan and thought the United States should rebuff such attempts by Japan.

47. Iwakuro, "Amerika," in Ikawa, *Nichibei kōshō shiryō*, 502.

48. Iwakuro recalls this as happening on Apr. 30, but the telegram in the Ikawa Papers reads Apr. 29; see Ikawa, *Nichibei kōshō shiryō*, 256, 418–21, 502–3. Hoover's daily calendar confirms the meeting took place on April 28 (www.ecommcode2.com/hoover/calendar/home.cfm).

49. Ikawa, *Nichibei kōshō shiryō*, 421.

50. Strauss was concerned about American war preparedness and was assigned to the Navy's Bureau of Ordnance in March 1941. Pratt to Hoover, Apr. 29, 1941, "Pratt," Post-Presidential Individual File, Herbert C. Hoover Papers; Ikawa, *Nichibei kōshō shiryō*, 256–57, 412–21; Iwakuro, "Amerika," in Ikawa, *Nichibei kōshō shiryō*, 502–3, 512–13; *Iwakuro Hideo-shi danwa sokkiroku*, 288–92; Heinrichs, *Threshold of War*, 125–26, 134–35, 141; transcript, Dr. Payson J. Treat Oral History Interview, Sept. 19, 1967, 17–18, Herbert C. Hoover Presidential Library; Butow, *The John Doe Associates*, 172–74, 391; and Ikawa, *"Nichibei kōshō hiwa*—hōi no Misshi," pt. 2, 59–63. Wikawa's and

Iwakuro's name cards with the date Aug. 1, 1941, are located in "Wight-Wikham," Post-Presidential General File, Herbert C. Hoover Papers.

51. Ikei, *Nihon gaikōshi gaisetsu*, 213–21.

52. Heinrichs, "The Russian Factor in Japanese-American Relations," 169–71, 173; idem, *Threshold of War*, 200–201, 206.

53. See entry for Aug. 7, 1941, in Kido, *Kido Kōichi nikki*, 2: 899–900. While in Sugamo Prison, Kido (*Kido Kōichi kankei bunsho*, 29) stressed that he wanted a peaceful southward expansion by Japan. On Oct. 9, Kido told Prime Minister Konoe that based on *gashin shōtan* Japan should concentrate on establishing a national defense state and nurturing national power under a ten–fifteen-year timetable. In the meantime, Japan should ignore America's economic pressure and concentrate on defeating the Chiang regime (see Kido, *Kido Kōichi nikki*, 2: 912).

54. Ayukawa, "Watashi no rirekisho," 336, has $5 billion. In Microfiche no. 163.1, Ayukawa Papers, the figure is $1 billion. Ayukawa mentioned that Miho's meeting with Baruch had taken place in the summer of 1941, but this is implausible because of the severe travel restrictions for Japanese traveling overseas at the time. In the 1953 draft memoir, Ayukawa stated that Miho's meeting with Baruch had taken place in summer of 1940; during this time Miho was meeting influential business executives with strong political connections to the White House (see Chapter 6; Microfiche no. 931.4, 93, Ayukawa Papers). Although the 1953 document is correct in this regard, Ayukawa is incorrect in saying that he made the aforementioned proposal to Commander Umezu in the summer of 1940 since there was no proposal for a Konoe-Roosevelt summit at the time. In the draft memoir (99–100), Ayukawa introduced a document that he had addressed to Umezu on June 29, 1940. Ayukawa had proposed that the Japanese government, in entering talks for a rapprochement with the United States, must include in the agenda the demand that the American government underwrite $1 billion worth of dollar-denominated Manchukuo government bonds so that Manchukuo could purchase much-needed machinery and other items from the United States for its industrialization. Ayukawa must have lobbied Umezu once in June and July 1940 and again in Aug. and Sept. 1941. Ayukawa was aware of secret talks between Grew and Konoe at Baron Itō's house; see his 1953 draft memoir, 101, Microfiche no. 931.4, Ayukawa Papers. For Ayukawa's meetings with Kido, see Kido, *Kido Kōichi nikki*, 2: 896, 907. For U.S.-Japan negotiations between Aug. and Oct. 1941, see Heinrichs, *Threshold of War*, 161–62, 184–88.

55. *New York Times*, Sept. 20, 1941.

56. Raoul E. Desvernine, "The Church, Democracy and the War," Newman Club Federation of New York Province, 23rd Annual Communion Breakfast, Feb. 1, 1942; and Desvernine to Hynes, Dec. 9, 1940; both in "Raoul E. Desvernine," Post-Presidential Individual File, Herbert C. Hoover Papers; see also the correspondence

between Desvernine and Lippmann between Feb. 13, 1939, and Dec. 10, 1941, Walter Lippmann Papers.

57. Nash et al., *The American People*, 843, 849; Marks, *Wind over Sand*, 278.

58. Hoover to Desvernine, May 25, 1936, and Desvernine to Hoover, May 19, 1936, "Raoul E. Desvernine," Post-Presidential Individual File, Herbert C. Hoover Papers.

59. Desvernine to Hoover, Nov. 6, 1939, "Raoul E. Desvernine," Post-Presidential Individual File, Herbert C. Hoover Papers.

60. Desvernine to Lippmann, Feb. 13, 1939, "Raoul E. Desvernine," Walter Lippmann Papers; and Hoover to Desvernine, Apr. 17, 1941, "Raoul E. Desvernine," Post-Presidential Individual File, Herbert C. Hoover Papers.

61. Desvernine to Hoover, Jan. 22, 1941, "Raoul E. Desvernine," Post-Presidential Individual File, Herbert C. Hoover Papers.

62. Desvernine to Lippmann, Nov. 22, 1941, "Raoul E. Desvernine," Walter Lippmann Papers; Baruch, *Baruch*, 288; and Memorandum, Feb. 10, 1942, "Pearl Harbor—Diaries and Events," Post-Presidential Subject File, Herbert C. Hoover Papers.

63. For examples, see Desvernine to Hynes, Dec. 9, 1940; Hynes to Richey, Jan. 7, 1941; Desvernine to Hoover, Jan. 8, 1941; Hoover to Desvernine, Jan. 9, 1941; Hoover to Desvernine, Jan. 9, 1941; Hoover to Desvernine, Jan. 14, 1941; Desvernine to Hoover, Jan. 27, 1941; Hoover to Desvernine, Jan. 31, 1941; Hoover to Desvernine, Apr. 17, 1941; Desvernine to Hoover, May 12, 1941; Desvernine to Hoover, Oct. 7, 1941; and Richardson to Desvernine, Oct. 8, 1941; all in "Raoul E. Desvernine," Post-Presidential Individual File, Herbert C. Hoover Papers.

64. Desvernine to Hoover, Oct. 18, 1941, "Raoul E. Desvernine," Post-Presidential Individual File, Herbert C. Hoover Papers; and Desvernine to Lippmann, Nov. 27, 1941, "Raoul E. Desvernine," Walter Lippmann Papers. In his letter to Lippmann, Desvernine wrote: "I have been in Washington most of the summer acting as one of the advisers to the Japanese in the present international negotiations." Desvernine was planning to tell Lippmann the inside story, and Lippmann was interested in hearing about it. But it is not certain if Lippmann and Desvernine met for a chat about this after the outbreak of Pearl Harbor (see Lippmann to Desvernine, Dec. 3, 1941; Desvernine to Lippmann, Dec. 8, 1941; and Lippmann to Desvernine, Dec. 10, 1941, "Raoul E. Desvernine," Walter Lippmann Papers).

65. Desvernine to Hoover, Oct. 18, 1941, "Raoul E. Desvernine," Post-Presidential Individual File, Herbert C. Hoover Papers. Kurusu Saburō (*Nichibei gaikōshi hiwa*, 122) noted in his memoir that Nishiyama's efforts had contributed to the realization of his meeting with Baruch.

66. *FRUS: The Far East, 1941*, 4: 1–2, 80–81.

67. The part on Moore and Desvernine's decision are mentioned in an Apr. 10 memo in Payson J. Treat Oral History Interview, 14, Herbert C. Hoover Presiden-

tial Library; the part in this memo that describes Desvernine's decision when Kurusu and Nomura visited him in New York is wrong if Hoover's diary is correct. With regard to Nomura's view of Moore, see Ikawa, *Nichibei kōshō shiryō*, 393.

68. Desvernine to Hoover, Oct. 25, 1941, and Hoover to Desvernine, Oct. 28, 1941, "Raoul E. Desvernine," Post-Presidential Individual File, Herbert C. Hoover Papers; and Oct. 31, 1941, "Pearl Harbor—Diaries and Events," Post-Presidential Subject File, Herbert C. Hoover Papers. It is not quite certain whether Hoover wrote this at the time or whether this entry was based on his discussions with Desvernine on Feb. 10, 1942, as were his entries for the portions of Nov. 29 and all entries for Nov. 30 through Dec. 5. See the Feb. 10, 1942, memorandum in the above "Pearl Harbor—Diaries and Events."

69. Payson J. Treat Oral History Interview, 14.

70. Desvernine to Hoover, Nov. 21, 1941, "Raoul E. Desvernine," Post-Presidential Individual File, Herbert C. Hoover Papers; and Nov. 23, 1941, "Pearl Harbor—Diaries and Events," Post-Presidential Subject File, Herbert C. Hoover Papers. It is not known when Hoover wrote this Nov. 23 memo. This memo is also in the Desvernine folder. Unlike this memo, a memorandum dated Apr. 10, 1942, records that Baruch, in his meeting with Kurusu and Desvernine, suggested that Chiang be included in the big power conference. Baruch's memoir does not mention such a conference (see Payson J. Treat Oral History Interview, 14, 16; and Baruch, *Baruch*, 289–90).

71. Ikawa, *Nichibei kōshō shiryō*, 363–64. The date of this letter is revealed in Ikawa's essay that describes his meetings with General Mutō between his return from the United States and Pearl Harbor. In this essay Ikawa provided a synopsis of this letter (see ibid., 479–81).

72. Microfiche no. 611.1, Ayukawa Papers. Aoki stated that there was a certain individual affiliated with a right-wing group who had worked for the three men as a liaison between them and the military. Aoki Kazuo expressed his views before the Pacific War on Japan's economic power and his support for siding with the United States and Great Britain in the notes he had written, probably in preparation for the war crimes investigation against him; see "Daitōa sensō to Aoki no tachiba," 17–21, Microfiche no. 163.3, Ayukawa Papers.

73. Hashimoto Tetsuma, "Makoto ni aikoku no Kyojin Nariki," 307–14. The cable and the quote are taken from Kranzler, *Japanese, Nazis & Jews*, 334–35.

74. Ayukawa, "Watashi no rirekisho," 336; Aoki Kazuo and Ayukawa Yoshisuke, "A Proposal to Avoid a War Between the U. S. and Japan," Nov. 23, 1941, Microfiche no. 611.1, Ayukawa Papers. There was another movement organized by Japan Chamber of Commerce chairman Fujiyama Aiichirō (1897–1985), who was also the president of the biggest sugar-refining company in Japan, and Chamber of Commerce board member Ishida Reisuke (1886–1978), who was a director of the Mitsui Trading

Company. In November a group of businessmen led by Fujiyama and Ishida, including Asano Ryōzō of Nihon kōkan, lobbied politicians and military officials against going to war, particularly with the United States. This effort was also too little, too late (see Fujiyama, "Senjika no zaikai no ugoki," 73–74). Mutō Akira, the director of military affairs, had been very reluctant to fight the United States. Around Jan. 3, 1942, Mutō told Yatsugi that as he had expected, Japan enjoyed initial victories, but he thought Japan had almost no chance of ultimate victory. What he hoped was for Japan to give it all it had in fighting. But Mutō now wanted to seek ways to end the war since he knew the tide would change soon. Mutō believed that a country that lost by fighting had a better chance of making a comeback some day than a country that did not fight; that was what he had learned from his study on the history of war. For this episode and for the tensions and rivalries that existed between Mutō and Tōjō, see Yatsugi Kazuo in *Gendaishi o tsukuru hitobito*, 4: 123–24, 127–28.

75. See entries for Nov. 25 and Dec. 1, 1941, in Kido, *Kido Kōichi nikki*, 2: 925, 931.

76. Nov. 25, 1941, "Raoul E. Desvernine," Post-Presidential Individual File, Herbert C. Hoover Papers. The same document can be found in "Pearl Harbor—Diaries and Events," Post-Presidential Subject File, Herbert C. Hoover Papers.

77. Butow, *The John Doe Associates*, 301.

78. Kurusu, *Nichibei gaikō hiwa*, 158.

79. Ibid., 159–60.

80. Tōgō, *The Cause of War*, 165–66; and Kurusu, *Nichibei gaikō hiwa*, 148, 158–60.

81. Kurusu, *Nichibei gaikō hiwa*, 148–57; Heinrichs, *Threshold of War*, 215; Nov. 27, 1941, Diaries and Itineraries (Microfiche), Franklin D. Roosevelt Papers; Tōgō, *The Cause of War*, 167; and Butow, *The John Doe Associates*, 304–5, 444–45.

82. Kurusu, *Nichibei gaikō hiwa*, 179. In contrast to the dates suggested in Baruch's memoir and Hoover's diary, Kurusu noted that he met with Nishiyama and Desvernine on Nov. 28 and that Baruch and Nishiyama met on Dec. 4.

83. Payson J. Treat Oral History Interview, 15.

84. Ibid., 16, for the part on protection. In addition, see Kurusu, *Nichibei gaikō hiwa*, 168–71; and Baruch, *Baruch*, 288–91. For the memorandum, see Dec. 1, 1941, "Pearl Harbor—Diaries and Events," Post-Presidential Subject File, Herbert C. Hoover Papers; and Dec. 1, 1941, "Raoul E. Desvernine: Correspondence, 1936–1942," Post-Presidential Individual File. The memorandum reads:

1. There was to be a slow withdrawal of Japanese troops from China, the withdrawal to be made under a joint Japanese and American Commission; the Japanese were to retain three or four garrisons there, the location and size of which to be agreed upon with the United States; they insisting that they had the same right to garrisons in China as the other powers who already had such rights there.

2. They stated that the Tri-Partite Treaty (the Axis treaty) was inoperative except in case of attack by some third power and that they had reserved the right to determine what attack comprised. That they would agree in a memorandum with the United States such an inter-

pretation as would make it impossible for any war between the United States and Japan to arise from that Treaty. In fact, the purpose of this was to set aside any possibility of the fact that the United States and Japan should go to war in case the United States should have war with Germany.

3. That the trade situation and the embargoes should be settled by negotiation of new treaties of commerce covering all relationships in the commercial field, thus to solve questions of embargoes and to resurrect the commercial treaty which Hull had denounced some time before.

4. These three projects were to be the basis of an international conference to be held at some neutral place agreed upon, and that pending the conclusions by this conference there should be an economic and military standstill agreement.

5. That pending the solutions of this Conference, there should be a relaxation of the embargo in respect to non-military commodities to be imported in normal quantities.

This memorandum differs from Baruch's recollection:

The following idea must come from President not from Government [*sic*] and is based upon the the [*sic*] expression of the President of his being the "introducer."

1. That they [Japan] will accept introduction and good offices of President in Chinese situation and that they will agree to confer with Chinese Government (Chiang kai-shek [*sic*]) as to a general settlement with China. They only have in mind keeping troops on Mongolian border with Russia & 1 or 2 garrison in North China all to be agreed to by military experts of Japan, China & U. S. All other troops in China to be slowly evacuated as military experts shall agree—this refers to only question of time. Southern troops to be withdrawn upon complete settlement.

2. Pending such conference, Japan agrees no further military advances—will freeze existing military situation & possibly have a general military truce.

3. Indo-China question entirely dependent upon settlement of Chinese incident.

4. If president desires he can secure commitment confidentially in advance of any announcement.

5. State Dept. will only represent Chinese cause & requires full agreements on all points in advance, whereas they [Japan] are willing to settle questions in course of conversations under President's introduction, thereby avoiding appearance of capitulation.

6. Axis treaty can be settled by formula.

7. Non-discriminatory trade purely matter of establishing details in a treaty to be negotiated and principle admitted.

8. Breaking down attitudes—peace possible.

9. Keep open.

According to Baruch's memoir (288–91), Kurusu suggested President Roosevelt send a personal envoy such as Harry Hopkins to Japan; this is mentioned in neither the Herbert C. Hoover Papers nor Kurusu's memoir. Furthermore, Kurusu drew a proposal "at my request and he dictated the substance of his proposals to Desvernine, who took them down in longhand." Finally, compared to the five proposals mentioned in Hoover's Dec. 1 diary entry, the Desvernine note Baruch reproduced in his memoir mentions neither a five-power conference—including the statement in Hoover's aforementioned 1942 memo that Baruch had proposed China's participation in such a conference—nor lifting the economic embargo of materials for civilian uses; Baruch's memo also differs from Hoover's Dec. 1 diary entry in that it mentions that the areas in China where the Japanese Army will be allowed to maintain garrisons will be decided by a committee consisting of military experts from China, the United States, and Japan rather than by a joint U.S.-Japan commission. The two documents also differ in that Baruch's memo states the settlement of the Indochina question is contingent on the Sino-Japanese settlement whereas Hoover's diary does not mention this precondition.

See also Terasaki, *Bridge to the Sun*, 64–67; and Jones, "An Adventure in Failure." Terasaki has the dates wrong. She wrote that Jones had sent this message to the president on Nov. 29 instead of Nov. 30. On the other hand, she is right about the fact that that message contained a request to the president to send a cable to the emperor to appeal for peace, whereas Jones wrote that this request was delivered verbally when he met the president on Dec. 3. The fact that Jones had sent a message to the president on Nov. 30 is confirmed by Roosevelt's memorandum to his secretary Marvin McIntyre on Dec. 2, 1941; see Roosevelt, *F.D.R.*, 4: 1248. In this memorandum Roosevelt instructed McIntyre as follows: "Will you answer [Jones] and say I was very grateful to him for his letter and that it is a coincidence that two days before I had taken up the procedure he suggested and may still use it."

85. Butow, *The John Doe Associates*, 304–5, 443; and Iriye, *The Origins of the Second World War in Asia and the Pacific*, 183–84.

86. Butow, *The John Doe Associates*, 306; and Kurusu, *Nichibei gaikō hiwa*, 160–61. Although Father Drought might have been an influencing factor at the time as Butow suggests, I tend to discount his role.

87. Schwarz, *The Speculator*, 418–19.

88. Blum, *Roosevelt and Morgenthau*, 420.

89. "Japan Pair 'Didn't Know': Envoys Still Maintain Pearl Harbor Surprise" and "Pre–Pearl Harbor Confabs Said Held with FDR Consent," *Pacific Stars and Stripes*, Dec. 7, 1951, Microfiche no. 136.1, Ayukawa Papers. In his 1960 memoir (288–89), Baruch wrote:

I told Desvernine that I could not see the Japanese envoy for so irregular a reason, and at so delicate a moment, without consulting the White House. I then called General Watson and told him of the strange request. After consulting the President, Watson advised me that the President would not meet Kurusu without Hull, but had no objection to my seeing the Japanese to find out what message he wished to transmit.

Accordingly, I met with Kurusu and Desvernine at the Mayflower Hotel on Wednesday, Dec. 3rd. What Kurusu had to say was truly extraordinary.

He assured me that he himself wanted peace, that the Japanese people and the Emperor wanted peace, but that the war lords were sitting with a loaded gun in each hand, as he put it, determined to shoot. He thought, however, that such a calamity might still be averted. It was imperative, he said, that he see the President privately; Secretary Hull, he claimed, was hostile and untrusting. If the President would set aside protocol and receive him without Hull's presence, Kurusu was sure that the proposals he would put before him would prove acceptable.

When I asked Kurusu what exactly were his proposals, he replied that it was paramount that President Roosevelt appeal directly and personally to the Emperor—which Kurusu felt would immobilize the military. He further proposed that the President act as intermediary in the war between Japan and China. He assured me that Japan would accept such an offer and that she was prepared to negotiate with Chiang Kai-shek on a general settlement. He stressed the need to keep the conversations going between his government and ours, and suggested that this could be done if the President sent a personal representative, such as Hopkins, to Japan, as Japan had sent Kurusu here.

The date on which Baruch met Kurusu is different in this memoir, the Hoover papers, and Kurusu's memoir. For details, see the main text.

90. "Pre–Pearl Harbor Confabs Said Held with FDR Consent," *Pacific Stars and Stripes*, Dec. 7, 1951, Microfiche no. 136.1, Ayukawa Papers.

91. Kurusu, *Nichibei gaikō hiwa*, 170.

92. Ibid., 167–70. The $1 billion episode is also mentioned in Kurusu Saburō to Ayukawa Yoshisuke, Sept. 6, 1946, Microfiche no. 511.1, and Kurusu to Prime Minister Yoshida Shigeru, Nov. 22, 1951, Microfiche no. 136.1, Ayukawa Papers. Kurusu's letter to Yoshida mentions that Baruch thought that providing $1 billion to Japan would calm the "Inferiority Complex" of the Japanese military. His other ideas introduced here are mentioned in Kurusu's memoir. For Baruch's view of international relations, see Schwarz, *The Speculator*, 329–31, 343–44, 349–58.

93. Baruch, *Baruch*, 288–91; and Kurusu, *Nichibei gaikō hiwa*, 168–170, 179.

94. Jones, "An Adventure in Failure," 614.

95. Ibid., 614; Kurusu, *Nichibei gaikō hiwa*, 167–170; Terasaki, *Bridge to the Sun*, 66–69; Prange, *At Dawn We Slept*, 396–400; Dec. 3, 1941, Diaries and Itineraries (Microfiche), Franklin D. Roosevelt Papers. Jones did not mention his remark to Roosevelt not to reveal Terasaki's name and Roosevelt's response to that, and Terasaki did not mention that Roosevelt was going to "force a reply" by publicly revealing the information that he had sent a cable to the Emperor.

96. Ikawa, *Nichibei kōshō shiryō*, 360–63. See Butow, *The John Doe Associates*, 306–7; I disagree with Butow's interpretation of "North Carolina" on 306. For Walsh's activities in Japan from June to Oct. 1941, see ibid., 194, 210, 280–83, 292–93.

97. Heinrichs, *Threshold of War*, 217.

98. For Roosevelt's decision to send the message and its subsequent delayed delivery, see Toland, *The Rising Sun*, 193–94, 199; and Hull, *Memoirs*, 2: 1091–94. For the text of President Roosevelt's message to the emperor, see *FRUS: The Far East, 1941*, 4: 723–25. See Tōgō, *The Cause of War*, 217–21.

99. Kurusu, *Nichibei gaikō hiwa*, 160.

100. For Hoover's views on policy toward Japan from the 1920s to Pearl Harbor, see Ninkovich, *Modernity and Power*, 92–97; Wilson, *Herbert Hoover*, 205, 242, 245–48; and Doenecke, "Anti-Interventionism of Herbert Hoover," 319–20.

101. Transcript, Payson J. Treat Oral History Interview, Sept. 19, 1967, 15; Aug. 21, 1945, memo, Herbert C. Hoover Presidential Library.

102. Microfiche no. 136. 2, Ayukawa Papers.

Chapter 8

1. For the text of Ayukawa's speech, see "Gijyutsusha no shokuba to shite no Manshū" at the Chōyukai Lecture Series (printed in the July 1939 edition of *Chōyu kaihō*), in Microfiche no. 922.22, 185–93, 196–97, 199–200, 202, 204–5, Ayukawa Papers.

2. Kobayashi, *Daitōa kyōeiken no keisei to hōkai*, 197, 200, 364–65.

3. As Chalmers Johnson (*MITI*, 117) points out, the 1918 law was "Japan's first basic law relating to industrial control during wartime"; "it defined military supplies broadly and authorized the government after a declaration of war to supervise, use, or expropriate the industries producing them."

4. Hara Akira, "Senkyūhyaku sanjūnendai," 81–87, 108–9; Ishikawa, "Shūsen ni itaru made no Manshū keizai kaihatsu," 743; and Kobayashi, *Daitōa kyōeiken no keisei to hōkai*, 111–17, 362.

5. Peattie, *Ishiwara Kanji*, 160, 166.

6. Ibid., 274–75.

7. Ibid., 293–308.

8. Ayukawa discussed the obstacles he had faced inside and outside Manchuria in managing MIDC in *Shinmonkiroku* 1: 18–25, Microfiche no. 163.1, Ayukawa Papers. Ayukawa stated in this document that the military officers and civil servants in Manchukuo interfered with MIDC's operations. He complained about this to Kishi Nobusuke and Hoshino Naoki, but their measures did not satisfy him; they were caught between MIDC's and the military's demands. In addition, those who felt their interests were threatened by MIDC interfered with MIDC's activities; these included SMR personnel, Manchukuo civil servants, and employees of Japan-Manchuria Trading Company. Hoshino Naoki also acknowledged in the Japanese transcript of his interrogation record that Ayukawa experienced interference from SMR personnel, Manchukuo civil servants, Kwantung Army officers, and civilians who perceived his industrialization scheme as contrary to their aim to establish a self-sufficient economy. Hoshino also admitted that the short-term imperatives of the national economy and war undermined Ayukawa's industrialization plan (see *Hoshino jinmonchōsho*, 22–23, Microfiche no. 163.3, Ayukawa Papers). Finally, see Awaya and Yoshida, *Kokusai kensatsukyoku (IPS) jinmonchōsho*, 247–48; Hara Akira, "Senkyūhyaku sanjūnendai," 111; Ishikawa, "Shūsen ni itaru made no Manshū keizai

kaihatsu," 750–51, 762, 774–75; and Kobayashi, *Daitōa kyōeiken no keisei to hōkai*, 75, 167–70. The percentage of capital under the original and revised plans going to the mining and industrial sectors remained unchanged at 26 percent for liquid fuel and changed from 23 to 19 percent for iron and steel, 12 to 8 percent for coal, 18 to 13 percent for electricity, 5 to 2 percent for light metals, 3 to 6 percent for pulp, salt, and soda ash combined, 0.6 to 0.2 percent for processed dairy goods, 6 to 4 percent for gold, copper, lead, zinc, and asbestos combined, 0 to 0.4 percent for machine tools, 1 to 5 percent for vehicles, and 8 to 16 percent for weapons and airplanes. In terms of the percentage of capital allocation, liquid fuel continued to receive top priority, and there was a fivefold increase in capital allocation for vehicles and a doubling of the allocation for weapons and airplanes. Although the capital allocated to iron and steel decreased, it still remained high.

9. Nissan jidōsha kabushikigaisha, *Nissan jidōsha sanjūnenshi*, 76–78. For Asakura's involvement in Ayukawa's quest to create a single company in the Japanese automobile industry and the government and corporate response to this idea, see the entries for Nov. 17, 1937; Feb. 8, 1938; Apr. 19 and 20, 1938; June 21, 1938; July 8, 12, 18, and 19, 1938; Aug. 11, 1938; Nov. 11 and 12, 1939; Dec. 12 and 13, 1939; Jan. 15, 17, 22, 24, and 25, 1940; and Feb. 3, 1940, in Asakura, *Nikki*, vol. 3. See also ibid., "Kaidai," 18–19, for a *Tōkyō Asahi* news report on the reorganization in the car industry.

10. Hoshino, *Mihatenu yume*, 289.

11. On Sept. 6, 1939, the *New York Times* ran an article on Yamamoto's visit to the United States with his American engineer, A. N. Little, who was introduced in the article as the man in charge of the company's Antung factory, which produced 120 trucks a year. Yamamoto claimed that he had been obligated to purchase German machinery, but the outbreak of the European war enabled him to propose a purchase of about $10 million worth of machines and diesel engines for the production of two-and-a-half ton trucks. The article stated that Yamamoto had not yet contracted for the purchase of diesel engines and it did not indicate whether he had succeeded in purchasing machines (see "Japanese Switch Order from Reich: Machinery for Truck Factory in Manchuria to be Bought Here," *New York Times*, Sept. 6, 1939, 41).

12. Hoshino, *Mihatenu yume*, 289.

13. See the entries for May 3, June 15, June 28, Aug. 5, and Nov. 21, 1939, in Asakura, *Nikki*, vol. 3.

14. Hoshino, *Mihatenu yume*, 290; in the postwar years the machines were used to produce Nissan's car engines, and they were still running in 1963 (*Jidōsha shiryō*, 2: 137–39).

15. See the entries for Apr. 2, 4, 5, 10, and 11; May 16, 17, and 24; and June 14, 1940, in Asakura, *Nikki*, vol. 3. See also ibid., "Kaidai," 22–23, for an excerpt of the Apr. 11, 1940, article from *Yomiuri shimbun* on Nissan Motors' move to Manchuria.

16. Hara Akira, "Senkyūhyaku sanjūnendai," 107–8; Ishikawa, "Shūsen ni itaru made no Manshū keizai kaihatsu," 757.

17. Jerome B. Cohen used Ayukawa's statement and other materials gathered during the postwar occupation to discuss the industrial control organizations in his *Japan's Economy in War and Reconstruction*, 59–66. Ayukawa's presentation of his idea for regulating the automobile market is mentioned in the entry for Sept. 22, 1940, in Asakura, *Nikki*, vol. 4; see also ibid., "Kaidai," 6–8. For a succinct explanation of Manchukuo's initial experimentation with economic programs in the 1930s, see the post-1945 recollection of Ikeda Sumihisa in his *Nihon no magarikado*, 269–76.

18. According to Takasaki (*Manshū no shūen*, 125), in 1943 Manchukuo produced 1,200 airplanes and over 1,000 airplane engines.

19. Ishikawa, "Shūsen ni itaru made no Manshū keizai kaihatsu," 757; and Kobayashi, *Daitōa kyōeiken no keisei to hōkai*, 416.

20. Hoshino, *Mihatenu yume*, 129; Kojima Naoki, *Ayukawa Yoshisuke den*, 91; and Hara Akira, "Manshū ni okeru keizai tōsei no tenkai," 252–53. I disagree with Johnson's (*MITI*, 131) argument that the Kwantung Army's intervention in the Manchurian economy diminished significantly after Kishi's arrival in Manchuria in Nov. 1936. Kishi (Itō et al., *Kishi Nobusuke no kaisō*, 22) mentioned in his memoir that he was aware of the Fourth Section's mishandling of the Manchukuo economy and of the rising criticisms in the business world. He stated that he had sent Shiina and other MCI bureaucrats in the hope of taking control of Manchukuo's industrial policy away from the Kwantung Army. Kishi also said that even as he sent his subordinates, he felt that he would have to join them eventually.

21. Hara Akira, "Senkyūhyaku sanjūnendai," 86–87.

22. Hara Akira, "Manshū ni okeru keizai tōsei seisaku no tenkai," 253–55.

23. For the figures that illustrate the unavailability of materials needed for production, see Kobayashi, *Daitōa kyōeiken no keisei to hōkai*, 200; Hara Akira, "Manshū ni okeru keizai tōsei seisaku no tenkai," 261–62, 293; and Takasaki, *Manshū no shūen*, 154–57.

24. Takasaki, *Manshū no shūen*, 67–69, 72; and Hara Akira, "Manshū ni okeru keizai tōsei seisaku no tenkai," 257.

25. Hara Akira, "Manshū ni okeru keizai tōsei seisaku no tenkai," 256–64; Takasaki, *Manshū no shūen*, 105–6; and Kobayashi, *Daitōa kyōeiken no keisei to hōkai*, 192–200.

26. Yoshino and his subordinate Kishi Nobusuke spearheaded the rationalization movement in the early 1930s. On relations between Itō and Yoshino and between Yoshino and Kishi, see Yoshino, *Omokaji torikaji*, 179–92, 275–76, 300–304. See ibid., 303–4, for Yoshino's discussion of relations between Ayukawa and Itō.

27. Yoshino, *Omokaji torikaji*, 326, 342–43, 395–409, 419, 421–22. In addition, see Kojima Naoki, *Ayukawa Yoshisuke den*, 88–89.

28. Ayukawa, "Watashi no rirekisho," 328. For Yoshino's comment about the Fourth Section of the Kwantung Army, his unpopularity in that section, and Ayukawa's proposal to Yoshino in spring 1940, see Yoshino, *Omokaji torikaji*, 430–32.

29. Hara Akira, "Manshū ni okeru keizai tōsei seisaku no tenkai," 265.

30. Takasaki, *Manshū no shūen*, 66–67, 86–87.

31. For the details of the Feb. 1941 corporate reorganization of MIDC, see "Mangyō no kikō kaikaku ni tsuite Ayukawa sōsai dan," Feb. 18, 1941, 229–32, Microfiche no. 922.22, Ayukawa Papers. For Mantō, see Hara Akira, "Manshū ni okeru keizai tōsei seisaku no tenkai," 276–77; Ishikawa, "Shūsen ni itaru made no Manshū keizai kaihatsu," 759; and Udagawa Masaru, "Nissan zaibatsu no Manshū shinshutsu," 70–71. Udagawa argues that although Ayukawa created Mantō to separate his Nissan interests in Japan from MIDC, Mantō further weakened Ayukawa's control over Nissan subsidiaries such as Japan Mining and Hitachi.

32. Hara Akira, "Manshū ni okeru keizai tōsei seisaku no tenkai," 282–83; and Takasaki, *Manshū no shūen*, 71. For the history of MIDC's troubles after its inception, see Manshū teikoku seifu, *Manshū kenkoku jūnenshi*, 571–73, 585–89.

33. "Zuisōroku Ayukawa sōsai dan," May 6, 1942, 244–46, in Microfiche no. 922.22, Ayukawa Papers. According to ibid., 244, the text of the speech was published in the appendix of *Nissan konwakai kaihō* 5, no. 12.

34. "Mangyō tainin no aisatsu," Jan. 7, 1943, 256–72; and "Zaidan hōjin gaishi kenkyūkai sōritsu ni tsuite," Aug. 15, 1948, 315, in Microfiche no. 922.22, Ayukawa Papers. For Ayukawa's attempts to reform the bureaucracy's economic regulations, see *Shinmonkiroku* 1: 55–82, Microfiche no. 163.1, Ayukawa Papers; and Awaya and Yoshida, *Kokusai kensatsukyoku (IPS) jinmonchōsho*, 245–50, 262–63, 277–79. For Ayukawa's discussion of his attempt to establish a general economic staff in Manchukuo, see Microfiche no. 163.1, 55–59, 81–82; and Awaya and Yoshida, 277. Ayukawa stated during his interrogation that the military withheld vital economic statistics in the name of national security; see Awaya and Yoshida, 246–47. See Ōuchi Hyoe's recollection of Ayukawa's Giseikai activities, including his support for other think tanks, in "Ayukawa-san to Ōhara shakai mondai kenkyūjo," in Ayukawa Yoshisuke sensei henshū kankōkai, *Ayukawa Yoshisuke sensei tsuisōroku*, 92–95. Ōuchi mentioned that Miyake Haruki of the *Oriental Economist* had helped Ōuchi contact Ayukawa. In the same book, see Morito Tatsuo, "Chigatta shiya kara fukai nagori o," 502–4; see also Ayukawa, *Hyakumi dansu*, 184–85. For Ōuchi's involvement in the Rōnō-ha of the Marxist economic school of thought in Japan, see Hoston, *Marxism and the Crisis of Development in Prewar Japan*, 36–37. Furthermore, see Ayukawa's 1953 draft memoir, 151–61, in Microfiche no. 931.4 of the Ayukawa Papers. Finally, with regard to the anti-Tōjō cabinet, see Hara Yoshihisa, *Kishi Nobusuke*, 96–99.

35. Fujiyama, "Senjika no zaikai no ugoki," 75.

Chapter 9

1. Yoshida Shigeru to Kurusu Saburō, Aug. 27, 1945, in Yoshida kinen jigyō zaidan, *Yoshida Shigeru shokan*, 553–54.

2. Kurusu to Ayukawa, Sept. 6, 1946, Microfiche no. 136.2, Ayukawa Papers; for Kurusu's son, see Itō, *Shōwaki no seiji (zoku)*, 157.

3. Kurusu to Prime Minister Yoshida Shigeru, Apr. 18, 1950, Microfiche no. 136.1, Ayukawa Papers. Ayukawa wrote a memorandum on Nov. 11, 1945, on how the GHQ was treating big business. He thought there were many unfounded reports by the media about big business executives. He was bothered by the fact that the media were demanding the wholesale resignation of current board members of big businesses. Ayukawa argued these men had risen to their current positions based on ability, not on feudalistic wealth. His aide Miho Mikitarō was talking to officials in the GHQ about the possibility that Ayukawa's business interests would be designated a zaibatsu. Ayukawa also wondered if GHQ would prosecute businessmen for their responsibility in Japan's war effort. At the time, Ayukawa was also talking to officials in the Ministry of Agriculture, leading business executive Ōkouchi Masatoshi (1878–1952), and former government officials Ishiguro Tadaatsu (1884–1960), Yoshino Shinji, and Hatta Yoshiaki about using the think tank he had established in 1943 to find ways to industrialize Japan's countryside. Ayukawa shared in the view that the countryside would have a surplus population because of people returning from the war fronts and Japan's former colonies and territories. Japan therefore had to find means to employ those extra workers. For Ayukawa's think tank, Giseikai, see Chapter 8. In Nov. 1945, Ayukawa thought that GHQ might allow the Giseikai to continue. He soon discovered that it would not. For Ayukawa's thoughts on what might happen to his business interests as the result of the Occupation, see his Nov. 12, 1945, memorandum, Microfiche no. 922.22, 304–13, Ayukawa Papers.

4. Kurusu to Ayukawa, Sept. 6, 1946, Microfiche no. 136.2, Ayukawa Papers. Kurusu proposed that American loans be received under the following scheme. He proposed to use as an indicator the average monetary amount of silk exports to America during a five-year period before the war in order to establish a dollar credit account in New York. This would be used as collateral to import such items as American cotton, Indian cotton, rubber, and wool for Japan's light industries. The amount of the loans would increase as Japanese industries recovered and business opportunities expanded.

5. Robert Moss to "Whom It May Concern," Oct. 21, 1946; and Robert Moss to Ayukawa, Jan., 9, 1950, in Microfiche no. 142.1, Ayukawa Papers. On Crane, see Howard B. Schonberger, "Zaibatsu Dissolution and the American Restoration of Japan." In addition to Robert Moss, Ayukawa's family and friends pleaded his innocence to GHQ; see Microfiche nos. 161 and 162, Ayukawa Papers. Furthermore,

Ayukawa's political ally Hashimoto Tetsuma aided this effort. Shortly before GHQ sent Ayukawa to prison, he had told Hashimoto that Hashimoto's criticisms shortly before and during the Pacific War regarding Japanese foreign policies toward the United States and Britain had been correct; as a token of appreciation, Ayukawa gave him a hefty amount of money. Hashimoto stated to occupation officials that Ayukawa had tried to convince Generals Tōjō and Mutō in late Nov. 1941 to achieve rapprochement with the United States and Britain by arguing this was possible with help from the Jewish conglomerates. Hashimoto also said he had frequently sought Ayukawa's advice in his endeavor to realize a rapprochement with the United States. His comments undoubtedly helped to clear Ayukawa's name. See Hashimoto Tetsuma, "Makoto ni aikoku no Kyojin Nariki," 307–14.

6. Awaya and Yoshida, *Kokusai kensatsukyoku (IPS) jinmonchōsho*, 265–74.

7. Ibid., 156.

8. Ibid., 78.

9. Ibid., 69.

10. Ibid., 78.

11. Kurusu Saburō to Bernard M. Baruch, July 7, 1947, Microfiche no. 136.1, Ayukawa Papers. The same letter can be found in its entirety in Kurusu's 1952 memoir, *Nichibei gaikō hiwa*, 172–78.

12. Takasaki to Hoover, Dec. 7, 1947, "Takasaki, T.," Post-Presidential Individual File, Herbert C. Hoover Papers. Takasaki briefly discussed his postwar attempts to attract American capital in "Watashi no rirekisho," 228–29.

13. See Levine, *Anvils of Victory*, 5–13, chap. 2; and Gillin and Myers., *Last Chance in Manchuria*, 1–52, particularly 1–2 for the quote, 21, and 24–25. See ibid., 31–34, for the conflicting opinions within the Chiang regime concerning economic cooperation with the Soviet Union in Manchuria, for the U.S. State Department's intention not to allow the Chiang regime to make any concessions to the Soviet Union other than the ones granted by Yalta, for the Sept. 1945 Sino-Soviet Treaty, and for the Soviet intention to maintain an economic sphere of influence in Manchuria. In addition, see ibid., 111–31, 161–74, and 177 for Chang's diary entries describing his negotiations and discussions with Soviet officials regarding the details of Sino-Soviet economic cooperation centered around how much of the assets were "Japanese" and "Manchurian (Chinese)" and whether the industries in Manchuria constituted "war booty," as the Soviets claimed. The Chinese resented the Soviets' excessive demands in their proposal for economic cooperation and their criteria of "war booty." These diary entries also mentioned Chang's and Soviet officials' discussions with former Japanese officials in Manchuria, including Takasaki Tatsunosuke. See also Takasaki, *Manshū no shūen*, 192–295, 333–34; Schaller, *The American Occupation of Japan*, 35; and Nagashima and Yasutomi, *Jūgonen sensō gokuhi shiryōshū hokan*, 5–24.

14. Walch and Miller, *Hoover and Truman*, 203–4.

15. Wilson, "Herbert Hoover's Plan for Ending the Second World War," 87–88, 94, 102; Walch and Miller, *Hoover and Truman*, 29–55 (51–52 for the quotations); Millis, *The Forrestal Diaries*, 52–53; ; Smith, *An Uncommon Man*, 321, 343–48; LaFeber, *The Clash*, 23, 38, 243–46; Hoopes and Brinkley, *Driven Patriot*, 208; Asada Sadao, "The Shock of the Atomic Bomb and Japan's Decision to Surrender"; Chace, *Acheson*, 106–7, 113–14; Heinrichs, *American Ambassador*, 154, 364–80; Alperovitz, *The Decision to Use the Atomic Bomb*, 392–99; Mar. 9 and May 28–29, 1945, William R. Castle, Jr., Diary, vol. 49, Harvard University, Houghton Library; and Castle to Hoover, May 2 and June 2, 1945, "Castle, William R.," Hoover to Stimson, May 15, 1945, "Stimson, Henry L.," Post-Presidential Individual File, Hoover Papers; May 8, 1945, Henry L. Stimson Diary, Yale University. As for post-surrender measures against Japan, Hoover thought the United States should rely on the liberal-minded "large middle class . . . which was the product of industrialization," because they had previously governed Japan. Hoover was wrong in believing that Japan had a strong middle class in the pre–Pacific War years, but the group he had identified as "middle class" were the internationally minded political moderates in the Japanese ruling class. Hoover thought they were "the only hope of stable and progressive government" since this should "save [America] the impossible task of setting up a military or civil government in Japan with all its dangers of revolutions and conflicts with our Allies." See Wilson, "Herbert Hoover's Plan for Ending the Second World War," 101; or Walch and Miller, *Hoover and Truman*, 53.

16. For growing anti-Soviet views among top policymakers, see Yergin, *Shattered Peace*, 95–96, 305–6, 442n26, 484n6.

17. Hoover to Richardson, Oct. 12, 1945, in "MacArthur," Post-Presidential Individual File, Herbert C. Hoover Papers.

18. "Famine Emergency Committee, General,—Herbert Hoover Diaries: Round World Trip," Post-Presidential Subject File, Herbert C. Hoover Papers. Hoover wrote the following:

Having lived in China the best part of three years and constantly travelling in the interior, China was not a strange country nor Chinese a strange people to me. I was already acquainted with some of its present officials and educators.

My first interest was, of course, the famine relief. At once I summoned meetings in Shanghai with the UNRRA and CINRA officials, the American Legation's economic staffs, the missionary leaders and the Shanghai business men. I quickly discovered that of some 260,000 tons of UNRRA food landed, 200,000 tons had been sold to merchants in Shanghai, Canton and Tientsin, purportedly to "keep prices down," although those cities were amply supplied from contiguous areas. Only 20,000 tons had actually reached the famine areas in the interior and 40,000 tons were purportedly en route. . . .

I therefore arranged meeting with T.V. Soong, vice-president of China, resident in Shanghai and brother of Madame Chang Kai shek [sic] and related to others of the Soong dynasty. . . . Soong defended this sale as a measure "to keep prices down." I suggested that prices had gone up steadily ever since the sale. . . . Soong said that was impossible in China. I said that the Japanese had done it all over China. He denied Japanese rationing and price control were effective. Residents tell me otherwise.

Hallam Tuck at my request went out to inquire into this transaction from the foreign banks and merchants. At once they said that if Mr. Hoover is inquiring into who got it that he will find it is T.V. Soong and his relative Kung. Some of these banks had re-discounted their warehouse receipts. . . .

In continuation of my inquiries as to who got some of the $20,000,000 graft from American charity, I asked General Gillem for the services of his G-a for a few days and instructed them to examine all of the principal warehouses in Shanghai. . . . Soong had said that the sale money had been turned over to the "China United Relief" for "rehabilitation." The head of the CIRA (who was a Chinese) had told me that his organization was broke and could not pay inland transportation of food. I did not pursue the matter further, but through our Consul General Monnett B. Davis, advised the State Department that inquiry was needed. The heads of UNRRA and CIRA were removed.

19. "Famine Emergency Committee, General,—Herbert Hoover Diaries: Round World Trip," Post-Presidential Subject File, Herbert C. Hoover Papers. Hoover wrote the following:

When discussing Russia, T. V. Soong said that nations only have to say NO! emphatically enough and that then the Russians stop. He said that when Russia demanded that they guard the Manchurian railways, he stopped them with an emphatic NO! He did not apparently use his "stop" effectively against their looting the country, taking over the railways, Port Arthur, Dalney, etc. . . .

Soong says that they have to keep their major armies scattered all over China, for the Communists infect the whole country and would rise up anywhere unless there were troops. He was undoubtedly frightened at the outlook and wanted to impress me that *China was our safety against Stalin "just as it was against Japan." I had not seen much safety in the latter* [italics added].

20. "Famine Emergency Committee, General,—Herbert Hoover Diaries: Round World Trip," Post-Presidential Subject File, Herbert C. Hoover Papers. Hoover wrote the following:

On the evening of May 3rd, I dined with Major General Alvin C. Gillem. He gave, in great detail with maps, the location of the Communist and Nationalist Armies. Communist movement is increasing, their armies better disciplined, better commanded, and organized from the bottom up; and also that they treat the people better. Nationalists control only south of the Yangtse River. The position north as far as the Wall, there are Communists interspersed with Nationalists. The Communists are constantly sabotaging the railways, thus preventing any movement of troops or of food. They control Shantung, all the areas around Peiping and Tientsin, Tong Shan, Ching Wan Tao. Were it not for the American marines in this area, all coal to Shanghai and the south would cease.

In Manchuria the Communists dominate the situation. . . .

I called on Generalissimo Chang Kai shek [*sic*], passed compliments for forty-five minutes but nothing important. He and Madame Chiang Kai shek [*sic*] saw me off at the airport. . . .

21. "Famine Emergency Committee, General,—Herbert Hoover Diaries: Round World Trip," Post-Presidential Subject File, Herbert C. Hoover Papers. Hoover wrote the following:

On May 3rd, I flew to Nanking and had long talks with General Marshall at his request. I stopped with him. Marshall is making a super-human effort to stop civil war. If he can do this and hold Manchuria in the Chinese Empire, he is a wonder. Marshall had made an agreement last January between the Nationalists and the Communists by which they were to stop fighting and organize a coalition government. He says both sides have violated the agreement. He says that the Communists have hold of the military situation in Manchuria today. He confirms Gillem on the layout. I ventured that he did not have one chance in ten of success. My contention was that he could not bring about a Communist coalition with Chiang Kai-shek's government without the Communists eating the government up as they had done in Eastern Europe. I gave him a detailed account of my observations in this matter in Poland, Czechoslovakia and Yugoslavia a few weeks before. *I said he could not mix oil and water. He said the so-called Communists are only a minority of real Communists, the majority being liberals. He said there was really no more difference between the two major groups than between Republicans and Democrats at home. He blamed Chiang Kai-shek far more than the Communists.*

My sum of Marshall was a man absolutely ignorant of ideological matters, somewhat dumb on everything but logistics and totally unfitted for our situation in China [italics added].

22. "Famine Emergency Committee, General,—Herbert Hoover Diaries: Round World Trip," Post-Presidential Subject File, Herbert C. Hoover Papers.

23. Schaller, *The American Occupation of Japan*, 35.

24. *FRUS: The Far East, 1946*, 6: 506–7, 592; for documents pertaining to the delay, see ibid., 123, 493–505, 579–80, 562–63, 566–67, 601–4. In addition, see Schaller, *Douglas MacArthur*, 138–39 and the notes to those pages; idem, *The American Occupation of Japan*, 33–41 and the notes to those pages; Schonberger, "Zaibatsu Dissolution and the American Restoration of Japan," 16–18 and the notes to those pages; and Fossedal, *Our Finest Hour*, 185.

25. Schonberger, "Zaibatsu Dissolution and the American Restoration of Japan," 21; Schaller, *The American Occupation of Japan*, 40–41.

26. "Famine Emergency Committee, General,—Herbert Hoover Diaries: Round World Trip," Post-Presidential Subject File, Herbert C. Hoover Papers. Ferrell, *Off the Record*, 83–85.

27. See the following in Herbert C. Hoover Papers: "Honolulu, May 7–8, 1946," "Famine Emergency Committee, Herbert Hoover Diaries: China," Post-Presidential Subject File; "Itinerary for Pauley," May 6, 1946, "Famine Emergency Committee, Countries: Japan, Correspondence," Post-Presidential Subject File; and Hoover to MacArthur, May 9, 1946, and Pauley to Hoover, Aug. 4, 1953, "Pauley," Post-Presidential Individual File. In addition, see *New York Times*, May 12, 1946, 23; the newspaper article reported that Pauley was going to submit a final report after he toured North Korea and Manchuria to assess Japanese economic assets. The article also stated that the United States was going to allow Japan to produce a prewar level

of "peace production," so that it could produce enough exports to pay for its food. On Truman's instructions to Hoover, see Truman to Hoover, May 4, 1946, in Walch and Miller, *Hoover and Truman*, 78–79.

28. Yergin, *Shattered Peace*, 171, and chaps. 7–14.

29. McCloy was a former partner at the New York law firm of Cravath, Henderson, and de Gersdorff. He had an illustrious career in government and business in the postwar years, including the chairmanship of the Chase Manhattan Bank. His ties to the Rockefellers were an important factor in his successes.

30. Bird, *The Chairman*, 18, 54–55, 266–67.

31. Schonberger, "Zaibatsu Dissolution and the American Restoration of Japan," 25, 25n64.

32. Brinkley and Hoopes, *Driven Patriot*, chap. 21; Kennan, *Memoirs*, 294–95, chaps. 11–15; and Yergin, *Shattered Peace*, 322–23.

33. Abramson, *Spanning the Century*, 383, 411; Yergin, *Shattered Peace*, 217–18, 254–55, 275, 283–84, 319–20 and the notes to these pages; Gaddis, *The United States and the Origins of the Cold War*, 312, chap. 11; Fried, *Nightmare in Red*, 3–36; Kennan, *Memoirs*, 368, 373–74; Schaller, *The American Occupation of Japan*, 88–93, 108, 141–50; Schonberger, "Zaibatsu Dissolution and the American Restoration of Japan," 21; Theodore Cohen, *Remaking Japan*, 152–53; Jerome B. Cohen, *Japan's Economy in War and Reconstruction*, 422–32; Hogan, *The Marshall Plan*, 33–35; Millis, *The Forrestal Diaries*, 255–56.

34. Hoover to Patterson, May 7, 1947, "MacArthur," Post-Presidential Individual File, Herbert C. Hoover Papers. In this letter, Hoover also stated:

Without giving more instances, it is safe to say that there was an underestimate of the thin margins of the Japanese economy and the destruction to it from war and her territorial separations.

Of the illusions, the first is that to demilitarize Japan it is necessary to do little more than to destroy or remove all arms fortifications and direct arms factories and to prevent *any* army, *any* navy, *any* air force, *any* munitions or aircraft manufacture, and to enforce such a regime over a generation or two until Japan loses the know-how of war.

The second illusion is the whole concept of control of "war potential" in industry of the type which can contribute to peace economy. All industry is "war potential" in total war. Very little industry is war potential (except arms manufacture) if a country has a forced demilitarization such as I assume above. Another part of this illusion is that these major "levels of industry" can be enforced and a nation function without a complete "planned economy" directed by foreign agents. On the other hand, to watch a major free economy, to see it is directed to no evil, is a simple problem of inspection. People are not going to manufacture for war where there is compulsory elimination of militarism.

The third illusion is that Japan can ever be self-supporting in food. That is impossible with only 15 % of arable land in a state the size of California with 80,000,000 people; in all her modern history she has imported 15 to 20 per cent of her food and now the population has been increased by six or seven million expellees. One third of the population of Japan must live by export industry.

The fourth illusion is that there is any consequential reparations to be had from the removal of industrial plants overseas. The buildings, foundations, water, electrical and other connections in such plants have no value for removal. All that is removable of any use is motive power and machine tools, all second hand. The cost of tearing them out, crating them, shipping them to some area where there is neither skilled labor nor skilled management and to build new foundations, buildings and connections, leaves even these values comparatively trivial.

These ideas in action or threat of action have created the present economic paralysis.

Hoover had sent to MacArthur a copy of this letter which he wrote to Patterson at Patterson's request. He told MacArthur this was not for publication and was "merely intended to be helpful support to [Patterson]." Schaller uses the letter Patterson received from Hoover; see *The American Occupation of Japan*, 93.

35. Schaller, *The American Occupation of Japan*, 93. For Hoover's economic programs and his beliefs behind them, see Wilson, "Herbert Hoover's Plan for Ending the Second World War," 86–90, 97–102. For discussions of the New Dealers' economic programs and those of their precursor, Herbert Hoover, see Schwarz, *The New Dealers*, 34–56. See also Alan Brinkley, "The New Deal and the Idea of the State," 90–91.

36. Schwarz, *The New Dealers*; Brinkley, "The New Deal and the Idea of the State."

37. Patterson, *Mr. Republican*, 79–80, 163; Smith, *Uncommon Man*, 360; Wilson, *Herbert Hoover*, 223; Schonberger, *Aftermath of War*, 134–60; Arnold, *Making the Managerial Presidency*, 118–59; Chace, *Acheson*, 185; Hoopes and Brinkley, *Driven Patriot*, 424; Hogan, *A Cross of Iron*, 191–208; Jan. 30, 1947, William R. Castle, Jr., Diary, vol. 52, and Jan. 9 and 14, Feb. 21, June 29, Aug. 16, 1948, William R. Castle, Jr., Diary, vol. 53; and Hoover to Pratt, June 26, 1947, "Pratt, Admiral William V., Correspondence, 1942–April 1953"; Dooman to Hoover, June 23, 1947, "Dooman, Eugene, 1947–1950"; Kern to Hoover, June 27, 1947, through June 26, 1948, "Kern Harry P., 1947–1953"; Castle to Hoover, June 23, 1948, "Castle, William R., Correspondence, 1948–1951," Post-Presidential Individual Files, Hoover Papers.

38. Kennan, *Memoirs*, 369–70.

39. FRUS: *The Far East, 1946*, 6: 506–7, 592; for documents pertaining to the delay, see ibid., 123, 493–505, 579–80, 562–63, 566–67, 601–4. See also Schaller, *Douglas MacArthur*, 138–39 and the notes to these pages; Schaller, *The American Occupation of Japan*, 33–41 and the notes to these pages; and Schonberger, "Zaibatsu Dissolution and the American Restoration of Japan," 16–18 and the notes to those pages.

40. Schaller, *The American Occupation of Japan*, 40–41; Schonberger, "Zaibatsu Dissolution and the American Restoration of Japan," 21–24.

41. Schonberger, *Aftermath of War*, 173, 174–77; see esp. 310n30 and 313n72, which compare the reparation figures in SWNCC 236/43, OCI (Overseas Consultants, Inc.), and the Johnston reports.

42. Schonberger, *Aftermath of War*, 178, 180–82, 190–94. The Johnston mission, in addition to the chairman and Draper, consisted of, among others, Paul G. Hoffman, former president of Studebaker and administrator of the Marshall Plan, and Robert F. Loree, chairman of the National Foreign Trade Council and former vice president of Morgan Guaranty Trust Company.

43. Schaller, *Douglas MacArthur*, 152–55; Schonberger, *Aftermath of War*, 187, 193, 195–97, 313n72; Schonberger, "Zaibatsu Dissolution and the American Restoration of Japan," 27–28.

44. For a biographical sketch of Simpson, see *Who's Who in America*. For Simpson's role in the Republican party, see Smith, *An Uncommon Man*, 249, 260, 264, 270, 282. Simpson died on Jan. 25, 1941, in his mid-forties.

45. For this section, see Ayukawa to Murray, Feb. 28, 1948; "Circular Letter," May 12, 1948; Murray to Aikawa (Ayukawa), May 26, 1948; Murray to Lowell, May 26, 1948; Lowell to Yaichi Aikawa (Ayukawa), June 13, 1948; Yamaoka to Aikawa (Ayukawa), June 21, 1948; Aikawa (Ayukawa) to Yamaoka, June 26, 1948; Lester H. White to Aikawa (Ayukawa), July 12, 1948; Mooney to Aikawa (Ayukawa), June 17, 1948; and Cress to Aikawa (Ayukawa), June 17, 1948, in Microfiche no. 142.1, Ayukawa Papers.

46. For the Foreign Capital Research Association and Ayukawa's views of cottage industries, see Ayukawa Yoshisuke, Aug. 15, 1948, "Zaidan hōjin Gaishi kenkyūkai sōritsu ni tsuite" (On the establishment of the Foreign Capital Research Association), Microfiche no. 922.22, 313–20, Ayukawa Papers. Shudō Yasuto was born in 1888. He joined the Bank of Japan upon graduation from the Tokyo Imperial University, a bank in which his father served as a high-ranking official. Shudo studied at Harvard Business School from 1916 to 1918, and from 1918 to 1919 he worked for the Old Colony Trust Company of Boston and the Guaranty Trust Company of New York (see Microfiche No. 412.1, Ayukawa Papers; and Earl Bryan Schwulst to Robert C. Alexander, Feb. 1, 1950, Microfiche no. 412.4, Ayukawa Papers). In Microfiche no. 136.3, see "The Highway Measures for Rehabilitation of Japan's Economy (Excerpt of a discourse delivered by Mr. Ayukawa Yoshisuke at the Noguchi Research Association on Nov. 22, 1949)"; and "The Rain, One of the Great Natural Resources of Japan (The gist of Ayukawa Yoshisuke's speech given at the lecture meeting on the tenth anniversary of the foundation of the Noguchi Research Association on Feb. 10, 1951)." Ayukawa discussed his activities to promote the modernization of small and medium-sized firms, and build roads and hydroelectric power plants in *Hyakumi dansu*, 205–10. In addition, see Ayukawa's 1953 draft memoir, 110–230, in Microfiche no. 931.4 of the Ayukawa Papers for his activities to promote the healthy growth of small and medium-sized firms, the construction of hydroelectric plants, and the building of roads and to attract foreign capital. With regard to debates between and within the Japanese government and SCAP on the issue of foreign

investments, see Miyazaki, "Ashida naikakuki no gaishi dōnyū mondai," pt. I, 85–90, and pt. II, 89–92, 94, 96–98; and Nakakita Kōji, *Keizai fukkō to sengo seiji*, 153–55, 166, 172. In addition, see Schonberger, *Aftermath of War*, 184–90.

47. Calder, *Strategic Capitalism*, 81–82. With regard to Yoshida and MITI, see Kōno, "Yoshida gaikō to kokunai seiji," 32–33, 37–38. For the Foreign Investment Research Society, see "Requests Concerning Foreign Investments," Feb. 4, 1949, RG 331, Box 1040, National Archives; and "Gaishi kenkyūkai nichigin sōsai ra," Feb. 3, 1949, *Asahi shimbun*; and an editorial in the Jan. 15, 1949, edition of the *Nikkei shimbun*.

Chapter 10

1. For the discussions of the Foreign Capital Research Association and Ayukawa's views of cottage industries, see Ayukawa Yoshisuke, Aug. 15, 1948, "Zaidan hōjin Gaishi kenkyūkai sōritsu ni tsuite" (On the establishment of the Foreign Capital Research Association), Microfiche no. 922.22, 313–20, Ayukawa Papers.

2. Borden, *The Pacific Alliance*, 101.

3. Fukao Mitsuhiro, Etō Kimihiro, and Ōmi Masao, "Tanka kawase rēto to bōeki min'eika," in Kōzai and Teranishi, *Sengo Nihon no keizai kaikaku*, 98–102.

4. Arisawa, *Nihon shōkenshi*, 50–54.

5. Borden, *The Pacific Alliance*, 99–100, 146–47. For details regarding Toyota's approach to Ford, see Wada and Yui, *Toyoda Kiichirō den*, 366–69.

6. "Gaishi dōnyū ni rakkan," Dec. 12, 1949, *Mainichi shimbun*; "Nichibei gōben no tōshi gaisha gaishi dōnyū," *Nikkei shimbun*, Dec. 14, 1949; and Draper to MacArthur, Dec. 2, 1949, and May 19, 1950, "Draper-MacArthur Correspondence," Douglas MacArthur Papers.

7. Shudō to Earl B. Schwulst, May 10, 1949, Microfiche no. 412.4, Ayukawa Papers.

8. Memorandum, June 13, 1949, Microfiche no. 412.1, Ayukawa Papers.

9. Shudō to Earl B. Schwulst, May 10, 1949, Microfiche no. 412.4, Ayukawa Papers. Shudō consulted F. Baker, advisor to ESS, as well as ESS officials Adams, Robinson, and Smith. See Shudō to William H. Draper, Jr., May 9, 1950; "Plan for Setting up New Japanese Investment Banking Corporation Jointly with an American Investment Banking Corporation," Mar. 31, 1950, Microfiche no. 412.4, Ayukawa Papers.

10. SCAP, "Announcement Concerning Private Commercial Entrants," GHQ Circular No. 1, Jan. 14, 1949 ("General Order No. 1"); "Announcement Concerning Foreign Business and Foreign Investment Activities in Japan," GHQ Circular No. 2, Jan. 14, 1949 ("General Order No. 2"); and "General Order No. 18," Oct. 21, 1949, RG 331 Box 1039, National Archives; SCAP, ESS, "Memorandum to the Members of the Foreign Investment Board," Jan. 20, 1949, RG 331 Box 1041, National Archives; Rabinowitz, *The Genesis of the Japanese Foreign Investment Law of 1950*, 397–426; and Mason, *American Multinationals and Japan*, 111–14.

11. Schwulst to Alexander, Feb. 1, 1950; MacArthur to Schwulst, Sept. 8, 1949, Microfiche no. 412.4, Ayukawa Papers.

12. Shudō to Major General W. F. Marquat, July 12, 1950, Microfiche no. 412.1; "Plan for Setting up New Japanese Investment Banking Corporation," Microfiche no. 412.4; Shudō to Draper, May 9, 1950, Microfiche no. 412.1, Ayukawa Papers.

13. Calder, *Strategic Capitalism,* 42.

14. Sugiura, "Sengo fukkōki no ginkō/shōken," 259–66.

15. Watanabe, *Watanabe Takeshi nikki,* 461; Sodei, *Yoshida Shigeru–MacArthur ōfuku shokanshū,* 297–302; and Rabinowitz, *The Genesis of the Japanese Foreign Investment Law of 1950,* 27–65, 485–506.

16. Shudō to Schwulst, July 18, 1949, Microfiche no. 412.4, Ayukawa Papers.

17. "Luncheon for Mr. Shudō Yasuto, Tuesday, Apr. 4, 1950," Microfiche no. 412.4, Ayukawa Papers.

18. "Plan for Setting up New Japanese Investment Banking Corporation," Microfiche no. 412.4, Ayukawa Papers.

19. Kurusu to Yoshida, Apr. 19, 1950, Microfiche no. 412.4, Ayukawa Papers; Ayukawa's unpublished 1953 memoir, Microfiche no. 931.4, Ayukawa Papers; Miyazawa, *Tokyo-Washington no mitsudan,* 40–81; Sakamoto, *Nichibei dōmei no kizuna,* 29; Borden, *The Pacific Alliance,* 99.

20. Shudō to Marquat, July 12, 1950, Microfiche no. 412.1, Ayukawa Papers. The following items were being considered by Dillon Read and Ayukawa's group.

Capitalization: Dillon Read and perhaps some other American interests would provide capital amounting to about $1 million. The Japanese interests will pay a yen equivalent of this amount. American interests might hold over 50 percent of the proposed firm's capital.

Management: The proposed firm will have a chairman of the Board of Directors and a president. One of them was to be a representative from Dillon Read, and Draper considered that this person would become chairman. Another representative from his firm was to become executive officer. Draper strongly desired that executive and administrative officers should be selected from competent bankers and industrialists to whom SCAP had no objections.

Participation of other firms: Draper stated that a consideration might be later given to the possibility of participation by British or other American interests.

In addition to this letter, see Shudō to Draper, May 9, 1950, Microfiche no. 412.2, Ayukawa Papers. Shudō met C. Douglas Dillon for the first time on Apr. 13; see cable from Shudō to Ayukawa (cable no. 6), Microfiche no. 412.2. Clarence Dillon's retention of his influence on his firm is discussed in Perez and Willett, *Clarence Dillon,* 129, 145–46.

21. Shudō to Marquat, July 12, 1950, Microfiche no. 412.1; Shudō to Ayukawa (cable no. 8); Shudō to Draper, May 9, 1950, undated cable from Shudō to Ayukawa;

Microfiche no. 412.2, Ayukawa Papers. Cable no. 8 is the Japanese transcript of Shudō's meeting with Draper, Wilkinson, and C. Douglas Dillon on Apr. 18. It indicates that Dillon's father still had a large influence over the firm, and the three told Shudō they would have to talk to Dillon's father and other partners of the firm about the proposed business investment banking firm. Draper considered sending a representative from his firm to continue talks in Tokyo and also consult with SCAP and Prime Minister Yoshida. See June 4, 1950, cable (cable no. 17) from Shudō, Microfiche no. 412.2, Ayukawa Papers. Shudō and Ayukawa were irritated by the slow response to their negotiations with Dillon, Read by BOJ Governor Ichimada and IBJ Governor Kawakita; see the following in Microfiche no. 412.2: May 13, 1950, cable (cable no. 14) from Shudō: May 19, cable (cable no. 16) from Shudō; Ayukawa to Shudō, June 7, 1950; Ayukawa to Ichimada, June 11, 1950. With regard to the Draper-Shirasu discussions, see Draper to MacArthur, May 19, 1950, "Draper-MacArthur Correspondence," MacArthur Papers.

22. Ayukawa's 1953 draft memoir, 225, Microfiche no. 931.4, Ayukawa Papers. It is unknown whether the proposed figure included or excluded taxes and expenses.

23. Shudō to Ayukawa (cable no. 8); Ayukawa to Shudō (cable no. 6), Apr. 28, 1950; Ayukawa to Shudō (cable no. 7), May 12, 1950; Microfiche no. 412.4, Ayukawa Papers.

24. Shudō to Schwulst, Feb. 12, 1952, Microfiche no. 412.1, Ayukawa Papers.

25. Rabinowitz, *The Genesis of the Japanese Foreign Investment Law*, 27–65, 506–27.

26. Ayukawa Yoshisuke, "The Highway Measures for Rehabilitation of Japan's Economy," Nov. 22, 1949, 7, Microfiche no. 412.4, Ayukawa Papers. This is an English translation of an excerpt of a speech delivered at the Noguchi Research Institute. See also Sodei, *Yoshida Shigeru*, 295–96; Kōzai Yasushi, "Kōdo seichō e no shuppatsu," 300–330; Industrial Consultants, Inc., "Plan to Hydro Power Exploitation of 10 Million KW and Its Relation to the Economy of Japan," Mar. 25, 1950, Microfiche no. 412.4, Ayukawa Papers; and Ayukawa's 1953 draft memoir, 107–25, Microfiche no. 931.4, Ayukawa Papers

27. Kōno, "Yoshida gaikō to kokunai seiji," 41–42, 44–45. On Kawasaki Steel, see Shinomiya, "Nishiyama Yatarō," 248–55; Yonekura, *Keiei kakumei no kōzō*, 182–200; idem, "Nihon tekkōgyō no kakushinsha"; and "Sengo Nihon tekkōgyō shiron."

28. In Microfiche no. 136.3, see Kurusu to Baruch, Apr. 22, 1950; Kurusu to Baruch, undated draft letter (probably 1950 since Kurusu thanked Baruch for helping Shudō meet Dillon Read executives); and Earl B. Schwulst to Col. Lawrence E. Bunker, June 16, 1950. See Ayukawa's 1953 draft memoir, 114–38, 141–50, Microfiche no. 931.4, Ayukawa Papers, for his activities to promote hydroelectric plants and roads and to attract foreign capital. There are materials here that do not appear in the materials cited above regarding his negotiations with Lilienthal and Yoshida for realizing TVA-type projects in Japan by obtaining Marshall Plan–type aid from the United States. In his diary

Lilienthal mentioned Baruch's request for Lilienthal to meet Shudō about "a hydro-project in Japan" (see entries for Apr. 4, 1950, and Mar. 9, 1951, entry on 125 in Lilienthal, *Journals*, 3: 3, 125). Finally, in Microfiche no. 412.4, see Shudō to Ayukawa (Japanese transcript of conversations between Shudō and Lilienthal), Apr. 10, 1950; Shudō to Ayukawa (Japanese transcript of conversations between Shudō and Baruch), Apr. 4, 1950; Shudō to Ayukawa (cable no. 5), Apr. 6, 1950; Kurusu to Ayukawa, Apr. 17, 1950; Shudō to Ayukawa (cable no. 10), May 2, 1950; Ayukawa to Shudō (cable no. 8), May 16, 1950; Shudō to Ayukawa (cable no. 17), June 5, 1950.

29. Lilienthal to Shudō, Apr. 10, 1950, Microfiche no. 412.4, Ayukawa Papers.

30. The Industrial Consultants, Inc., "Plan of Hydro Power Exploitation of 10 Million KW and Its Relation to the Economy of Japan," Mar. 25, 1950; Shudō to Ayukawa, Apr. 10, 1950; Lilienthal to Shudō, May 6, 1950; Ayukawa to Shudō (cable no. 6), Apr. 28, 1950; Microfiche no. 412.4, Ayukawa Papers.

31. Draper to MacArthur, Feb. 13, 1951, "Draper-MacArthur Correspondence," MacArthur Papers.

32. Shudō to Lilienthal, undated cable; Lilienthal to Shudō, Jan. 29, 1950; Microfiche no. 412.1, Ayukawa Papers.

33. Lilienthal, *Journals*, 3: 117, 127–28.

34. Ibid., 3: 88, 90–92, 106, 109, 111–13, 160; and Schwarz, *The New Dealers*, xvi–xvii, chap. 10, 328–30, 336–40.

35. Lilienthal, *Journals*, 3: 130.

36. Ibid., 3: 127.

37. Ibid., 3: 125–26, 128.

38. Lilienthal to Dulles, Apr. 17, 1951, David E. Lilienthal Papers.

39. On the meeting with Acheson on May 4, see Lilienthal, *Journals*, 3: 156–57.

40. Ibid., 3: 133.

41. See ibid., 3: 154–55, for Lilienthal's talk with Dulles on May 2.

42. In Microfiche no. 136.3, Ayukawa Papers, see David E. Lilienthal to Yoshi-suke Aikawa (Ayukawa), May 3, 1951; Aikawa (Ayukawa) to Lilienthal, May 16, 1951; Aikawa (Ayukawa) to Lilienthal, May 16, 1951; Shudō Yasuto to Earl B. Schwulst, May 17, 1951; and Lilienthal to Aikawa (Ayukawa), June 18, 1951.

43. Kurusu to Yoshida, Apr. 18, 1950, Kurusu to Yoshida, Nov. 12, 1951, Yoshida to Kurusu, Jan. 1, 1952, Microfiche no. 136.1, Ayukawa Papers; Ayukawa to Yoshida ("Nihon no dengen kaihatsu gaishi wa wagahō to shite naze Marsharu puran hōshiki no seiji shakkan o erabubeki de aruka"), Apr. 1951, Microfiche no. 911.8, Ayukawa Papers; Shudō to Schwulst, Feb. 12, 1952, Schwulst to Shudō, Mar. 4, 1952, and Shudō to Schwulst, Mar. 17, 1952, Microfiche no. 412.1, Ayukawa Papers; and Lilienthal, *Journals*, 3: 125–28; Borden, *The Pacific Alliance*, 149–51.

44. Shibata, "Sekai ginkō no tai-Nichi karyoku hatsuden shakkan," 96, 99–107; Kraske et al., *Bankers with a Mission*, 93; Kōzai, "Kōdo seichō e no shuppatsu," 300–

302; Jyūnenshi hensan iinkai, *Nihon kaihatsu ginkō jyūnenshi,* 374–75; and "Taidan: Nihon no saiken," *Fūsei,* Nov. 1953, in Microfiche no. 912.2, Ayukawa Papers.

45. Borden, *The Pacific Alliance,* 149, 222.

46. Ibid., 93, 150, 167, 187–90, 218.

47. For Ayukawa's discussions of his efforts to organize a political lobbying organization for small and medium-sized firms, see Ayukawa, "Watashi no rirekisho," 341–43; "Chūshō kigyō joseikai o ashiba ni ugokidashita Ayukawa Yoshisuke-shi," *Jinji tsūshin,* Apr. 1953, no. 282, Microfiche no. 912.2, Ayukawa Papers; and Ayukawa, *Hyakumi dansu,* 301–5. For his idea about attracting overseas Chinese capital to the Atō Bank, see "Yushutsu kankei no chūshō kigyō ni taisuru ichi josei keikaku," July 1951, in Microfiche no. 911.8 of the Ayukawa Papers. Finally, see Ayukawa's 1953 draft memoir, 161–230, in Microfiche no. 931.4. Ayukawa states that one of the overseas Chinese who approached him was a former finance minister of Manchukuo.

48. For the discussions between Ayukawa and Kishi on their ideas about the Japanese political and economic situation, see "Taidan: Nihon no saiken," *Fūsei,* Nov. 1953, in Microfiche no. 912.2 of the Ayukawa Papers. Ayukawa also made similar arguments on these issues in the following published reports in the same microfiche: Miki Yōnosuke, "Zaikai no backbone, Ayukawa Yoshisuke," *Bungei shunjū,* Aug. 1947, 182–84; "Chinmoku o yabutta Ayukawa Yoshisukeshi: naze kanzen san'in senkyo ni shutsubashitaka," *Ōsaka keizai* 3, no. 4: 33; Ayukawa Yoshisuke, "Kakumei o matsu kokoro," *Bungei shunjū,* Nov. 1953, 102–7; and Ayukawa Yoshisuke, "Nihon kakumei kuruka," *Jitsugyō no sekai zōkan,* Aug. 1953, 26–29. Ayukawa ("Watashi no rirekisho," 343) acknowledged that in 1956 Kishi's support had secured the passage of the Law on the Organizations for Small and Medium-Sized Firms. Many laws for small and medium-sized firms were passed during the Kishi cabinet (1957–60); for a list, see Ayukawa, *Hyakumi dansu,* 305.

49. Wolferen, *The Enigma of Japanese Power,* 388–89.

Conclusion

1. Dower, *Embracing Defeat,* 558.

2. Zeiler, *Free Trade, Free World;* 172–73; Johnson, *MITI,* 223–24; Calder, *Strategic Capitalism,* 216; Shimizu, *Creating People of Plenty,* chap. 2.

3. Gotō Akira, "Gijutsu dōnyū: sengo Nihon no keiken," in Kōzai and Teranishi, *Sengo Nihon no keizai kaikaku,* 238–42, 245.

4. Johnson, *MITI,* 217; Calder, *Strategic Capitalism,* 33.

5. Fukao Mitsuhiro, Etō Kimihiro, and Ōmi Masao, "Tanka kawase rēto to bōeki mineika," in Kōzai and Teranishi, *Sengo Nihon no keizai kaikaku,* 102.

6. Johnson, *MITI,* 217.

7. Noguchi, *1940 nen taisei,* 100–101.

8. "Sekai sangyō shinchizu no. 20: saihen wa chikara, Ōbeizei ga shihai," *Asahi shimbun*, Aug. 19, 2001.

9. Calder, *Strategic Capitalism*, 43. Although the Securities Exchange Act in early 1948 took away "regulatory authority over securities from MOF to a U.S.-style Securities Commission . . . and bann[ed] banks from trading in or underwriting securities," the commission was abolished and its authority transferred back to MOF only three months after the Occupation ended. Furthermore, even though SCAP attempted to create a U.S. Federal Reserve–style Policy Board in the Bank of Japan, this became a nominal entity, because of resistance by MOF and Bank of Japan officials. See Calder, *Strategic Capitalism*, 43; and Noguchi, *1940 nen taisei*, 84–85, 88–89.

10. Calder, *Strategic Capitalism*, 44.

11. Ibid., 29–30; Noguchi, *1940 nen taisei*, 31–34; and Teranishi Jūrō, "Shūsen chokugo ni okeru kin'yū seido kaikaku," in Kōzai and Teranishi, *Sengo Nihon no keizai kaikaku*, 134, 144. Teranishi (144) argues that investors avoided purchasing corporate bonds, many of them issued by quasi-governmental entities and most of them with returns guaranteed by the government because of the lack of financial disclosure.

12. Noguchi, *1940 nen taisei*, 31, 35.

13. Arisawa, *Nihon shōkenshi*, 7–14.

14. Calder, *Strategic Capitalism*, 42, 158–59.

15. Arisawa, *Nihon shōkenshi*, 45–53, 64–68, 97–101. See also Noguchi, *1940 nen taisei*, 85.

16. Noguchi, *1940 nen taisei*, 100–101.

17. Ibid., 102–3. American interference in Japan's trade with China may have contributed to the weakening of small and medium-sized firms because those firms in the textile and other low-tech industries could not export as much as they wanted to China; see Borden, *The Pacific Alliance*, 159, 213.

18. Calder, *Strategic Capitalism*, 33.

Epilogue

1. Noguchi, *1940 nen taisei*, 170–71.

2. "Gaishi wa hashiru," *Nikkei shimbun*, Aug. 15, 1998.

3. "Gurobaruka no naka de towareru jiritsu," *Nikkei shimbun*, Aug. 15, 1998.

4. "Kuni o kaeru," *Nikkei shimbun*, Aug. 23, 1998; "Kigyō jiritsu e kisei teppai," *Nikkei shimbun*, Aug. 5, 1998; "Gaishi katsuyō okureru Nihon," *Nikkei shimbun*, May 19, 2001. With regard to Nissan's negotiations with European and American automakers, see *Nikkei Business*, Mar. 22, 1999, 6–19, Apr. 5, 1999, 6–7, and Dec. 18/25, 2000, 5–6. For articles on Nissan's managerial and financial reforms, see *Nikkei Business*, Nov. 13, 2000, 26–47, Mar. 5, 2001, 82–85, 155–57, and Apr. 2, 2001, 27–28. See the interesting article on the talks between Toyota Motors and Ford in *Nikkei Business*, Dec. 18/25, 2000, 4–12. In contrast to Nissan, the managerial and financial

reforms of Mitsubishi Motors have not fared as well under Daimler-Chrysler; see *Nikkei Business*, Mar. 5, 2001, 4–7; and *BusinessWeek*, May 14, 2001, 22–25. *BusinessWeek* lauded Carlos Ghosn as one of its twenty-five top managers of the year; see *BusinessWeek*, Jan. 8, 2001, 35, 40.

5. "China's Pirates," *BusinessWeek*, June 5, 2000, 20–25; "China Coping with Its New Power," *BusinessWeek*, Apr. 16, 2001, 38–45; "Tai-Chū sēfugādo sōsetsu," *Nikkei shimbun*, Aug. 18, 2001; "Bei 'tai-Nichi jūshi' suitai no kanōsei," *Nikkei shimbun*, Aug. 19, 2001; *Nikkei Business*, Nov. 20, 2000, 4–9, Nov. 27, 2000, 26–49, Aug. 20, 2001, 26–34; *Shūkan Diyamond*, Aug. 25, 2001, 38–41.

Bibliography

Unpublished Materials

Duke University, Durham, North Carolina
  Robert L. Eichelberger Papers

Franklin D. Roosevelt Presidential Library, Hyde Park, New York
  Franklin D. Roosevelt Papers: President's Personal File
  Franklin D. Roosevelt Papers: Diaries and Itineraries (microfiche)
  White House Usher's Diary (microfiche)

Georgetown University Library Special Collections Division, Washington, D.C.
  James D. Mooney Papers

Harvard University, Baker Library, Boston, Massachusetts
  Thomas W. Lamont Papers

Harvard University, Houghton Library, Cambridge, Massachusetts
  Joseph C. Grew Diary and Papers
  William R. Castle, Jr., Diary

Herbert C. Hoover Presidential Library, West Branch, Iowa
  William R. Castle, Jr., Papers
  Herbert C. Hoover Commerce Papers Series Subject File
  Herbert C. Hoover Post-Presidential General File
  Herbert C. Hoover Post-Presidential Individual File
  Herbert C. Hoover Post-Presidential Subject File
  Arthur Kemp Oral History Interview
  Lewis L. Strauss Papers

Payson J. Treat Oral History Interview
Gerald P. Nye Papers

Hoover Institution on War, Revolution and Peace, Stanford University, Palo Alto, California
Stanley K. Hornbeck Papers

Library of Congress, Washington, D.C.
Roy Howard Papers

MacArthur Memorial Bureau of Archives, Norfolk, Virginia
Douglas MacArthur Papers

The National Archives, Washington, D.C.
Supreme Commander of the Allied Powers, RG331 Boxes 1039–41
United States Department of State, Record Group 59, Decimal File 711.94 Category. 1940–1944 (Microfilm LM 136 reel nos. 1–3)

The National Diet Library, Tokyo, Japan
Wikawa (Ikawa) Tadao Papers
Ayukawa (Aikawa) Yoshisuke Papers (microfiche)

Naval War College, Newport, Rhode Island
William V. Pratt Papers

The Nevada Historical Society, Reno, Nevada
H. Foster Bain Papers

Princeton University, Seeley G. Mudd Manuscript Library, Princeton, New Jersey
John F. Dulles Papers
David E. Lilienthal Papers

Yale University Library, New Haven, Connecticut
Walter Lippmann Papers
Henry Stimson Diary and Papers

Other Works

Abramson, Rudy. _Spanning the Century: The Life of W. Averell Harriman, 1891–1986_. New York: William Morrow, 1992.

Alperovitz, Gar. _The Decision to Use the Atomic Bomb_. New York: Vintage Books, 1995.

Amos, Paul Stoddard. "American Commercial Interests in Manchuria Since the Japanese 'Occupation' of 1931." Master's thesis, University of Chicago, 1941.

Anzai Masao. "Watashi no rirekisho." In _Watashi no rirekisho_, ed. Nihon keizai shimbunsha, 42: 7–86. Tokyo: Nihon keizai shimbunsha, 1964.

Arisawa Hiromi. _Gakumon to shisō to ningen to: wasureenu hitobito no omoide_. Tokyo: Mainichi shimbunsha, 1957.

Arisawa Hiromi, ed., *Nihon shōkenshi*. Tokyo: Nihon keizai shimbunsha, 1995.

Arita Hachirō. *Baka Hachi to hito wa iu: gaikōkan no kaisō*. Tokyo: Kōwadō, 1959.

Arnold, Peri E. *Making the Managerial Presidency: Comprehensive Reorganization Planning, 1905–1980*. Princeton: Princeton University Press, 1986.

Asada Sadao. "The Shock of the Atomic Bomb and Japan's Decision to Surrender: A Reconsideration." *Pacific Historical Review* 67 (Nov. 1998): 477–512.

Asakura Tsuneto. *Asakura Tsuneto nikki*, vols. 2–4, 6. Tokyo: Yamakawa shuppansha, 1985–91.

————. "Ōyō bōsha shisō zuihitsu." In *Ayukawa Yoshisuke Sensei Tsuisōroku*, ed. Ayukawa Yoshisuke sensei henshū kankōkai, 14–26. Tokyo: Ayukawa Yoshisuke sensei henshū kankōkai, 1968.

Awaya Kentarō. *Shōwa no rekishi*, vol. 6. Tokyo: Shōgakkan, 1988.

Awaya Kentarō and Yoshida Yutaka, eds. *Kokusai kensatsukyoku (IPS) jinmonchōsho*, vol. 29. Tokyo: Nihon tosho sentā, 1993.

Ayukawa Yoshisuke. *Gomokumeshi: zuihitsu*. Tokyo: Daiyamondosha, 1962.

————. *Hyakumi dansu: Ayukawa Yoshisuke zuihitsushū*. Tokyo: Aizōbon kankōkai, 1964.

————. "Manshū keizai shihai no kii pointo." *Bessatsu chisei*, special issue: *Himerareta Shōwashi*, Dec. 1956, 188–200.

————. *Mono no mikata kangaekata*. Tokyo: Jitsugyō no Nihonsha, 1937. English trans.—*Searching for Truth*. Tokyo: Jitsugyō no Nipponsha, 1938.

————. *Watashi no jinsei sekkei*. Tokyo: Ōkura shuppan, 1955.

————. *Watashi no kangaekata*. Tokyo: Daiyamondosha, 1954.

————. "Watashi no rirekisho." In *Watashi no rirekisho*, vol. 24, ed. Nihon keizai shimbunsha, 24: 267–358. Tokyo: Nihon keizai shimbunsha, 1966.

Ayukawa Yoshisuke sensei henshū kankōkai, ed. *Ayukawa Yoshisuke sensei tsuisōroku*. Tokyo: Ayukawa Yoshisuke sensei henshū kankōkai, 1968.

Bain, H. Foster. "Manchuria: A Key Area." *Foreign Affairs*, Oct. 1946, 106–17.

Barnhart, Michael. *Japan Prepares for Total War*. Ithaca, N.Y.: Cornell University Press, 1981.

Baruch, Bernard M. *Baruch: The Public Years*. New York: Holt, Rinehart & Winston, 1960.

Best, Gary Dean. *Herbert Hoover: The Post-presidential Years, 1933–1964*. 2 vols. Stanford: Hoover Institution Press, 1983.

Bird, Kai. *The Chairman: John J. McCloy, the Making of the American Establishment*. New York: Simon & Schuster, 1992.

Blum, John Morton. *Roosevelt and Morgenthau: A Revision and Condensation of "From the Morgenthau Diaries."* Boston: Houghton Mifflin, 1970.

Borden, William S. *The Pacific Alliance: United States Foreign Policy and Japanese Trade Recovery, 1947–1955*. Madison: University of Wisconsin Press, 1984.

Borg, Dorothy. *The United States and the Eastern Crisis of 1931–1938: From the Manchurian Incident Through the Initial Stage of the Undeclared Sino-Japanese War.* Cambridge, Mass.: Harvard University Press, 1964.

Brinkley, Alan. "The New Deal and the Idea of the State." In *The Rise and Fall of the New Deal Order, 1930–1980,* ed. Steve Fraser and Gary Gerstle, 85–121. Princeton: Princeton University Press, 1986.

———. *The Unfinished Nation: A Concise History of the American People.* New York: McGraw-Hill, Inc., 1993.

Butow, R. J. C. *The John Doe Associates: Backdoor Diplomacy for Peace, 1941.* Stanford: Stanford University Press, 1974.

Calder, Kent. *Strategic Capitalism: Private Business and Public Purpose in Japanese Industrial Finance.* Princeton: Princeton University Press, 1993.

Chace, James. *Acheson: The Secretary of State Who Created the American World.* New York: Simon & Schuster, 1998.

Chernow, Ron. *The House of Morgan: An American Banking Dynasty and the Rise of Modern Finance.* New York: Simon & Schuster, Touchstone Book, 1991.

———. *The Warburgs.* New York: Vintage Books, 1994.

Chō Yukio. "Amerika shihon no Manshū dōnyū keikaku." In *Nichibei Kankeishi,* III, *Gikai/seitō to minkandantai,* ed. Hosoya Chihiro, Imai Seiichi, Michio Rōyama, and Saitō Makoto, 113–70. Tokyo: Tōkyō daigaku shuppankai, 1971.

———. "An Inquiry into the Problem of Importing American Capital into Manchuria: A Note on Japanese-American Relations, 1931–1941." In *Pearl Harbor as History: Japanese-American Relations, 1931–1941,* ed. Dorothy Borg and Shumpei Okamoto, 377–410. New York: Columbia University Press, 1973.

———. *Shōwa kyōkō: Nihon fashizumu zen'ya.* Tokyo: Iwanami shoten, 1994.

Chūnichi shimbun, Shakaibu, ed. *Jiyū e no tōsō: Sugihara visa to yudayajin.* Tokyo: Tōkyō shimbun shuppankyoku, 1995.

Clauss, Errol MacGregor. "The Roosevelt Administration and Manchukuo, 1933–1941." *Historian* 32, no. 4 (Aug. 1970): 595–611.

Cohen, Jerome B. *Japan's Economy in War and Reconstruction.* Minneapolis: University of Minnesota Press, 1949.

Cohen, Theodore. *Remaking Japan: American Occupation as New Deal.* New York: Free Press, 1987.

Cohen, Warren I. *The Chinese Connection: Roger S. Greene, Thomas W. Lamont, George E. Sokolsky and American–East Asian Relations.* New York: Columbia University Press, 1978.

Coit, Margaret L. *Mr. Baruch.* Boston: Houghton Mifflin, 1957.

Cumings, Bruce. *The Origins of the Korean War,* Vol. 2, *The Roaring of the Cataract, 1947–1950.* Princeton: Princeton University Press, 1990.

Cusumano, Michael A. *The Japanese Automobile Industry: Technology and Management at Nissan and Toyota.* Cambridge, Mass.: Harvard University, Council on East Asian Studies, 1985.

Dallek, Robert. *Franklin D. Roosevelt and American Foreign Policy, 1932–1945.* Oxford: Oxford University Press, 1979.

Doenecke, Justus D. "Anti-Interventionism of Herbert Hoover." *Journal of Liberterian Studies* 8 (Summer 1987): 311–40.

———. *In Danger Undaunted: The Anti-interventionist Movement of 1940–1941 as Revealed in the Papers of the America First Committee.* Stanford: Hoover Institute Press, 1990.

———. *Storm on the Horizon: The Challenge to American Intervention, 1939–1941.* Lanham, Md.: Rowman & Littlefield, 2000.

Dower, John W. *Embracing Defeat: Japan in the Wake of World War II.* New York: New Press, 1999.

Eguchi, Keiichi. *Jūgonen sensō shōshi.* 2d ed. Tokyo: Aoki shoten, 1991.

Etō Kimihiro, Fukao Mitsuhiro, and Oumi Masao. "Tanitsu kawase rēto saiyō to bōeki min'eika." In *Sengo Nihon no keizai kaikaku: shijō to seifu,* ed. Kōzai Yasushi and Teranishi Jūrō, 87–105. Tokyo: Tōkyō daigaku shuppankai, 1993.

Ferrell, Robert H., ed. *Off the Record: The Private Papers of Harry S. Truman.* New York: Harper & Row, 1980.

Fletcher, William Miles. *The Japanese Business Community and National Trade Policy, 1920–1942.* Chapel Hill: University of North Carolina Press, 1989.

———. *The Search for a New Order: Intellectuals and Fascism in Prewar Japan.* Chapel Hill: University of North Carolina Press, 1982.

Forsberg, Aaron. *America and the Japanese Miracle: The Cold War Context of Japan's Postwar Economic Revival, 1950–1960.* Chapel Hill: University of North Carolina Press, 2000.

Fossedal, Gregory, A. *Our Finest Hour: Will Clayton, the Marshall Plan, and the Triumph of Democracy.* Stanford: Hoover Institution Press, 1993.

Fried, Richard M. *Nightmare in Red: The McCarthy Era in Perspective.* New York: Oxford University Press, 1990.

Fujiyama Aiichirō. "Senjika no zaikai no ugoki." In *Kataritsugu Shōwashi: gekidō no hanseiki,* ed. Asahi shimbunsha, 4: 57–80. Tokyo: Asahi shimbunsha, 1976.

Furukawa Takahisa. *Shōwa senchūki no sōgō kokusaku kikan.* Tokyo: Yoshikawa kōbunkan, 1992.

Gaddis, John Lewis. *The United States and the Origins of the Cold War, 1941–1947.* New York: Columbia University Press, 1972.

Garon, Sheldon, *The State and Labor in Modern Japan.* Berkeley: University of California Press, 1987.

Gendaishi shiryō, vol. 7, *Manshū jihen;* vol. 8, *Nichū sensō.* Tokyo: Misuzu shobō, 1964.

Gillin, Donald G., and Ramon H. Myers, eds. *Last Chance in Manchuria: The Diary of Chang Kia-Ngau.* Stanford: Hoover Institution Press, 1989.

Goodman, David G., and Miyazawa Masanori. *Jews in the Japanese Mind: The History and Uses of a Cultural Stereotype.* New York: Free Press, 1995.

Gordon, Andrew. *Labor and Imperial Democracy in Japan.* Berkeley: University of California Press, 1991.

Gotō Akira. "Gijutsu dōnyū: sengo Nihon no keiken." In *Sengo Nihon no keizai kaikaku: shijō to seifu,* ed. Kōzai Yasushi and Teranishi Jūrō, 237–74. Tokyo: Tōkyō daigaku shuppankai, 1993.

Hagiwara Tōru. *Nihon gaikōshi,* vol. 30. Kashima heiwa kenkyūjo shuppankai, 1973.

Halberstam, David. *The Reckoning.* New York: Avon Books, 1987.

Hara Akira. "Manshū ni okeru keizai tōsei seisaku no tenkai: Mantetsu kaiso to Mangyō setsuritsu o megutte." In *Nihon keizai seisakushiron,* ed. Andō Yoshio, 209–96. Tokyo: Tōkyō daigaku shuppankai, 1976.

———. "Senkyūhyaku sanjūnendai no Manshū keizai tōsei seisaku." In *Nihon teikokushugika no Manshū,* ed. Manshūshi kenkyūkai, 1–114. Tokyo: Ochanomizu shobō, 1972.

Hara Akira and Nakamura Takafusa. "Kaidai." In *Nichiman zaisei kenkyūkai shiryō: Izumiyama Sanrokushi kyūzō,* ed. Hara Akira and Nakamura Takafusa, 1: 1–18. Tokyo: Nihon kindai shiryō kenkyūkai, 1970.

Hara Yoshihisa. *Kishi Nobusuke: kensei no seijika.* Tokyo: Iwanami shoten, 1995.

Harada Kumao. *Saionji Kō to seikyoku,* Vols. 5 and 7. Tokyo: Iwanami shoten, 1951, 1952.

Hashimoto Jurō. *Daikyōkōki no Nihon shihonshugi.* Tokyo: Tōkyō daigaku shuppankai, 1984.

———. "Kigyō shisutemu no 'hassei,' 'senren,' 'seidoka' no ronri." In *Nihon kigyō shisutemu no sengoshi,* ed. Hashimoto Toshiaki, 1–42. Tokyo: Tōkyō daigaku shuppankai, 1996.

———. "'1940 nen taisei' wa genzai to chokketsu shiteinai." *Economist,* May 9, 1995, 64–69.

Hashimoto Tetsuma. "Makoto ni aikoku no Kyojin Nariki." In *Ayukawa Yoshisuke sensei tsuisōroku,* ed. Ayukawa Yoshisuke sensei henshū kankōkai, 307–14. Tokyo: Ayukawa Yoshisuke sensei henshū kankōkai, 1968.

———. *Nichibei kōshō hiwa.* Tokyo: Shiunso, 1946.

———. *Nihon no haisen kōfuku rimenshi.* Tokyo: Shiunsō, 1986.

Hayashi Shigeru and Tsuji Kiyoaki, eds. *Nihon naikaku shiroku.* Tokyo: Daiichi hōki shuppan, 1981.

Heinrichs, Waldo. *American Ambassador Joseph C. Grew and the Development of the United States Diplomatic Tradition.* Little, Brown, 1966.

———. "The Russian Factor in Japanese-American Relations, 1941." In *Pearl Harbor Reexamined: Prologue to the Pacific War,* ed. Hilary Conroy and Harry Wray, 163–77. Honolulu: University of Hawaii Press, 1990.

———. *Threshold of War: Franklin D. Roosevelt and American Entry into World War II.* New York: Oxford University Press, 1988.

Hill, Frank Ernest, and Mira Wilkins. *American Business Abroad: Ford on Six Continents.* Detroit: Wayne State University Press, 1964.

Hogan, Michael J. *A Cross of Iron: Harry S. Truman and the Origins of the National Security State, 1945–1954.* Cambridge, Eng.: Cambridge University Press, 1998.

——. *Informal Entente: The Private Structure of Cooperation in Anglo-American Economic Diplomacy, 1918–1928.* Chicago: Imprint Publications, 1991.

——. *The Marshall Plan: America, Britain, and the Reconstruction of Western Europe, 1947–1952.* Cambridge, Eng.: Cambridge University Press, 1987.

Hoopes, Townsend and Douglas Brinkley. *Driven Patriot: The Life and Times of James Forrestal.* New York: Vintage Books, 1992.

Horikoshi Teizō. *Keizai dantai rengōkai zenshi.* Tokyo: Keizai dantai rengōkai, 1962.

Hoshino Naoki. *Mihatenu yume: Manshūkoku gaishi.* Tokyo: Daiyamondosha, 1963.

Hosoya Chihiro. *Nihon gaikō no zahyō.* Tokyo: Chūō kōronsha, 1979.

Hoston, Germaine A. *Marxism and the Crisis of Development in Prewar Japan.* Princeton: Princeton University Press, 1986.

Howard, Graemer K. *America and a New World Order.* New York: Charles Scribner's Sons, 1940.

Hu, Shizhang. *Stanley K. Hornbeck and the Open Door Policy, 1919–1937.* Westport, Conn.: Greenwood Press, 1995.

Hull, Cordell. *The Memoirs of Cordell Hull,* vol. 2. New York: Macmillan, 1948.

Ienaga Saburō. *Taiheiyō sensō.* Tokyo: Iwanami shoten, 1986.

Iguchi Haruo. "Amerika no kyokutō seisaku: Herbert C. Hoover to Nichibei kankei." In *Kantaiheiyō no kokusai chitsujo no mosaku to Nihon,* ed. Itō Yukio and Kawada Minoru, 5–43. Tokyo: Yamakawa shuppansha, 1999.

——. "Ayukawa Yoshisuke no sengo dengen kaihatsu kōsō to Beikoku: 1950–1952." *Dōshisha Amerika kenkyū,* no. 37 (Mar. 2001): 79–85.

——. "Herbert Hoover moto daitōryō to Nichibei sensō: shinjuwan chokuzen no Hoover nikki no shinpyōsei." *Dōshisha Amerika kenkyū,* no. 35 (Mar. 1999): 103–13.

——. "A Quest for Peace: Ayukawa Yoshisuke and U.S.-Japan Relations, 1940." *Journal of American–East Asian Relations* 5, no. 1 (Spring 1996): 15–35.

——. "An Unfinished Dream: Yoshisuke Ayukawa's Economic Diplomacy Toward the U.S., 1937–1940." *Journal of American and Canadian Studies,* no. 16 (Spring 1998): 21–47.

——. "Senryōki Nihon no keizai seisaku to Nichibei kankei: Ayukawa Yoshisuke no sengo fukkō kōsō o chūshin ni." In *Nijūseiki Nichibei kankei to Higashi Ajia,* ed. Kawada Minoru and Itō Yukio, 236–65. Nagoya: Fūbaisha, 2002.

Ikawa (Wikawa) Tadao. "Nichibei kōshō hiwa: hōi no misshi." 2 pts. *Keizai hyōron,* Jan. 1952, 81–91; and Mar. 1952, 54–64.

——. *Nichibei kōshō shiryō.* Tokyo: Yamakawa shuppansha, 1982.

Ikeda Sumihisa. *Nihon no magarikado: gunbatsu no higeki to saigo no gozenkaigi.* Tokyo: Senjō shuppan, 1968.

Ikei Masaru. *Nihon gaikōshi gaisetsu,* rev. ed. Tokyo: Keio tsūshin, 1982.

Iokibe Makoto. *Beikoku no Nihon senryō seisaku: sengo Nihon no sekkeizu.* 2 vols. Tokyo: Chūō kōronsha, 1985.

Iriye Akira. *Across the Pacific: An Inner History of American–East Asian Relations.* New York: Harcourt, Brace & World, 1967.

———. *The Origins of the Second World War in Asia and the Pacific.* London: Longman, 1987.

———. *Pacific Estrangement: Japanese and American Expansion, 1897–1911.* Chicago: Imprint Publications, 1994.

———. *Power and Culture: The Japanese American War, 1941–1945.* Cambridge, Mass.: Harvard Unversity Press, 1981.

Ishikawa Shigeru. "Shūsen ni itaru made no Manshū keizai kaihatsu: sono mokuteki to seika." In *Taiheiyō sensō shūketsuron,* ed. Nihon gaikōshi gakkai, 737–79. Tokyo: Tōkyō daigaku shuppankai, 1958.

Itō Takashi. *Shōwaki no seiji.* Tokyo: Yamakawa shuppansha, 1983.

———. *Shōwaki no seiji (zoku).* Tokyo: Yamakawa shuppansha, 1993.

———. *Taishō-ki "Kakushin"-ha no seiritsu.* Tokyo: Hanawa shobō, 1978.

Itō Takashi and Momose Takashi. *Jiten Shōwa senzenki no Nihon: seido to jittai.* Tokyo: Yoshikawa kōbunkan, 1990.

Itō Takashi, Kishi Nobusuke, and Yatsugi Kazuo. *Kishi Nobusuke no kaisō.* Tokyo: Bungei shunjūsha, 1981.

Iwakuro Hideo-shi danwa sokkiroku. Tokyo: Tōkyō daigaku, Shakai kagaku kenkyūjo, 1977.

Izumiyama Sanroku. *Tora daijin ni naru made: yo ga hansei no omoide.* Tokyo: Shinkigensha, 1953.

Jidōsha shiryō, vol. 1, *Nihon jidōsha kōgyōshi zadankai kirokushū;* vol. 2, *Nihon jidōsha kōgyōshi kōjyutsu kirokushū;* vol. 3, *Nihon jidōsha kōgyōshi gyōsei kirokushū.* Tokyo: Shadanhōjin jidōsha kōgyō shinkōkai, 1973, 1975, 1979.

Johnson, Chalmers. *MITI and the Japanese Miracle: The Growth of Industrial Policy, 1925–1975.* Stanford: Stanford University Press, 1982.

Jones, E. Stanley. "An Adventure in Failure: Behind the Scenes Before Pearl Harbor." *Asia and the Americas* 45, no. 12 (Dec. 1945): 609–616.

Jones, F. C. *Manchuria Since 1931.* London: Royal Institute for International Affairs, 1949.

Jyūnenshi hensan iinkai, ed. *Nihon kaihatsu ginkō jyūnenshi.* Tokyo: Nihon kaihatsu ginkō, 1963.

Karl, Barry D. *The Uneasy State: The United States from 1915 to 1945.* Chicago: University of Chicago Press, 1983.

Kasuga, Yutaka. "Mitsui zaibatsu to Chūgoku/Manshū tōshi." In *Nihon no kindai to shihonshugi: kokusaika to chiiki,* ed. Nakamura Masanori, 39–85. Tokyo: Tōkyō daigaku shuppankai, 1992.

Katakura Tadashi. "Ayukawa Yoshisuke-shi to Mangyō no omoide." In *Ayukawa Yoshisuke Sensei tsuisōroku*, ed. Ayukawa Yoshisuke sensei henshū kankōkai, 111–29. Tokyo: Ayukawa Yoshisuke sensei henshū kankōkai, 1968.

Kennan, George F. *Memoirs, 1925–1950*. Boston: Little, Brown, 1967.

Kennedy, David. *Over Here: The First World War and American Society*. New York: Oxford University Press, 1980.

Kido, Kōichi. *Kido Kōichi kankei bunsho*. Tokyo: Tōkyō daigaku shuppankai, 1966.

———. *Kido Kōichi nikki*. 2 Vols. Tokyo: Tōkyō daigaku shuppankai, 1966.

Kitaoka Shin'ichi. "Yoshida Shigeru ni okeru senzen to sengo." In *Sengo gaikō no keisei*, ed. Kindai Nihon kenkyūkai, 105–31. Tokyo: Yamakawa shuppansha, 1994.

Kobayashi Hideo. *Daitōa kyōeiken no keisei to hōkai*. Tokyo: Ochanomizu shobō, 1975.

———. *"Nihon kabushikigaisha" o tsukutta otoko: Miyazaki Masayoshi no shōgai*. Tokyo: Shōgakkan, 1995.

Kobayashi Michihiko. "Seitō seiji to Manshū keiei: Shōwa seikōsho mondai no seiji katei." In *Kokusai kankyō no naka no kindai Nihon*, ed. Kurosawa Fumitaka, Saitō Seiji, and Sakurai Ryōju, 199–232. Tokyo: Fuyō shobō shuppansha, 2001.

Kojima Naoki. *Ayukawa Yoshisuke den: akai yuhi no Shōwashi*. Tokyo: Nihon keiei shuppankai, 1967.

Kojima Tsunehisa. "Inoue, Takahashi zaisei no higeki to zaisei no gunjika." *Senkyūhyaku sanjūnendai no Nihon: daikyōkō yori sensō e*, ed. Kojima Tsunehisa, 168–202. Kyoto: Hōritsubunkasha, 1989.

Kōno Yasuko. "Yoshida gaikō to kokunai seiji: Tsusanshō sechi kara denryoku shakkan dōnyū made." In *Sengo kokka no keisei to keizai hatten: senryō igo*, ed. Nihon seiji gakkai, 29–52. Tokyo: Iwanami shoten, 1992.

Kōzai Yasushi. "Kōdo seichō e no shuppatsu." In *Nihon keizaishi*, vol. 7, *"Keikakuka" to "minshuka*," ed. Nakamura Takafusa, 284–321. Tokyo: Iwanami shoten, 1989.

Kōzai Yasushi and Teranishi Shigeaki, eds. *Sengo Nihon no keizai kaikaku: shijō to seifu*. Tokyo: Tōkyō daigaku shuppankai, 1993.

Kranzler, David. *Japanese, Nazis & Jews: The Jewish Refugee Community of Shanghai, 1938–1945*. New York: Yeshiva University Press, 1976.

Kraske, Jochen, et al. *Bankers with a Mission: The Presidents of the World Bank, 1946–1991*. New York: Oxford University Press, 1996.

Kubo, Naoyuki. *Manshū no tanjō: Nichibei masatsu no hajimari*. Tokyo: Maruzen, 1996.

Kurusu Saburō. *Hōmatsu no sanjūgonen*. Tokyo: Bunkashoin, 1949.

———. *Nichibei gaikō hiwa*. Tokyo: Sōgensha, 1952.

LaFeber, Walter. *The Cambridge History of American Foreign Relations*, vol. 2, *The American Search for Opportunity, 1865–1913*. New York: Cambridge University Press, 1993.

———. *The Clash: U.S.-Japanese Relations Throughout History*. New York: W. W. Norton, 1997.

Lash, Joseph P. *Roosevelt and Churchill, 1939–1941: The Partnership That Saved the West*. New York: W. W. Norton, 1976.

Leffler, Melvyn P. *The Specter of Communism: The United States and the Origins of the Cold War, 1917–1953.* New York: Hill & Wang, 1994.

Leuchtenburg, William E. *Franklin D. Roosevelt and the New Deal, 1932–1940.* New York: Harper Torchbooks, 1963.

Levine, Steven L. *Anvil of Victory: The Communist Revolution in Manchuria, 1945– 1948.* New York: Columbia University Press, 1987.

Lilienthal, David E. *The Journals of David E. Lilienthal,* vol. 3, *Venturesome Years, 1950– 1955.* New York: Harper & Row, 1966.

Lotchin, Roger W. *Fortress California, 1910–1961: From Warfare to Welfare.* New York: Oxford University Press, 1992.

Manchuria Industrial Development Company. Tokyo: Oriental Economist, 1938.

Manshū teikoku seifu. *Manshū kenkoku jūnenshi.* Hsinking, 1941; reprinted—Tokyo: Hara shobō, 1969.

Marcus, George E., and Peter Dobkin Hall. *Lives in Trust: The Fortunes of Dynastic Families in Late Twentieth Century America.* Boulder, Colo.: Westview Press, 1992.

Marks, Frederick W., III. *Wind over Sand: The Diplomacy of Franklin D. Roosevelt.* Athens: University of Georgia Press, 1988.

Marshall, Jonathan. *To Have and Have Not: Southeast Asian Raw Materials and the Origins of the Pacific War.* Berkeley: University of California Press, 1995.

Masland, John W. "Commercial Influence upon American Far Eastern Policy, 1937–1941." *Pacific Historical Review* 11 (Sept. 1942): 281–99.

Mason, Mark. *American Multinationals and Japan: The Political Economy of Japanese Capital Controls, 1899–1980.* Cambridge, Mass.: Harvard University, Council on East Asian Studies, 1992.

Matsui Haruo. *Keizai sanbō honburon.* Tokyo: Nihon hyōronsha, 1934.

Millis, Walter, ed. *The Forrestal Diaries.* New York: The Viking Press, 1951.

Mitarai Tatsuo. *Minami Jirō.* Tokyo: Seikatsu no tomosha, 1957.

Miyajima Hideaki. "Zaibatsu kaitai." In *Nihon keizai no hatten to kigyō shūdan,* ed. Hashimoto Jurō, Hōsei daigaku sangyō jōhō sentā, and Takeda Haruoto, 203–54. Tokyo: Tōkyō daigaku shuppankai, 1992.

Miyazaki Masayasu. "Ashida naikakuki no gaishi dōnyū mondai." 2 pts. *Shinshū daigaku kyōiku gakubu kiyō,* no. 60 (1987): 13–24; no. 61 (1987): 9–20.

Miyazawa Kiichi. *Tokyo-Washington no mitsudan.* Tokyo: Chūkōbunko, 1999.

Morison, Elting E. *Turmoil and Tradition: A Study of the Life and Times of Henry L. Stimson.* Boston: Houghton Mifflin, 1960.

Morito Tatsuo. "Chigatta shiya kara fukai nagori o." In *Ayukawa Yoshisuke sensei tsuisōroku,* ed. Ayukawa Yoshisuke sensei henshū kankōkai, 502–4. Tokyo: Ayukawa Yoshisuke sensei henshū kankōkai, 1968.

Murakami Ryūsuke. "Ayukawa sensei no tsuisō." In *Ayukawa Yoshisuke sensei tsuisōroku,* ed. Ayukawa Yoshisuke sensei henshū kankōkai, 389–94. Tokyo: Ayukawa Yoshisuke sensei henshū kankōkai, 1968.

Nagashima Katsusuke and Yasutomi Ayumu. *Jūgonen sensō gokuhi shiryōshū hokan 13: Kantōgun sanbōbu sakusei sōdōin kankei chōsa shiryō.* Tokyo: Fuji shuppan, 2000.

Nakagane, Katsuji. "Manchukuo and Economic Development." In *The Japanese Informal Empire in China, 1895–1937,* ed. Peter Duus, Ramon H. Myers, and Mark R. Peattie, 133–57. Princeton: Princeton University Press, 1989.

Nakakita Kōji. *Keizai fukkō to sengo seiji: Nihon shakaitō, 1945–1951.* Tokyo: Tōkyō daigaku shuppankai, 1998.

Nakamura Takafusa. *Economic Development of Modern Japan.* Tokyo: Ministry of Foreign Affairs, 1985.

———. *Economic Growth in Prewar Japan.* New Haven: Yale University Press, 1983.

———. "Gaisetsu, 1937–1954." In *Nihon keizaishi,* vol. 7, *"Keikakuka" to "minshuka,"* ed. idem, 1–68. Tokyo: Iwanami shoten, 1989.

———. *Shōwa keizaishi.* Tokyo: Iwanami shoten, 1986.

———. *Shōwa kyōkō to keizai seisaku.* Tokyo: Kōdansha gakujutsu bunko, 1994.

Nash, Gary B., et al. *The American People: Creating a Nation and a Society.* New York: Addison-Wesley, 1998.

NHK, ed. *Dokyumento Shōwashi,* vols. 3 and 6. Tokyo: Kadokawa Shoten, 1986.

Nihon kōgyō kurabu gojūnenshi hensan iinkai ed. *Zaikai kaisōroku.* 2 vols. Tokyo: Nihon kōgyō kurabu, 1967.

Ninkovich, Frank. *Modernity and Power: A History of the Domino Theory in the Twentieth Century.* Chicago: University of Chicago Press, 1994.

Nishimura Shigeo. "Nihon seifu no Chūka minkoku ninshiki to Chō Gakuryō seiken." In *Manshūkoku no kenkyū,* ed. Yamamoto Yūzō. Kyōto: Kyōto daigaku, Jinbun kagaku kenkyūjo, 1993.

Nishimuta Yūji. *Nachizumu to Doitsu jidōsha kōgyō.* Tokyo: Yūhikaku, 1999.

Nissan jidōsha kabushikigaisha, Sōmubu, Chōsaka. *Nissan jidōsha sanjūnenshi.* Tokyo: Nissan jidōsha kabushikigaisha, 1965.

Noguchi Yukio. *1940 nen taisei: saraba "senji keizai."* Tokyo: Keizai shinpōsha, 1995.

Ōhata Tokushirō. *Nihon Gaikōshi.* Tokyo: Seibundō, 1986.

Okazaki Tetsuji. "Nihongata kigyō system no genryū." In *Nihon no kigyō system dai 4 kan: kigyō to shijō,* ed. Itami Hiroyuki, Itō Motoshige, and Kagono Tadao, 183–213. Tokyo: Yūhikaku, 1993.

Okazaki Tetsuji and Okuno Masahiro. "Gendai Nihon no keizai system to sono rekishiteki genryū." In *Series Gendai keizai kenkyū 6: Gendai Nihon keizai system no genryū,* ed. Okazaki Tetsuji and Okuno Masahiro, p. 1–34. Tokyo: Nihon keizai shimbunsha, 1993.

Ōuchi Hyōe. "Ayukawa-san to Ōhara shakai mondai kenkyūjo." In *Ayukawa Yoshisuke sensei tsuisōroku,* ed. Ayukawa Yoshisuke sensei henshū kankōkai, 92–95. Tokyo: Ayukawa Yoshisuke sensei henshū kankōkai, 1968.

Patterson, James T. *Mr. Republican: A Biography of Robert A. Taft.* Boston: Houghton Mifflin, 1972.

Peattie, Mark R. *Ishiwara Kanji.* Princeton: Princeton University Press, 1975.

Perez, Robert C., and Edward F. Willett. *Clarence Dillon: Wall Street Enigma.* Lanham, MD: Madison Books, 1995.

Perry, John Curtis. *Facing West: Americans and the Opening of the Pacific.* Westport, Conn.: Praeger, 1994.

Prange, Gordon W. *At Dawn We Slept: The Untold Story of Pearl Harbor.* New York: Penguin Books, 1982.

Rabinowitz, Richard W. *The Genesis of the Japanese Foreign Investment Law of 1950.* Publication of the German-Japanese Lawyers' Association, vol. 10. Hamburg: Alster Media & Werbung, 1999.

Rauch, Basil. *Roosevelt: From Munich to Pearl Harbor.* New York: Creative Age Press, 1950.

Roosevelt, Franklin D. *F.D.R.: His Personal Letters, 1928–1945,* vol. 4, ed. Elliot Roosevelt. New York, 1950.

Rosenberg, Emily S. *Financial Missionaries to the World: The Politics and Culture of Dollar Diplomacy, 1900–1930.* Cambridge, Mass.: Harvard University Press, 1999.

Sakamoto Kazuya. *Nichibei dōmei no kizuna: anpo jōyaku to sōgosei no mosaku.* Tokyo: Yuhikaku, 2000.

Samuels, Richard J. *"Rich Nation, Strong Army": National Security and the Technological Transformation of Japan.* Ithaca, N.Y.: Cornell University Press, 1994.

Sawada Setsuzō. *Sawada Setsuzō kaisōroku: gaikōkan no shōgai.* Tokyo: Yuhikaku, 1985.

Schaller, Michael. *The American Occupation of Japan: The Origins of Cold War in Asia.* New York: Oxford University Press, 1985.

———. *Douglas MacArthur: The Far Eastern General.* New York: Oxford University Press, 1989.

Schonberger, Howard B. *Aftermath of War: Americans and the Remaking of Japan: 1945–1952.* Kent, Ohio: Kent State University Press, 1989.

———. "Zaibatsu Dissolution and the American Restoration of Japan." *Bulletin of Concerned Asian Scholars* 5, no. 2 (Sept. 1973): 16–31.

———. *Japanese Connection: Kaiun Ō K. Sugahara gaiden.* Tokyo: Bungei shunjūsha, 1995.

Schulzinger, Robert D. *U.S. Diplomacy Since 1900.* New York: Oxford University Press, 1998.

Schwarz, Jordan A. *The New Dealers: Power Politics in the Age of Roosevelt.* New York: Vintage Books, 1994.

———. *The Speculator: Bernard M. Baruch in Washington, 1917–1965.* Chapel Hill: University of North Carolina Press, 1981.

Shibata Shigeki. "Sekai ginkō no tai-Nichi karyoku hatsuden shakkan." *Dōshisha daigaku, Jinbun kagaku kenkyūjo shakai kagaku,* no. 64 (Jan. 2001): 95–123.

Shillony, Ben-Ami. *The Jews and the Japanese: The Successful Outsiders.* Rutland, Vt.: Charles E. Tuttle, 1991.

———. *Revolt in Japan: The Young Officers and the February 26, 1936 Incident.* Princeton: Princeton University Press, 1973.

Shimizu, Sayuri. *Creating People of Unity: The United States and Japan's Economic Alternatives, 1950–1960.* Kent, Ohio: Kent State University Press, 2001.

Shinomiya Masachika. "Nishiyama Yatarō: sengo tekkōgyō no inobētār." In *Kēsubook Nihon no kigyōka katsudō,* ed. Hōsei daigaku, Sangyō jōhō sentā and Udagawa Masaru, 247–55. Tokyo: Yūhikaku, 1999.

———. "Senzen no jidōsha sangyō to 'Manshū': senzen no jidōsha sangyō seisaku ni shimeru 'Manshū' no ichi o megutte." *Keiei shigaku* 27, no. 1 (Apr. 1992): 1–30.

Shiozaki Hiroaki. *Nichieibei sensō no kiro: Taiheiyo o meguru seisenryaku.* Tokyo: Yamakawa shuppan, 1984.

Smith, Richard Norton. *An Uncommon Man: The Triumph of Herbert Hoover.* Worland, Wyo.: High Plains Publishing, 1984.

Sodei Rinjirō, ed. and trans. *Yoshida Shigeru-MacArthur ōfuku shokanshū.* Tokyo: Hōsei daigaku shuppankyoku.

South Manchuria Railway Company. *Sixth Report on Progress in Manchuria to 1939.* Tokyo: Herald Press, 1939.

Strauss, Lewis L. *Men and Decisions.* Garden City, N.Y.: Doubleday, 1962.

Sudō Shinji. *Nichibei kaisen gaikō no kenkyū: Nichibei kōshō no hottan kara haru nōto made.* Tokyo: Keiō tsūshin, 1986.

Sugiura Seishi. "Sengo fukkōki no ginkō/shōken: 'main bankusei' no keisei o megute." In *Nihon kigyō system no sengoshi,* ed. Hashimoto Toshiaki, 249–96. Tokyo: Tōkyō daigaku shuppankai, 1996.

Sun, Kungtu C. *The Economic Development of Manchuria in the First Half of the Twentieth Century.* Cambridge, Mass.: Harvard University East Asian Research Center, 1969.

Suzuki Takashi. "Manshū keizai kaihatsu to Manshū jūkōgyō no seiritsu." *Tokushima daigaku gakugeikiyō: shakaikagaku* 13 (1963): 97–114.

———. *Nihon teikokushugi to Manshū,* vol. 2, 1900–1945. Tokyo: Hanawa shobō, 1992.

Takahashi Makiko. *Shizukanaru tate: Yonai Mitsumasa.* 2 vols. Tokyo: Hara shobō, 1990.

Takasaki Tatsunosuke. *Manshū no shūen.* Tokyo: Jitsugyō no Nihonsha, 1953.

———. "Watashi no rirekisho." In *Watashi no rirekisho,* ed. Nihon keizai shimbunsha, 2: 203–32. Tokyo: Nihon keizai shimbunsha, 1957.

Takebe Rokuzō. *Takebe Rokuzō nikki.* Ed. Taura Masanori, Furukawa Takahisa, and Takebe Kenichi. Tokyo: Fuyō shobō.

Tatematsu Kiyoshi. "Dokusen: jūkagaku kōgyōka to shinkyū zaibatsu no kyōsō." In *Senkyūhyaku sanjūnendai no Nihon: daikyōkō yori sensō e,* ed. Kojima Tsunehisa, 203–34. Kyōto: Hōritsu bunkasha, 1989.

Teranishi Jūrō. "Shūsen chokugo ni okeru kinyū seido kaikaku." In *Sengo Nihon no keizai kaikaku: shijō to seifu,* ed. Kōzai Yasushi and Teranishi Jūrō, 131–52. Tokyo: Tōkyō daigaku shuppankai, 1993.

Terasaki, Gwen. *Bridge to the Sun.* Chapel Hill: University of North Carolina Press, 1957.

Thorne, Christopher. *The Issue of War: State, Societies and the Far Eastern Conflict of 1941–1945.* New York: Oxford University Press, 1985.

Tōgō, Shigenori. *The Cause of War.* New York: Simon & Schuster, 1956.

Toland, John. *The Rising Sun: The Decline and Fall of the Japanese Empire, 1936–1945.* New York: Random House, 1970.

Tomoda Juichirō, ed. *Ayukawa Yoshisuke jūōdan.* Tokyo: Sōgensha, 1953.

Udagawa, Masaru. "Business Management and Foreign-Affiliated Companies in Japan Before World War II." In *Foreign Business in Japan Before World War II,* ed. Takeshi Yuzawa and Masaru Udagawa, 1–30. Tokyo: University of Tokyo Press, 1990.

———. "Kokusanka seisaku no gaishi: jidōsha seizō jigyōhō to Ford, GM." In *Nihon kigyō no keiei kōdō 1: Nihonteki keiei no seisei to hatten,* ed. Itami Hiroyuki, Kagono Tadao, Miyamoto Matao, and Yonekura Seiichirō, 322–47. Tokyo: Yūhikaku, 1998.

———. "Nissan zaibatsu no jidōsha sangyō shinshutsu ni tsuite." 2 pts. *Keiei shirin* 13, no. 4 (Jan. 1977): 93–109; 14, no. 1 (Apr. 1977): 73–95.

———. "Nissan zaibatsu no Manshū shinshutsu." *Keiei shigaku* 11, no. 1 (June 1976): 46–74.

U.S. Department of State. *Foreign Relations of the United States: Japan, 1931–1941,* vol. 1. Washington, D.C.: Government Printing Office, 1955.

———. *Foreign Relations of the United States: Japan, 1952–1954,* vol. 14, pt. II. Washington, D.C.: Government Printing Office, 1985.

———. *Foreign Relations of the United States: The Far East, 1939,* vol. 3. Washington, D.C.: Government Printing Office, 1955.

———. *Foreign Relations of the United States: The Far East, 1940,* vol. 4. Washington, D.C.: Government Printing Office, 1955.

———. *Foreign Relations of the United States: The Far East, 1941,* vol. 4. Washington, D.C.: Government Printing Office, 1956.

———. *Foreign Relations of the United States: The Far East, 1946,* vol. 6. Washington, D.C.: Government Printing Office, 1971.

Wada Kazuo and Yui Tsunehiko. *Toyoda Kiichirō den.* Nagoya: Nagoya daigaku shuppankai, 2002.

Walch, Timothy, and Dwight M. Miller, eds. *Herbert Hoover and Harry S. Truman: A Documentary History.* Worland, Wyo.: High Plains Publishing, 1992.

Watanabe Takeshi. *Watanabe Takeshi nikki.* Tokyo: Tōyō keizai shinpōsha, 1983.

Who's Who in America: A Biographical Dictionary of Notable Living Men and Women, vol. 21, 1940–1941. Chicago: A. N. Marquis, 1940.

Who's Who in America: A Biographical Dictionary of Notable Living Men and Women, vol. 25, 1948–1949. Chicago: A. N. Marquis, 1948.

Who's Who in American Jewry: A Biographical Dictionary of Living Jews of the United States and Canada, vol. 3, *1938–1939*. New York: National News Association, 1939.

Wilkins, Mira. "America keizai to kyokutō mondai." In *Nichibei kankeishi, III, gikai/seitō to minkandantai*, ed. Hosoya Chihiro, Imai Seiichi, Rōyama Michio, and Saitō Makoto, 171–236. Tokyo: Tōkyō daigaku shuppankai, 1971.

———. "Kyōdōtōron." In *Nichibei kankeishi, III: gikai/seitō to minkandantai*, ed. Hosoya Chihiro, Imai Seiichi, Michio Rōyama, and Saitō Makoto, 238–54. Tokyo: Tōkyō daigaku shuppankai, 1971.

———. "The Role of U.S. Business." In *Pearl Harbor as History: Japanese-American Relations, 1931–1941*, ed. Dorothy Borg and Shumpei Okamoto, 341–76. New York: Columbia University Press, 1973.

William R. Gorham-shi kinenjigyō iinkai, ed. *William R. Gorham den*. Tokyo: n.p., 1951.

Williams, William Appleman. *The Contours of American History*. Cleveland: World Publishing, 1961.

Wilson, Joan Hoff. *American Business and Foreign Policy, 1920–1933*. Lexington: University Press of Kentucky, 1971.

———. *Herbert Hoover: Forgotten Progressive*. Boston: Little, Brown, 1975.

———. "Herbert Hoover's Plan for Ending the Second World War." *International History Review* 1 (Jan. 1979): 84–102.

Wolfren, Karel van. *The Enigma of Japanese Power: People and Politics in a Stateless Nation*. New York: Vintage Books, 1990.

Woo, Jung-En. *Race to the Swift: State and Finance in Korean Industrialization*. New York: Columbia University Press, 1991.

Yamamoto Kazuto. "Bōeki no henka to kokusaitairitsu no gekika." In *Senkyūhyaku sanjūnendai no Nihon: daikyōkō yori sensō e*, ed. Kojima Tsunehisa, 235–73. Kyōto: Hōritsu bunkasha, 1989.

Yamamuro Shin'ichi. *Kimera: Manshūkoku no shōzō*. Tokyo: Chūō kōronsha, 1993.

Yamazaki Kazuyoshi. *Fūunji Ayukawa Yoshisuke*. Tokyo: Tōkai shuppansha, 1937.

Yatsugi Kazuo. "Yatsugi Kazuo" (oral history). In *Gendaishi o tsukuru hitobito*, ed. Hara Akira, Itō Takashi, and Nakamura Takafusa, 4: 45–140. Tokyo: Mainichi shimbunsha, 1972.

———. *Rōdōsogi hiroku*. Tokyo: Nihon kōgyō shimbunsha, 1979.

———. *Shōwa dōran shishi*, vol. 1. Tokyo: Keizai ōraisha, 1971.

Yergin, Daniel. *Shattered Peace: The Origins of the Cold War*. Rev. ed. New York: Penguin Books, 1990.

Yonekura Seiichirō. *Keiei kakumei no kōzō*. Tokyo: Iwanami, 1999.

———. "Nihon tekkōgyō no kakushinsha: Nishiyama Yatarō (Kawasaki seitetsu)." In *Kēsubook Nihon kigyō no keiei kōdō dai 4 kan: kigyōka no gunzō to jidai no ibuki*, ed. Itami Hiroyuki, Kagono Tadao, Miyamoto Matao, and Yonekura Seiichirō, 174–97. Tokyo: Yūhikaku, 1998.

————. "Sengo Nihon tekkōgyō shiron: sono renzokusei to hirenzokusei." In *Nihon no kigyō system dai 2 kan: soshiki to senryaku*, ed. Itami Hiroyuki, Kagono Tadao, and Itō Motoshige, 184–217. Tokyo: Yūhikaku, 1993.

Yonemoto Jirō. *Denki Kuhara Fusanosuke ou o kataru*. Tokyo: Riburu, 1991.

Yoshida kinen jigyō zaidan, ed. *Yoshida Shigeru shokan*. Tokyo: Chūō kōron shinsha, 1994.

Yoshino Shinji. "Mangyō jidai no omoide." In *Ayukawa Yoshisuke sensei tsuisōroku*, ed. Ayukawa Yoshisuke sensei henshū kankōkai, 445–48. Tokyo: Ayukawa Yoshisuke sensei henshū kankōkai, 1968.

————. *Omokaji torikaji—urakara mita Nihon sangyō no ayumi*. Tokyo: Tsushō sangyō kenkyūsha, 1962.

Zaikaijin shisō zenshū, vol. 2, *Keiei tetsugaku, keiei rinen (Shōwa-hen)*. Tokyo: Daiyamondosha, 1972.

Zeiler, Thomas W. *Free Trade, Free World: The Advent of GATT*. Chapel Hill: University of North Carolina Press, 1999.

Index

Harvard East Asian Monographs

(* out-of-print)

Harvard East Asian Monographs

Harvard East Asian Monographs